# HOUSING UNDER PLATFORM CAPITALISM

# ijurr
**INTERNATIONAL JOURNAL
OF URBAN AND REGIONAL RESEARCH**

## IJURR STUDIES IN URBAN AND SOCIAL CHANGE BOOK SERIES

The IJURR Studies in Urban and Social Change Book Series has been a cornerstone in global urban studies since its founding in 1992 and has pushed the boundaries of critical, interdisciplinary, and theory-driven urban research. Contributors have conducted pathbreaking, theoretically informed empirical studies on inequality, informality, politics, environmental justice, gentrification, and segregation across the Global North and South. The common thread underlying these diverse interventions has been to respond to the urban question: How are cities both sites of significant inequality and repression and incubators of transformative cultural and political movements? Partnering with University of California Press since 2024, the IJURR Book Series continues to be a central intellectual hub for understanding the complex challenges facing cities in the twenty-first century.

# HOUSING UNDER PLATFORM CAPITALISM

The Contentious Regulation of
Short-Term Rentals in European Cities

THOMAS AGUILERA
FRANCESCA ARTIOLI
CLAIRE COLOMB

UNIVERSITY OF CALIFORNIA PRESS

University of California Press
Oakland, California

Library of Congress Cataloging-in-Publication Data

Names: Aguilera, Thomas, author. | Artioli, Francesca, author. | Colomb, Claire, author.
Title: Housing under platform capitalism : the contentious regulation of short-term rentals in European cities / Thomas Aguilera, Francesca Artioli, Claire Colomb.
Other titles: IJURR studies in urban and social change book series.
Description: Oakland, California : University of California Press, [2025] | Series: IJURR Studies in Urban and Social Change Book Series | Includes bibliographical references and index.
Identifiers: LCCN 2024061733 (print) | LCCN 2024061734 (ebook) | ISBN 9780520418073 (cloth) | ISBN 9780520418080 (paperback) | ISBN 9780520418097 (epub)
Subjects: LCSH: Rental housing—Law and legislation—European Union countries—21st century. | Rent control—European Union countries—21st century. | Vacation rentals—Law and legislation—European Union countries—21st century. | Tourism and city planning—European Union countries--21st century. | Electronic commerce. | Disruptive technologies.
Classification: LCC KJE1741 .A93 2025 (print) | LCC KJE1741 (ebook) | DDC 346.404/344—dc23/eng/20250202
LC record available at https://lccn.loc.gov/2024061733
LC ebook record available at https://lccn.loc.gov/2024061734

GPSR Authorized Representative: Easy Access System Europe,
Mustamäe tee 50, 10621 Tallinn, Estonia, gpsr.requests@easproject.com

34  33  32  31  30  29  28  27  26  25
10  9  8  7  6  5  4  3  2  1

# Contents

# Illustrations

## TABLES

# Acknowledgments

THIS SIX-HANDED MANUSCRIPT, co-authored by three colleagues and friends, is the result of a long journey and intellectual companionship that started in the mid-2010s. We
met while attending several international workshops of the
comparative research network What Is (Not) Governed in
the Large Metropolis (WHIG) and discovered that we were
developing parallel research projects—respectively on the
regulation of short-term rental housing; on the social movements and public policy debates around touristification; and
on digital platforms, technologies and urban governance in
several European cities. We decided to join forces to start
researching what was (at the time) an emerging set of issues.
We had different scientific interests in the matter—housing,
property ownership, new technologies, informality, urban
planning, tourism and social movements—but we shared an
overarching interest in the *comparative study* of urban politics,
policies and governance in European cities. As the debates

around, and regulation of, platform-mediated short-term rentals were rapidly evolving, we decided to carry out a medium-term, incremental piece of research. This allowed us to cover a sufficient period to test and slowly build a coherent comparative design and to collect and analyse data for 12 European cities. We did not receive any large research grant, but benefitted from the help and support of several institutions and an extensive number of people.

We would first like to warmly thank Tatiana Moreira de Souza (previously at University College London, now at the University of Liverpool) for her contribution to the fieldwork in Amsterdam, Lisbon and London; her support to Claire Colomb in preparing the report that served as our initial empirical basis for comparing short-term rental regulations in 12 European cities (Colomb and Moreira de Souza 2021); and her intellectual input on the regulation of the private housing rental sector more broadly. The report was partly funded by a small research grant from the Property Research Trust (formerly RICS Research Trust) in 2018–2019: we would like to thank the trustees for their support (in particular Sarah Sayce, who passed away prematurely, and Richard Holt). We also thank the Royal Town Planning Institute (RTPI) for awarding the report the 2022 Sir Peter Hall Award for Excellence in Research and Engagement.

We warmly thank Murray Cox, the founder of Inside Airbnb, for producing some of the data and maps presented in the book, for our conversations on the role of data in platform capitalism and STR regulation and more generally for his tireless work as a data activist concerned with housing justice.

Thank you to all the interviewees from different sectors and organisations across Europe who agreed to speak to us and share their expertise, experiences and often opposed positions. We have tried to represent their arguments and differing views faithfully.

In Paris, we would like to thank Ian Brossat (deputy mayor for housing of the City of Paris, 2014–2023) and his office for their invaluable help. We also thank the team of the Office for the Protection of Residential Dwellings (BPLH), in particular Franck Affortit, François Plottin, Mélanie Gidel, Jeanne Richon, Nicolas Billotte, Amandine Zancanaro and the inspection agents whom we were able to follow in their daily work. Thanks to Stéphanie Jankel, Clément Boisseuil and their team at the Atelier Parisien d'Urbanisme (APUR). Thanks to the members of the citizen collectives ParisVsBnb, Collectif National des Habitants Permanents and others in Douarnenez and Saint-Malo, more particularly to Franck and Véronique.

In Milan, we would like to thank the staff and elected officials of the City of Milan and the Region of Lombardy for talking to us. Thanks also to colleagues at the University of Milano Bicocca and the Politecnico di Milano for our insightful exchanges regarding the 'Milano model' over the years: Alberta Andreotti, Guido Anselmi, Massimo Bricocoli, Veronica Conte, Alessandro Coppola, Valeria Fedeli and Marco Peverini have helped us make sense of the city. Serena Vicari has left us too soon: we would like to pay tribute to her kindness and research. Thanks to many other Italian colleagues and grassroots initiatives working on short-term rentals in Italian cities, in particular Sarah Gainsforth, Giovanni Semi, Marta Tonetta, Alessandra Esposito, the members of the collectives Alta Tensione Abitativa and Chiediamo Casa Milano and the Short Term City project team.

In Barcelona, we would like to thank Albert Arias for insightful discussions on the governance of tourism and for inviting Claire Colomb to carry out a small exploratory study of the regulations of short-term rentals in Europe for the Tourism Department of the Ajuntament de Barcelona in 2016. Thanks to Joan Torella, Rosa Bada, Silvia Flores and other members of that department at the time for their invitation to exchange knowledge with the municipal administration between 2016 and 2018. Thanks to the inspection team of the Department of Urban Planning for sharing insights on their work. Thanks to Yolanda Martínez Mata, lawyer at Marimón Abogados and associate professor at the

University of Barcelona, for her clear explanations of EU law. Thank you to Reme Gómez and Daniel Pardo for our conversations and their commitment to a more just Barcelona that remains liveable for its residents. Finally, *moltes gràcies* to the many colleagues in Catalonia and Spain with whom we had the opportunity to discuss our research, and who provided valuable feedback over the years: Ernest Cañada, Agustín Cocola-Gant, Javier Gil, Toni López-Gay, Claudio Milano, Oriol Nel·lo, Marc Pradel, Paolo Russo and Jorge Sequera, among others.

In the other cities covered in this book, we would like to thank the colleagues who facilitated access to data or interviewees, in particular Juliana Martins and Sandra Marques in Lisbon and Petr Návrat, Daniel Cohn and Michaela Píxova in Prague.

More broadly, thanks to the participants at the many seminars, public lectures and conferences in which we have presented this work, for inspiring feedback and discussions—among those we have not mentioned yet, Mara Ferreri, Nicole Gurran, Justin Kadi, Romola Sanyal and Luke Yates.

This book finds its roots in the comparative research network WHIG, initiated by Patrick Le Galès, CNRS research professor at Sciences Po Paris (Centre for European Studies and Comparative Politics, Urban School). A special thanks to Patrick: we would not have met without him, and he has been a great source of inspiration and support for our comparative work. Thanks to all the colleagues involved in the WHIG network in Paris, London, São Paulo, México City and Milan for our intellectual exchanges and their support over the years, in particular Alberta Andreotti, Charlotte Halpern, Eduardo Marques, Mike Raco, Vicente Ugalde and Tommaso Vitale. We also thank François Bonnet, Marine Bourgeois, Antoine Courmont, Marco Cremaschi, Renaud Epstein, Antoine Guironnet, Gilles Pinson, Pauline Prat and Julie Pollard for their inspiring work and our discussions, and other colleagues associated with the Cities Are Back in Town research group at Sciences Po. Thank you, too, to our colleagues from RC21, the

Research Committee on the Sociology of Urban and Regional Development of the International Sociological Association, which has provided us with an invaluable and friendly intellectual space over the years.

From Thomas Aguilera: warm thanks to Tom Chevalier, Benoit Giry, Eileen Michel, Pierre Wokuri, Sébastien Segas, Bleuween Lechaux and the Mixed-Methods Group from Rennes for their daily support and their valuable feedback on the book. Thanks to Marylène, Brice, Jean-Pierre, Karine, Elsa and the ARENES UMR 6051 staff. Thanks to Romain Pasquier and the TMAP Chair. Thanks to Alan Smart, Jacques de Maillard and Paul Watt for their inspiring works, their kindness and their intellectual companionship. Thanks to my PhD students in Rennes—Adrien Mével, Fabien Meslet, Mathias Seguin—and Pierre Burban, who have nourished me daily with their visions of cities. Thanks to the University of Rennes, Sciences Po Rennes, Sciences Po Paris and the Centre for European Studies and Comparative Politics, which have given us the resources needed for this research.

From Francesca Artioli: thanks to the Paris colleagues and friends of the Ecole d'Urbanisme de Paris, the Lab'Urba, the GT-POUM (Labex Futurs Urbains), and the LATTS for our inspiring discussions about urban policies. A warm thanks to Christine Lelévrier, Félix Adisson, Ludovic Halbert, Claire Carriou, Claire Aragau, Joël Idt and Ana Christina Torres for their everyday support and their enthusiastic scrutiny of housing and real estate dynamics and the inequalities they produce. Thanks to Sophie Didier, Julien Aldhuy, Nadia Arab and Jennifer Buyck for their encouragement as directors of the Lab'Urba; to Sabine Hermenault for navigating administrative issues; and to Sabine Bognon for co-directing the Master 1 in urban planning during the completion of this book. This research has also benefitted from financial support from the Young Researchers program of the University of Paris Est-Créteil (BQR-JC) and the research program Internationalising Cities (LATTS-PUCA) led by Olivier Coutard and Christian Lefèvre, whom I would like to thank. Thanks to Léa de Frémont for her study on the conversion of commercial premises into short-term rentals, as part of her internship at the Lab'Urba.

From Claire Colomb: thanks to Johannes Novy for introducing me, a decade ago, to the social and political conflicts surrounding the visitor economy in cities and for his inspiring work. I owe a lot to the intellectual companionship and friendship of my former colleagues at University College London, among others Sonia Arbaci, Elisabete Cidre, Michael Edwards, Nick Gallent, Barbara Lipietz, Claudio de Magalhães, Juliana Martins, Susan Moore, Mike Raco, Yvonne Rydin, Uta Staiger, John Tomaney, Mark Tewdwr Jones and Joanna Williams. A warm thank you to supportive colleagues and friends across the world, in particular Talja Blokland, Paola Briata, Stefanie Dühr, Adrian Favell, Yuri Kazepov, Penny Koutrolikou, Christine Lelévrier, Margit Mayer, Lucia Alexandra Popartan, Nathalie Rivère de Carles, Sanjay Srivastava, Elena Vacchelli, Bas van Heur and many others. Thank you to my colleagues at the University of Cambridge for welcoming me in 2023/2024, as this book was being finished.

A heartfelt thank you to the members of the editorial board of the IJURR SUSC Book Series and to the series editor, Walter Nicholls, who believed in this project from the beginning and accompanied us through the process. We are grateful to the anonymous reviewers for their constructive comments, and to Diane Bowden and Sharon Langworthy for their careful editing of the manuscript. Thanks to Kim Robinson at the University of California Press, and her collaborators, for bringing this book to light.

Our final and most affectionate thanks go to our loved ones: this book owes everything to their support, love and patience. Thomas warmly thanks Camille, Yuna, Mathieu, Maïlys, his parents and his friends from Paris, Toulouse and Tinténiac. Francesca warmly thanks Romain, Sofia, Emilia, her parents and her lifetime friends from Bologna and Paris. Claire wholeheartedly thanks her parents, her brother and the friends who have stood by in stormy weather.

# Abbreviations

| | |
|---|---|
| AHTOP/ATOP | Association Représentative des Acteurs de l'Hébergement et du Tourisme Professionnels, later renamed Association pour un Tourisme Professionnel (Association for a Professional Tourism, France) |
| AIGAB | Associazione Italiana Gestori di Affitti Brevi (Association of Short-Term Rentals Managers, Italy) |
| APARTUR | Asociación de Apartamentos Turísticos de Barcelona (Association of Tourist Rentals, Spain) |
| API | application programming interface |
| B&B | bed and breakfast |
| B2C | business-to-consumer |
| BPLH | Bureau de la Protection des Locaux d'Habitation (Office for the Protection of Residential Dwellings, Paris) |

| | |
|---|---|
| CAV | case e appartamenti per vacanze (holiday homes and flats, Milan) |
| CJEU | Court of Justice of the European Union |
| CoR | European Committee of the Regions |
| DG | Directorate-General (European Commission) |
| DG GROW | Directorate-General for Internal Market, Industry, Entrepreneurship and SMEs, European Commission |
| DMA | *Digital Markets Act* (EU legislation) |
| DSA | *Digital Services Act* (EU legislation) |
| EC | European Commission |
| EHHA | European Holiday Home Association |
| ETTSA | European Technology & Travel Services Association |
| EU | European Union |
| FEVITUR | Federación Española de Asociaciones de Viviendas y Apartamentos Turísticos (Spanish Federation of Holiday Rentals Associations) |
| GDPR | *General Data Protection Regulation* (EU legislation) |
| HOTREC | Association of Hotels, Restaurants, Pubs and Cafes (and similar establishments in Europe) |
| ISS | information society service (EU legal terminology) |
| IUT | International Union of Tenants |
| MEP | Member of the European Parliament |
| NGO | non-governmental organisation |
| OECD | Organisation for Economic Co-operation and Development |
| P2P | peer-to-peer |
| PEUAT | Pla especial urbanístic d'allotjaments turístics (Special Plan for Tourist Accommodation, Barcelona, Catalonia) |
| STR | short-term rental |

| | |
|---|---|
| UK | United Kingdom |
| UMIH | Union des Métiers et des Industries de l'Hôtellerie (Hotels association, France) |
| UNPLV | Union Nationale pour la Promotion de la Location de Vacances (National Union for the Promotion of Holiday Rentals, France) |
| URL | uniform resource locator |
| USA | United States of America |
| VRBO | Vacation Rentals by Owner (company) |

# INTRODUCTION

FIFTEEN YEARS AFTER the birth of Airbnb in California in 2008, most of the world's major cities have experienced conflicts involving the regulation of what are known as *short-term rentals* (hereafter STRs), suspected of exacerbating the effects of tourism and of removing permanent dwellings from the housing stock for the exclusive use of visitors. Since the mid-2010s, large European cities—which together form one of the world's largest tourism markets—have been at the heart of these conflicts, often leading urban governments to take measures to regulate the phenomenon. Yet what is striking is the diversity of forms taken by these conflicts and the modes of regulation that were subsequently developed. By adopting a perspective that combines the comparative sociology of public policies, of multi-level governance, and the political economy of urban capitalism, this book seeks to explain *how* and *why* local governments—faced with the same global phenomenon of 'platform capitalism'—have adopted different modes of regulation; how regulations have been implemented; and what the socio-political effects of these regulations are on the political economy of cities.

## FROM A SILICON VALLEY UNICORN TO THE RISE OF AN URBAN PUBLIC PROBLEM IN EUROPE

In 2008, shortly after the beginning of the subprime crisis in the United States of America (USA), three graduates living in San Francisco set up a website called Airbed&breakfast, allowing travellers to rent inflatable mattresses or spare beds in people's apartments. Their start-up, rebranded Airbnb in 2009, quickly became portrayed as the archetypal Silicon Valley 'unicorn success story' of 'how three ordinary guys disrupted an industry, made billions, and created plenty of controversy' (Gallagher 2018:n.p.; Stone 2018). Airbnb rapidly expanded within and outside the USA, becoming a highly valuable venture-capital-backed company and the unrivalled world leader in the online offer of STR accommodation. In 2019, 17.4% of the global offer of active listings on Airbnb were in the USA, nearly 50% in Europe, and the rest of the offer was growing in East Asia, Oceania and South and Central America (Adamiak 2022). When the company was introduced in the Nasdaq stock exchange in December 2020, it was valued at nearly $100 billion—twice the value of the largest hotel operator Marriott (Rushe 2020). In December 2023, its website boasted 7.7 million active listings from over 5 million hosts in 100,000 cities and towns in more than 220 countries, and a total of 1.5 billion all-time guest arrivals recorded since the company's beginnings.[1] This exponential growth proved disruptive for the conventional tourist accommodation and housing sectors and quickly provoked strong social and political contestations. This first happened in the very birthplaces of Airbnb: grassroots mobilisations emerged in 2015 in San Francisco and New York City, eventually pushing local governments to take measures aimed at protecting housing for permanent residents.

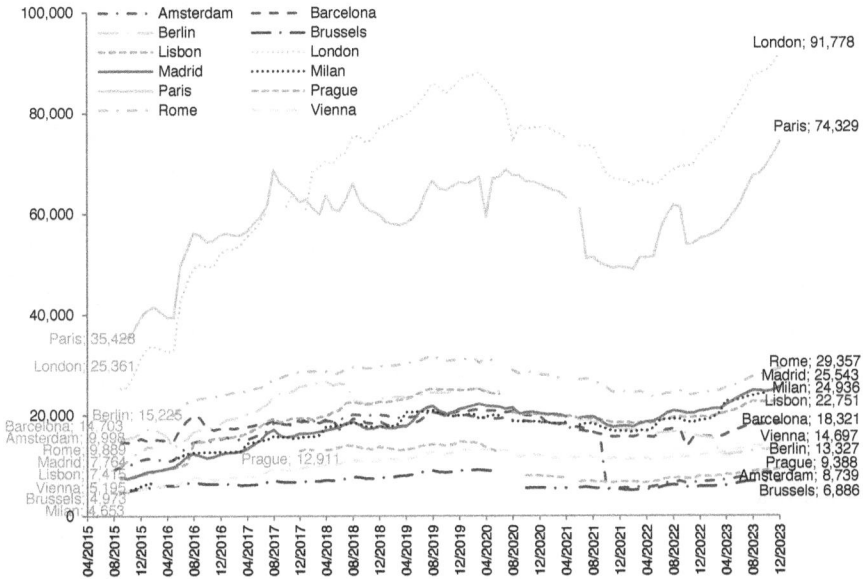

**Figure 1.** Evolution of short-term rental listings in 12 major European cities (2015–2023). *Source*: Compiled by the authors based on Inside Airbnb data.

In Europe, in the first five years after the start of Airbnb's operations on the continent in 2011, the number of reservations grew exponentially: from 0 to 18,000 listings in Amsterdam, 26,000 in Berlin, 28,000 in Barcelona, 48,000 in London and just over 60,000 in Paris (Coyle and Yu-Cheong Yeung 2016). By the mid-2010s, Europe-based listings represented over half of Airbnb's business (Airbnb 2014). Overall, the STR sector in Europe was estimated to provide 20 million beds—twice the number of hotel beds (EHHA 2016)—and generated an annual turnover of €15 billion (Vaughan et al. 2016). This growth continued unabated until the onset of the COVID-19 pandemic in early 2020, as shown in Figure 1 for 12 large European cities. At that point in time, Italy, Spain and France were Airbnb's biggest market after the USA.

Just over a decade after the start of Airbnb, a group of 22 European city leaders, representing large capital and second-tier cities across the continent, wrote a letter to the European Commission, one of the institutions

of the European Union (EU), asking for 'better EU legislation of platforms offering short-term holiday rentals' (Eurocities 2020a) and stating:

> We, European cities, will go at length to welcome the many tourists who
> wish to visit us in the coming decades. We recognise the opportunities in
> this that come with short-term holiday rentals. But we have at the same time
> a primary duty to accommodate the people who wish to live and work in
> our cities. And we need urgently to secure the liveability of our neighbour-
> hoods and therefore find the right balance when facing these challenges. A
> 'carte blanche' for short-term holiday rentals cannot be the answer.

This statement from city governments directed to the supranational
institutions of the EU was a stark symbol of the transformation of
platform-mediated STRs into a global public problem addressed by various levels of government with different priorities. How did this happen?

The STR of a property or part thereof was not, in the European context, a new phenomenon: holiday villas, bed and breakfast (B&B) and
guesthouses had existed for a long time. However, since the beginning
of the 2010s, STR accommodation has expanded in an unprecedented
way, due to three dynamics of socio-economic change addressed in
this book: the rise of platform capitalism, the growth of urban tourism
and other forms of human mobility and the reshaping of housing markets through the assetisation of housing. New digital platforms have
mediated a growing demand for STRs, fuelled by visitors and 'temporary city users', while contributing to shape this demand. Platform-
mediated STRs have consolidated a new opportunity for property
owners and investors to extract revenue from the housing stock, part
of which has been redirected toward the needs of a temporary clientele. It is precisely because platform-mediated STRs are entangled in
those three dynamics of socio-economic change that they constitute
a 'wicked' policy object (Rittel and Webber 1973) worthy of in-depth
study. They emerged as part of a new wave of platform-mediated activities connecting transnational and local processes. They first seemed

to 'escape' regulations and state oversight. They cut across established economic and policy sectors, and did not call for any obvious single, best regulatory solution, but rather trade-offs that would favour some interests, social groups and goals at the expense of others.

While STR operators, platforms and pro-tourism politicians have defended the unimpeded growth of STRs, in the mid-2010s a diverse range of voices began to criticise their adverse impacts on people and places, warning of the risks of unregulated practices. In North America and Europe, fierce debates and conflicts erupted, first in large cities with tight housing markets, and more recently in small or medium-sized tourist cities. Various groups started to mobilise to demand more regulatory intervention: residents' associations concerned about the impacts of mass tourism on their neighbourhoods, hotel industry representatives denouncing unfair competition and local activists and politicians worried about the loss of affordable housing. The globalising phenomenon of platform-mediated STRs quickly turned into an object of contention and controversy, in the public debates of the media and in the political arenas of many countries, regions and cities. Their impacts on local economies, housing markets, urban spaces and everyday life became increasingly scrutinised by researchers, activists, public authorities and other interest groups.

## EXPLAINING THE DIVERSITY OF STR REGULATION IN EUROPEAN CITIES

In response to such controversies, public authorities have been under pressure to develop existing, or create new, forms of regulation to manage and control STRs and the activities of platforms. In the Global North, city governments have been at the forefront of regulatory attempts, alone or alongside regional or national governments. In the USA, the city governments of San Francisco and New York City, Airbnb's first two large markets, went through several years of political and legal battles until they managed to pass restrictive, 'one-host-one-home' regulations in 2016 (for an overview, see Hoffman and Schmitter Heisler 2020). In Europe, the first regulatory wave started in the mid-2010s, in cities like Berlin, Barcelona and Paris, where the issue was politicised early on. European media began to publish news articles with often sensationalist titles that referred to various measures being taken 'against Airbnb' in those cities (Croft 2015; Hery 2015; The Guardian 2016),[2] that is, the enactment of new, seemingly highly restrictive regulations. In 2014 the Parliament of the city-state of Berlin passed a law banning the use of residential units as STRs without a permit (which most districts systematically refused in order to protect the long-term rental residential stock). In Barcelona, the new city government elected in 2015 froze new licences for STRs (effectively capping the size of the legal market) and strengthened controls to curtail the illegal STR offer.

However, such restrictive measures were not witnessed everywhere in Europe: in 2015, the United Kingdom (UK) Parliament abolished the obligation to apply for planning permission to rent out residential properties on a short-term basis for fewer than 90 nights a year. In the view of the then Conservative government, the measure was meant to bring 'London up to speed with the internet age' and 'free homeowners from the "bureaucratic headache" of applying for planning permission just to rent their home out for a few weeks' (UK Ministry of Housing, Communities & Local Government 2015). In other cities, like Lisbon, STR regulatory measures were developed a few years later, in the late 2010s, after changes were made in national legislation. By the early 2020s some cities still had very minimal regulation, such as Prague, Milan and Rome, but proposals for more restrictive measures were under discussion. Small and medium-sized city governments, in particular in desirable coastal, rural and mountain areas, were also becoming increasingly concerned about STRs and trying to find ways to regulate the phenomenon.

At the end of 2023 there were very few large cities in Europe where STRs mediated by digital platforms had *not* been the object of some form of regulatory intervention—or where debates had not started about that possibility. But in 10 years, public authorities have not all reacted in the same way, and they have experimented with a wide diversity of modes of regulation that this book seeks to analyse. New rules have been initiated by different levels of government—municipal, metropolitan, regional and national. They have stemmed from different policy sectors and have had different rationalities: controlling the effects of tourism on living conditions in Barcelona; protecting the housing stock in Berlin or Paris; or, on the contrary, legalising STRs in London or Milan to boost urban attractiveness. Beyond the common goal of giving a legal framework to STRs, regulations have sought to impose more or less strict limitations on this market through different instruments (from bans to light registration schemes, via rules distinguishing between different types of STR or urban areas). Regulations have also changed, sometimes several times in the space of a few years, in the same city, as has been the case in Berlin (from very strict to middle-range regulation) and Lisbon (from no to strict regulation).

How can we account for and explain such a diversity of regulation in European cities, in the face of a global, disruptive phenomenon that has developed so quickly everywhere, shaped by transnational corporate platforms? The diversity of modes of (urban) regulation could be deemed surprising by those who hypothesise that the dynamics of economic globalisation, neoliberalisation and financialisation cause relatively similar transformations, or even convergence, in national and/or urban policies. Policy responses would tend to converge around urban attractiveness strategies geared towards the attraction of inward investment and visitors, influenced by the international circulation of urban policy models in a context of competition between cities at the global scale. However, comparative social scientists have long analysed the multiplicity of forms taken by capitalism, its regulation, its transformations and the ways in which national and local societies seek to respond to exogenous and endogenous changes. This has constituted the starting point, and initial puzzle, of various strands of scholarship in comparative political economy and urban studies, which contribute to explain the diversity, variety or variegation of capitalism and its regulation at different scales. The diversity we unpack in this book is not only the expression of small variations in a sea of common political and economic mechanisms; it is of significance and has to be explained through detailed comparative empirical research (Hay 2004). As we will show, existing works on STR regulation do not always make it possible to *explain* regulatory diversity, due to a lack of attention to causal mechanisms and institutional frameworks at multiple scales.

The book examines the ways in which European city governments and other collective actors (such as national governments, European institutions, firms and social movements) have taken up the issue of platform-mediated STRs and attempted to regulate it. It addresses this general question through four objectives:

- First, the book aims to describe, measure and make explicit the diversity of regulations—to what extent, and how, city governments have sought to govern this new phenomenon through a variety of regulatory approaches.

- Second, it seeks to explain why city governments have adopted different regulatory approaches in the face of a 'globalised public problem', in a complex multi-level governance landscape shaped by local, regional, national and transnational actors and interest groups with sometimes diametrically opposed views on regulation.

- Third, it analyses the challenges of implementing and enforcing regulations in an era of digital platform capitalism, global human mobility and transnational investment flows.

- Fourth, it explores the social, political and institutional effects of those regulations and the reshaping of the urban political economy and governance of (urban) platform capitalism, tourism and housing.

At a broad level, the book addresses the question of how state actors, in particular urban/local governments (alongside regional, national and supranational ones), regulate transnational platforms, platform-mediated activities, tourism and housing markets, as well as the mechanisms through which social and interest groups collectively mobilise to shape (urban) policies and regulatory interventions. It therefore seeks 'to identify the mechanisms through which a (new) phenomenon is made governable, i.e. by whom, how and for what purpose, activities and groups are organised and steered through mechanisms of political regulation' (Jacquot and Halpern 2015:57). The policy issue at stake is twofold: STRs themselves and the digital platforms that mediate the practice.

Platforms have built their economic and rent extraction model around *data*: they appropriate and exploit user-generated data for their activities, creating a system of information asymmetry that underpins their power in the face of public authorities. The lack of visibility of digitally mediated STR economic practices makes any attempt to enforce regulations by public authorities challenging. Those authorities try to regulate, while at the same time attempting to know precisely what the object of regulation is.

STRs are both an economic activity and a specific type of land/building use, mediated by digital corporations. Regulatory choices therefore involve political compromises between the right to freely use one's property, conduct an economic activity or offer a digital intermediation service, and the demands for the protection of collective, 'public interest' objectives, for example a sufficient stock of affordable housing for long-term residents. In a fast-expanding market, regulations play a crucial socio-economic and political role: to rephrase Harold Laswell's classical argument (1936), they contribute to determining 'who gets what, when and how' (and where) from the concurrent development of platform capitalism and the STR economy. Regulations contribute to recomposing the relations between urban, regional, national and European governments; large transnational companies such as digital platforms; and the actors of the housing, real estate and tourism sectors. They shape different STR markets (more or less liberalised). This produces winners and losers by defining who can most benefit from the extraction of value and land rent, as well as how benefits and losses are individually and collectively distributed. As the book will show, the contentious politics of STR housing has been, to a large extent, a matter of conflicting claims, rights and distributional conflicts around regulatory choices.

Thus, while the book focuses on STRs, its broader significance lies in illuminating how cities as collective actors, and states, regulate capitalism. The study of STRs offers a fascinating take on how an innovation—*platform capitalism*—that appeared and rapidly spread in many countries simultaneously has been met with and mediated by radically different responses in different places. The analysis of the diversity of STR regulations is not only about STRs, digital platforms and housing: it is about the differential capacity of state actors, in particular city governments, to regulate transnational corporations and flows, about the variety of urban capitalisms and about the multi-level political and institutional features that shape this variety. By studying and explaining the emergence of different STR regulations, additionally, the book shows the ways in which STR markets have become institutionalised differently from one city to another and the varying degrees of opportunity they offer for capital accumulation.

## REGULATING URBAN PLATFORM CAPITALISM AND STRs: A NEW CHALLENGE FOR URBAN POLICY AND URBAN STUDIES

Since the 2010s a number of objects, problems and corporations related to the rise of platform capitalism have entered local governments' agendas and have received intense media coverage. Whether ride-hailing (Uber), electric scooters (Lyme), food delivery (Deliveroo) or short-term accommodation (Airbnb), new activities have developed and opened up urban markets, often outside existing legal frameworks. This has plunged local governments into situations of uncertainty, while giving them some room for manoeuvre to elaborate new forms of regulation, push for specific agendas and increase their political power and distinctiveness. Among these new policy problems, platform-mediated STRs have undoubtedly been one of the most salient.

This salience can be explained by the very characteristics of housing—a central aspect of daily life. In Europe and elsewhere, existing problems of housing accessibility and affordability have, in many places, been further challenged by the emergence of STR platforms. This 'disruptive innovation' in visitor accommodation (Guttentag 2015) has transformed housing markets and jeopardised access to housing in urban centres that were already under pressure from pre-existing gentrification and touristification dynamics. The salience of STRs can additionally be explained by the 'wicked nature' of the issue, which stands at the crossroads of the digital economy, tourism and housing sectors. This cross-sectoral nature makes it a contentious object that has triggered collective action by many actors: social movements fighting for the right to the city, local officials seeking to promote affordable housing, the hotel industry defending its grip on tourist accommodation, property owners seeking to extract STR revenues, and governments embracing the promises of the start-up and tech industry. Finally, this salience can also be explained by the fact that platform-mediated STRs have challenged the modes of regulation of urban (and national) economies (Artioli 2018): How can city governments have a hold on transnational corporations; issues of taxation; regulation of property rights; and the free movement of goods, people and capital? In the face of a global phenomenon and its locally contentious politics, can local governments regulate it at all, if they so wish in the first place?

## Bringing Back Politics and Institutions into the STR Regulation Field

While limited until 2015, the social sciences literature on platform-mediated STRs is now abundant—and still growing. The phenomenon has been well researched in various parts of the world, addressed through a diversity of perspectives and themes. While few comprehensive monographs have been published so far, with the notable exceptions of Oskam's (2019) and Hoffmann and Schmitter Heisler's (2020) books, a large number of articles have been published on the development of platform-mediated STRs; their consequences for tourism activities and industries; their effects on cities, housing markets and local conflicts; and the challenges of regulation. Existing scholarship stems from tourism studies, geography, sociology, planning, economics, law, political science, management, business and technology studies.

However, it took longer for scholars to focus on how governments have reacted to the phenomenon. In an in-depth review of this growing body of scholarship in Chapter 2, we show that existing research on STR regulation has produced four main findings. First, STRs are difficult to regulate because they often fall outside existing legal frameworks and thus—at least initially—fall into spaces of 'a-legality' or illegality. Platforms and STR operators, through various strategies, seem to outpace the expertise and watchdog capacity of public administrations. Second, the first regulatory measures were taken at the local level by city governments to address a new phenomenon that national authorities were slow to respond to. Third, regulations have varied widely across cities, from complete bans to laissez-faire. Fourth, where new regulations have been put in place, they do produce effects on the STR offer yet appear to be difficult to enforce—particularly due to a lack of data and grip on the digital sphere by public authorities.

This body of scholarship covers a wide range of geographical areas and develops useful typologies and robust econometric models of the impacts of regulations on the STR offer. However, there are two short-comings that we address in this book. First, with rare exceptions (e.g., Benli-Trichet and Kübler, 2022), researchers take the diversity of reg-ulations as an independent variable to explain differences in effects, rather than as a fully fledged dependent variable to be explained in and of itself. Second, STR regulatory instruments are often treated in isolation from other public policies and institutions: most exist-ing studies confine themselves to a 'command and control' under-standing of regulatory instruments, without studying the relations between these instruments and other policy sectors and between dif-ferent institutions, actors and levels of government. They also neglect the processes of politicisation that play out in each city, the politics of implementation and enforcement and the effects of regulations in terms of urban governance. The (now numerous) studies of what hap-pens *after* the enactment of new regulations are focused on the eval-uation of quantitative effects on the STR offer, without taking into account how implementation works in practice. This is, however, a complex and crucial aspect to investigate for a meaningful analysis of public policies.

The present book seeks to respond to these shortcomings by propos-ing a comparative framework to capture and explain the diversity of modes of STR regulation in a dozen cities. To address the problem of causal inference, we propose a comparative, mixed methods and multi-site research design combining a variable-oriented approach (a com-parison of 12 cases) and a case-oriented approach (a process tracing of 3 cases). To address the crucial lack of understanding of the diversity and complexity of regulatory policies, we move beyond a formal comparison of regulatory outputs by drawing on comparative political economy and on the political sociology of public policies and multi-level governance to explain the political origins, policy process, implementation and socio-political outcomes of regulations.

## Political Mobilisation, the Regulation of Urban Capitalism and Multi-Level Governance

This book is about STR regulation in large European cities as a matter of politics and governance. The regulation of STRs is not merely achieved through the use of specific *instruments*, even if they are the most visible face of such regulation. Regulation and government activities should also be seen in the context of institutions, on the one hand, and of relations between actors, discourses, representations and symbols, on the other hand. We cannot understand and explain regulation without taking into account the national and local institutional arrangements between governments, firms and markets, and the processes of politicisation that have played out between citizens, interest groups and political leaders at the local, national and transnational levels—all of this in a socio-economic and housing context specific to each city and country. Besides, STRs are not just about the provision of tourist accommodation: they are connected to the transformation of capitalism in cities; changes in travel, tourism and working practices; the financialisation of the global economy; the housing crisis; urban inequalities; and other eminently political issues. This has implications for the ways in which public policy practitioners or citizens involved in social mobilisations might consider the issue: to govern platform-mediated STRs, we must not simply regulate STRs but also consider broader policy interventions related to housing, taxation, the digital economy and tourism.

In this book, altogether, we show that there is a diversity of regulatory regimes in European cities that we classify into *three worlds of STR regulation*. The first encompasses cities where regulations are aimed at legalising and taxing a competitive STR market without curbing it, in order to support tourism attractiveness and property-based revenues within liberalised housing markets dominated by homeowners. By contrast, the second and the third worlds include cities with stricter STR regulations aimed at curbing the expansion of STR markets and mitigating their adverse effects on housing availability and neighbourhood life. The second world is one of touristic cities with robust housing institutions and local governments acting as initiators of STR regulation. The third world comprises cities characterised by 'new municipalist' local governments receptive to active grassroots mobilisations.

To make sense of the diversity of STR regulations, our argument combines four types of explanatory strands. Those strands have emerged from both our review of existing scholarship and our original theoretical framework (presented in Chapter 2). Our empirical analysis shows that none of the variables and mechanisms identified under each strand can be isolated; they work in combination to explain differences between modes of regulation.

- The first explanatory strand concerns politics. Following a fairly classical perspective in comparative political science, we examine the extent to which the political alignment (partisan variable) of local governments on the one hand, and the presence of local social mobilisations that politicise the STR issue on the other, play a role in the observed differences in regulation.

- The second explanatory strand concerns the role of socio-economic and structural conditions in the cities studied, drawing on the comparative urban studies literature. We examine whether differences in the characteristics of the housing stock and housing markets on the one hand, and in tourist flows and the quantity of STRs on the other, explain the regulatory variations observed between cities.

- The third explanatory strand goes beyond the urban level to tackle a hypothesis that stems from the scholarship on the political economy of welfare states and housing systems. We analyse the extent to which the diversity of STR regulations in cities can be explained by the diversity of national welfare/housing regimes.

- The last explanatory strand refers to the importance of relations between levels of governments—well addressed in scholarship on multi-level governance. We examine the extent to which STR regulations in cities are influenced by the distribution of competences between cities, regions, national states and the EU, and by the (changing) power relations between those levels.

First, to what extent do politics matter? Whether it concerns markets, humans or the environment, the choices leading to regulation are political: they are guided not only by economic, technical or administrative considerations, but also by distributional conflicts and trade-offs between different interest groups. A first hypothesis emerges: the intensity and type of STR regulation would depend on the cities' ruling majorities and their political agenda, which would shape problem framing and public policy choices. At first sight, one might expect left-wing city governments to regulate the activities of urban platform capitalism more quickly and more strongly than right-wing ones, in order to protect residents' access to affordable housing. We will show that this hypothesis is partly true: in Berlin, Barcelona, Amsterdam, Paris and Lisbon, more stringent STR regulations were adopted when those cities were governed by left-wing parties or coalitions, who justified regulation by the urgent need to curb residents' displacement and the increase in house prices and rents. But this hypothesis is not completely confirmed by empirical evidence: for instance, how can we explain the significant differences in regulations between Paris and Barcelona, the latter being more stringent than the former? And how can we explain the fact that local authorities led by right-wing parties have sometimes pushed for more regulation (e.g., some boroughs in London)?

The other dimension of the (urban) politics variable refers to the mobilisation of citizens, through organised social movements or informal grassroots collectives. An initial observation of the history of STR regulations in the USA or in European cities such as Berlin or Barcelona led us to formulate the hypothesis that the more local social movements critical of STRs are present and vocal, the more local governments will be led to regulate strongly in response to public pressure. Yet we will show that this hypothesis is only partially confirmed: while it holds true in cases such as Barcelona, Madrid and Berlin, it does not in cases such as Paris, where social movements have been weaker and latecomers, but STR regulation has been relatively early and strong.

Second, we analyse to what extent policy responses to STRs depend on urban socio-economic and structural conditions, more specifically: the structure of the housing stock (tenure split, share of public/social housing), the housing market (rents, house prices, housing affordability), the relative intensity of tourist flows and the quantity of STR accommodation. Those variables all have strong explanatory potential for inter-city variance in STR regulations, and we have tested a number of hypotheses related to each of them. However, as we have argued before (Aguilera et al. 2021) and show more extensively in this book, those hypotheses are not completely satisfactory. They do not explain the variance in our sample (synchronic variation: cities with relatively similar structural conditions such as Barcelona, Paris and Milan have adopted very different STR regulations) or the changes over time (diachronic variation: cities such as Lisbon or Berlin may have changed their strategy over time, even though local conditions have not changed fundamentally). Here again, without dismissing the weight of local conditions, the book shows that political processes and the interplay of individual and collective actors with local and national institutions play a greater role in explaining what policy decisions are made and implemented in relation to STRs.

Third, for scholars working on the political economy of capitalism and its diversity (Hall and Soskice 2001; Hay 2004), regulatory differences are actually not surprising: they can be explained by the diversity of types and trajectories of welfare states and national styles of regulation of capitalism. They represent a diversity of articulations between states, firms and social groups in the organisation of the economy and in citizens' social protection. Over time, welfare state reforms and state restructuring have followed clearly identifiable trajectories through path-dependency (Pierson 1994). Thus, a transformation or a crisis shared on a global scale will never impose itself uniformly and linearly on all countries. It will be intermediated by actors whose representations, room for manoeuvre and decisions may vary from one country to the next (Hay and Rosamond 2002), and by existing institutional arrangements. For the proponents of a territorialised and 'urban' variation of such political economy approaches (Lorrain 2005; Guironnet et al. 2016; Pinson and Journel 2017), the diversity of capitalism and welfare regimes is expressed not just at the national level, but also at the regional and local levels. They identify regimes of urban capitalism that can be very diverse between cities in the same country (as has been the case in Europe). This diversity is rooted in a variety of central–local relations that influence the autonomy of local governments in decision-making and in the design and implementation of modes of regulation in specific sectors. Similarly, for urban and economic geographers, different forms of urban 'variegated capitalism' reflect a diversity of (local) modes of extraction and regulation of urban rent, and of articulations of neoliberalisation processes and resistance to them, in a multi-level perspective (Peck and Theodore 2007). As we will argue, when it comes to housing specifically, scholarship on the variety of welfare/housing systems (Arbaci 2019), and on housing assetisation and financialisation (Schwartz and Seabrooke 2009; Aalbers 2017), can also be mobilised to explain the diversity of STR regulations—though we will see that the variety of welfare/housing regimes in which our 12 cities are located does not explain all the variance in our sample.

Fourth, the diversity of policy choices formulated and implemented by local governments in Europe—in the face of the transformations of the global economy and the retreat of the Keynesian state—cannot be explained without taking into account the multi-level governance dimension (Le Galès 2002). At its simplest, the concept of multi-level governance refers to the dispersion of authority within and beyond national states (Hooghe et al. 2023). On the one hand, there is a diversity of forms of European states (*polity*) and of organisation of competences and power relations between local, regional and national governments (*politics* and *policies*) (Artioli 2016), even if researchers have observed certain dynamics of convergence in the territorial organisation and politics of European states following the 2008 crisis (Goldsmith and Page 2010; Cole et al. 2015; King and Le Galès 2017). Moreover, in the context of the EU, a set of supranational institutions plays a crucial role in the regulation of platform capitalism (Thelen 2018; Culpepper and Thelen 2020), in particular regarding STRs, as we will see in Chapter 7. On the other hand, the relationships between local governments and non-state actors such as private firms can vary within the same national context, producing a variety of modes of governance and market regulation at the local level (Lorrain 2005). Thus, in this book we argue that taking into account the relationships between different tiers of government, and between state, market and civil society actors, is crucial to explain the public policy choices of municipal officials at particular moments in time.

Altogether, the theoretical framework underpinning this book is therefore located at the crossroads of three broad lines of scholarship: the *political sociology of public policies*—to explain issue framing, agenda-setting and implementation processes; the *comparative political economy* of national and urban capitalism—to explain the diversity of articulations between national and local governments, urban policies, firms and markets; and *urban and multi-level governance*—to explain the relations between public and private actors at different scales in specific territories (here, large European cities) in the context of the global spread of platform capitalism. We thus hope to contribute to the strengthening of the dialogue and cross-fertilisation between political science, political sociology and the other various disciplines that make up urban studies (Colomb 2023; Marques 2024).

The book compares 12 European large, touristic cities (Amsterdam, Barcelona, Berlin, Brussels, Lisbon, London, Madrid, Milan, Paris, Prague, Rome, Vienna), but focuses more precisely, in some chapters, on three ideal-typical cases selected through typological work (Barcelona, Milan and Paris). Our sample focuses on capital and second cities that are among the top tourism destinations in Europe, are economically dynamic and are thus faced with demographic pressures and tense housing markets (see Chapter 2). We did not study smaller historic towns and cities whose economies have, for a long time, been dominated by tourism (e.g., Venice), or medium-sized cities, small towns and villages in coastal, mountainous or rural settings. Our analysis does not necessarily apply to destinations that have much less concentration of STRs and visitors, that is, 'ordinary cities' (Semi and Tonetta 2021, based on Robinson 2006) and peripheral territories where the negative impacts of STRs discussed in Chapter 1 might be less prevalent. However, it is worth noting that the socio-political mobilisation of diverse actors, including local governments, around the growth and impacts of STRs has in recent years expanded geographically to a variety of small and medium-sized towns across Europe.

The choices underpinning our research design are explained in Chapter 2, with more details on the methods given in the Appendix. The book combines a *variable-oriented analysis* focused on the factors that have produced similarities or differences between cases and a *case-oriented analysis* attentive to the cross-case histories and causal mechanisms that led to particular types of STR regulations. Our mixed methods approach combined in-depth fieldwork through semi-structured interviews and repeated periods of ethnographic observations in three cities (Barcelona, Milan, Paris); shorter periods of qualitative research combining documentary analysis and/or interviews in nine other cities; and the creation and analysis of a quantitative dataset covering the 12 cities. All this empirical work was carried out between 2016 and 2022. The analysis of STR regulations offered in the book was up-to-date as of the end of 2023.

## STRUCTURE OF THE BOOK

The first part of the book contextualises platform-mediated STRs as an object of regulation and establishes the theoretical foundations of the research. The emergence of STRs as a major issue for European cities reflects the broader transformation of capitalism, through the emergence of the digital platform model, shifts in tourism and mobility practices and changes in housing systems and markets. Chapter 1 examines how platform-mediated STRs lie at the crossroads of these three fields of analysis. It helps the reader to grasp the multiple facets of the phenomenon and the challenges it poses for public authorities that seek to regulate a 'wicked issue'. Chapter 2 sets out the book's theoretical framework and research design. It offers a detailed, critical review of existing international scholarship on the regulation of STRs, before presenting our theoretical approach and mixed method, multi-level comparative research design.

The second part of the book brings the reader fully into our empirical analysis and explanation of the diversity of STR regulatory regimes in European cities. In Chapter 3 we present an ideal-typical typology of our 12 European cities. We explain how we constructed an Intensity of Regulation Index (IRI) that enabled us to classify cities according to the number and types of STR regulatory instruments adopted.

We then build an ideal-typical typology of three types of regulatory regimes that we call the 'three worlds of STR regulation' in Europe. Chapter 4 subsequently adopts a more explanatory and case-oriented perspective: we carry out a detailed process-tracing analysis of the three central cases of each 'world' (Paris, Barcelona and Milan) to identify the causal mechanisms behind the diversity of adopted modes of regulation.

The third part of the book analyses how European city governments have all been facing common challenges in the implementation of STR regulations, that nevertheless produce different socio-political effects in the three worlds. In Chapter 5, based on in-depth fieldwork carried out in Barcelona, Paris and Milan, we analyse the issues at stake in the *implementation* and *enforcement* of STR regulations at three levels: city politics, street-level bureaucrats, and courts. In all cities, enforcement efforts are confronted with the challenges and uncertainty that stem from platforms' proprietary data strategies. Chapter 6 focuses on the interest group politics and power relationships between the various stakeholders involved in STR governance across our European cities. It analyses and compares how corporate platforms, STR operators and 'hosts', social movements and the hotel industry have contributed to shape, oppose or, on the contrary, support new regulations. Chapter 7 analyses the judicialisation and transnationalisation of local STR regulatory conflicts at the European level in the early 2020s. It shows that EU institutions play a key (and contested) role in shaping the legal and regulatory interventions of national and local authorities.

The conclusion offers a broader reflection on the implications of our explanatory model for understanding the diversity of STR markets and the limits of STR regulations. It concludes with a discussion of how our findings can contribute to a better understanding of the (urban) politics and regulation of platform-mediated STRs, and more generally of platform capitalism, beyond Europe.

## POSITIONALITY AND AUDIENCE OF THE BOOK

We are three European researchers whose disciplinary backgrounds combine sociology, political science, geography, planning and urban studies. We have tenured positions in French and British universities, which has been a source of stability, albeit accompanied by a heavy administrative and teaching load. Combined with the fact that we did not receive a large grant to pursue this research, this has meant that we carried the work underpinning this book incrementally, over several years. As EU citizens, however, we were able to move freely across European borders to carry out regular periods of fieldwork in the cities covered here—a privilege that many scholars and students who struggle with restrictive or hostile visa or immigration policies, and racism, might not have.

Our respective prior research had mostly focused on comparative urban governance, public policies, planning conflicts and social movements in Western and Southern European cities. Our knowledge of several European languages means that we have drawn on multiple sources and intellectual traditions, not just from Anglophone urban studies and social sciences, but also from French, Italian, Spanish, Catalan and German ones. Embedding non-Anglophone scholarship and materials into a book written in English, along with our mixed methods and multidisciplinary approach, contributes, we hope, to the ongoing pluralisation of perspectives in comparative urban studies.

We wrote this book as an academic text whose primary objective is to develop an ambitious comparative research framework to explain the diversity of STR regulatory regimes and the politics and socio-political effects of regulation. Beyond STR, the book aims to contribute to empirical and theoretical knowledge-building in relation to several contemporary themes of social scientific inquiry: the rise of platform capitalism and its regulation; the transformation of human mobilities and tourism; the reshaping of housing in an era of globalised assetisation and financialisation; and the implications of those dynamics for the fabric of cities, urban governance and public policies. The book will therefore be of interest to scholars in urban studies, political science, sociology, geography, political economy and a wider range of social science disciplines.

The book does not seek to evaluate policy effectiveness in a quantitative sense, nor to propose normative solutions to the issues at stake. Equally, while we assess critically the activities of actors such as STR operators and digital platforms in specific contexts, it is not a manifesto against platform-mediated STRs. Nevertheless, researchers are also citizens with political opinions about the topics they investigate and are often involved in, or close to, social movements and grassroots campaigns in the cities where they live and work. They may be partial and more sympathetic to the voices of certain actors compared to others. We are no exception to this, but have consciously sought, in this book, to represent fairly the different—sometimes opposed—positions and arguments of the various actors involved in regulatory debates.

That being said, the standpoint underpinning our research is that European cities are deeply unequal; that recent land, housing and real estate development trends and political-economic dynamics have compounded those inequalities; and that social science research on public policies should broadly contribute to improve our understanding of the role that such policies can play to prevent or tackle inequalities. We believe in the right to housing for all and in the right of democratically elected local governments to enact public policies and forms of regulation that seek to ensure this right. When we wrote this book, we lived, respectively, in the city-regions of Rennes, Paris and London, where STRs have been a major political issue. When doing fieldwork, we deliberately chose not to stay in STR accommodation. As citizens concerned with urban and housing inequalities, we have taken part in social debates on STRs and their regulation in parallel to, and drawing on, our work as academic researchers. We have contributed to public meetings and debates; responded to public consultations by presenting evidence to different tiers of government; spoken to journalists; shared knowledge with social activists involved in housing- or tourism-related grassroots campaigns; and written non-academic, advocacy-oriented texts. We hope that the book will therefore be of interest to a wider audience beyond academic circles, such as policy-makers in various tiers of governments, economic actors, journalists, activists and curious citizens.

# PART I

# PLATFORM CAPITALISM, SHORT-TERM RENTALS AND THEIR REGULATION

**A Framework**

# 1

# THE RISE OF SHORT-TERM RENTALS

Between Corporate Platforms, Tourism Flows
and Housing Assetisation

THE UNPRECEDENTED GROWTH of STRs since the early 2010s in many parts of the globe lies at the intersection of three dynamics of socio-economic change: (1) the emergence of digital platforms as a new type of firm, (2) the growth of tourism and other forms of human mobility and (3) the assetisation of housing. In this chapter we present how STRs are simultaneously a consequence of, and a contributor to, these dynamics.[1] STRs have been fuelled by new start-ups turned multinational corporations, by the growing demand from tourists and 'temporary city users' and by the new sources of revenue that this activity represents for property owners. In turn, the growth of STRs has expanded the reach of digital platforms over the urban realm, has brought more short-term users into residential buildings and has reinforced the transformation of housing into a lucrative investment opportunity.

We discuss how STRs are entangled in these broader dynamics (see Figure 2) for two main purposes. First, this

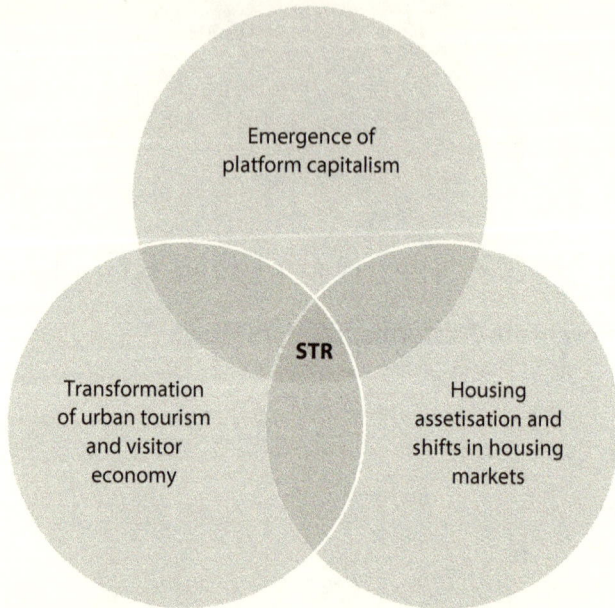

**Figure 2.** Platform-mediated short-term rentals: a 'wicked' policy object at the intersection of three dynamics of urban change. *Source*: Authors.

allows us to introduce STRs as a phenomenon and as an object of controversy, to assess their novelty and to situate them within broader socioeconomic and spatial transformations. Second, it helps us to understand the regulatory challenges connected to their growth, which is crucial for our subsequent analysis of the consolidation of different regulatory regimes that turned this 'disruptive' innovation into a policy object and a (more or less) regulated market.

## THE RISE OF PLATFORM CAPITALISM

While the STR of accommodation units to visitors is not new, the emergence of digital platforms that match supply and demand at a global scale has expanded this practice dramatically. In the STR sector, during the 2010s mergers and acquisitions consolidated the role of a small number of large corporate platforms operating internationally, that is, Airbnb, Vacation Rentals by Owner (VRBO, from the Expedia group), Booking.com and TripadvisorRentals.[2] Beyond those giants, smaller national platforms offer different types of STR accommodation through a variety of business models (peer-to-peer [P2P], business-to-consumer [B2C] or both). STR platforms have been described as a 'disruptive innovation' radically transforming the tourism industry (Dredge and Gyimóthy 2015; Guttentag 2015; Oskam and Boswijk 2016; Prayag and Ozanne 2018; Oskam 2019). They are part of the broader emergence of 'platform capitalism' (Srnicek 2016) or the 'platform economy' (Kenney and Zysman 2016), characterised by the bundling together of technology, digital economic circulation, and social and business practices organised around *platforms*. Digital platforms represent a new kind of firm, market intermediary and form of social ordering.[3] They have transformed entire markets: urban mobility, accommodation, labour, finance, goods, online social activities and content production.

## From the 'Sharing Economy' to 'Platform Capitalism'

In the mid-2010s, digital platforms were initially described as the backbone of a new 'sharing' or 'collaborative' economy (Codagnone and Martens 2016; Arcidiacono et al. 2018). The term referred to the temporary access to, rather than the ownership of, goods and services (Belk 2007; McLaren and Agyeman 2015), for example, occasionally renting an electric drill from someone rather than buying one. Under the banner 'What's Mine is Yours' (Botsman and Rogers 2011), advocates heralded the potential of the sharing economy to democratise capitalism via bottom-up cooperation and the sustainable use of 'underused' resources. Early analyses of STR embraced this optimistic view, celebrating new ways of travelling and fostering encounters between a new global community of 'hosts' and 'guests'. The rhetoric of 'sharing' between ordinary people became a central plank of the marketing and public policy narratives developed by corporate STR platforms, such as Airbnb, to promote their activities (Sharp 2018).

Yet initial hopes faded quickly. The 'sharing euphoria' has given way to 'platform disillusion' (Grabher and König 2020:96), through increasing evidence of negative externalities for those affected by platforms' operations: service providers, customers, incumbents, communities and the government (Mosaad et al. 2023). In many sectors, a handful of corporate for-profit platforms have acquired quasi-monopolistic positions, while local, smaller, not-for-profit or cooperative experiments have disappeared, remained marginal or become monetised. The advertised goods or services on offer have rapidly been appropriated by commercial actors, rather than amateur 'peers'. And the precarity and insecurity of labour conditions in the platform-based 'gig economy' has become well documented (O'Regan and Choe 2017; Berg and Furrer 2018; Prassl 2018; Vallas 2018; Woodcock and Graham 2019), as well as the gendered and racialised exploitation and inequalities hidden by promotional narratives celebrating 'platform labour' (van Doorn 2017). The rhetoric of sharing has thus been described as 'sharewashed neoliberalism' (see also Cockayne 2016; Törnberg 2021).

It has also become clear that platform-mediated market exchanges often reproduce class, racial, gender and other forms of inequalities and exploitation (Schor 2021; Schor and Vallas 2021). In the case of platform-mediated STRs, there has been evidence of discrimination by hosts on- and offline, along lines of gender, disability (Randle and Dolnicar 2019; Ameri et al. 2020), sexual identity, national origin and race (Edelman et al. 2017; McCloskey 2018; McLaughlin 2018; Verhaeghe et al. 2023), through active practices of guest screening (Ravenelle 2016). Other studies from the USA showed that conversely, guests showed a preference for White hosts, which allowed the latter to charge higher prices (Marchenko 2019; Jaeger and Sleegers 2023) and led to lower average earnings for African American (Edelman and Luca 2014; Gold 2020) or

Asian American hosts (Gilheany et al. 2015; Luca et al. 2024). Such findings echo existing scholarship on racial discrimination and dispossession in the private rental housing sector in an era of emergent 'rentier capitalism' (Wolifson et al. 2023), financialisation (Fields and Raymond 2021) and 'platform real estate' (McElroy 2020; Fields and Rogers 2021). More widely, this evidence should be placed within broader debates on the entanglement of platform capitalism, racial capitalism (McMillan Cottom 2020) and (neo)colonialism (Törnberg and Chiappini 2020).[4]

## Platforms as a New Type of Firm

Digital platforms are not just digital marketplaces between suppliers and consumers (in Airbnb's language, *hosts* and *guests*). They also represent a new kind of firm that relies on an external labour force, a network of coopted users, the production of value through data analytics and algorithms, and 'winner-take-all' or 'winner-take-most' strategies (Rahman and Thelen 2019; Stark and Pais 2020). Rahman and Thelen (2019) see the *platform* as the latest form taken by the *vanguard firm* in contemporary capitalism: after the 'large industrial firm' of the mid-century (e.g., General Motors or Ford) and the 'network of contracts' firm of the 1990s (e.g., Nike), a new 'platform business model' epitomised by Uber, Amazon and Airbnb has emerged. This model combines existing and new features.

First, platforms have pushed the process of 'individualisation and flexibilisation of the labour force' to the extreme (Montalban et al. 2019:9). They do not employ the suppliers of the goods or services they mediate and thus bear 'no responsibility for workers' wages, hours or benefits' (Rahman and Thelen 2019:183). Platforms foster workers' precarity in four ways: 'low, irregular pay; the opacity of algorithmic management; health and safety risks; and the lack of social protection' (Kriz 2023:30). This has generated new forms of labour mobilisations among 'gig economy' workers in the Global North and South. In parallel, the emergence of platform-mediated services has put pressure on, and triggered protests from, incumbent providers, as demonstrated by the debates on the effects of Uber on taxis or of STRs on the hotel industry.

Second, the organisational model of the platform is based not on making or buying, but on *coopting* things that are not owned by the firm: 'physical assets, R&D, workforce, salesforce, market research, and the creative energies of customers' (Stark and Pais 2020:53). Platforms thus rely on *network effects:* the more numerous the coopted users, the more useful and valuable the platform becomes for everyone who joins (Srnicek 2016:45). Increasing the number of users and transactions is vital to the platforms' capacity to both create and capture value (Kenney and Zysman 2016; Srnicek 2016; Langley and Leyshon 2017). Gallagher (2018) narrates the efforts of the founders of Airbnb to recruit new hosts in San Francisco and New York in 2007–2008. The increasing size of the network subsequently locks in existing platform users and incentivises those who are still outside to jump in: for someone renting a property on a short-term basis, it has become difficult to stay out of Airbnb. Moreover, in the digital 'reputation economy' (Hearns 2010), it is not easy to move to a different platform, since the ratings acquired in one cannot be transferred to another.

Third, platforms generate and extract value thanks to their dual role as intermediary between users, and as data-gathering infrastructure (Srnicek 2016). On the one hand, platforms take a commission for the intermediation between supply and demand (in the case of Airbnb, this amounts to a service fee of 3% of the booking subtotal for hosts and 14% for guests). On the other hand, users' activities and searches on the platform provide the firm with huge quantities of data. Such data are at the heart of the platform business model, and software engineers and data scientists are the technical elite behind this model. Data feed into, and educate, algorithms to refine the platform's operations, optimise its matching capacities and help it expand the market (Yeung 2018:507). Platform algorithms serve the purpose of matching, but also rating, ranking and rewarding users (e.g., on Airbnb, through the attribution of the 'superhost' status to highly rated responsive hosts). This *algorithmic management* represents a specific form of social ordering engineered in a highly opaque and asymmetric manner (Yeung 2018; Stark and Pais 2020) and has raised significant challenges for social science researchers (Kitchin 2018). Altogether, the platform model is characterised by an unprecedented asymmetry in the production, holding and treatment of data (Langley and Leyshon 2017; Voytenko Palgan et al. 2021).

Finally, platform development has been backed by a new form of 'patient capital' that relies on 'winner-take-all' market strategies (Rahman and Thelen 2019:181). Acting on a high risk/high return basis, 'patient' venture capital has been invested in numerous platforms with the expectation that a few of them would acquire a dominant market share that ultimately generates high returns (Langley and Leyshon 2017; Montalban et al. 2019). Investors have thus financed platforms that operate in the red for several years, supporting their aggressive expansion aimed at reaching quasi-monopolistic positions. This enabling financial regime, first developed in the Silicon Valley in the USA, has been a precondition for the birth of large corporate digital platforms as we know them (Kenney and Zysman 2020). For instance, in 2009 Sequoia Capital funded Airbnb (which only had 1,000 hosts then) with over half a million US dollars, followed by over US$7 million from Greylock Partners in 2010 and US$112 million from other venture capital funds (Gainsforth 2019). Yet it was only in 2022 that Airbnb reported its first profitable year.

## From Market Power to Political Power

Large-scale cooptation, network and lock-in effects, algorithmic management, winner-take-all strategies and market dominance are the main reasons platforms are often compared to the classical monopolies and oligopolies of the past (Srnicek 2016; Rahman and Thelen 2019;

Peck and Phillips 2020). Similarly to the latter, platforms exhibit not just *market power* but also *political power*. Scholars have underlined that platforms share classical *instrumental power* with other types of businesses (Culpepper and Thelen 2020; Valdez 2023): they mobilise corporate resources to advance their interests through active lobbying at different tiers of government (as carried out, for example, by content and social media platforms Google and Facebook at the EU level since the mid-2010s). The extent of such practices, and the receptive answer they have received from many national governments, was vividly illustrated by the 'Uber Files' revelations of the International Consortium of Investigative Journalists (ICIJ 2022), which argued that the Uber platform 'broke laws, duped police and secretly lobbied governments' (The Guardian 2022).

The political power of platforms, however, cannot be reduced to instrumental business power. According to Culpepper and Thelen (2020), platforms also exhibit a new, specific form of 'platform power' derived from their close relationship with consumers, who depend on, and benefit from, the immediate reach of platform-provided services and goods. As a result, the political terrain is 'tilted in favour of platforms' (2020:294), making policy-makers reluctant to oppose the tacit alliance between platform owners/investors and consumers. In Culpepper and Thelen's words (2020:288), we are 'all Amazon primed', up to the point when social mobilisations and political struggles might eventually reveal how the interests of particular social groups or citizens can be at odds with those of consumers as a whole. Valdez, in her work on Uber, takes the argument one step further by arguing that platform power rests not just on consumers, but more broadly on the dependence that such firms create among all economic actors. This 'infrastructural power' (Valdez 2023) comes from the fact that large platform companies become essential to the interactions between producers, workers, consumers and even the public sector. Sellers need access to Amazon and need to be listed on Google, as much as drivers need Uber to earn money and owners need Airbnb to rent a property. This is the source of the platforms' political strength. Consequently, the power struggles surrounding regulation involve corporate platforms and governments, but also investors, consumers, providers and all the socio-economic actors in the platforms' networked ecosystem, as we will see. Furthermore, the data collected by large platforms have turned them into 'urban big data oligopolies' (Boeing et al. 2021). As will be discussed in Chapters 5 and 6, data ownership—and the decision to release data, to whom and to what extent—is another dimension of platforms' 'infrastructural power'.

Importantly, platform power has not emerged by chance, nor is it simply the result of rapid technological change. As argued by Mazur and Serafin (2023) in the case of Uber, it is the result of deliberate strategies, in which buying time has been a key part of the business plan. Corporate platforms have taken advantage of the initial legal uncertainty surrounding their activities to develop aggressively and grow 'too big to ban' (Pollman and Barry 2017:16). Having taken control of large shares of a market, platforms then have more leverage to ask for legalisation and to shape the terms of the regulatory debate and the solutions applying to them. Since many platforms started their business in a context of lack of legal clarity or even prohibition (e.g., ride-hailing without licencing), influencing the law has been a key part of their business plan and one of the conditions of their survival. Platforms are thus 'regulatory entrepreneurs' (Pollman and Barry 2017). As shown by scholars working on STR regulation (see Chapter 2), STR platforms have been no exception to those strategies. We investigate more precisely their political activities and relationships with governments in Chapter 6.

## The Platformisation of the Urban

While platform capitalism is not a specifically urban phenomenon, it has urbanised thoroughly. Big cities were the birthplaces and testbeds for platform development and political strategies: in the case of Airbnb, San Francisco (McNeill 2016) and New York (Stabrowski 2017). The diffusion of digital platforms that mediate the provision of goods and services in cities has been extremely rapid across the world, driven by either the international expansion of firms initially born in the USA or Europe (in early 2024, Airbnb operated in over 220 countries, VRBO in 190 countries, Uber in 72 countries) or by firms born and operating in specific markets (e.g., in China, STR firms Tujia or Xiaozhu, Airbnb having announced its withdrawal from the Chinese market in 2022).

More generally, platform capitalism takes hold in, feeds from and reshapes cities (Artioli 2018; Hodson et al. 2020; Sadowski 2020). Platform-mediated exchanges have thrived thanks to the population density, spatial proximity and socio-economic specialisation of urban agglomerations. Large urban markets have made it easier to attract, pool and match producers, consumers, goods and assets (Rauch and Schleicher 2015). A small number of large transnational companies has acquired a particular visibility in the landscape of our cities, operating in the fields of transportation (e.g., Uber), food delivery (e.g., Deliveroo), services (e.g., TaskRabbit), and short-term accommodation (e.g., Airbnb). Platforms have taken over core services related to everyday life. These platforms rely on, and contribute to, the 'digital skin of the city' (Rabari and Storper 2015), namely the entanglement of ubiquitous mobile technologies, virtually mediated relations and augmented digital maps connecting people, companies, infrastructure, and the built environment. This increasingly shapes 'the ways city users and inhabitants choose what to do, where and with whom to do it, what is exchanged, and how, where, when and on what terms choices are made' (Artioli 2018:3).

A growing body of scholarship (sometimes labelled 'digital geography'; Ash et al. 2018a) has explored how socio-spatial practices, the built environment and capitalist accumulation processes in the city have been reconfigured by digital technologies and firms, by 'documenting geographies produced through, produced by, and of the digital' (Ash et al. 2018b:25). Under the neologisms of 'platform urbanism' (Barns 2020; Hodson et al. 2020; Sadowski 2020) or the 'platformisation' of the urban (Hodson et al. 2020:2), scholars have captured this new stage of the urbanisation of technology capital, in which multiple platforms are enmeshed with urban infrastructure, knowledge, data, the production and appropriation of value and daily life in cities. As Bauriedl and Strüver (2022:13) stress, 'not everyone uses digital platforms mediating information, goods, and services, but everybody is influenced by the implications of service platforms on the housing and labour market and the use of public space'.

It is crucial to be aware of the key features of the functioning of platforms to understand the subsequent regulatory conflicts and political strategies analysed in this book. However, the regulation of platforms also depends on the sector(s) to which the services or goods they mediate belong to: it is not the same to seek to regulate ride-hailing, food delivery or STRs. The socio-economic actors, the issues at stake and the rules shaping each sector are different. Platform-mediated STRs are specifically embedded in two key fields of socio-economic life and public policy that are explored in the next sections: tourism and housing.


## THE CHANGING VISITOR ECONOMY OF CITIES

### The Demand for STRs: Tourists, 'Digital Nomads' and 'Temporary City Users'

The exponential growth of STRs in European cities is due to a multiplicity of factors, some supply-related (new technologies making the activity easier; economic incentives for STR providers) and others demand-related, associated with the changing contours of tourism and other forms of short-term mobility. In the classical definition of the United Nations World Tourism Organization (UNWTO), a visitor is 'a traveller taking a trip to a main destination outside [their] usual environment, for less than a year, for any main purpose . . . other than to be employed by a resident entity in the country or place visited'. A visitor is classified as a tourist if their trip includes an overnight stay (United Nations 2008).[5] Global flows of tourism have grown at an extraordinary pace since the Second World War: international arrivals have increased fortyfold, from 25 million in 1950 to more than 1.1 billion in 2014 (UNWTO 2015). This has been facilitated by the decreasing cost of air travel, rises in living standards and changes in consumption patterns among middle- and upper-income groups of the Global North and fast-developing economies of the Global South. In that context, *urban* tourism has been one of the fastest growing segments of the global travel market (Bock 2015). European cities, including the 12 covered in this book, have witnessed a significant increase in tourist numbers in the first two decades of the twenty-first century (Zekan and Wöber 2022). While some were tourist magnets for a long time (e.g., Paris or Rome), other cities not previously considered 'world tourism cities' (Maitland and Newman 2009) became popular destinations from the early 1990s onwards, such as Barcelona and Berlin. This increasing demand has fuelled the explosive growth in STRs (as illustrated in Figure 1 in the Introduction). Moreover, visitors have increasingly sought to experience ordinary spaces off the beaten track (Maitland and Newman 2009; Novy and Huning 2009), something that an STR platform like Airbnb has capitalised on and actually encouraged through one of its slogans, 'live like a local'.

The outbreak of the COVID-19 pandemic in 2020–2021 seems to have only put a temporary halt to those trends. In the spring of 2020, as the pandemic spread, governments all over the world enacted lockdowns and heavy restrictions on international and domestic travel. The UNWTO (2021) estimated the drop in international tourist arrivals in 2020 at 74%, while in countries of the Organisation for Economic Co-operation and Development (OECD) it was estimated at 80%. This led to mass cancellations of STR bookings and a weak demand throughout 2020 (AirDNA 2020). In Europe, destinations that were heavily reliant on international tourism were hit hardest, while coastal and rural regions with strong domestic tourism markets were less severely affected (Böhme 2021; Gössling et al. 2021). The number of guest nights booked via the largest four tourist accommodation platforms (Airbnb, Booking, Expedia Group and Tripadvisor) fell from 512 million in 2019 to 272 million in 2020. However, it grew again to 364 million in 2021 and 547 million in 2022 (Eurostat 2023), exceeding pre-pandemic levels (see Figure 3).

The popularity of city tourism suffered during the pandemic, but European cities have rapidly recuperated their attractiveness: 41 cities recorded more than one million guest nights in 2022 (Eurostat 2023). The highest numbers of STR bookings made that year via the four above-mentioned platforms were recorded in Paris (13.5 million guest nights), Barcelona (8.5 million), Lisbon (8.5 million), Rome (8.0 million) and Madrid (6.7 million) (Eurostat 2023).

Yet the growth of STRs has not been fuelled only by classic tourists.[6] The boundaries between tourism and other forms of mobility, temporary migration and visits for study, work or leisure have become increasingly blurred (Selby 2004; Ashworth and Page 2011). In Europe, the rapid growth of low-cost airlines and high-speed trains, and the visa-free movement of EU citizens that exists between countries of the Schengen area,[7] have facilitated travel across the continent for a broader range of social groups. Flexible working practices in the creative and knowledge industries have encouraged new forms of temporary mobility whereby a person can spend a few weeks in a location combining work and leisure. This blurring of boundaries has been depicted in the media through neologisms such as *workation* (*work* and *vacation*) or *half-tourist* (Turner 2020). New forms of temporary lifestyle migration, for example, of high-income households who buy a second home in another country and live transnational lives, have grown more prominent (Benson and O'Reilly 2009; Janoschka and Haas 2014; Sigler and Wachsmuth 2020). Business travellers on short-term assignments in London, owners of second homes in Paris, university researchers

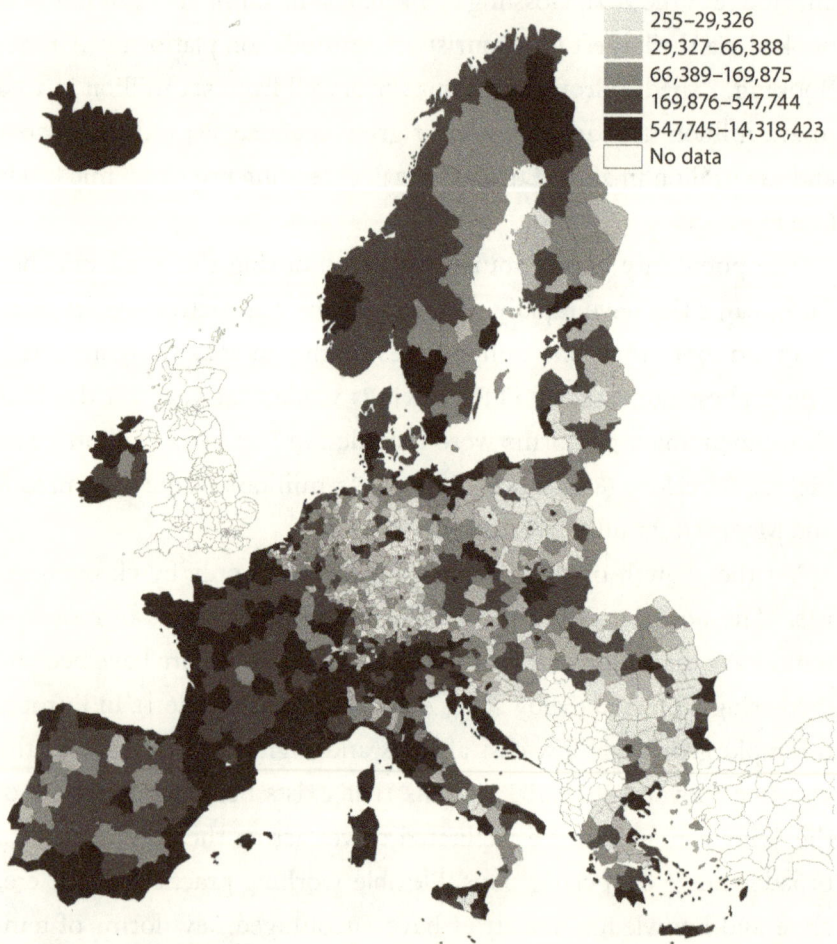

**Figure 3.** Map showing the number of guest nights spent at short-stay accommodation offered via four platforms in 2022. *Source*: Elaborated by the authors based on Eurostat data.

doing fieldwork in Barcelona, artists in temporary residence in Berlin, students going on a semester of study in Lisbon and 'translocal' workers on seasonal contracts in low-skilled occupations moving back and forth between Eastern and Western European countries are very different in nature. Yet their practices blur the boundaries between traditional tourists, visitors and residents (Brollo and Celata 2023). They are all 'temporary city users'—a term originally coined by Italian sociologist Guido Martinotti (Martinotti 1993; Costa and Martinotti 2003). Their simultaneous presence in the city have visible impacts on urban spaces, housing markets and socio-economic relations, as explained later on (Novy 2018; Brollo and Celata 2023).

The increasingly blurred distinction between short-, medium- and longer-term mobilities—and between tourism and other practices of place consumption—was sharpened during the COVID-19 pandemic. The stay-at-home orders of 2020 and 2021 accelerated the spread of remote working practices in the economic sectors where it was possible to do so. In Europe, this was accompanied by temporary outflows of households who could afford to go away from large urban areas towards greener, less dense locations. This had an impact on the demand for second homes and STRs in desirable coastal or rural locations or in attractive cities such as Lisbon, Barcelona and Prague that were already magnets for expatriates and 'digital nomads' (Reichenberger 2018; Colomb and Gallent 2022). Firms, entrepreneurs and investors—big and small—were quick to capitalise on that demand, as illustrated by new, dedicated medium-term rental platforms such as Flatio, NomadX, Flown and Outsite (Smith and Gillet 2020) or the flourishing of co-working spaces. Additionally, some national, regional and local governments have developed policies to encourage remote workers, that is, specific visa rules (Cook 2020) that supplement the existing Golden Visa or citizenship policies conditional upon real estate ownership that were set up by countries like Portugal (Surak 2022). During the pandemic, marketing campaigns were launched in the province of Barcelona and in small Italian towns to encourage workations. The municipal governments of Florence and Venice created platforms to promote medium-term rentals for 'remote workers, digital nomads, freelancers' and 'international students, startuppers and co-workers' (cited in Brollo and Celata 2023).

The COVID-19 pandemic outbreak did not, in the end, generate a long-term, marked demographic exodus away from large European cities (Colomb and Gallent 2022). But the changes in working practices that it has fuelled and the return of intense tourism flows from 2022 onwards mean that the demand for short- and medium-term rental accommodation has remained very high in many desirable rural, coastal and urban locations in Europe. Notwithstanding the threat of another pandemic or of supply-side shocks resulting from terrorism, natural catastrophes, wars or sharply rising energy prices, already heavily visited European towns and cities are expected to see further increases in visitors and 'temporary city users', compounding local tensions and conflicts.

### The Shaping of a New Accommodation Offer

The exponential growth of the STR offer has thus responded to a growing demand. But the supply of STRs has also partly *shaped* that demand, albeit in ways that are difficult to quantify. A platform like Airbnb has grown spectacularly because consumers have found it convenient and financially attractive to book short-term accommodation at the click of a button, with the relative security provided by the online payment and rating systems. At the same time, platforms themselves have shaped consumer demand. Airbnb has, from the beginning, proactively created its own markets, through marketing campaigns that promote particular locations, experiences and lifestyles. In countries like France and Italy, the company has partnered with local government associations to encourage the development of STRs away from big city centres, in less visited rural locations. In response to the pandemic,[8] Airbnb has promoted the offer by hosts of new 'online experiences', as well as of medium-term rentals for remote workers (Sequera et al. 2022).[9]

Besides platforms, STR operators, tourism marketing organisations and some public authorities have encouraged the growth of the STR market by arguing, first, that STRs would democratise access to travel through lower accommodation costs and more flexible options for consumers, thus benefiting families or people with limited budgets. The rising price of STRs in desirable locations and frequent reports of unpleasant STR experiences in the media have tempered that argument over time. But STRs have also been promoted as encouraging beneficial forms of social and cultural encounters between hosts and guests (Paulauskaite et al. 2017; Tussyadiah and Pesonen 2018)—a claim valid only in the case of home-sharing in a strict sense.

STR advocates have also underlined the economic benefits of this form of accommodation. Hosts who share their home benefit from extra income, an argument discussed in the next section. In a series of city-based reports, starting with San Francisco in 2012 (Airbnb 2018a), Airbnb emphasised positive impacts for consumers and the tourism industry, for neighbourhoods and local businesses, and for hosts. The company argued that its STR offer contributes to a better territorial spread of tourist accommodation and generates 'trickle-down effects' for local economies—claiming that 42% of guests' spending 'stays local' (Airbnb 2018a). Since then, independent studies have explored the geographical spread of Airbnb listings in particular cities, revealing a mixed picture. Listings have indeed spread over time from central areas to more distant ones that have a smaller hotel supply and higher residential stock (see Quattrone et al. 2016 on London or Balampanidis et al. 2021 on Athens).[10] However, this process of dispersion does not invalidate the fact that, in all cities, the STR offer tends to remain highly concentrated in central touristic neighbourhoods or culturally desirable areas near major leisure opportunities, as shown in the maps in Figure 16 (Chapter 4) in Barcelona, Milan and Paris (see Arias Sans and Quaglieri Domínguez 2016; Gutiérrez et al. 2017 on Barcelona; Picascia et al. 2017 on Italian cities; Oskam 2020a on 26 European cities).

Furthermore, unlike on-demand app-based platforms offering ride-hailing, food delivery or casual work services, STR platforms do not rely directly on a large mass of self-employed, independent contractors. However, the daily operation of platform-mediated STRs depends on the externalisation of on-demand labour via other apps and companies. An entire economy of associated intermediary services—'complementors' (Kenney and Zysman 2016:65)—has developed around the exponential increase in STRs, involving the refurbishment and photography of properties, the professional management of hosts' profiles, online communication with guests, cleaning, key-picking and check-in/out services (Sigala 2018). These services may be offered by individuals or by companies, some delivering highly professionalised packages (e.g., Hostmakers or Airsorted). Studies of the labour involved have shown the frequent reliance on low-paid, precarious workers (often women and non-White workers, sometimes in the shadow economy) (Cañada and Izcara Conde 2021; Vyas 2021). This mirrors the well-documented precarity that characterises significant parts of the wider platform economy and tourism sector. Even in cases of 'self-entrepreneurship', in which a host manages an STR themselves, scholars drawing on feminist political economy have unpacked the unpaid, physical, emotional labour that goes into 'playing host': this labour of 'performing home' enables the digital economy to function and is enrolled in the creation of value for the platform (Spangler 2020; Kluzik 2022).

As they became confronted with the rapid expansion of STRs in the early 2010s, the incumbent economic actors in the field—hotel operators—immediately perceived STR as a direct form of competition. As we will see in Chapters 4 and 6, hotel representatives have played a key role in the politics of STR regulation in European cities. Their main argument has been that STRs escape the strict requirements that hotels must comply with in terms of fire safety, accessibility, health and service standards and taxation. They criticise STRs for generating unfair competition for hotels, in particular those at the lower end (Zervas et al. 2016)—though evidence is not clear-cut (Coyle and Yu-Cheong Yeung 2016).

More broadly, the issue of taxation in relation to this new form of accommodation became controversial at three levels: the tax minimisation strategies of large platforms; the possible tax evasion by individual STR operators who might not declare the income generated by that activity; and the question of the collection and remittance of the city or tourist tax (where it exists) by hosts and platforms.

## Touristification and the Public Debates on 'Overtourism'

For decades, in many parts of Europe, tourism growth has been prioritised by local political and economic elites of all political colours as a driver of job creation and development. Urban political economy scholars have analysed the role of the (local) state in the production of tourism, leisure and consumption destinations as part of a shift towards new forms of urban entrepreneurialism in a post-Fordist era (Harvey 1989; Judd and Fainstein 1999; Hoffman et al. 2003; Selby 2004; Spirou 2011; Colomb 2012; Wijburg et al. 2023). A diverse range of local policies have provided a suitable environment for the tourism industry to thrive, ranging from 'the outsourcing of the governance of tourism to private bodies or commercial tourism marketing organisations' to the 'favourable regulatory or tax conditions offered to major tourism industry actors (e.g. hotel chains) without consideration of the potential opportunity costs' (Novy and Colomb 2019:5). In Europe, in particular in the southern part, the 2008 economic and financial crisis, and subsequent sovereign debt crisis and austerity policies, have reinforced the priority already given to tourism in many cities and 'peripheral economies' (Cocola-Gant 2018).

While tourism can create economic and socio-cultural benefits for local communities, the intensification and geographical spread of visitors have also led to increasing negative externalities on urban spaces and residents (Novy and Colomb 2016, 2019). These may include disruptions to daily life through noise, litter, traffic congestion or disorderly behaviour caused by 'party tourism' (Nofre et al. 2018). Tourism also generates structural impacts in terms of changing land and building uses, from grocery stores serving local needs to shops or entertainment venues mostly targeting visitors, and from long-term residential units to short-term holiday rentals (Novy and Colomb 2016). Such processes have been referred to as 'touristification' (van der Borg et al. 1996) or 'tourism gentrification' (Gotham 2005; Gravari-Barbas and Guinand 2018), a particular form of gentrification that entails residential, commercial and cultural displacement (Cocola-Gant 2023). Ironically, it is the low-paid, precarious tourism sector workers who are often at a higher risk of residential displacement (see Valente, Zaragozí, et al. 2023 on Barcelona).

The significant growth in tourist numbers in European cities and the mounting evidence of their adverse impacts on people and places have led to intense academic and policy debates on *overtourism*, a term that appeared in the mid-2010s (Milano 2017; Koens et al. 2018; Milano, Cheer, et al. 2019; Oskam 2020b). The concept became quickly appropriated in the media and in local political debates and electoral campaigns, for example in Amsterdam (Oskam and Wiegerink 2020), as well as in the transnational policy area (NHL Stenden University of Applied Sciences 2018; Peeters et al. 2018). In many parts of Europe, since the 2000s bottom-up social mobilisations have begun to explicitly challenge overtourism and the negative impacts of the visitor economy, putting pressure on city governments to act. This has happened not just in 'heritage cities' like Venice (Vianello 2016), but also in larger cities like Berlin (Novy 2016), Amsterdam (Oskam and Wiegerink 2020) and Barcelona (see Chapter 4). The grassroots mobilisations that have taken issue with the touristification of urban space have been very diverse in scope, social composition and focus (Novy and Colomb 2016, 2019). In some cities, such as Barcelona, a new coalition geared towards challenging overtourism and 'touristification' has emerged. In other cities, existing residents' associations or social movements have integrated aspects of the tourism question into their agenda, for example, housing activists (Novy and Colomb 2016, 2019). In those contexts, the proliferation of STRs has been a focus of contestation by grassroots movements from the mid-2010s onwards. The Airbnb platform has often been mentioned in protests as a shorthand term for STR in general.

Many of these social mobilisations have challenged the attitude of city governments towards the visitor economy, which has, in their view, not been 'governed or regulated enough—or merely governed in the interest of a narrow range of actors' (Novy and Colomb 2019:3). Such mobilisations have not been systematically present, however, in all European cities confronted with high tourist flows and a rapid increase in STRs. In the mid-2010s, in touristic cities like Paris, Rome, London, Vienna and Milan, there were no, or at least less visibly organised, social mobilisations against touristification as such, compared to Venice, Barcelona and Lisbon. Importantly, in the latter cities, tourism is not the only focus of collective mobilisation; it often crystallises 'the discontent which exists in a latent way with regard to various processes of urban and neighbourhood change [that] have negatively affected residents over the years' (Novy and Colomb 2016:15), for example, rent deregulation, speculative real estate development or large-scale regeneration. In Lisbon, the network of grassroots organisation Morar em Lisboa (Living in Lisbon) has taken issue with the intricate interplay between financialisation, touristification and gentrification processes in the transformation of the city (Morar em Lisboa 2017).

In some of the cities in our sample, as will be further discussed, the social demands for more regulation of STRs have thus been embedded in calls for a better governance of the visitor economy. But governing tourism at the urban level for the benefit of the resident population is not an easy task. Only a small number of European city governments have, over the past decade, put new policy measures in place to seek to do so (Novy and Colomb 2019), most notably Amsterdam (Gerritsma 2019; Novy 2021) and Barcelona between 2015 and 2023 (see Chapter 4).

## SHORT-TERM RENTALS AND THE ASSETISATION OF HOUSING

### Who Owns and Runs STRs? From 'Home-Sharing' to Professionalised Management

The extraordinary development of STRs has relied mostly on the shifting use of the existing housing stock for temporary accommodation purposes. Housing represents a central aspect of daily life, owing to its use value as a home. In private-property-based market economies, it is also a good and an asset that can be exchanged, invested in, accumulated and speculated upon. Housing, as an immobile and inelastic good, makes large proportions of urban dwellers captive and sensitive to price variations. Those very characteristics make housing a very sensitive social and political topic.

The early rhetoric of a company like Airbnb presented STR accommodation as a form of home-sharing by individual owner-occupiers (or tenants) who rent a room—or their entire home—on an occasional basis, as a supplementary source of household income. The company argued that it was 'democratising capitalism by expanding the economic pie for ordinary people, allowing them to use their home, typically their greatest expense, to generate supplemental income to pay for costs like food, rent, and their children's education' (Airbnb 2016a:1). Home-sharing has been portrayed as 'part of the solution to the housing crisis' (Airbnb 2018b)—a contested argument, as we will see. Some research has indeed shown that a number of households engage in STR practices out of need. North American and European urban dwellers who have suffered from stagnant or declining incomes have turned into 'micro-entrepreneurs' and commodified their domestic property by listing it on an STR platform (Stabrowski 2017). In European countries affected by the post-2008 crisis, or in cities with high housing costs, lower- and middle-income homeowners and tenants have sometimes used STR as an 'income maintenance strategy' (see Semi and

Tonetta 2021 on Turin; Balampanidis et al. 2021 on Athens; Söderström and Mermet 2020 on Reykjavík; Maier and Gilchrist 2022 on female hosts in London; Yrigoy et al. 2022 on Palma de Mallorca). In the Platform Labor project,[11] van Doorn has conceptualised 'home-sharing' as a 'platform fix', a 'way to finance the rising costs of social reproduction' in cities in the context of the weakening of European welfare states (van Doorn 2022). Hosting on STR platforms can, for example, help women excluded from the mainstream labour market or precariously employed to survive (Goyette 2021; Maier and Gilchrist 2022), though the practice has been criticised as 'a type of neo-liberal feminism, which endorses individualization and market-based solutions to employment' (Shade 2018:35).

Other studies have stressed how the opportunity to own property and to exploit it as STR is shaped by existing class, income, wealth, and racial inequalities (Schor and Attwood-Charles 2017). Individual operators of STRs tend to be disproportionately White property owners (sometimes tenants); educated; and in possession of particular forms of cultural, social or financial capital (Frenken and Schor 2017; Schor 2017; Mermet 2021). One may include in this category small-scale amateur landlords who operate one flat besides their own home (e.g. in Vienna see Kadi et al. 2022). As noted by Gurran (2018:301), 'those with spare and marketable space to rent to tourists are generally not the primary sector of the population experiencing the greatest housing need'. This does not exclude the possibility that some lower-income households facing precarious housing situations (through rising rent or mortgage repayments) may depend on STR practices in order to 'stay put'.

At the level of individual households, investing in one or several STR properties can become part of a broader strategy of 'asset-based welfare', that is, using property assets as a source of income or equity in a context of declining redistribution by the welfare state (Doling and Ronald 2010; Whitehead 2016). This form of household investment in property is not new. However, the easiness of entry into the STR market, especially in the early 2010s when STR practices were in a grey area, made this particular form of investment increasingly popular. Some banks started to offer specific 'buy-to-let' mortgage products to support the purchase of flats to be rented as STR via platforms, factoring the much higher revenue to be generated into their calculation of the loan-to-value ratio.

Professional operators who can 'further concentrate property through acquisition investments' (Salerno and Russo 2022:1051) and professionalise the management of their STR portfolios are therefore able to crowd out amateur landlords (Cocola-Gant, Jover, et al. 2021; e.g., Katsinas 2021; Bosma 2022), reinforcing property-led class inequalities. Additionally, many European cities have become desirable locations for transnational real estate investments by non-residents buying a second home, a 'safe haven' or a profitable asset (see Paris 2009 on second-home ownership; DeVerteuil and Manley 2017 on 'high net-worth individuals' and 'pied-a-terre urbanism' in London; Montezuma and McGarrigle 2019 on lifestyle migrants in Lisbon). In some cases, those properties are put on the STR market while their owners do not use them, thus serving a combination of leisure and investment purposes.

Unsurprisingly, many studies show that the nature of the STR offer on platforms such as Airbnb has changed in the space of a few years. That offer now entails a much higher or even dominant share of *professionalised* STR landlords or operators who advertise multiple entire dwellings—and no longer a spare bedroom in their home. Multi-property operators do not necessarily own all STR units; professionalised property managers have consolidated their role as 'second-tier platforms' (Anselmi and Conte 2021) running STRs on behalf of owners. The professionalisation and concentration of the STR market was first shown in North American cities (e.g., Samaan 2015 on Los Angeles; Hoffman and Schmitter Heisler 2020). Crommelin et al. (2018), in their study of Paris, London, New York, Sydney and Hong Kong, showed that in 2016, between a quarter and half of all Airbnb listings were traditional holiday-let businesses, rather than home-sharing. In Europe, various studies have shown similar patterns of professionalisation and of rapid concentration of the Airbnb offer among a small number of multi-property operators, for example, Barcelona (Arias Sans and Quaglieri Domínguez 2016); Paris (Chareyron et al. 2015); Rome (Celata et al. 2017); Amsterdam (Oskam et al. 2018), Madrid (Gil and Sequera 2022); Athens, Lisbon and Milan (Amore et al. 2020); and eight Southern European cities (Iacovone 2023). In their review of the evolution of STR listings in 12 European cities in the five years before the pandemic, Anselmi et al. (2021) demonstrate that the concentration of listings sharply increased in several cities (e.g., Milan, London, Barcelona, Seville and Lisbon).

Aggregate data obtained from Inside Airbnb confirm this finding for the 12 European cities covered in this book (see Figure 10 in Chapter 3 and Table 3 in the Appendix, and also Demir and Emekli 2021). In August 2019, in 8 out of 12 cities, more than 35% of the STR offer on Airbnb was composed of entire units available for more than 60 days (reaching 48% in Prague)—thus unlikely to be someone's primary residence. In another 7 out of 12 cities, the proportion of units listed by hosts who had multiple listings was above 35%, reaching 63% in Lisbon. In December 2023, this proportion of multi-listings was above 40% in 9 out of 12 cities, reaching 74% in Prague. This pattern of professionalisation and concentration has been accompanied by an unequal distribution of revenues among hosts: in Paris in 2015, almost 27% of hosts earned less than US$ 1,000, while 3.4% earned more than US$ 30,000 (Coyle and Yeung 2016). In the second half of the 2010s, in the 12 European cities studied by Anselmi et al. (2021), in almost every city (except Amsterdam) the distribution of STR revenues among hosts (measured through the Gini index) became more concentrated.

More recently, emerging research has shown that institutional investors (pension funds; real estate investment, private equity and wealth management companies) have entered the STR market (in the USA, see Hoffman and Schmitter Heisler 2020). Such a trend is still relatively under-researched and difficult to quantify. In Spain, hedge funds have been reported to have penetrated the STR market (Gil and Sequera 2022). In Lisbon, the pioneering work of Cocola-Gant and Gago (2021) and Jover and Cocola-Gant (2023) has shown that investment firms and institutional investors are increasingly present in the STR market. While we know relatively little about the diversity of institutional investors that have entered into the STR asset class, we can hypothesise that there are strong variations between cities (Esposito 2023b): existing literature on institutional landlords in Europe has shown different levels of entry and penetration into national and local housing markets (Wijburg and Aalbers 2017; Taşan-Kok et al. 2021; Gabor and Kohl 2022; Gimat et al. 2022; Brill et al. 2023).

Altogether, in many high-demand locations the STR market has shifted from an individual practice to 'a large-scale, strategic management of real estate property' (Balampanidis et al. 2021:2). This has led several scholars to interpret the exponential growth of STRs as part of a broader trend towards the 'assetisation' and 'financialisation' of housing (Marcuse and Madden 2016; Aalbers 2017; Gurran 2018; Hoffman and Schmitter Heisler 2020; Grisdale 2021; Tulumello and Allegretti 2021; Gil 2024), including in the Global South (e.g., in South America, see Rolnik et al. 2021; Jolivet 2024 on Cuba). As assets— defined as 'anything that can be controlled, traded, and capitalized as a revenue stream' (Birch and Muniesa 2020:2)—STRs are a vehicle for wealth and investment whose value lies in their rental income flow, and eventually, capital gains. The transformation of STRs into an asset class has been assisted by the platforms themselves and by a proliferation of specialised commercial data analytics and consultancy companies, which advise individuals on how to start an STR property portfolio and maximise the profits from investing into STRs. Other scholars have framed STR investors as part of the growth of 'rentier capitalism' (Christophers 2022) or 'housing market rentierisation'

(Ryan-Collins and Murray 2023), that is, the increasing role of *property* as a source of income (as opposed to *labour*) for a growing segment of the population (Müller et al. 2021). Wijburg et al. (2023) have conceptualised 'tourism-led rentier capitalism' as a particular economic and spatial expression of rentier capitalism, characterised by the 'incorporation of tourism-oriented rent seeking, value producing and extracting activities in mainstream actions of property investors around the globe' (730). It entails a 'highly heterogenous group of actors [who] develops, owns, manages, and purchases tourism property' (715), but whose core business is *not* tourism, by contrast with the post–World War II patterns of tourism property investment that were dominated by tourism-related actors.

During the heat of the COVID-19 pandemic, there was much speculation about what would happen to the thousands of STR listings in European cities suddenly deprived of visitors. Those landlords whose main source of revenue depended on STRs (some of whom had heavy mortgage debt) lost their income overnight. In the first months of the 2020 lockdowns, in cities such as London, Paris, Barcelona and Madrid, a proportion of listings were returned to the long-term market. But this has been a short-term trend (for Paris, see APUR 2021 and Pérez Mendoza and Casado 2021; for Madrid, see Sequera et al. 2022). Sequera et al., drawing on their study of four Spanish cities, argue that the pandemic shook 'the material foundations of Airbnb' in 2020–2022 but ultimately 'strengthened the function of the platform as a device of platform capitalism' (2022:3). Smaller-size STR managers unable to face their liquidity problem went out of business, while more professionalised managers overcame the crisis by transforming their activity (Sequera et al. 2022; see also Gyódi 2024), shifting to 'medium-term rentals' of a few weeks or months (APUR 2021 comes to a similar conclusion for Paris). Shifting between or within platforms now gives property owners the option to move flexibly between short-, medium- and long-term rental markets serving different types of consumers, which 'broadens the forms and possibilities for the commodification of housing' (Sequera et al. 2022:4).

## More STRs, Fewer Permanent Dwellings?
## Impacts on Housing Markets

In many parts of the world where platforms have fuelled the expansion of STRs, the question of their impacts on the local housing supply has been at the centre of intense social, political and academic debates. It is important to note from the outset the differences between the potential impacts of different types of STRs (to which we will return in Chapter 3): strictly speaking, the following discussion relates primarily to accommodation units that are not anyone's primary residence and are instead used year-round as STRs. This can impact housing markets if many property owners decide to remove housing units from the long-term residential market to convert them into STRs. Other things being equal (e.g., assuming little or no growth of the total number of housing units in an area), this would decrease the supply of units available in the long-term private rental or owner-occupation markets. This would also put upward pressure on house prices and long-term rents (Sheppard and Udell 2016; Horn and Merante 2017). This is more likely to be noticeable in cities or neighbourhoods that already have a tight rental housing market with high demand and low supply, and where the opening of new STRs does not result from new purpose-built units like 'apart-hotels' in coastal resorts.

There are, however, significant methodological challenges in measuring those impacts. The first one is related to the absence of accessible, precise and reliable data on STRs available for researchers, public authorities and other interested parties, as discussed further in Chapter 5. The second is that it is not easy to isolate the effect of STRs from other variables that may influence the rental housing supply, rental prices, sale prices and more broadly demographic change in neighbourhoods. This being said, a number of methodologies have been developed by housing scholars, economists and geographers to quantify the impacts of STRs on the housing markets of particular cities (see, e.g., Wachsmuth 2017; Wachsmuth and Weisler 2018; Grisdale 2021; Valente, Bornioli, et al. 2023), leading to a rapid increase in published studies over the past years.

In a prior report (Colomb and Moreira de Souza, 2021:Table 4), we summarised the evidence produced by the first North American and European studies of STR impacts on local housing markets, more specifically those focusing on the 12 cities addressed in this book. In a nutshell, in cities popular with visitors, many studies have shown that the rapid growth of STRs has contributed to a decrease in the supply of housing available for long-term occupation and induced an increase in rental prices (and sometimes an increase in sale prices). In Paris, for example, just before the COVID-19 pandemic, between 15,000 and 25,000 flats were rented on Airbnb throughout the year, diverted from the traditional rental market without the required authorisation for 'change of use' (Cox and Haar 2020). However, all studies show that those impacts are much more visible and quantitatively significant in *specific neighbourhoods* than at the scale of the city as a whole. In Barcelona, Cocola-Gant estimated in the mid-2010s that in the historical central district of Ciutat Vella, 17% of all housing units were listed on Airbnb (against 2% for the city as a whole), and that in some of the most popular streets of the Gothic Quarter, this amounted to up to 50% of the housing stock (Cocola-Gant 2016a). In the historical centre of Rome, around the same period 19% of housing units were listed on Airbnb (Celata et al. 2017). In those areas, the existing social and economic fabric has been affected by the high ratio of STRs relative to their total housing stocks, through knock-on effects on shops and social and public infrastructure. In some cases, entire buildings were converted into STRs, becoming de facto 'cottage hotels' (Salerno and Russo 2022).

The effects of STRs on housing supply, rents and prices are explained by a variety of mechanisms that incentivise the conversion of accommodation units into STRs. Those units were often previously used for residential purposes, but in some cases they may have served other functions, for example as ground-floor shops or small offices. The main incentive is economic in nature: the monthly or annual income that can be generated by renting short-term rather than long-term is at least three to four times higher, according to early research from North America (Wachsmuth et al. 2018; Grisdale 2021) and to the testimonies of interviewees in the European cities we studied. STRs have created a new form of 'rent gap' (Wachsmuth and Weisler 2018; Yrigoy 2019; Amore et al. 2020; Bosma and van Doorn 2022), that is, the disparity between the potential ground rent and the actual ground rent capitalised under the present land use (Smith 1979). In the case of STRs, this gap is 'driven by sharply rising potential revenue, rather than gradually falling actual revenue' (Wachsmuth 2017:n.p.), because STRs are often located in 'culturally desirable and internationally recognizable' neighbourhoods (Wachsmuth and Weisler 2018:1147). The gap is also 'globally-scaled' (Sigler and Wachsmuth 2020:3195), shaped by the demand of transnational flows of visitors.

Platforms themselves have been a key agent and facilitator in the production of the STR rent gap in two ways. First, as digital marketplaces, they have 'dramatically reduce[d] the establishment, search and transaction costs associated with holiday home accommodation, exponentially expanding their potential market' (Gurran 2018:299) at the global scale. STR platforms are part of a growing ecosystem of 'platform real estate' (Shaw 2020; Fields and Rogers 2021), characterised by the increasing automation, digitalisation and platform intermediation of the tasks involved in housing search, property management, real estate transactions and investments. Cocola-Gant and Gago (2021) argue that a platform like Airbnb has increasingly become designed to turn STR into a desirable asset class for investors. Second, large platforms themselves have contributed to the production and exploitation of the rent gap through their role as data analysts and *price setters* (Bosma and van Doorn 2022). Careful data monitoring 'that provides insights into what type of listings on the platform could potentially generate higher rents', accompanied by an algorithmic management that recommends price levels to hosts, are key mechanisms for 'ensuring the continued growth of the company's revenues, profitability, and financial value' (Bosma and van Doorn 2022:6). This makes the platform a 'facilitator of rentier relations' (Sequera et al. 2022).

## The 'Airbnbfication' of Cities

In desirable cities and neighbourhoods, the outcome of this platform-mediated and STR-induced rent gap is that long-term tenants are priced out: they are 'no longer bidding against the local residential rent price, but instead against the extra profit that STRs can bring' (Lee 2016:238). Long-term rental contracts might not be renewed by landlords turning to STRs. Sometimes, tenants may also be displaced through evictions, including practices that are violent or illegal (e.g., in Barcelona; see Chapter 4). As for owner-occupiers, the effects of the concentration of visitors in their neighbourhood or building (e.g., noise nuisances) may lead them to move elsewhere voluntarily, selling their homes or offering them as STRs on a platform. When a property is put up for sale, if it has a good potential for high returns as an STR, or a licence for this activity, its price increases, potentially crowding out first-time or lower- to middle-income buyers.

In this context, many scholars have analysed STRs in relation to broader dynamics of gentrification (Sequera and Nofre 2018; Aalbers 2019; Sigler and Wachsmuth 2020; López-Gay et al. 2021), as well as previously mentioned processes of touristification (Cocola-Gant 2016b; Gravari-Barbas and Guinand 2018; Oskam 2019; Celata and Romano 2020; Cocola-Gant et al. 2020; Sequera and Nofre 2020). It is worth noting here that the link between tourism, STRs and residential and commercial gentrification is complex: tourism pressures and the proliferation of STRs are often among several factors that drive changes in neighbourhoods. In popular tourist cities, the process of displacement of lower-income groups and traditional retail from historic centres had started before the emergence of Airbnb and has multiple endogenous and external causes (Venice being the most extreme European case of what Salerno and Russo [2022] have called the 'short-term city'). However, the new rent gap created by STRs has sharply intensified those processes—opening new urban frontiers of gentrification (Cocola-Gant, Hof, et al. 2021).

Moreover, recent scholarship on 'transnational gentrification' in Southern European cities shows how the attractiveness of a particular neighbourhood 'for visitors and for a wider palette of transnational dwellers feeds one another' (López-Gay et al. 2021:1).[12] These processes lead to a decrease in the number of long-term residents (i.e., Carvalho et al. 2019 on Porto; Cocola-Gant et al. 2021 on Barcelona, Lisbon and Sevilla; Jover and Díaz-Parra 2022 on Seville; López-Gay et al. 2021 on Barcelona). Sequera and Nofre (2020:3169) argue that 'the Airbnbisation of former lower-class central urban areas of post-recession southern European cities emerges as the newest, most aggressive form of urban accumulation by dispossession and spatial displacement against the working and middle-lower classes (both locals and migrants) of the "tourist city"'. It is not surprising, therefore, that in some European cities—but not all of them, as explained in Chapters 3 and 4—the impacts of STRs on housing markets and the sharpening of existing property-based inequalities have become a focus of discontent by citizen mobilisations. Housing activists have attempted to publicly problematise the interplay between processes of gentrification, touristification, housing assetisation and financialisation.

While the conversion of units into STRs has been a global trend driven by a variety of actors with different motivations and economic power, such conversion processes are, crucially, mediated by national and local housing systems, policies and market conditions. Local property and tenure structures, existing housing legislation, the tightness of the housing market, the state of conservation of the residential stock and local economic conditions can make the process more or less easy and profitable. As in all gentrification and touristification processes, institutions and public policies play a key mediating role (Bernt 2022). For instance, historic city centres that had suffered decline, abandonment and vacancy, as was the case in Lisbon and Athens, have offered easy opportunities for owners or investors to turn empty or decaying properties into STRs (Balampanidis et al. 2021). Similarly, the conditions under which a long-term rental contract can be terminated, or a tenant evicted, vary significantly from one country or region to another; this creates different opportunities for the conversion of long-term rentals into STRs. This is why, as will be explained in Chapter 2, we embed our study of the variety of STR regulations in European cities in the broader comparative scholarship on housing systems and 'welfare/ housing regimes'.

National taxation and public policies that have facilitated (domestic or foreign) investment in real estate have additionally been stressed by scholars as key factors. The case of Lisbon is paradigmatic. From 2012 onwards, a combination of national reforms in the fields of taxation, visa, citizenship and rental legislation have strongly incentivised foreign investments in Portuguese real estate, attracting foreign retirees and mobile professionals. Those reforms made it easier for long-term tenants to be displaced and had a dramatic impact on the rate of conversion of housing units into STRs (Mendes 2018; Sequera and Nofre 2020; Cocola-Gant and Gago 2021; Tulumello and Allegretti 2021; Marques Pereira 2022; Estevens et al. 2023). Between 2015 and 2019, the number of STRs increased from 3,174 to 20,014 (Marques Pereira 2022). A national law providing municipal governments with the instruments to try to contain this process was only promulgated in 2018.

## CONCLUSION

The emergence and growth of platform-mediated STRs have been driven by, and contributed to, broader dynamics in (urban) economies, societies and the built environment. The digitalisation of markets, flexible work arrangements, the touristification of cities and the housing crisis were already present in many cities *before* digital platforms like Airbnb, but those dynamics have been reshaped and intensified by the growth of platform-mediated STRs. The significant amount of published (Anglophone) scholarship on the subject has focused on trends at play in North America, Europe and Australia, with relatively less publications on the rest of the world, despite the growing prevalence of the three dynamics explored in this chapter around the globe. This new phenomenon poses specific challenges to public authorities, including how to regulate a digitally intermediated, transnational and cross-sectoral object. At the beginning of the 2010s, when major platforms expanded in Europe, STRs displayed the typical features of a 'wicked' policy object (Rittel and Webber 1973), for four reasons.

First, new platform-mediated activities have opened up markets outside of, or bluntly contravening, existing legal and regulatory frameworks. Platform companies initially seemed to disrupt 'not only the economic sectors they enter[ed], but also the regulatory regimes that govern those sectors' (Collier et al. 2018:2). They enabled a 'grey zone of economic exchanges' (Kovács et al. 2017) that seemed to escape quantification, state control and all kinds of existing rules pertaining to taxation, safety, housing and land use planning. As suggested above, this was not the result of technological determinism, whereby innovation systematically outpaces 'slow' administrations, nor of an enchanted success story of start-ups becoming 'unicorns'. The growth of STRs has been pushed by specific market and political strategies.

Second, STR growth has involved transnational capitalist activities, actors and flows that are outside local jurisdictions: USA-based venture capital, multinational firms, international visitors and service providers from all over the world interact online. Yet their activities materialise locally, contributing to reshape local housing markets, employment, urban spaces and neighbourhood life. The regulation of STRs has therefore called into question governments' capacity to extend their reach over transnational actors, processes and strategies, as well as to steer their localised effects (to boost or constrain them).

Third, STRs have developed across policy sectors. Many policy fields can therefore be relevant to address them: tourism, housing, local economic development, land use planning, taxation and so on. The actors involved in those fields are heterogeneous: platforms, hotels, property owners, investors, real estate companies, social movements, tenants, non-governmental organisations (NGOs), local residents and all kinds of government administrations at different tiers. Importantly, before the irruption of platform-mediated STRs, those different policy sectors were already organised as dense political and economic spaces of policies, regulations, interest groups and institutions, structured at different levels of government. They reacted to STR growth in different ways.

Fourth, STRs have been a subject of both vocal praise and intense criticism on multiple grounds, as discussed in this chapter. These contrasting narratives intersect with, and represent, broader interest groups. Any attempt at regulating STRs means dealing with different and often contradictory claims and interests and leads to distributional tensions. The freedom to use one's property and conduct an economic activity collides with the protection of the long-term residential stock by public authorities. Housing is seen by some as an asset that remunerates investors and by others as a fundamental right. Politicians and urban elites disagree on whether urban spaces and services should be adjusted to attract visitors or, conversely, to first serve the needs of long-term residents. Regulating STRs does not call for any obvious single, best regulatory solution, but it has been a matter of arbitrating between specific goals and interests: negotiating with the actors who have mobilised around those interests and navigating between the institutional arrangements that sustain them.

These four regulatory challenges help us understand why platform-mediated STRs have become a conflictual field of intervention and regulation. In the next chapter we introduce a framework to study the contentious politics of STR regulation and explain the diversity of STR regulations in European cities.

# 2

# THEORISING AND RESEARCHING THE REGULATION OF PLATFORM-MEDIATED SHORT-TERM RENTAL HOUSING

WHILE INITIAL RESEARCH on platform-mediated STRs had mainly focused on the description of a phenomenon 'disrupting' tourism practices, housing markets and cities, there is now a significant body of research dealing with STR regulations. In the first part of the chapter, we summarise the key contributions of this existing body of work and identify the main limitations we address in this book. In the second and third parts of the chapter, we present the conceptual framework we use to answer the core question of the book: how to explain the variety of regulations of platform-mediated STRs in large European cities. This means elucidating how STR regulatory instruments, approaches and modes of governance were arrived at; how and why choices were made, at what times and under what conditions; and which actors weighed in on the choices.

To do that, we need to 'embed' regulations—which do not happen in a socio-economic, political and institutional vacuum—and to (re)politicise them. We propose a broader conceptual approach to regulation that combines insights from the sociology of public policy and urban/multi-level governance, on the one hand, with the political economy of regulation on the other. This implies, in particular, embedding STR regulatory instruments into the different institutional arrangements that organise housing systems. This also means integrating into the analysis the relationships between the regulators and the regulated (STR operators and platforms); the history and politics of collective mobilisations, political competition and regulatory change; and the multi-level governance systems in which STR regulations emerge. In the fourth part of the chapter, we present the research design that aimed at capturing and explaining STR regulatory diversity in 12 European cities. To address the problem of causal inference, we crafted a comparative, mixed methods and multi-site research design combining a variable-oriented approach (a comparison of 12 cases) and a case-oriented approach (a process tracing of three cases).

## MEASURING AND EXPLAINING STR REGULATORY DIVERSITY AND ITS EFFECTS: CONTRIBUTIONS AND LIMITATIONS OF EXISTING SCHOLARSHIP

Scholars in tourism, management and business studies, law and economics have published the most on STR regulation, often based on quantitative assessments of regulatory differences and their effects. In the field of urban studies, geographers, sociologists and planners have also published on the issue, mostly in the form of qualitative studies of regulatory change, which do not explain variety across cities and countries. Surprisingly, political scientists or comparative political economists have published little on the regulation of STRs, often dealing with other types of platforms or platform capitalism more generally. Altogether, there is now a cumulative body of work and a degree of interdisciplinary dialogue on measuring STR regulatory stringency and approaches, identifying more or less collaborative modes of governance with platforms and quantitatively assessing the effects of regulations on STR supply and housing markets. However, only a small number of studies to date have addressed STR regulation as a dependent variable, and as the result of socio-political processes.

## Profiling Cities in Terms of Regulatory Stringency, Approaches and Modes of Governance

The existing literature has captured the diversity of STR regulation in different ways (Hijrah Hati et al. 2021:13), focusing on the variety of instruments, degrees of regulatory stringency, regulatory approaches (more or less favourable to STRs) and modes of governance (more or less collaborative). Most comparative studies begin with an inventory of the instruments used in the cities under consideration. Instruments have been classified according to a few types (Nieuwland and van Melik 2020; Hübscher and Kallert 2023): quantitative restrictions (limitations of the number of STR overnight stays, listings per host, guests per accommodation) (Gottlieb 2013; Guttentag 2015; Jefferson-Jones 2015); qualitative restrictions (rental of a whole housing unit or part of it, rental of a primary or secondary residence, compulsory host presence in rented accommodation, health and safety standards, compliance with condominium rules, compulsory contact details, insurance) (Jefferson-Jones 2015); and spatial restrictions (specific limitations on STR densities in certain districts, maximum ratio of STRs to permanent residences, distances between listings) (Gurran and Phibbs 2017; Hübscher and Kallert 2023). Some distinguish regulations that apply to hosts in the form of administrative requirements (declaration, licence, tax remittance) (Jefferson-Jones 2015). Others add instruments that ensure the collection of information and data (reporting, mapping) (von Briel and Dolnicar 2020).

Based on these inventories, the most widespread approach has been to compare cities according to their level of regulation. Such a tactic is quite intuitive and helps answer a question that matters for researchers and practitioners (including investors): In which cities are STRs regulated the most? A number of quantitative indicators of levels of regulation have been developed. They are based on scores calculated from the number of instruments present in each city. Authors often use them for statistical analysis in combination with STR data drawn from various sources (Hong and Lee 2018; Nieuwland and van Melik 2020; von Briel and Dolnicar 2020; Furukawa and Onuki 2022; Bei and Celata 2023; Hübscher and Kallert 2023).

Nieuwland and Von Melik (2020) and Hübscher and Kallert (2023) have built a continuous 'scale of stringency' that ranges from laissez-faire to *full ban*, based on the number of instruments in a sample of European and USA cities. Von Briel and Dolnicar (2020) proposed a comparative and systematic longitudinal study of the modes of STR regulation in 11 European and USA cities by aggregating scores corresponding to 10 instruments that cities had gradually adopted (or not) since the appearance of Airbnb. This indicator made it possible to distinguish between a range of approaches (from 'unregulated' to 'extremely restrictive') and, by comparing the timing of regulations, to identify 'precursor' or 'follower' cities and their evolution. Bei and Celata (2023) developed a continuous scale of 'degree of stringency of STR regulation' in 16 European cities between 2011 and 2022 with the aim of evaluating their effects on the STR offer. Their indicator is based on the addition of scores for the adoption, partial adoption or non-adoption of a dozen instruments,[1] leading to a continuous scale from the most to the least regulated. They distinguish, as we do (see Box 1 in Chapter 3), between different types of STR accommodation (whole commercial professional dwelling, whole non-commercial dwelling, secondary dwelling, partial rental).

Finally, economists or political scientists influenced by public interest and regulatory capture theories have adopted the opposite perspective, asking not 'which cities regulate the most' but 'which cities are the most welcoming to STR'? They work on the assumption that public policy-makers often serve, or are captured by, the interests of their political clienteles (e.g., the traditional hotel industry). Furukawa and Onuki (2022) built an indicator of 'STR friendliness' in 17 USA cities, and Hong and Lee (2018) characterised a 'favourable policy environment' for STRs in 59 USA cities. Both sets of authors argue that the hotel industry has pressured city governments into regulating its STR competitors, particularly when the relative size of this industry is important (Furukawa and Onuki 2022) and when local political competition is low (Hong and Lee 2018).

Altogether, those works on regulatory differences have made important contributions to the measurement and comparison of regulatory stringency. They favour synchronous comparison and longitudinal follow-up, but they do not explain the diversity of regulations.

TYPOLOGIES OF REGULATORY APPROACHES:
CONNECTING INSTRUMENTS TO POLITICAL OBJECTIVES

Part of the scholarly literature (in particular from management, law or technology and innovation studies) is normative and starts from the assumption that the objective of STR regulations should be to allow the development of innovation without stifling the activities of platforms and operators, while containing the negative externalities whose costs weigh disproportionately on third parties (e.g., residents). Moving away from this assumption, scholars closer to analytical social sciences have empirically observed that different political objectives underpin regulations—that is, to protect housing, limit 'overtourism' or generate tax income—and are linked to specific combinations of instruments. By crossing instruments, levels of stringency and policy objectives, several authors have proposed an ideal-typical profiling of STR regulatory approaches that differentiate cities.

Oskam and Boswijik (2016) proposed 'scenarios of regulation' in different types of tourist cities based on the place-specific challenges of tourism attractiveness. Nieuwland and Von Melik (2020) highlighted different 'rationales behind STR policies' from which they developed a typology of cities' regulatory approaches: cities that seek to reduce and limit the pressure of overtourism through a partial or total ban on STRs (such as Barcelona); cities that seek to protect affordable housing by banning the rental of entire dwellings and limiting overnight stays (such as Berlin); and cities that seek to protect residential living conditions by banning the rental of second homes and limiting overnight stays (such as Amsterdam or Paris). The authors showed that most city governments (particularly in Europe) were not trying to stifle STR development, but on the contrary sought to take advantage of their economic benefits. At the same time, many of those governments were attempting to curtail visible negative externalities (e.g., impacts on affordable housing shortage, neighbourhood change and gentrification), especially in cities already subject to overtourism, and to regulate 'unfair' competition with hotels. However, the authors did not explain those differences, and neither did Hübscher and Kallert (2023) in a similar piece of work.

An interesting temporal dimension to differentiate regulatory approaches was added by Von Briel and Dolnicar (2020). They distinguished between cities that already had rules governing STRs before Airbnb and whose regulatory activity ultimately consisted in 'deregulating' to adapt to STRs ('end-run' cities such as London) and cities that did not have such rules and thus had to create new ones ('gap cities', such as Amsterdam, Berlin, Paris and Barcelona). Finally, Furukawa and Onuki defined six 'approaches for regulating STRs' (from 'laissez-faire' to 'prohibitive cities') based on different policy objectives and types of instruments, and crossed them with the above-mentioned quantitative STR friendliness indicator (Furukawa and Onuki 2022:3252).

An ideal-typical profiling of regulatory approaches has the advantage of giving overall coherence to different groups of cities, which facilitates comparison. However, the existing models are sometimes based on an exceedingly coherent vision of the policy-making process, as if policy objectives necessarily materialise into perfectly adapted instruments that produce the expected results. While we also adopt an ideal-typical perspective, we consider that it is crucial to unpack how political processes, actors' strategies and institutional arrangements shape these relationships, which are not necessarily so linear.

## MODES OF GOVERNANCE AND RELATIONSHIPS WITH PLATFORMS

Some authors have shifted the focus from policy instruments to characterising regulations in terms of *modes of governance*, that is, classifying different types of relationships between actors (governments, platforms, hosts, tourist accommodation professionals and possibly citizens). One of the key normative assumptions shared in this literature is that collaboration with platforms allows for the development of more adequate (and potentially acceptable) rules that allow cities to benefit from the positive externalities of STRs (Edelman and Geradin 2016; Avdimiotis and Poulaki 2019; Voytenko Palgan et al. 2021).

Finck (2018) distinguishes between *self-regulation* of the STR market (letting platforms regulate themselves and implement their own rules of operation), *state regulation* (command and control) and *co-regulation* (close collaboration between firms and governments to identify common interests and develop appropriate rules). The author recommends co-regulation, albeit with possible borrowing from the other two approaches when necessary. Tedds et al. (2021) also argue that traditional sectoral regulations are not fine-grained and adequate enough to produce the targeted effects (e.g., by regulating commercial STRs but not occasional ones). Co-regulation is seen as a solution, but the authors argue that it can only work if governments trust platforms enough to regulate their own users, which is not always the case (Tedds et al. 2021). Li and Canelles (2021) also deductively define two ideal types of styles of governance: *hierarchical governance* (a governmental monitoring activity aimed at limiting the negative externalities of STRs) and *adaptive governance* (a close collaboration between government and platforms to co-construct rules).

Taking a more critical perspective, authors from urban geography, sociology and political economy have focused on the political mobilisation strategies and lobbying activities of corporate STR platforms and STR operators (so-called hosts). Their research has mainly investigated the global and national policy initiatives of the largest platform, Airbnb, as well as local socio-political responses to contested local/national regulations, first in the USA and then in Europe. To maintain control of their regulatory environment, platforms have pushed for standardising STR rules across jurisdictions, offering self-regulation and resisting unwanted laws (Stabrowski 2017; Ferreri and Sanyal 2018; Boon et al. 2019; van Doorn 2020; Aguilera et al. 2021). They have deployed a large variety of repertoires of action. Besides classical lobbying, they have developed an intense political activity that relies on producing narratives about the STR market—framed as a market of ordinary citizens renting out their home occasionally—in order to shape the terms of policy debates (van Doorn 2020). Platforms have also mobilised their user base (Culpepper and Thelen 2020), in particular the hosts (McNeill 2016; Yates 2023, 2025). This body of works is crucial to explain policy change and has been an important source of inspiration for our analysis. Through a comparative approach, however, we aim to emphasise the differentiation of the configuration of actors and their relationships from one city to the other and to consider platforms and hosts in relation to other interest groups (e.g., the hotel industry or social movements).

## Understanding Enforcement and Measuring the Effects of Regulation on STRs and Housing Markets

A rather different stream of research has addressed STR regulations from the perspective of their implementation and effects. First, planning and housing scholars have noted that traditional zoning and planning control mechanisms are not very effective in curbing STRs because of significant difficulties with enforcement on the ground (Gurran and Phibbs 2017; Gurran 2018; Holman et al. 2018; Leshinsky and Schatz 2018; Ferreri and Sanyal 2019). Some of those difficulties are not new and reflect long-standing challenges associated with the control of illegalities in the built environment (Colomb and Moreira de Souza 2024), in particular informal or illegal housing uses, such as squatting or overcrowded rental housing, which may be undetectable from the street.

Moreover, those authors stress that the digitally mediated nature of STR practices creates both challenges and opportunities for regulatory enforcement authorities. STR platforms do not share their data with regulators unless constrained. This has generated what Hoffman and Schmitter Heisler (2020) have called, in the context of the USA, 'data wars' between city governments and large platforms. In Europe, a few scholars have highlighted the tensions around platform data and the uneven power balance between platforms and (local) policy-makers in enforcement in the context of individual cities (Ferreri and Sanyal 2018; Holman et al. 2018 on London; Söderström and Mermet 2020 on Reykjavík). In Chapter 5, we offer a comparative analysis of regulatory implementation and analyse how local governments develop do-it-yourself (DIY) strategies of enforcement to cope with the lack of data.

A more recent and growing literature has studied the effects of regulations on STRs and housing markets, in particular in the USA (van

Holm 2020; Chen et al. 2021; Koster et al. 2021; Bekkerman et al. 2022; Yeon et al. 2022; Bibler et al. 2023) and Europe (Bei and Celata 2023; Hübscher and Kallert 2023; Robertson et al. 2024). Those studies converge in showing that regulations do produce effects on STR supply (measured through the volume of listings and the level of professionalisation of the offer), on STR density in central districts and on the housing market (sale prices and rents). Stricter regulations seem to diminish the number of STR listings and contribute to reducing the share of accommodation units that are used intensively as STRs on platforms (Hübscher and Kallert 2023). Bei and Celata (2023), in their study of 16 European cities, also show that stricter regulations change the composition of the STR market, with a relative de-professionalisation and decreasing rates of multiple listings and entire apartments. Yeon et al. (2022) have also observed drops in monthly STR revenues after regulation. Studies showing downward effects on house sale prices and long-term rents are rare, but the effect seems to exist (Koster et al. 2021; Bibler et al. 2023).

Some analyses focus on understanding the specific effects of different instruments. Time caps (i.e., limitations on the number of days per year a property can be rented on the STR market), safety standards and eviction restrictions (that 'prohibit units that have recently been subject to eviction from being registered as an STR') are argued to reduce the number of listings and multi-listings (see Chen et al. 2021:4 on the USA; Bei and Celata 2023 on Europe). Other studies show that instruments such as licences, registration and taxation-related instruments have a temporary effect: they form a barrier to the entry of newcomers into the STR market, which encourages incumbent operators to increase their prices. This makes the market more attractive and ultimately encourages new entrants (Chen et al. 2021). Finally, specific regulations may affect the spatial organisation of the STR offer, contributing to its geographical dispersion (van Holm 2020; Robertson et al. 2024).

Three salient points emerge from this body of research. First, instruments do not seem to have lasting effects (von Briel and Dolnicar 2020;

Chen et al. 2021), above all because the targeted actors (hosts, platforms and pro-STR organisations), over time, find ways to evade or circumvent regulations (Piganiol 2021; Colomb and Moreira de Souza 2024; Richon 2024). Second, most authors conclude that, to produce effects, regulations must be differentiated and target specific objectives (reducing, dispersing or controlling the market, recovering housing for permanent residence), specific types of STR operators (professionals or amateurs) or specific types of accommodation (entire units, shared rooms) (Wegmann and Jiao 2017; Tedds et al. 2021). These results seem to converge with the arguments of law and management scholars who criticise overly generic regulations on the basis that they would stifle an innovative market (Edelman and Geradin 2016). Regulations might also produce the unwanted effect of professionalising the market by discouraging small operators, who cannot cope with too strict or too many rules. Finally, most quantitative studies suggest that collaboration and agreements with platforms considerably reinforce the effects of each instrument.

The effects of regulation differ according to the cities, the combination of regulatory instruments and the types of STR that are targeted by regulations (professionalised STRs, occasional or both). While our research did not seek to measure the effects of regulations through econometric models, taking into account the findings from existing scholarship on the topic matters: over time, the perceived effects of regulations can retroactively contribute to the evolution of these regulations (e.g., unexpected effects or a lack of effect of certain instruments can lead citizens to ask for new rules or lead politicians to adjust existing ones).

## Diversity as a Dependent Variable: Political Processes and Pre-Existing Institutions

Within existing scholarship on STR regulations, few studies seek to explain *why* STRs were regulated differently. Some do so via quantitative methods of correlation and regression tests (e.g., Hong and Lee

2018) that leave out the political, social and economic mechanisms at work. A very small number of studies take regulatory diversity as a dependent variable to be explained through the qualitative study of processes of politicisation, institutional trajectories, political conditions and sectoral norms. They provide important hypotheses, on which we have built in this book.

According to Benli-Trichet and Kübler (2022), who have worked on the regulation of Airbnb and Uber in six Swiss cities, four factors and mechanisms explain differences in regulatory stringency between cities. First is the *level of salience*: the more politicised, debated, publicised and contentious the issue is at the local level, the more urban governments are encouraged to take strong measures to regulate in order to respond to mobilised clienteles and stakeholders. The second explanation is the level of *stakeholder* mobilisation, including incumbent providers (e.g., the hotel industry) and citizen movements. These factors are, however, necessary but not sufficient: political and institutional conditions play a major role in determining whether local politicisation is reflected in strong regulations. The authors identify two such conditions: *a stable governmental agenda* that leads to an institutionalisation of regulations and the *intensity of pre-existing sectoral regulations* (in this case, housing and accommodation). As the authors argue, 'pre-existing regulations in a policy sector shape the options that policymakers have at their disposal to address public issues. . . . [I]t is easier for local governments to control platform-mediated activities when targeted markets (here housing) are already regulated as they do not have to create a new law from scratch' (Benli-Trichet and Kübler 2022:740). This argument is fundamental to our approach, as we contend that pre-existing institutional and policy instrument density in the housing sector is one of the key strands of explanation for STR regulatory diversity.

Cassell and Deutsch (2023) have also sought to explain the variation in STR regulations in 10 cities in Germany, a country in which local governments have strong political and legal autonomy. They show that the perception of negative externalities by local populations and elected officials plays an important role in explaining the strictest regulations. However, in contrast to the quantitative assessments of regulations presented earlier in this chapter, those papers do not measure regulatory diversity in a formalised manner and focus on within-country comparisons, which does not allow for the testing of national variables.

Other authors have also researched the politicisation of the STR issue via single-city case studies, identifying factors that can nevertheless be embedded in a comparative analysis of STR regulatory diversity. Marques Pereira (2022), in her study of Lisbon, demonstrates the need to consider both *local* and *national political trajectories and agendas*, without which it is impossible to explain changes in local STR regulation in Lisbon from laissez-faire to strong regulation. Ferreri and Sanyal (2018) highlighted the opposite trajectory in London, which moved from a well-regulated to a deregulated STR market, due to intervention from the UK central government favourable to STRs and the platform economic model.

The early work we produced on some of our case study cities (Aguilera 2016 on Paris and London; Artioli 2020 on Milan; Aguilera et al. 2021 on Barcelona, Paris and Milan) shares similarities with the conclusions of the above-mentioned studies regarding the importance of issue salience, stakeholder mobilisations and pre-existing institutional and instrumental thickness to explain variation in STR regulations. We also insisted on the role played by *multi-level conflicts* (between municipal, regional and national governments, as well as EU institutions) and by competition between different *policy sectors* (housing, spatial planning, tourism, economic development, etc.).

## BROADENING, POLITICISING AND RE-EMBEDDING STR REGULATION: A CONCEPTUAL FRAMEWORK

With rare exceptions, existing studies on the regulation of STRs are often based on a restrictive understanding of regulation as the intentional and

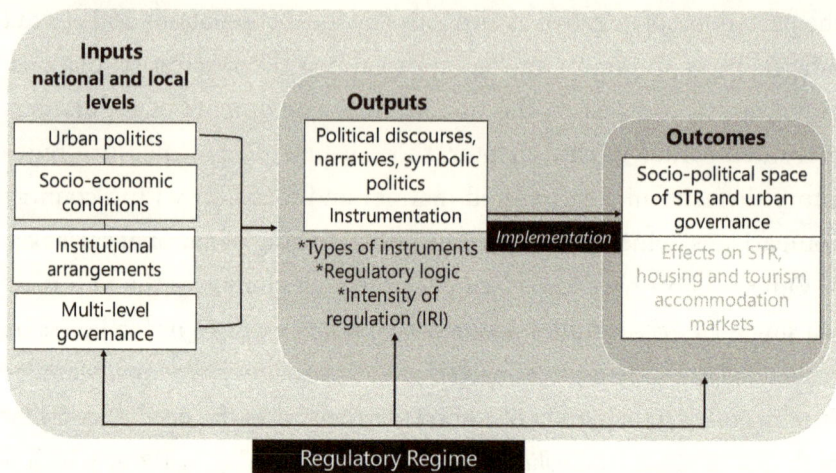

**Figure 4.** Conceptualisation of a regulatory regime. *Source:* Authors.

direct 'intervention in the activities of a target population'—involving binding standard-setting, monitoring and sanctioning, exercised by public sector actors targeting the activities of private sector actors (Koop and Lodge 2017:105). Regulating is about setting rules that establish spaces where actors negotiate a political and regulatory equilibrium that allows them to exchange goods and develop their activities. These rules define what is authorised and prohibited in a given place. In our case, STR rules set the conditions for accessing, operating and maintaining STR activities—for extracting rent and profits in markets that are constituted and guaranteed by the state. Under this classic approach, most works on STRs list the instruments designed and implemented by governments to regulate the STR market (via platforms and/or operators).

Such an understanding of regulation is precise, facilitating the delimitation of the object of study and the development of comparisons. In this book, we take this approach to characterise what we call the *outputs of regulation* (see Figure 4), that is, the instruments designed or recycled to target STRs, their regulatory logics and the intensity of regulations (through the development of an indicator; see Chapter 3).

But sticking to this understanding of regulation runs the risk of isolating these instruments and rules from the rest of the governmental activities and governance processes. This is why we associate it with a broader perspective on regulation, conceptualised at the crossroads of the sociology of multi-level (urban) governance, the New Political Economy, and the study of welfare/housing systems.

## Regulation from a Multi-Level Governance Perspective

The sociology of multi-level urban governance considers cities and local governments as important political collective actors that regulate European societies and economies (Le Galès 2002; Mossberger et al. 2012), while being attentive to other *scales of regulation* and the role of the state. Drawing on such approaches, we consider regulation as a *set of institutional arrangements that shape a space between political institutions and economic market activities*, where interests are defined and negotiated, and where strategies and preferences of firms and regulators are delineated.[2] In the medium and long run, regulation represents a specific relationship between the state and capitalism that can give rise to a *diversity* of institutional configurations (depending on the time, the country, the sector and the level of public action) (Hall 1986; Boyer 2003). These arrangements are rather stable (in each country), but several factors (innovations, crises, reforms, etc.) can change the interests, preferences and strategies of actors (Woll 2016).

In this book, we make explicit the role played by institutional arrangements at the national and local levels over time: the regulation of platform and STR activities is the result of power relations and negotiation between a variety of actors with different interests and at different scales, which can take very diverse forms that need to be explained (Thelen 2018; Aguilera et al. 2021; Benli-Trichet and Kübler 2022). This perspective helps us to take STR regulation out of the sole domain of tourist accommodation, to link it to the regulation of housing and platform capitalism more broadly. We do so at a *meso-level* of analysis that empirically considers the roles of, and forms of coordination between, tiers of governments, platforms, hosts, tourism professionals, housing professionals and civil society, but also investigates how resources are allocated and conflicts are structured between those actors (Lange and Regini 1989).

In the context of state reconfiguration (King and Le Galès 2017), Europeanisation, the rise of cities as major political actors and the transformation of urban capitalisms (notably platform capitalism; see Artioli 2018), cities represent major and complex political spaces in which we find, overall, a layering of various modes of regulation. The task of multi-level and comparative urban governance research is therefore to characterise modes of regulation and governance in cities, emphasising the role of politics in the coordination of actors, and to explain the diversity and effects of such modes on the construction of public policies at multiple scales (Le Galès 1998).

In concrete terms, studying the multi-level governance of platform-mediated STRs in major European cities means explaining how urban governments organise their relations with their socio-political and economic environments; how they coordinate actors and their interests; and how they implement regulatory public policies via instruments, discourses and procedures. This includes considering the political capacity of city governments to impose choices and enforce policies and the articulation between different sectoral regulations in the same locality. This also comprises the political capacity from local governments to mobilise at upper levels—from the regional to the national to the EU— to ask for political and legislative actions that would provide them with new regulatory means and instruments. However, it is important to stress that while local governments can be the initiators of regulations, sometimes they are not. Altogether, 'local' STR regulations are in fact a combination of national, regional and local provisions (to which supra-national, European legal and court decisions must be added).

## The Political-Economic Dimension of Regulations

The New Political Economy pays particular attention to the relationships between regulators and regulated entities in an era of regulatory governance, while taking into account the very political dimension of regulation (Benoît 2021). This dimension is left aside by most existing research on STRs. When this dimension is included, it is within the framework of public interest or regulatory capture theories (Hong and Lee 2018; Li and Canelles 2021; Furukawa and Onuki 2022), which conceive decision-making in a simplistic way: regulators work for the general interest, and profit-driven firms try to influence them. However, the relationships between private and public actors are non-linear and complex (Carrigan and Coglianese 2011). Furthermore, regulating a new and fast-expanding STR market entails more than a technical question of how to grasp a 'disrupting innovation'. We investigate how, through STR regulations, choices and balancing acts are formulated and imposed—which reflect specific values and representations of what housing is, who public policies are intended for, to whom cities belong and who has the right to (use) the city (property owners, visitors, residents). Whether and how governments have regulated STRs has been part of broader political agendas regarding tourism, economic development, housing, the digital and platform economy and so on, as the phenomenon is at the intersection of those different fields, as discussed in the previous chapter. This is often connected to partisan politics and electoral competition.

Finally, the political dimension of regulation comes from the conflicts that emerge between all kinds of organisations defending their legitimacy and their interests: between public administrations operating/competing in different policy sectors; between the central state, regional and local authorities and European institutions; between courts in various jurisdictions; and between public authorities, corporate firms, experts, advocacy groups, social movements or citizens.

In this book, we thus draw on the perspectives adopted by scholars of regulation who have sought to 'understand how regulation gets made and implemented—and who influences regulatory decisions in order to get what, when and how' (Carrigan and Coglianese 2011:106). This goes beyond the simple comparison of the set of legal rules and instruments applied to STRs and platforms, to encompass a search for explanation of their emergence and form. This is done by linking the study of socio-economic and political conditions, national and local institutional arrangements, instrumentation processes and the effects that all of this produces on the configurations of actors.

## STR Regulations as Part of Welfare/Housing Regimes

Finally, to move away from STR regulations conceived as isolated interventions, we argue that they must be analysed in the context of broader housing systems. A platform such as Airbnb is not like Uber or Deliveroo: STR is about *housing* and not about a cab ride or a burger delivery. As discussed in Chapter 1, housing is a good, a policy field and an asset with very specific characteristics that make it a crucial node in the regulation of societies and markets. It is a vital and essential good that concerns all individuals and a symptom and vector of socio-economic inequalities, in particular wealth inequalities (Rodríguez-Pose and Storper 2020; Adkins et al. 2021). It crystallises a significant part of the financialisation of the economy via the real estate activities of investment funds and banks, as the 2008 crisis has revealed (Aalbers 2016). It contributes to determining citizens' political preferences, depending on their housing tenure, towards redistribution and the welfare state (Ansell 2019).

As argued by scholars in comparative housing studies and neo-institutionalist political economy, countries can be differentiated according to their housing systems, which are shaped by, and contribute to, wider social, political and economic structures of regulation of capitalism in a broader sense. As stressed by Bernt, 'the general dynamics of [housing] commodification are universal in capitalist societies, whereas the ways in which markets are embedded into societies and the variations in which social rights are perceived, negotiated and legislated are not' (2022:4). This is why we explicitly integrate, in our comparative analysis of STR regulations, 'welfare/housing regimes' as a particular set of institutional arrangements.

Inspired by Esping-Andersen's typology of welfare states, the welfare/housing regimes line of research has demonstrated that 'each welfare regime cluster determines a distinctive housing system cluster, according to the conception of society and the redistributive mechanisms' (Arbaci 2019:70, based on Kemeny 1995; Balchin 1996; Allen et al. 2004; Stephens 2020). A housing regime comprises both a tenure system (i.e., in most European countries, the relationship between owner-occupation, the private rental sector and the public/social housing sector) and a provision system (the supply and demand side of housing markets) (Arbaci 2019:70). Housing regimes are characterised by different degrees of redistribution through state intervention, from the active promotion of social and non-profit rental housing to limited and residualist intervention. Countries are clustered in liberal, socio-democratic, corporatist and familistic 'welfare/housing regimes'.[3] In general, more decommodified regimes tend to be associated with lower rates of home-ownership, fewer social inequalities and less spatial segregation (Musterd and Ostendorf 1998; Arbaci 2019). They filter the urban socio-spatial polarisation brought about by economic globalisation (Marcuse and Van Kempen 2000).

After the 2008 financial crisis, the 'variety of residential capitalism' thesis (Schwartz and Seabrooke 2009) connected the housing sector to the 'variety of capitalism' debate (Hall and Soskice 2001). To make sense of the different forms taken by the 2008 real estate boom and bust, those authors differentiated countries based on the different degrees of financial liberalisation (measured by mortgage debt in relation to GDP) and homeownership rates, which made them more or less exposed to global financial pressures. Aalbers (2016) has also shown that global financial capital was more or less 'absorbed' by national housing markets. In the book, we borrow more from the 'welfare/housing regime' clustering than from the 'variety of residential capitalism' clustering, because the first one directly addresses the role of the state in rental markets and ownership (key to the STR issue). Yet the two clusters partially overlap, and both have helped to connect the scholarly fields of housing and urban studies to the comparative political economy of capitalism and welfare states.

A number of authors have cautioned against the possible temporal limitations of such national typologies of welfare/housing regimes: they are always a snapshot at one point in time and need to be put into historical perspective and subjected to constant, repeated empirical scrutiny (Stephens et al. 2015; Blackwell and Kohl 2019; Cucca and Ranci 2019). With those caveats in mind, we argue that the welfare/housing regime approach can potentially help us make sense of differences across European cities and countries in the responses to the phenomenon of platform-mediated STRs, in the context of global pressures towards the financialisation, assetisation and 'platformisation' of residential real estate detailed in Chapter 1.

## INVESTIGATING POLITICISATION, INSTRUMENTATION AND IMPLEMENTATION: A POLITICAL SOCIOLOGY OF STR REGULATIONS

The adoption of a broader definition of regulation goes hand in hand with the adoption of a theoretical framework at the crossroads of the political sociology of public policy (how an issue is grasped in terms of framing, politicisation and instrumentation), governance (how political, economic and citizen actors coordinate their action) and political economy (how political actors and institutions shape the strategies of economic actors and vice versa). Our book focuses on *regulation as a socio-political process* giving rise to the design or recycling of instruments and the production of frameworks for the coordination of actors with the aim of solving the STR problem, within pre-existing institutional, political and socio-economic arrangements that are more or less stable.

## How STRs Become a Public Problem: Politicisation, Framing and Agenda-Setting

Building on our previous work (Aguilera et al. 2021), we seek to explain the politicisation of STRs and their appearance on governmental agendas. A social, political or economic 'fact' becomes perceived as problematic and as requiring policy intervention through a process of socio-political construction (Spector and Kitsuse 1977). Various actors coordinate or confront each other to impose their representation of an issue in the public arena, in order to defend their interests and influence future political decisions (Gusfield 1984). They mobilise to draw attention to a problem or, on the contrary, to contest the recognition of a problematic situation: these 'policy entrepreneurs' (Kingdon 1984) can include citizens' movements, professional and economic interest groups, local politicians and researchers. They aim to provoke a reaction from decision-makers, who—usually—only act when a large part of the population is affected (Schattschneider 1960). Public problems are therefore constituted and 'framed' by actors, who mobilise to formulate a diagnostic (identifying and characterising a problem) and a prognostic (solutions) (Cress and Snow 2000).

To understand the conditions and mechanisms through which public problems emerge, we need to link the characteristics of the problems themselves, the social (state of public opinion) and political contexts (regimes, political opportunity structures) and the types of actors who mobilise and their resources. Sometimes the weight of the dramatic intensity of a situation—relayed by the media, particularly in crisis contexts—is crucial (Hilgartner and Bosk 1988). As we will see in Chapter 4, this was the case where citizens movements and local elected officials framed the negative externalities of STRs in the context of the post-2008 housing crisis that has affected many citizens, and therefore laid the ground for a rather receptive public opinion on the issue of STR regulation.

But these 'expanders' of a policy issue (Cobb and Coughlin 1998) may clash with 'opponents' (here, platforms, STR operators, 'home-sharing clubs', tourism professionals, etc.), who will want to restrict the issue to the private sphere (i.e., not requiring a public intervention) or will reject the existence of a problematic situation. The latter may deploy strategies to delegitimise the 'policy entrepreneurs' (Cobb and Ross 1997), showing that there is no problem at all or that the 'problem' is in fact a solution (e.g., that STRs are an important source of revenue for households and cities). This often relies on the production of counter-evidence and counter-expertise to 'reframe' the problem, for example, as we will see by highlighting the benefits of STRs and lobbying local, national and European governments.

## STRs as a Priority for (Some) Local Governments: Agenda-Setting from a Comparative Perspective

The framing and agenda-setting processes are neither homogeneous nor linear. This is so first because the type of actors who mobilise, the causalities of the problem they formulate in their narratives and the field in which they act all shape the framing as well as the political responses that follow. In earlier exploratory research, we have shown that modes of STR regulation (types and intensity) varied according to the framing of STR as part of a specific policy sector with its own instruments (housing, tourism, economic development); the type of actors who mobilised in the first place (the hotel industry, tourism professionals, politicians, administrations, social movements, platforms or sharing economy advocates); and the scale of government that was activated (municipal, regional, national) (Aguilera et al. 2021). Despite the dynamics of globalisation and the transnational circulation of 'public problems' such as STRs (Neveu and Surdez 2020), framings must be studied locally and comparatively to explain diversity at the infranational scale (Benli-Trichet and Kübler 2022). Agenda-setting is, second, not a linear but a highly selective process: not all public problems are addressed by political authorities. Some stakeholders oppose the agenda-setting of an issue that calls for regulation, because they would lose out if regulation were put in place. These actors then mobilise resources and develop strategies not just to reframe an issue but to take it out from the governmental agenda (Cobb and Ross 1997).

Our book takes into account the interplay of actors involved in order to explain why some city governments put STR regulation on the agenda very early on, while others delay it or put STR on the agenda as an economic opportunity to be supported rather than limited. Furthermore, as we will show through comparison, framing, however consensual and dominant it may be, does not always completely determine the policy measures subsequently taken. Sometimes there is a dissonance between the dominant framing, the decisions taken and the instruments chosen (Bergeron et al. 2014): in some cities, despite a strong politicisation of STR-related problems, regulations were of average intensity (i.e., Berlin in 2022) or slow to emerge (i.e., Lisbon in 2018), whereas in some cities where the social salience of the issue was low, strong measures have been taken to limit STRs (i.e., Brussels).

Finally, the arrival of STRs on governmental agendas depends on the availability of solutions. Policy-makers are only willing to give serious attention to a problem if they see a pool of potential solutions: it is only when a public problem finds a solution, in an advantageous political context, that a 'political opportunity window' opens (Kingdon 1984). This reversed causality ('solutions seek their problems') injects a dose of contingency and politics into the analysis of STR regulations. This distances our approach from common approaches in law and policy studies, that too often consider that the rationalities guiding public policy choices involve designing and selecting the most suitable and effective instruments in an informed and rational manner (see critique by Le Galès 2022). As we shall see, politicians open their agendas to the STR issue when they know that there are existing instruments to regulate it, at least in part, and that they can gain political capital by using them. In the absence of a solution, few politicians take the risk of tackling a problem as complex as STRs, which could explain the time lag between different cities' regulatory actions. This is why, to understand regulatory policies and explain their outputs and outcomes, we need to study the full materiality of governmental activity: the concrete conditions under which policies are implemented and their instruments.

## A Sociology of Policy Instrumentation: Scrutinising Regulatory Change and Implementation

Studying policy instruments—as socio-political institutions and not just technical devices (Lascoumes and Le Galès 2007)—is relevant for studying 'wicked issues' that are not clearly part of a given sector and whose boundaries are not very stabilised (Jacquot and Halpern 2015). This is clearly the case for platform-mediated STRs. Knowledge of the set of problems posed by the choices and use of these instruments (what is referred to as *instrumentation*) is relevant to understand how not-yet-institutionalised objects come to be governed (Halpern and Galès 2011). An analysis of STR regulatory instruments also helps in locating the institutionalisation of explicit STR policies that can become autonomous, thus ensuring a form of routinisation of government activity in the field. This is why we have designed an indicator to measure, characterise and compare the 'instrumental thickness' (intensity) of STR regulations in different cities (presented in Chapter 3).

The study of instrumentation is also particularly appropriate to think about the change and diversity of regulations. Decision-makers often put forward innovations and radical changes in the instruments they use, particularly in the face of crises or phenomena that appear to be new, disruptive and unprecedented, as is the case with STRs, but these are sometimes merely symbolic policies (Edelman 1971). Instrumental innovations usually remain limited, and actors often give the illusion of radical change while 'recycling' old instruments (Hood 1983). The main room for manoeuvre lies in assembling new combinations in different contexts to pursue different goals. This instrument-based approach enables us to trace change by 'dismantling appearances' and deconstructing 'surface changes' (Palier 2004). A focus on instruments sheds light on changes that are often gradual rather than radical and take place through the *layering* of policy programmes (Streeck and Thelen 2005; Mahoney and Thelen 2010).

However, the study of STR regulatory decisions and instruments is not enough to explain policy outputs and outcomes. Between what is decided or voted on and what happens on the ground, policies change in content, instruments, involved actors and sometimes even goals (Pressman and Wildavsky 1973). Regulatory instruments are designed, brought to life, fine-tuned and implemented by government officers and 'street-level bureaucrats' (Lipsky 2010), who make them applicable on the ground and tackle the resistance from targeted audiences (e.g., STR operators or platforms). From a bottom-up perspective, street-level bureaucrats (in the field of STR regulation, mostly housing/planning inspectors) often operate without having the necessary data, room for manoeuvre and human and financial resources to do so efficiently. In this book, we therefore study the ways in which they develop discretionary and pragmatic strategies to cope with these shortcomings and make public policy viable. In Chapter 5 we analyse how STR regulatory policies are implemented and enforced on the ground, facing many challenges. Chapter 6 shows how their implementation transforms the relations between key actors (governments, platforms, STR operators, the hotel industry, etc.). By so doing we emphasise the importance of the symbolic and political dimensions of public policy (Edelman 1971). Public policy has two faces: that of a potential problem-solver of a 'wicked' issue such as platform-mediated STRs, and that of a central element in the structuring of a field of political and strategic action, between political and economic players who clash or cooperate to ensure that their interests prevail.

## THE RESEARCH DESIGN OF THE BOOK

### Comparing STR Regulatory Regimes

In this book we study the processes of politicisation of the STR issue contextualised in different socio-economic, political and institutional conditions that contribute to shape the dominant narratives and instruments of STR regulation (referred to as *outputs*). We then unpack their implementation and how STR policies transform the relationships between political and economic actors in the medium term (*outcomes*) (Figure 4). Altogether, we study the emergence and institutionalisation of different *STR regulatory regimes* that we define as *more or less stabilised configurations of actors, instruments, and narratives around the regulation of STRs, embedded in multi-level welfare/housing regimes, territorial institutions and socio-economic conditions.*

As developed in the introduction of the book, our study is located at the crossroads of four explanatory stands that constitute the point of departure (*inputs*) of our conceptualisation of STR regulatory regimes. First, we investigate urban politics in terms of political offer and the mobilisation of grassroots movements and economic actors around STRs. Second, we consider the socio-economic conditions of cities before the arrival of platform-mediated STRs: this includes the relative volume of tourism flows, but also housing market conditions and tenure

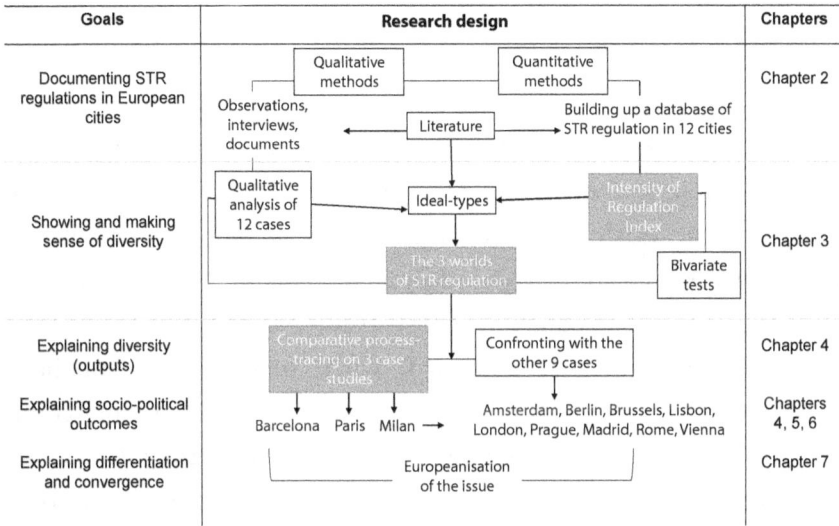

**Figure 5.** The research design of the book. *Source:* Authors.

structures. Third, we take into account the pre-existing institutional arrangements that define welfare/housing regimes. Fourth, we study the implications of the differential distribution of power and responsibilities across levels of governments. For each of these strands, we identified sets of variables which were first tested as part of a descriptive counterfactual statistical (variable-oriented) analysis (Chapter 3) in order to identify the potential pre-existing conditions that played a role in explaining the diversity of our 12 cases, and that should be taken into account in the definition of three ideal types. Then, through in-depth case studies of three cities (Paris, Barcelona and Milan, selected as representative of each ideal-typical group), we unpack the mechanisms and processes that lead to regulatory differences (Chapter 4). Therefore, through comparative analysis, we explained this diversity both in terms of *outputs* (political discourse and narratives, types of instruments adopted and implemented, intensity of regulation) and of *outcomes* (socio-political and economic effects on urban governance, housing and STR markets, in Chapters 5 and 6) (see Figure 5).

## Case Selection: Large European Visitor Cities

Our study focuses on STR regulation in 12 major European cities. By focusing on European cities of reasonably comparable size, which are the capitals and/or second cities of nine countries, we can control some variance in the socio-economic dimensions mentioned above. In the context of a comparison of an intermediate number of cases, it seemed reasonable to compare cities that share a fairly similar political and economic history (Lijphart 1971), where local governments have a relatively high degree of political capacity compared to other continents, and where the central state has been playing a strong, yet changing, role (Le Galès 2002). This is why comparing European cities thus makes sense both intellectually and methodologically.

European countries (particularly France, Spain and Italy) and their respective capitals or major cities (Paris, Barcelona and Madrid, Rome and Milan) are among the world's top destinations for visitors from all over the world and among the top destinations for STR listings on Airbnb. The challenges are therefore very high when it comes to regulating platform-mediated STRs—against the backdrop of the post-2008 crisis and a quasi-structural housing affordability crisis (as discussed in Chapter 1). For practical reasons related to time, financial and linguistic resources, we chose not to study the entire population of European capitals and second-largest cities, but an intermediate number of 12 cases from among Europe's most touristic cities in the mid-2010s: Barcelona, Paris, Milan, Amsterdam, Berlin, Brussels, Lisbon, London, Rome, Madrid, Prague and Vienna. The aim was to understand how European cities confronted with the highest tourism and STR numbers had reacted.

It is important to stress that we compare cities in multi-level and transnational settings. This has implications for our comparative analysis. First, 'cities' are considered here as urban governments; as the territorial jurisdictions for the application of the STR regulations under study; as the privileged arena of regulatory collective action, negotiations and conflicts; and as the crucible of the struggles shaping platform capitalism, the visitor economy and housing. But cities are part of national spaces that shape their characteristics and the politics that unfold within them—inter-state differences are significant and must be fully taken into account in comparative analysis (Therborn 2023). Second, we are not just comparing policies implemented by local authorities, but also regulatory measures from various tiers of government, developed in negotiation and conflicts with local, national and international public and private players, social movements and organisations. Third, although we are comparing regulations enacted in reaction to STR activities facilitated by multinational corporate platforms, the latter do not behave in the same way everywhere, and their relationships with regulatory authorities are highly differentiated (see Chapters 5 and 6). Therefore, platform strategies cannot be considered simply as factors exogenous to the local arenas under study. The transnationalisation of firms, the globalisation of platform capitalism and the transboundary circulation of policy ideas and knowledge between cities, countries and other actors do not erase national and sub-national variations (Hay 2004). The neoliberalisation of the urban world (of which platform capitalism is a new avatar) does not have the same effects everywhere (Le Galès 2016; Pinson and Morel Journel 2016), and public authorities do not react in the same way to the transformations and crises of capitalism. In the medium and long runs, this leads to important differences in who benefits and who loses from the spread of platform-mediated STR markets. In comparative urban and housing studies, methodologically and analytically, this calls for a middle-ground approach that pays due attention to the influence of transnational actors, regulations and markets that may lead to possible 'common trajectories' between cases embedded in very different contexts, without presuming convergence or divergence (Aalbers 2022).

## Ideal-Typical Comparison, Cross-Case Analysis and Mixed Methods

Our comparative research design consists in grasping and explaining the diversity of modes of regulation adopted in cities that we consider to be different. In this sense, we had to find a middle ground between the most common comparative designs in comparative political studies, whether quantitative large-N comparisons or rather qualitative small-N comparisons (Post 2023), including those inspired by Mill's comparative method (Lijphart 1971) or Qualitative Comparative Analysis (Rihoux and Ragin 2009). We first collected comprehensive data about our 12 cases and made causal mechanisms explicit in a small number (three) of these cases, before coding data aimed at developing our medium-N comparison. Our approach thus converges with emerging research perspectives in urban studies, that rely on the in-depth qualitative analysis of a small number of cases and incrementally identify similarities and differences between these cases (Pinson 2023).

Our comparison is divided into three main stages combining a variable-oriented and a case-oriented approach (Della Porta 2008), which are justified on empirical, theoretical and methodological grounds. The adoption of an ideal-typical perspective makes it possible to give meaning to a diversity of STR regulations established in different socio-economic, institutional and political situations. To do this, we mobilise quantitative methods to test the hypotheses derived from existing scholarship (counterfactual analyses), to document our cases and classify them, and qualitative methods to describe the differences between some cases and the similarities between other cases (Chapter 3). We construct three ideal types (our three 'worlds of STR regulation') from which we select three cases (Paris, Barcelona, Madrid), subsequently analysed through an in-depth process-tracing analysis. Our second stage is a cross-case analysis that enables us to show how these three cases are illustrative of their respective 'world', to explain the causal mechanisms that have led to regulatory differences and finally, to compare these results with the other cases in the sample (Chapter 4). We then move to the analysis of the processes of convergence or differentiation at the implementation stage (Chapter 5) and of the reconfiguration of actors' relationships at the local and national levels (Chapter 6) and at the European level (Chapter 7).

PART II

# VARIETIES OF REGULATORY REGIMES

The Three Worlds of STR Regulation
in Europe

# 3

# THE THREE WORLDS
# OF SHORT-TERM RENTAL
# REGULATION IN EUROPEAN CITIES

IN 2022, just over a decade after the emergence of Airbnb in Europe, the vast majority of medium and large European cities had taken a position on the issue of STR regulation. In some cities, local governments reacted quickly in the mid-2010s, as in Barcelona, Berlin and Paris, with a view to limiting the negative externalities of the phenomenon. In other cities, regulations came later, influenced by changes in national legislation, either to seek to contain STRs, as in Lisbon, or to allow their development as a legal activity, as in London. As we will see here, when looking more closely at the instruments of regulations, two observations can be made. On the one hand, STR regulations have been using a limited number of policy instruments: overall, about a dozen quantitative, qualitative or spatial tools (Nieuwland and van Melik 2020; Hübscher and Kallert 2023). On the other hand, the combinations of these instruments are rather diverse, revealing a highly contrasting landscape of regulatory logics and intensities, a diversity that constitutes the initial puzzle of this book.

This chapter substantiates those observations by mobilising quantitative and qualitative material derived from the coding and analysis of a database of detailed STR regulations in 12 European cities in 2022 (see the Appendix for details on data sources and methods; Colomb and Moreira de Souza 2021 for the original qualitative database). It has three complementary objectives, addressed in turn. First, we aim to empirically show the diversity of STR regulations. How are STRs regulated in European cities? What exactly is regulated, how, and by whom? How much? And how do regulations differ from one city to the other? While most of the research discussed in Chapter 2 has captured regulatory diversity through continuous indexes—from 'less' to 'more' regulated (Nieuwland and van Melik 2020; von Briel and Dolnicar 2020; Furukawa and Onuki 2022; Bei and Celata 2023; Hübscher and Kallert 2023), we develop a multi-dimensional approach that allows systematic comparison and correlation testing but is also sensitive to the different origins and logics of instrumentation. We grasp STR regulations as different combinations of (more or less numerous) policy instruments, that can target various STR practices (professional rentals, rental of a primary or secondary residence, rental of a room), carry different logics, and emanate from different levels of government and policy sectors. The detailed database of STR regulations, once coded, allowed us to measure STR regulatory intensity through a continuous quantitative Intensity of Regulation Index (IRI) that gives a measure of the intensity of regulation in each city.

Second, we seek to test a series of hypotheses that stemmed from existing scholarship and from our theoretical framework. These hypotheses are part of the explanatory strands that structure our analysis regarding the effects of local socio-economic, housing and political/institutional conditions on the intensity of STR regulations. Are STRs more regulated in the most touristic cities with the highest quantity of STRs relative to population? Do local housing market conditions, tenure split and welfare/housing regimes matter? Do the political colour of the ruling majority in the city government or the presence of social movements challenging STRs make a difference? Using the IRI to investigate the effect of selected groups of variables, we show that there is no direct and straightforward correlation: these variables impact regulation in some cases, but not always and not in isolation. Those tests offer partial results that cannot be used for further frequentist statistical modelling given our small-N sample of 12 cities, but they allow us to move towards a deductive approach to describe and explain the diversity of regulations.

Based on the previous observations, the third goal of this chapter is to make sense of regulatory diversity by building up a *typology of cities regulating STRs*. We outline three ideal types of STR regulatory regimes—'three worlds'. The first is the world of cities in which regulation aims at making the STR market legal, taxable and competitive, and to promote tourism attractiveness and property-based revenues in liberalised housing markets dominated by homeowners. The second and third worlds are those of cities with more intense regulations that have sought to limit the development of STR markets and contain their negative externalities on housing and neighbourhood life. The second world comprises touristic cities with strong housing institutions and local governments that acted as policy entrepreneurs of STR regulation. The third one entails cities with active grassroots mobilisations and 'new municipalist' governments responsive to these mobilisations.

## WHAT IS REGULATED AND BY WHOM?

### A Variety of Targeted Types of Short-Term Rental Accommodation Practices

Before the rise of digital platforms, most countries had established regulations for non-hotel types of tourist accommodation, such as the seasonal letting of a holiday home (e.g., villas on the seaside in summertime) or B&B establishments. However, at the beginning of the 2010s, these rules were challenged by the unprecedented increase, diversification and geographical expansion of platform-mediated STR activities, resulting in legal uncertainty and regulatory grey areas (presented in Chapter 1). Political struggles have emerged around how to adapt the existing legal frameworks and/or create new ones. Legal qualifications of *what* constitutes a STR, and henceforth what rules apply to it, have been built through various pieces of legislation specific to each national and/or local jurisdiction. This has produced new demarcations between what is legal or illegal in the STR of a property, that vary between places.

STR regulation has targeted both corporate platforms (to which we will return in Chapters 5 and 6) and a variety of STR practices, summarised in Box 1. These practices range from the commercial and full-time rental of

---

### BOX 1: MAIN TYPES OF SHORT-TERM RENTAL PRACTICES MEDIATED BY DIGITAL PLATFORMS

In 2020, the Court of Justice of the European Union defined STR as 'the repeated short-term letting, for remuneration, of furnished accommodation to a transient clientele which does not take up residence there', whether on a professional or non-professional basis (CJEU 2020a). Within that definition, we distinguished three main types of STR for analytical purposes (this typology does not entirely match the exact legal categories used in all cities and countries, but works as a comparative analytical tool):

- **Type i: Professional short-term rental:** the short-term letting on a commercial basis of an entire property not used as a primary residence.
- **Type ii: Short-term rental of a primary (or secondary) residence:** the short-term letting of an entire dwelling which is normally used as a primary (or secondary) home while the main resident is away on a temporary basis.
- **Type iii: Short-term rental of part of a primary residence:** the short-term letting of part of a primary residence (e.g., one or more rooms) while the host is usually present (home-sharing).

*Source*: Colomb and Moreira de Souza (2021).

a unit to the occasional rental of a primary residence, or of a room within it. As city governments became increasingly concerned with the shift of long-term residential units towards the short-term accommodation market, one of the most controversial issues in policy debates became the extent to which STR rules should differentiate between the *occasional* rental of a residence or part of it (STR types ii and iii) and the full-time commercial operation of a holiday let (type i). Several city governments have sought to find a middle ground between maintaining the city's attractiveness to visitors; protecting the long-term residential housing stock; and allowing tenants, mortgage-holders and homeowners to supplement their income through the occasional rental of their home. They have done so by differentiating between the three types of STR in their regulatory approaches, as detailed in the following sections.

## Who Regulates? Levels of Government and Policy Sectors

In the process of regulation of platform-mediated STRs, different levels of government have been called into action, depending on the territorial organisation of each country (unitary, regionalised or federal). In most cities, the competence over the legal definitions of both tourism-related establishments and rental housing is not in the hands of city governments, but of higher levels. For Paris, Lisbon, London and Prague, it is the national government (of France, Portugal, the UK and the Czech Republic, respectively). The transformation of the London STR regulation in 2015 was, for example, the outcome of changing national legislation. For Barcelona and Madrid, it is the regional government (of Catalonia and the Autonomous Community of Madrid, respectively) that legally defines what *accommodation for touristic use* is, while rental law is mostly in the hands of the national government. In Milan and Rome too, the regional governments (of Lombardy and Lazio, respectively) have legislative power in the field of tourism, and the national government has control over rental law. In all these cases, municipal governments have no control over the legal definition of STRs, but are in charge of the instruments (e.g., registration, licencing, authorisation schemes, etc.) that regional or national laws allow them to use. Two cities—Berlin and Vienna—have the status of city-states in federal countries and thus have broader powers than municipal governments in unitary states, such as Lisbon or Paris.

Often, as will be discussed in Chapters 4 and 7, there has been a lack of cooperation or even diverging goals, between different tiers of government regarding the approach to STR regulation. Several local governments have advocated more interventionist agendas that clash with those of regional or national governments, more favourable to housing deregulation, the platform economy and the growth of the tourism sector. Examples include the 'new municipalist' left-wing city governments of Barcelona (2015–2023) and Madrid (2015–2019), which faced regional governments led by centre-right or right-wing parties, and the centre-left city governments (in the second half of the 2010s) of London, Paris, Prague and Vienna facing national governments led by centre or right-wing parties. Other city governments have proactively lobbied national parliaments to demand new legislation that would give lower tiers of governments stronger powers to regulate STRs, as was the case with Amsterdam (leading to new legislation being approved by the Dutch Parliament in October 2020) and Prague (to no avail so far).

As discussed in Chapter 1, STRs are also at the intersection between the rise of the platform economy, the tourism/visitor economy and the transformation of housing. Unsurprisingly, therefore, they have become regulated through different policy sectors (see Colomb and Moreira de Souza 2021:66–92). In some cities, STR regulations have stemmed from the housing regulatory apparatus, which influences the uses of the residential stock, the conditions of its transformation, its safety requirements, new housing development and sometimes social housing and housing affordability. This has been the case in Amsterdam, Berlin, Paris and Vienna, often complemented by land use planning tools. In other cities, the regulatory framework has originated from the tourism regulatory apparatus, concerned with the definition of various types of tourist accommodation, their quality and safety and the possibilities and the conditions of their development and location. This was the case, initially, in Lisbon, Barcelona, Madrid, Rome and Milan. Interestingly, in both Milan and Barcelona, while STRs at first fell under tourism sector rules, the two cities later exemplified radically different approaches to regulation, laissez-faire in Milan and rigorous control over STR proliferation in Barcelona via land use planning, as detailed in Chapter 4. This shows that there is no clear-cut correlation between the chosen policy sector and the intensity of STR regulation. Importantly, STR regulations sometimes have also stemmed from *both* the housing and the tourism fields (Amsterdam).

It is relevant to note that in about half of the cities covered in this book, at some point in time STRs have been also framed by city governments as part of a broader policy agenda supportive of the sharing or collaborative economy, understood in its initial meaning (Vith et al. 2019). This was exemplified by the 'Milano Sharing City' strategy (2014), the 'Action Plan Sharing Economy' of the Municipality of Amsterdam (2016), the strategy 'Turning the Sharing Economy into a Fair Economy' in Vienna (2016), the 'Circular Economy Agenda' of the City of Paris (2015) and the 'Impetus Plan for the Social and Solidarity Economy of the Ajuntament de Barcelona' (2016). Those five cities, as well as Lisbon and Madrid, signed the declaration of 'Common Principles and Commitment for City Sovereignty Regarding the Platform Economy' adopted at the third Sharing Cities Summit in 2018. Its content reflected a concern with the challenges posed by the platform economy for cities' sovereignty, but also the desire of city governments to achieve a balancing act between the promotion of the initial spirit of the sharing economy and the regulation of corporate platforms.

The EU also framed STRs as part of its policy agenda in support of the growth of the digital economy and the strengthening of the Single Market. As we will see in Chapter 7, this specific sectoral view of STRs and the importance of the EU legal framework has turned the European level into a key arena for the contestation of local STR regulations by corporate platforms and other pro-STR interest groups.

## HOW ARE STRs REGULATED? COMPARING
## INSTRUMENTATION AND MEASURING INTENSITY

### Instruments and Their Logics

How exactly have STRs been regulated in European cities? As explained in Chapter 2, one way of grasping STR regulation is through its instruments and their combinations. Table 1 lists all the instruments we identified inductively in the 12 European cities under study (as of mid-2022). These instruments stemmed from various levels of government (national, regional, municipal) and policy sectors. Figure 6 shows the frequency of each instrument across the 12 cities for each type of STR.

The use of different instruments is linked to different representations of the STR issue and reveals a heterogeneity of underlying targets, criteria and rationalities. We have identified two main regulatory logics at play. On the one hand, some instruments regulate how companies and individuals *operate* in the STR market: they define the requirements to be fulfilled vis-à-vis public authorities, customers and third parties. They set the ground rules for a market of legal activities, but without steering its development pace, growth or volume. By contrast, other instruments regulate the *access* to the STR market in the first place, by establishing compulsory steps through which a dwelling

TABLE I

STR Regulatory Instruments in European Cities

| Number | Name | Description | Type |
|---|---|---|---|
| 1 | Authorisation, licence | Authorisation or licence requirement to conduct an economic activity and/or to change the use of a property | Access |
| 2 | Time cap | Maximum cumulative number of days of rental per year allowed for STR types ii and iii | Access |
| 3 | Quantitative restrictions | Quantitative restrictions (or ban) on STR at the city or neighbourhood level | Access |
| 4 | Spatial restrictions | Spatial differentiation regulating the presence of STR in certain areas | Access |
| 5 | Obligation of residency | The listed unit must be the host's primary residence for STR types ii and iii | Access |
| 6 | No social housing | Prohibition of STR in social housing for STR types ii and iii | Access |
| 7 | Third parties | Requirements for permission to use the property as STR from relevant private parties (possibility of veto or prohibition by those parties) | Access |
| 8 | Registration | Registration requirements | Operate |
| 9 | Guest reporting | Guest reporting requirements (for public order, immigration or statistical purposes) | Operate |
| 10 | Space/people limit in unit | Space limit and/or maximum number of guests in the rented unit | Operate |
| 11 | Safety/quality | High requirements in terms of safety and quality standards | Operate |
| 12 | Tourist tax | Subject to tourist or city tax | Operate |

SOURCE: Authors.

unit/a property can be redirected towards the STR economy (or not). Through regulating market access, such instruments seek to *control* and possibly *limit* the growth of STR rentals, their amount, their type and their location in a city. We can analyse these two regulatory logics in detail.

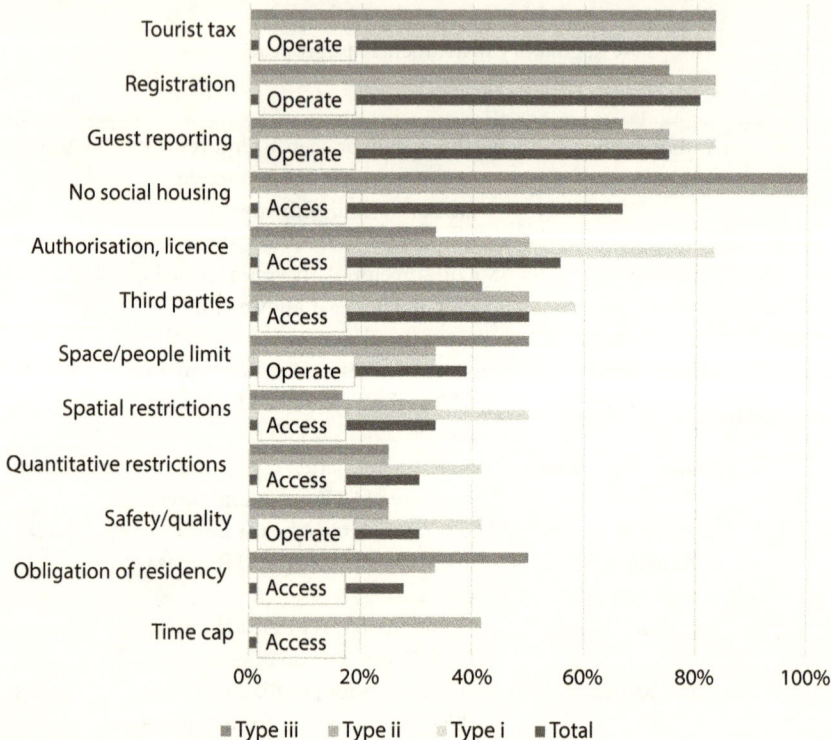

**Figure 6.** Frequency of STR regulatory instruments in 12 European cities, per type of STR. *Source:* Authors' STR Regulatory Database (2022).

REGULATING MARKET *OPERATION*:
LEGALISING AND NORMALISING STRs

As of May 2022, apart from the prohibition from letting social housing units on a short-term basis (which existed in all cities), the most widespread instruments were of the 'operate' type (Figure 6). This means that the most common regulatory logic in Europe has been to set rules to ensure that the market works legally. Faced with a steep increase in STRs, one of the first concerns of public authorities was the lack of knowledge about a phenomenon operating in grey areas. Some of the new rules aimed at making STR graspable and *countable*: they embodied the classical regulatory logic of 'seeing like a state' (Scott 1999) and making 'things' (rented units, operators, guests, etc.) visible, enumerable and thus governable, to public authorities. In around 80% of the cases (all cities and all types of STR), a *registration scheme* for STR units and an obligation of *guest reporting* were in place. With the exception of London and Prague, all cities had a compulsory registration scheme for STR operators that applied to all types of STR. Such schemes must be distinguished from a system of authorisation/licence: the latter can be refused by public authorities, while in the former, a registration number is automatically granted after self-declaration or self-registration. The obligation to report the number and/or identities of guests for statistical or security reasons is also an instrument that made STR users countable, just like hotel guests.

In addition, an activity which is registered becomes more easily *taxable*: all the cities which had a tourist tax applied to overnight stays in traditional forms of tourist accommodation have extended it to the STR market. The direct collection of the tourist tax by platforms and their remittance to local governments has helped the enforcement of this tax to STRs as a new form of tourist accommodation and has been strategically used by platforms to show signs of goodwill and cooperation with city governments (see Chapter 6). Other instruments of the operate type reflect the governing logic of *setting standards* for the accommodation offer, its quality and minimum specifications. Several cities have established safety and quality requirements that regulate how STRs must operate regarding customers and third parties.[1] This has sometimes been presented as 'levelling the playing field' with hotels, who are subject to well-established rules on this matter.

REGULATING MARKET *ACCESS*:
LIMITING THE EXPANSION OF STRs

By contrast, other instruments regulate the *access* to the STR market, under the logic of *steering* and eventually *curbing* the shift of the long-term residential (and sometimes non-residential) stock towards the short-term market. They also seek to influence what property owners can do, and act as (dis)incentives that influence which kind of real estate asset class private capital can flow into.

Some instruments directly control the transformation of the uses of the built environment that STRs entail. The most frequent ones are *authorisation or licencing schemes* for STRs, either for the exercise of an economic activity (tourist accommodation) and/or for a change of land use (from residential to commercial).[2] Here, the STR activity cannot be performed until a positive response from the relevant administration is issued after an application is submitted. The authorisation can be granted, or denied, according to local governments' considerations regarding the balance of uses in urban space. Ten city governments out of the 12 examined in this book (Amsterdam, Barcelona, Berlin, Brussels, Lisbon, London, Madrid, Paris, Prague and Vienna) have developed a system of licences or authorisations. Five city governments have also developed instruments that seek to explicitly *limit, or reduce, the overall number of STRs*—either in the city as a whole or in specific neighbourhoods (Amsterdam, Barcelona, Madrid, Lisbon, Vienna), by setting a maximum number of granted authorisations and/or implementing restrictions in defined geographical zones.

In Barcelona, as detailed in Chapter 4, the Special Plan for Tourist Accommodation (PEUAT) was approved in 2017 and applies to all types of tourist accommodation (hotels, hostels and STRs). It is based on a principle of zero growth of the existing total number of licences for such forms of accommodation (standing at just under 10,000 for STRs). It aims to rebalance the territorial distribution of STRs away from the over-congested historical centre, through a zoning system that bans new licences for any type of new tourist accommodation in central areas but allows a replacement of extinguished licences, or a very modest growth, in other areas. In Madrid, the city government has used its competence in urban planning to seek to control STR types i and ii (which are defined in a regional law amended in April 2019). In March 2019, a special plan for the uses of tourist accommodation was approved (*Plan Especial de Usos del Hospedaje*) by the left-wing government led by the political force Ahora Madrid that governed the city between 2015 and 2019. The plan aimed to protect residential buildings against the proliferation of STRs by imposing strict conditions for the granting of a licence, requiring, in particular, an STR unit to have a separate entrance and lift from those used by the residents of the building. These rules have been applied to specific zones defined in the plan, which cover the historic centre and surrounding neighbourhoods. These strict requirements de facto turned 95% of the existing registered STR offer in Madrid (approximately 10,000 flats) into illegal stock, as the central districts of the city are made of apartment blocks with a single communal entrance.

In Vienna, in December 2018 the commercial letting of residential space for short-term accommodation (STR type i) was prohibited in the 'residential zones' (*Wohnzone*) that cover large parts of the historic centre. Municipal guidance specified that the prohibition against STRs in such zones did not apply to people who occasionally rent out their own home in order to earn some extra money, if in terms of time and space their own residential use continues to predominate. In Lisbon, in November 2019 the city government introduced two types of 'containment areas' (*zonas de contenção*) in the historic centre and other neighbourhoods popular with visitors. 'Absolute' containment areas must have a ratio between the number of licenced STRs and the number of permanent dwellings no greater than 20%; a ratio lowered to between 10% and 20% in 'relative' containment areas. This means that in theory, no new registration of STRs has been allowed in absolute containment areas, or only under strict conditions in relative containment areas.[3] In Amsterdam, in July 2020 the city government banned all vacation rentals from three city centre districts in the old town (Burgwallen-Nieuwe Zijde, Burgwallen-Oude Zijde and the

Grachtengordel-Zuid), responding to concerns about overtourism. However, the ban was overturned and declared illegal by the Court of Justice of Amsterdam on 12 March 2021.[4]

It is important to underline that, in many cases, these instruments (licencing, quantitative and spatial restrictions) do not apply to all types of STR in the same way (see Figure 6). In many cities, regulations impose stricter requirements on type i STR (professional STR of a full property not used as a primary residence), but entail lighter requirements on the rental of a primary or secondary residence and home-sharing (types ii and iii). This is meant to allow—and even support—STR as a source of extra income for urban dwellers occasionally renting their residence. However, this has raised the issue of the distinction, from a legal standpoint, between occasional and full-time STRs. Often, *time caps* have been the answer to this issue: the authorisation to let a primary residence was limited to 30 days per year in Amsterdam, 90 in London and 120 in Paris and Brussels (for the category of STR type ii called *meublé de tourisme*). Yet the distinction is blurred and complex. In some cities (Vienna and Berlin), the nature of a primary residence has been assessed more qualitatively, often clarified through court rulings following an appeal. Sometimes, rules for STR types ii and iii only apply to the primary residence, and the occasional rental of a second home falls into a more stringent system (Paris, Amsterdam). In Berlin, second homes can be rented short-term but with a time cap (90 days per year). Finally, only a few cities had specific, explicit rules that treated room rental in someone's home differently (Amsterdam and Barcelona). The City Council of Barcelona took the controversial measure, in 2021, of prohibiting the rental of a room for less than 31 days. In other cities, the rental of a room has fallen under existing rules for B&Bs (if breakfast is served) or lodgings (e.g., the Rent a Room scheme in the UK/London).

In all cities, the public or social housing stock remains outside of the remit of the licencing system, given the blanket and generalised prohibition of STRs in this form of tenure. This has the potential to keep a significant part of the housing stock outside the STR markets in those cities with a large share of public or social housing units (especially London, Paris, Vienna and Amsterdam, where they represent between 20% and 40% of the housing stock), though illegal STR practices occur with more or less frequency.

Finally, under the scope of private law, condominium or home-owners associations that exist in the multi-storey apartment blocks typical of many continental European cities (e.g., *copropriété* in France or *comunidad de propietarios* in Spain) can vote on whether a landlord is allowed to convert a unit into STR type i. Mortgage, leasehold and private tenancy agreements also often explicitly forbid the STR of the associated housing unit. STRs are, in that sense, also regulated as part of contractual relationships between private parties.

## Intensity of Regulation: Measuring Instrumental Thickness

Regulations also vary in terms of the *number of instruments* in place. Figure 7 displays, for each city of our sample, the number of instruments per type of STRs and the IRI. The IRI is a continuous indicator that measures the constraints applying to an individual or a company putting a unit on the STR market, either on a commercial basis (type i), or occasionally in the case of a primary or secondary residence (type ii), or through the rental of a room (type iii) (see the Appendix for methodological explanations and Chapter 2 for the review of existing indicators). The IRI was calculated by coding, counting and adding up the presence or the absence of each STR regulatory instrument, with a higher value corresponding to a higher number of regulatory instruments applying to the STR market. This indicator thus characterises the regulatory/instrumental *thickness* more than a level of stringency per se. Drawing from Knill and Tosun (2020:217), it combines two characterisations of instrumentation: *policy density*, the area covered by

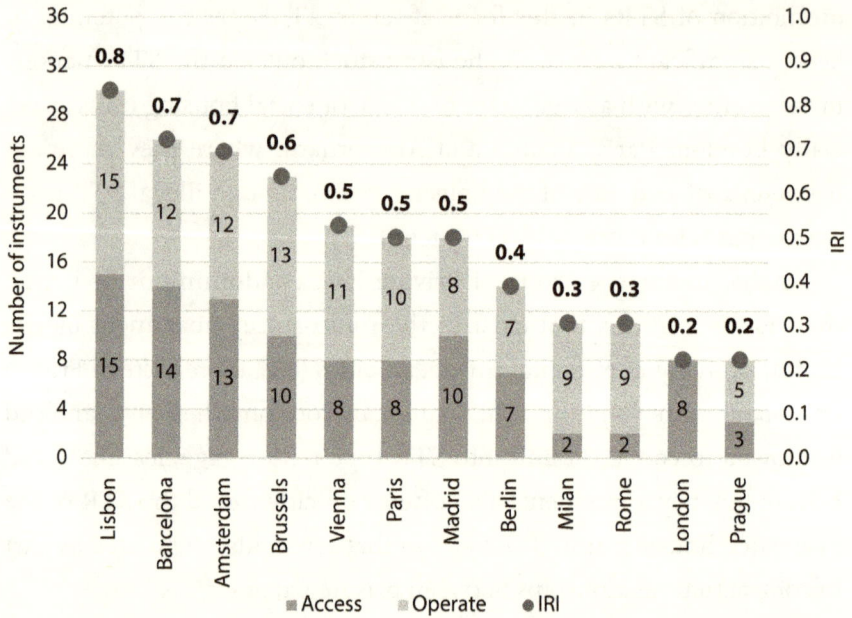

**Figure 7.** Number of STR regulatory instruments per type (access/operate, all types of STR) and Intensity of Regulation Index (0–1), per city. *Source*: Authors' STR Regulatory Database (2022).

government activities and their degree of penetration of that area (in this case, the targeted types of STR and the number of instruments addressing them), and *policy intensity*, the level of public intervention (here, policy strictness or laxness regarding STR). Of course, regulatory intensity does not imply policy effectiveness and actual implementation: there are significant challenges to the implementation and enforcement of STR regulations on the ground, which will be discussed in detail in Chapter 5.

As of May 2022, while there was no instance of 'zero regulation' in our sample, the intensity of regulation measured by the IRI varied greatly: from around 0.2 in Prague to around 0.8 in Lisbon. Between these extremes, the IRI was distributed on a continuum, with no major breaks. In some cities, regulation has been characterised by a high number of instruments combined to regulate STRs: Lisbon, Barcelona and Amsterdam (IRI of 0.7 and more). These cities all had an authorisation scheme for all types of STRs as of mid-2022. Lisbon and Barcelona also have zoning plans controlling the spatial concentration of STRs (though with different levels of effective implementation—weak in Lisbon and stronger in Barcelona). In some other cities, including Brussels, Madrid, Paris, Vienna and Berlin, the regulation is less thick (i.e., instruments) but still restrictive. While all these cities had some kind of authorisation scheme, the latter did not apply uniformly. Brussels and Madrid had complex requirements and conditions attached to the granting of an authorisation, close to the ones of the previous group. By contrast, Paris, Vienna and Berlin were typically characterised by the distinction between commercial STRs for which a permit was needed, and the occasional rental of a primary residence, which attracted lighter obligations. Finally, in some cities STR activities were regulated through only a few instruments, which were more of the operate type: Milan, Prague and Rome. In London and Prague, authorisations were needed for commercial STRs: a pre-existing trade licence system for commercial accommodation activities in Prague and planning permission for change of use in London. However, the rental of a primary residence in London (up to 90 days) remained widely unregulated. It was also the only city with no operate instruments. Finally, the two Italian cities of Milan and Rome had several operate types of instruments (compulsory registration schemes, guest reporting, etc.) but no access limitations (apart from the prohibition of STR in public housing).

Another way to read these results from the IRI description is to cross the intensity of regulation with the type of instruments (see Figure 8). We observe a correlation between the level of regulation and the dominance of access-type rules (i.e., cities in which market entry is more regulated). This will be explained qualitatively in the next chapter, where we will show that the cities with more intense regulation express the political goal of seeking to limit the development of the market rather than simply legalising it.

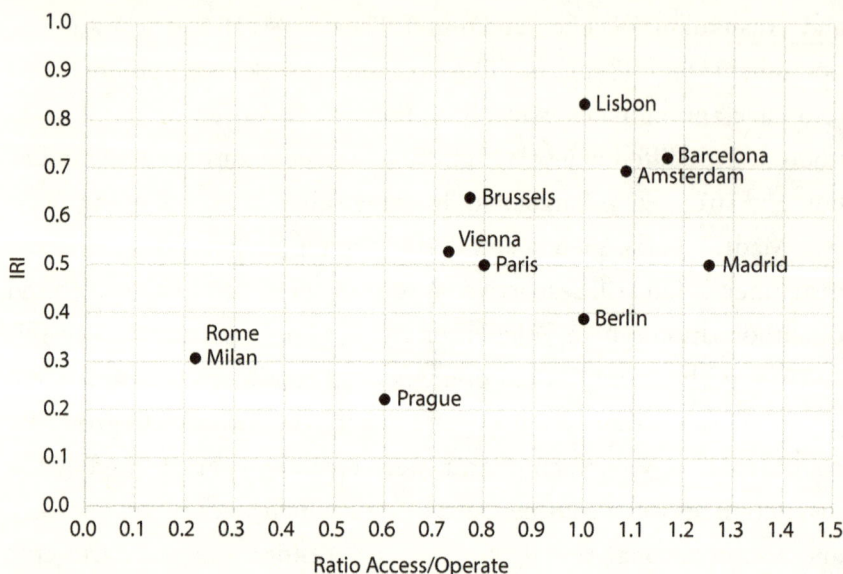

**Figure 8.** Dominant type of instruments (ratio access/operate) and Intensity of Regulation Index (IRI). London is not included since it has no operate instruments. *Source*: Authors' STR Regulatory Database (2022).

The construction of the IRI allowed us to test explanatory hypotheses for the diversity of regulations in European cities, in order to move towards a more precise understanding of the causes of such diverse policy responses.

## EXPLAINING DIVERSITY: TESTING AND NUANCING THE EFFECTS OF TOURISM, HOUSING AND POLITICAL CONDITIONS ON STR REGULATION

As shown in Chapter 2, the literature on STR regulation offers a number of arguments that help to explain the diversity of regulations, to be tested through comparative analysis and quantitative or qualitative methods. In this section we address three main explanatory strands and test hypotheses that emerged at the crossroads of the STR literature and our theoretical framework: the effects of the tourism/STR pressures, of welfare/housing regimes, and of political conditions on the IRI.

## Is There More Stringent Regulation in Tourist-Saturated Cities? Nuancing the Salience Argument

A first explanation for regulatory diversity, often shared in academic scholarship and public debates, suggests that the more a city has been saturated with tourists and STRs, the more (and the earlier) local government has regulated STRs (van Holm 2020). Following this hypothesis, regulatory stringency would be a direct response to the tourism/STR pressure, with a strong correlation between the two. The underlying public policy causal mechanism would be the salience one: the bigger the problem (intensity), the bigger its political prominence in the public arena (salience), the more likely local government is to take action and regulate firmly (Nieuwland and van Melik 2020; Benli-Trichet and Kübler 2022). Beyond a certain threshold of tourists and STRs, citizens would put pressure on local politicians to act.

Were the cities with the highest (relative) number of tourists or STRs also the ones with stricter regulations in our European sample?[5] Our analysis shows that this hypothesised link is not so straightforward, or at least that it does not explain completely the variance between cities. First, if we consider the absolute volume of tourists, it appears that high figures are not a sufficient condition for strong regulation: London and Paris, top tourist destinations in the world in absolute numbers (with respectively 19 and 18 million visitors in 2016), had respectively one of the less stringent regulations (London: IRI of 0.2) and a middle-ground regulatory approach (Paris: IRI of 0.5). If we consider relative values of both tourist and STR numbers per inhabitant, a slightly different picture appears. Figure 9 shows that one group of cities—Amsterdam, Lisbon, Barcelona and to a lesser extent Paris, that had high ratios of tourists and STR per inhabitant in 2016—exhibited more stringent regulations in 2022. They seem to have responded to the tourism/STR pressure. Yet a second group of cities—Vienna, Brussels, Madrid, Berlin, Milan, Rome, London and Prague—have lower ratios of tourist and STR per inhabitant, but exhibit among themselves entirely different regulatory approaches. Figure 9 (bottom graph) shows that in 2016, cities with less than one Airbnb listing per 100 inhabitants developed regulations that ranged from laissez-faire (London: IRI of 0.2) to stringent (Brussels: IRI of 0.6) and covered the whole spectrum of possible approaches to STRs. There is thus no clear-cut correlation between the IRI and tourism/STR intensity.

Beyond the volume and share of listings in cities, it is also necessary to take into account the structure of STR markets. As we will analyse in detail in Chapter 6, an important variable, politically speaking, is the share of multi-listings, namely the share of STRs run by hosts that operate more than one rental. Against the idea of an STR market run by individuals occasionally renting their homes, a high share of multi-listings indicates the concentration and professionalisation of the STR market: hosts with multiple listings are more likely to be running a business and are unlikely to be living in the property, which is therefore solely used for visitors.[6] Before the implementation of STR regulations, this share varied a lot between the cities in our sample: in 2015, it ranged from less than 20% in Paris, Amsterdam and Berlin to more than 50% in Lisbon and Prague (in 2017) (Figure 10).[7] Extending the hypothesis whereby the intensity of the phenomenon leads to more stringent rules, cities with higher shares of multi-listings would have more intense regulations, as decision-makers would attempt to fight against overtourism or the threat to permanent housing. Yet again, we observe clear counterfactual cases: how can we explain that Lisbon and Prague, which have a relatively similar ratio of multi-listings, had such different regulatory intensities? How can we explain that Paris and Madrid, which have a relatively similar IRI, reacted similarly to such differently structured STR markets?

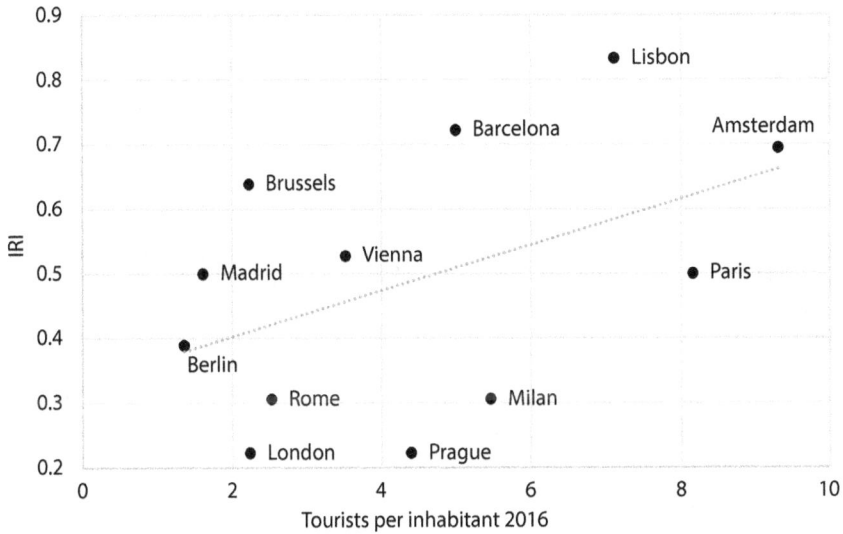

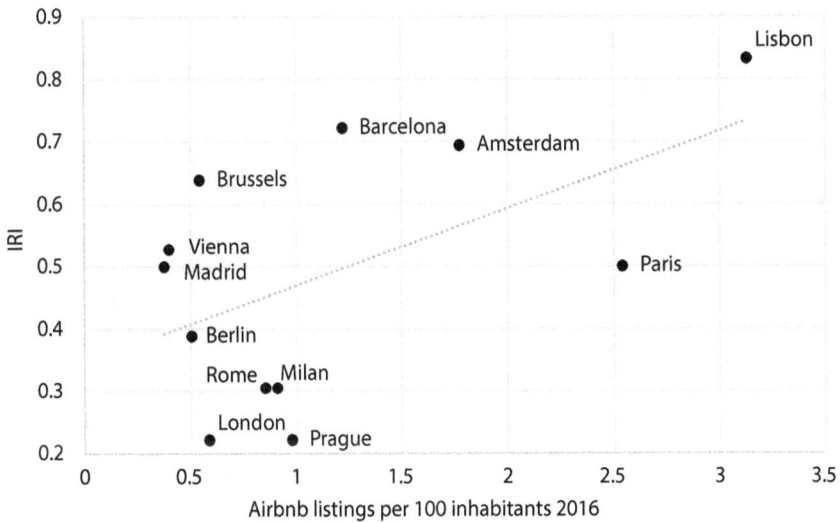

**Figure 9.** Number of tourists per inhabitant (top) and number of Airbnb listings per 100 inhabitants (bottom) and Intensity of Regulation Index (IRI). *Source*: Authors' STR Regulatory Database (2022), MasterCard Global Destination Cities Index (2016), and data from Inside Airbnb (2016).

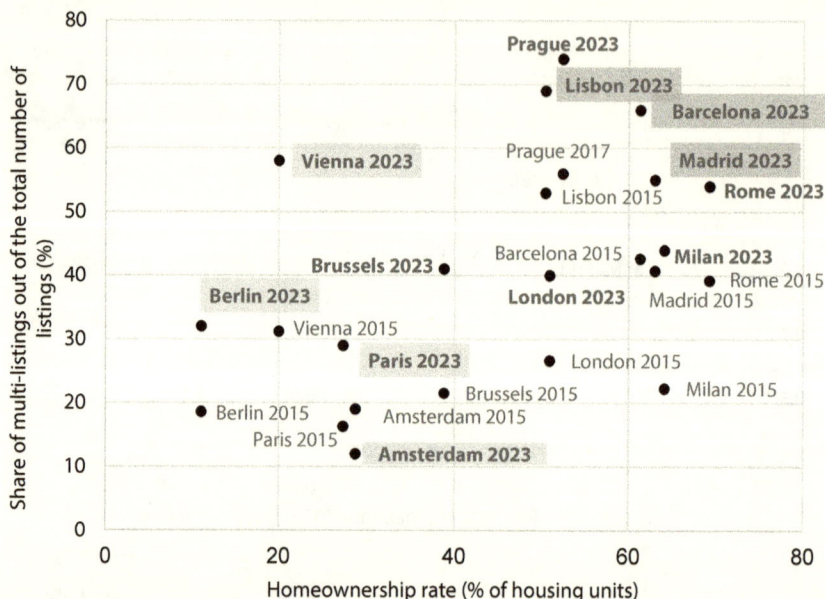

**Figure 10.** Share of multi-listings out of the total number of listings and share of homeownership (%). The cities with a higher IRI are highlighted in dark grey, those with a medium IRI are in light grey, and those with a low IRI are not highlighted. *Source*: Authors' STR Regulatory Database (2022), national and municipal statistics (see the Appendix).

Additionally, decision-makers often did not have data about the STR market structure (and thus their potential targets) when they shaped their regulations. We will even see discrepancies in the framing of the 'public problem': in Paris, for example, where the weight of multi-listings was the lowest, local elected officials greatly problematised the STR issue around multiple investors who were deemed to have removed units from the housing stock to develop an STR business (see Chapter 4).

In sum, considered alone, the tourism/STR intensity variable and the STR market structure are not enough to differentiate STR regulatory responses from one city to the other. From a counterfactual testing perspective, these findings nuance the commonly held view that there is a direct effect between the intensity of an issue and the intensity of political intervention. Other variables and processes have to intervene in between, as we will see.

## Do Housing Conditions Matter? A Partial Explanation

STR regulation does not take place in an institutional vacuum but rather in the context of a set of pre-existing institutions, particularly in the field of housing. Some large European cities have a large public/social housing stock, while others are characterised by a dominant share of homeownership or private rental (Figure 11). Different local tenure splits are also connected to differences in national housing systems and welfare regimes in European countries (Allen et al. 2004; Schwartz and Seabrooke 2009; Arbaci 2019; Stephens 2020; Bernt 2022). The second group of hypotheses tested here is whether differences in STR regulations are related to the diversity in housing contexts and institutional arrangements, which function as filters leading the same transnational phenomenon to be met with different policy responses. Some researchers have argued that STR regulation depends on local housing market conditions in terms of vacancy rate, affordability or housing shortage. But these conditions have been found to have contradictory effects. For instance, a high level of house prices and rents can have two opposite consequences: if governments believe that STRs generate extra incomes for households struggling with high housing costs, they may regulate less; conversely, if they believe that STRs are the cause of these high levels, they will have an incentive to regulate strongly (Chen et al. 2021).[8] To test those variables in our sample, we have broadened the argument and taken into account the housing systems of our cities/countries in order to link housing markets, welfare/housing regimes and policy responses.

We first looked at the structure of urban housing markets: a standard political economy hypothesis would posit that STR regulation is linked to different tenure splits, characterised by different combinations

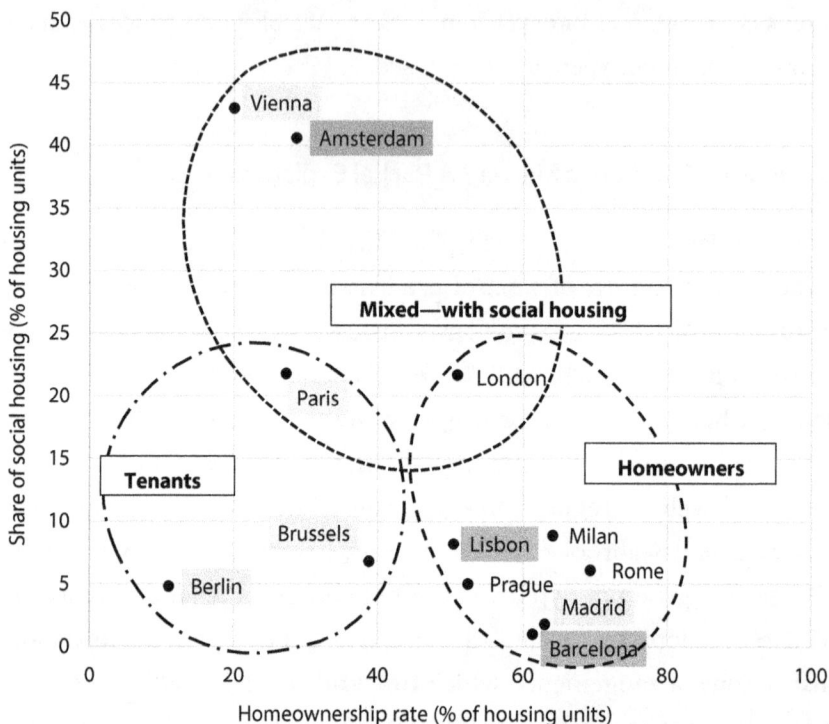

**Figure 11.** Housing tenure in European cities and Intensity of Regulation Index (IRI). The cities with a higher IRI are highlighted in dark grey, those with a medium IRI are in light grey, and those with a low IRI are not highlighted. *Source*: Authors' STR Regulatory Database (2022), national and municipal statistics (see the Appendix).

of owner-occupation, private and non-profit/social rental housing and their associated interest groups. In the face of the development of STRs, one would expect cities dominated by homeownership (in Southern and Eastern Europe especially) to be less regulated. Property owners have specific preferences to preserve their interests: in contexts of housing price appreciation, they tend to be less favourable to redistribution and regulation policies (Ansell 2014; Ansell and Cansunar 2021). The defence of their 'right' to freely rent their property on a short-term basis would be vocally upheld where the rate of homeownership is higher. Conversely, in cities with large shares of private long-term rental tenants, as well as in cities with large shares of public/social housing, STR regulations are expected to be more stringent. Tenants would react to the proliferation of STRs threatening the availability and the affordability of long-term rents, alerting public authorities, possibly participating in social movements and eventually pushing local governments to regulate.

However, this hypothesis is not entirely met, as shown by notable counterfactuals in our sample: Barcelona, Madrid and Lisbon—cities with a majority of homeowners (though this rate has been declining since the 2008 financial crisis)—were among the most regulated cities. Figure 11 shows the housing tenure split in the 12 European cities: cities of homeowners (from 50% in Lisbon to 70% in Rome), cities of tenants (from 50% in Paris to 80% in Berlin) and cities with mixed tenure systems including significant shares of non-profit and social housing (from 20% in London and Paris to 40% in Amsterdam and Vienna). It can be easily seen that, among the category of 'homeowners cities', one can find both the most interventionist (Lisbon, Barcelona) and the less interventionist (Prague, Italian cities, London) in terms of STR regulations. There was no correlation between this specific tenure structure and the intensity of regulation. By contrast, cities with a majority of tenants and large shares of public/social housing all displayed approaches that ranged from middle-ground to stringent. This result was puzzling and suggested that housing tenure played some role in differentiating cities, but not in isolation and not systematically.

Other aspects of the local housing markets were also not correlated with the intensity of STR regulation. Factors such as the local level of affordability of long-term rents (in relation to the average monthly salary) or the share of vacant homes, which played a role in structuring market opportunities for STR operators (as explained in Chapter 1), were not directly correlated to more or less stringent regulations.

To further investigate the role played by housing, we looked at STR regulations from the perspective of the national welfare/housing regimes that differentiate European countries in the relationship between owner-occupation and rental markets/sectors, as well as in

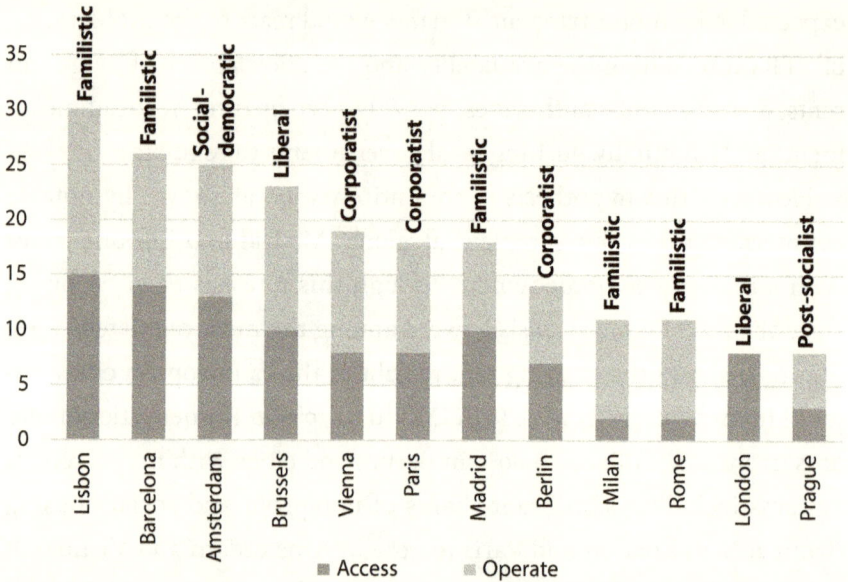

**Figure 12.** Welfare/housing regime and intensity of regulation. *Source*: Authors' STR Regulatory Database (2022), drawing on Arbaci (2019) classification.

the degree of redistribution by state intervention (Figure 12). Since STRs may contribute to reducing the stock of long-term rental housing, shifting housing units into assets for investment and in some cases, reducing affordability, one would assume that different welfare/housing clusters lead to different STR regulatory approaches. The main mechanism at play here would be the critical mediating role of macro-institutional arrangements: they provide specific contexts for local actors, structuring a mix of constraints, opportunities and worldviews, which may explain differences. They also tend to be sticky, which contributes to explaining why national systems respond differently to global events or trends and often remain on pre-existing paths (Aalbers 2022). Such a perspective assumes that urban local policies are first and foremost shaped by national arrangements.

According to this hypothesis, one would expect stricter STR regulations to be found in social-democratic systems (The Netherlands), characterised by a significant non-profit rental sector and the state promotion of various forms of rented housing, as well as in corporatist systems (Germany, Austria and France), with a predominant private rental sector and the state promotion of the private and social rented sector as a remedy for market imperfection. By contrast, regulations would be expected to be lighter in liberal countries (UK, Belgium), familistic ones (Spain, Italy) and post-socialist ones (Czech Republic), which share a predominance of owner-occupation, and where the state fosters home ownership and free market housing provision. Yet this was not completely the case nor always so in our sample. On the one hand, the corporatist group (to which Vienna, Paris and Berlin belong) was quite coherent in terms of their middle-ground intensity of STR regulation. The city of our sample belonging to the social-democratic cluster (Amsterdam) had an intense regulation, in line with the hypothesis. Cities belonging to the liberal (London) and post-socialist (Prague) clusters were also coherent in terms of lighter regulations. On the other hand, however, the internal variance within the familistic group was the same as the whole sample (Lisbon and Barcelona had the most intense STR regulations, while Milan and Rome were among the least-regulated cities). This produces a major counterfactual argument and limits the capacity of explaining the diversity of STR regulations merely based on different welfare/housing regimes.

## Do Local Politics Matter? Governing Majorities and Social Mobilisations

Finally, the issue of STRs has been highly politicised over the past decade, but not always in the same way and with the same intensity in all cities. Whether such variation relates to differences between the political colour of local governments, between types of ruling coalitions, or between the intensity of citizen mobilisations, one could expect these differences to play a role in explaining the diversity of regulations in two ways. First, the partisan aspect of (local) politics: one could easily assume that the more left-wing a municipal government is, the more it tends to regulate (Marques Pereira 2022); the more right-wing/economically liberal a municipal government is, the less it tends to regulate (Ferreri and Sanyal 2018). Some scholars, however, have shown that the political colour of local governments does not seem to play an important role (Benli-Trichet and Kübler 2022), or at least not in terms of the left–right cleavage but rather in terms of level of political competition between parties (the higher the competition is, the lighter the regulation, according to Hong and Lee 2018). The second relevant aspect of (local) politics relates to the mobilisations by various actors and citizens: the more social movements, the hotel industry and public opinion explicitly mobilise against STRs, the more intense STR regulation would be.

The partisan hypothesis that assumes left-wing local governments have regulated STRs more was verified in part of our sample. Cities governed by a political majority belonging to what has been described as the new left or 'new municipalist' movement adopted stricter and more intense regulations than others (see Figure 13). As discussed in Chapter 4, Barcelona exemplifies the effect that this political factor has had, with the arrival of Mayor Ada Colau and the political force Barcelona en Comú in 2015, that stemmed from citizen movements. Similarly, in Madrid the political shift to the left with the election of Manuela Carmena in the same year changed the STR agenda (though late in her mandate) and led to the adoption of measures that the previous right-wing government had not considered. The difference is visible when comparing these cities with right-wing, centre-right and/or populist city governments (as in Prague in 2014–2018, or Rome under the populist government of the Five-Star Movement, 2016–2021). But it is less obvious when compared with cities that were governed by centre-left parties or left-wing coalitions (Paris, London, Lisbon, Brussels, Berlin, Amsterdam, Milan): that group was highly heterogeneous in terms of regulation. Finally, in some cities like Lisbon and Amsterdam, STR

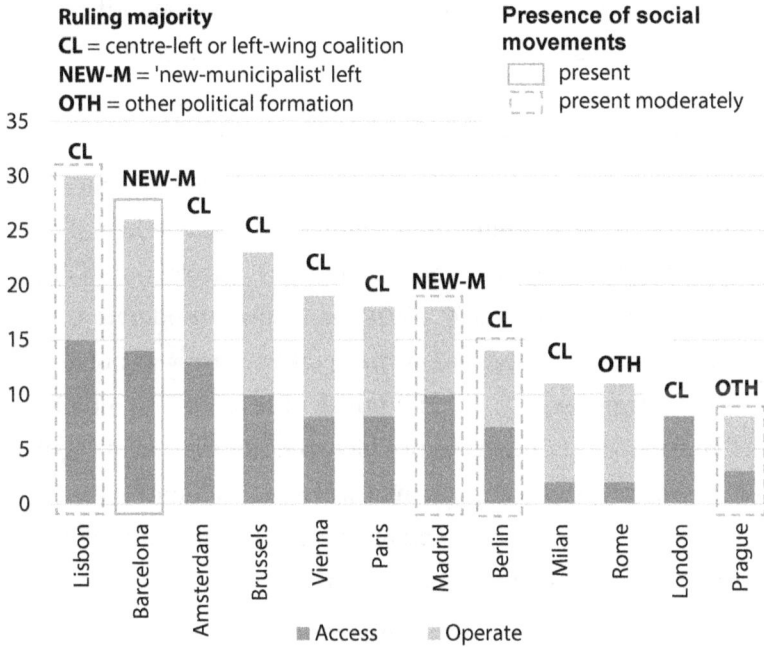

**Figure 13.** Ruling majority (at time of first STR rules), presence of social movements advocating STR regulation (prior to first STR rules) and intensity of regulation. *Source*: Authors' STR Regulatory Database (2022).

regulations were more intense than in cities qualified as new municipalist left: the correlation is thus not linear. Altogether, this empirical evidence suggests that new municipalist governments have pushed for more regulation, but it also leads us to nuance the assumed straightforward correlation between local politics and regulatory policy.

The other political variable to be considered is the role of social movements and citizen mobilisations around touristification, housing shortages and gentrification (see Figure 13). The hypothesis whereby a strong politicisation of the issue by social movements pushes local elected officials to adopt stronger regulations is partly demonstrated. However, our sample does not allow us to test it sufficiently and to put forward a completely significant result. The city of Barcelona is a paradigmatic case: as detailed in Chapter 4, a strong mobilisation in favour of stricter regulation (or even of a ban) was anchored in anti-touristification and anti-gentrification social movements that existed since the mid-2000s. Combined with the above-mentioned local political change in 2015, the presence of these movements played a strong role in the politicisation of the issue on the one hand, and in the agenda-setting and decision-making towards more intense STR regulation, on the other.

However, the difference between cities where anti-STR, pro-regulation mobilisations have taken shape (even moderate ones) and cities where no such mobilisations have taken place was not as significant as one might expect. At an equivalent level of low mobilisation, cities like Paris and London did not have the same levels of regulation. Another issue remained unexplained without a qualitative causal analysis: in some cities citizen movements were a strong source of influence over local agendas (in Barcelona and Berlin in alliance with ruling left-wing parties), whereas in others they followed earlier mobilisation by the hotel industry or local elected officials (Paris, Madrid). In Prague, despite the long-standing presence of some social mobilisations in the historic centre (Pixová and Sládek 2016), STR rules were extremely light in 2022, which again produces a counterfactual argument inviting us to nuance the direct correlation between social movements and the intensity of regulation.

Finally, one important interest group has played a major role since the emergence of Airbnb and major platforms in the early 2010s: hotel operators, their professional federations and unions and more broadly the hotel industry. As we will discuss in Chapters 4 and 6, they took up the issue of STRs very quickly in all European cities. Of course hotel operators have not mobilised in the same way, at exactly the same time, with the same framing and the same effects all over Europe. Still, at this level of analysis, they were present everywhere, and henceforth this variable does not meaningfully allow for a differentiation of STR regulations.

To sum up, the 12 European cities faced with STRs we consider here have different socio-economic contexts and institutional arrangements:

they are more or less attractive to tourists and have different levels of STR concentration, the structure of their housing stock and housing system differs, they have been governed by different political parties, and they have witnessed different levels of social mobilisation around STRs. All these differences must be taken into account, but our empirical analysis shows that none of them seems to explain, in isolation, the diversity of STR regulations. It is not possible to establish clear correlations based on simple bivariate tests because of important counterfactual cases. The intensity of tourist flows sometimes correlates with stringent rules, but not always. Cities of tenants and with larger shares of non-profit/social housing, as well as cities belonging to the sociodemocratic and corporatist housing/welfare clusters, clearly have tended to have stricter rules, but cities with a majority of homeowners have displayed very heterogenous regulatory approaches. The same is true for cities belonging to the liberal, familistic and post-socialist clusters. Finally, the 'new municipalist' left and vocal social movements were present in cities with stringent regulations, but such a regulatory approach was also found in cities that had more classical centre-left coalitions, with no or limited social movements around STRs. All in all, these results have two major implications. First, they push us to move from a logic of bivariate correlation testing towards a typological profiling and multiple factor approach (in the next section). Second, they clearly show that this initial statistical testing must be supplemented by qualitative analysis to unpack causation and understand the processes and mechanisms underlying these observed trends (Chapter 4).

## THE THREE WORLDS OF STR REGULATION: A TYPOLOGY

To make sense of the diversity of STR regulation, we move from a variable-oriented to a case-oriented approach and develop a Weberian, ideal-typical classification. The purpose is to identify different profiles of cities sharing similar STR regulatory regimes, that is, similar configurations of regulatory instruments and intensity, socio-economic and political-institutional features (for the data, see the Appendix). Each ideal type is defined as a 'world' about which a story can be told, and with which we can then confront our 12 empirical cases. We distinguish three worlds of STR regulation in European cities: (1) laissez-faire cities of homeowners favourable to STR markets, (2) touristic cities with robust housing institutions, and (3) cities of social movements and responsive governments. While the first group refers to cities with light STR rules that legalise the market, the second and third groups refer to cities where STR rules have explicitly sought to control and limit the development of STRs, although through different paths. This typology allows us to classify our 12 cities according to the criteria that bring them together or differentiate them, and to explain how these cities are similar or different (Figure 14). It also allows us to sample the most representative cities of each world to illustrate and explain the causal trajectories leading to different regulations (Chapter 4).

## World 1, 'La Dolce Vita' of STR Operators: Laissez-Faire Homeowners' Cities

The first world is that of *cities where STR regulation is not very intense*, where a small number of instruments exist that are intended not to limit and curb the expansion of STRs, but rather to regulate the functioning of the market to make it legal, competitive and taxable (through safety standards, tourist tax, guest reporting and registration). The underpinning aim is to support property-based STR revenues; promote local economic development; and maintain or strengthen the city's attractiveness to visitors, property investors and owners. It comprises cities characterised by a majority of homeowners (albeit to various degrees) and belonging to welfare/housing regimes marked by a residual public intervention in the rental market (in contrast with the second group of

Touristic large European cities

Cities with regulations that legalise STR to facilitate market development, taxation, competition, the free use of property ownership

Cities with regulations that limit STR market development to protect affordable housing and permanent residence, and to struggle against overtourism

**World 1**
Cities favourable to platforms + attractiveness as policy goal + supportive of property owners

**World 2**
Touristic cities + strong housing institutions + local governments as policy entrepreneurs

**World 3**
STR-related social movements + new-municipalist left + reactive governments

| | | Prague | Rome | Milan | London | Brussels | Paris | Amsterdam | Vienna | Berlin | Lisbon | Madrid | Barcelona |
|---|---|---|---|---|---|---|---|---|---|---|---|---|---|
| **Tourism intensity** | Tourism intensity | medium | low | medium | low | low | high | high | medium | low | high | low | medium |
| | STR intensity | medium | medium | medium | low | low | high | high | low | low | high | low | medium |
| **Housing system** | Housing welfare regime | post-socialist | familistic | familistic | liberal | liberal | corporatist | social-democratic | corporatist | corporatist | familistic | familistic | familistic |
| | Tenure profile | homeowners | homeowners | homeowners | mixed | tenants | mixed | mixed | mixed | tenants | homeowners | homeowners | homeowners |
| **Politics (at time of first STR rules)** | Ruling majority | other formation | other formation | centre-left | centre-left | centre-left | centre-left | centre-left | centre-left | centre-left | centre-left | new municipalist | new municipalist |
| | Social movements mobilisations | moderately present | absent | absent | absent | absent | absent | absent | absent | moderately present | moderately present | moderately present | strongly present |
| | Hotel industry mobilisations | yes | yes | yes | yes | yes | yes | yes | yes | yes | yes | yes | yes |
| **Territorial organisation** | State type | unitary | regionalised | regionalised | unitary | regionalised | unitary | unitary | regionalised | regionalised | unitary | regionalised | regionalised |
| **Intensity of regulation** | IRI | low | low | low | low | medium | medium | high | medium | medium | high | medium | high |

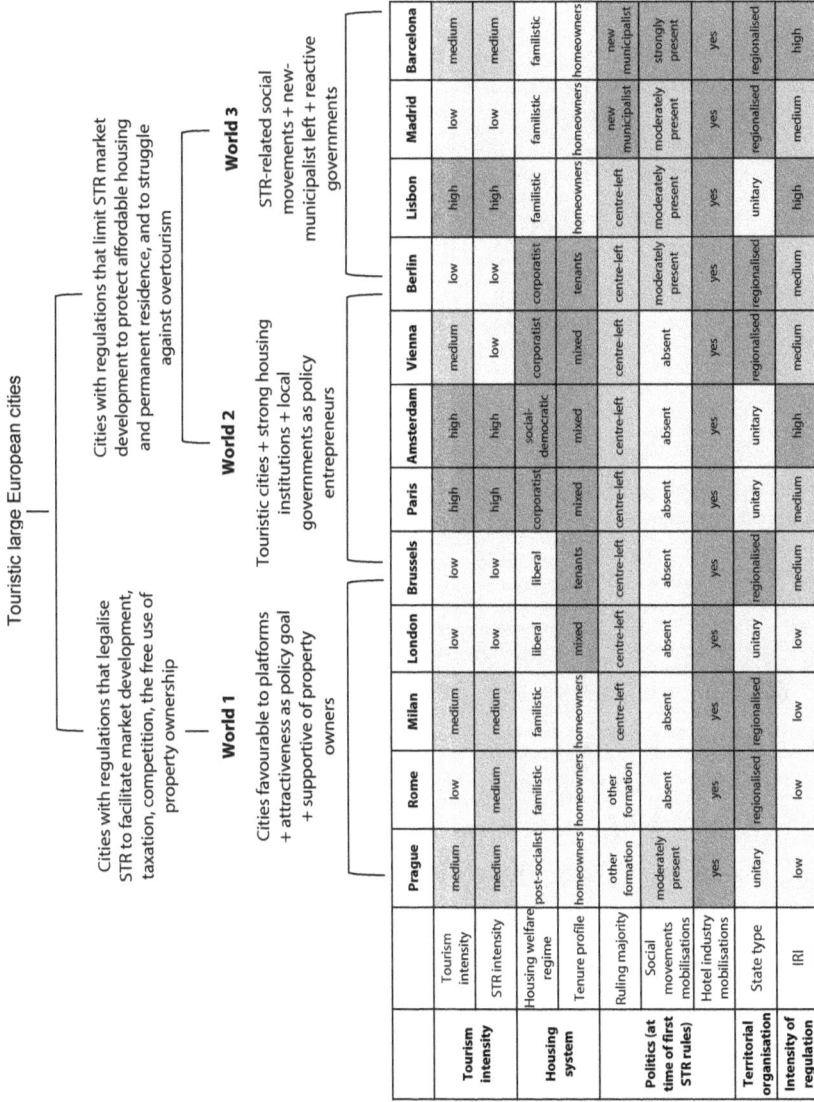

**Figure 14.** European cities facing STR: a typology. *Source:* Authors' STR Regulatory Database (2022).

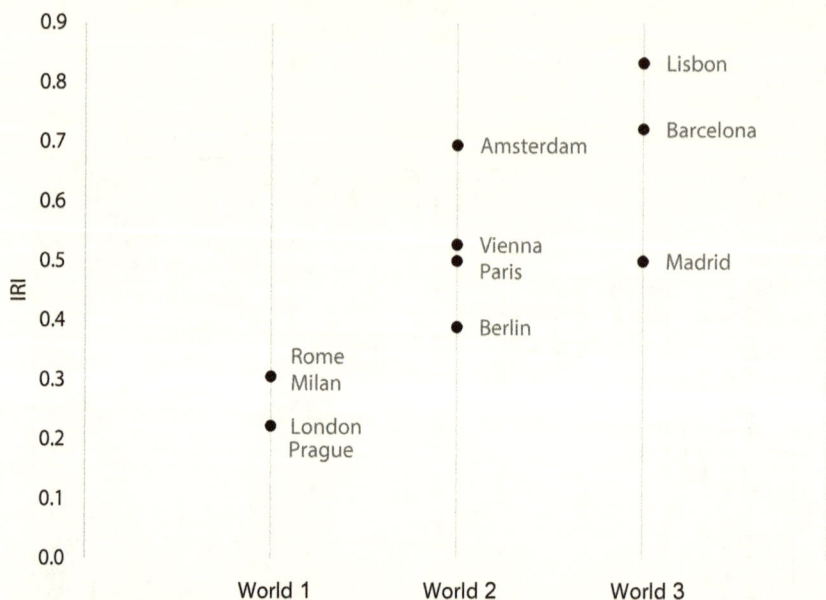

**Figure 15.** Intensity of regulation in each 'world'. Brussels has been excluded from this representation because it did not completely fit in any of our worlds (as of 2022). *Source*: Authors' STR Regulatory Database (2022).

cities). In these cities, the STR market tends to be dominated by opera-tors who own or manage several listings (the average share of multi-listings is significant, as in World 3). In the extreme case of Prague, the 50 largest hosts accounted for almost a quarter of the STR offer in 2023. Finally, in these cities, there were no or limited social movements that advocated for regulation *prior* to the passing of the first STR rules (in contrast with the third group). The most vocal organised group oppos-ing STRs has tended to be the hotel industry.

In our sample, in 2022 this world included Prague, Milan, Rome and London. Internally, it was the most homogenous group with a low IRI (Figure 15). While tourism and STRs were developing, their growth and impacts were at first not opposed by citizen organisations or by the gov-erning coalitions. The latter were either indifferent or keen on sustain-ing the visitor economy. Homeowners form a significant share of the local electorate. Those cities' welfare/housing institutions, power relations and housing market structures are favourable to homeowners, which were all potential (and often actual) STR operators. The two Italian cities are a good example of such a combination since the variables that, in the previous testing, seem to be associated with more interventionist regulations were all absent here (no STR grassroots mobilisations, no new municipalist coalitions, no welfare/housing regime with significant public intervention into the rental market). On the contrary, local policy agendas have been favourable to the visitor economy in a multi-level governance system marked by administrative and political conflicts between the regional governments (in charge of tourism) and the central state (in charge of housing rental law) (see Chapter 4).

The case of London is both archetypical and specific in this profile of cities. It is archetypical because social and affordable housing institutions have been greatly weakened at the national and urban levels, in a residual liberal welfare regime and a city where visitor attractiveness is crucial in the local agenda. It is also in London where we find the largest STR market in Europe (82,663 listings in 2023) and the biggest STR operators (in 2023, the 10 largest providers managed 300 listings each on average). But it is also a particular case because some STR regulatory instruments in London are of the *access* type (dissuasive entry barrier), while the other cities from World 1 have a majority of *operate* instruments (market rules without barriers). This is due to the fact that London is a case of deregulation (enforced by the national government) of a previously existing obligation of planning permission for a change of use, to support the development of a 'legal' STR market. While STRs were prohibited since 1973 unless a change of use was granted, in 2015 the national government (Ministry of Business, Innovation and Skills) heavily amended this prohibition (with the *Deregulation Act*) by enabling STRs without a change of use if a unit is rented under 90 days a year. Interestingly, this deregulation did not come with any instrument meant to actually oversee the growth of this market (e.g., a registration scheme, which is present in most cities, did not exist until a new law proposed to introduce one at the end of 2023).

While this world of *laissez-faire homeowners' cities* was the most homogeneous, it is also one that could possibly evolve with political changes. Indeed, in Prague (and the Czech Republic) as well as in Rome and Milan (and elsewhere in Italy), more and more voices have emerged from civil society and left-wing parties advocating for stricter STR rules. After the pandemic, social movements related to both housing and tourism have become more visible, as addressed in Chapter 6. Some municipal governments have asked their national parliaments to pass new legislation that would empower them to enact stricter rules. Yet whatever regulatory change might happen, the combination of factors highlighted here remains crucial to understanding the fact that these cities were regulatory latecomers. It also shows that, in those contexts where rental housing and housing market provision is mostly left to market forces, political factors became central in the push for new STR regulations. This is what happened in Barcelona and Madrid but had not, as of May 2022, taken place in Milan or Rome.

## World 2, 'Emily in Paris': Touristic Cities with Robust Housing Institutions

The second world is *the world of touristic cities with robust housing institutions (high share of non-profit/social housing, protected rental market) and medium to stringent regulations*. In this group, STR regulations have been developed by city governments to curb STR markets and limit their negative externalities, which are considered politically unacceptable in relation to local housing policy agendas. In our sample, in 2022 this world included Amsterdam, Paris, Vienna and Berlin. Housing policies are highly institutionalised, with a tradition of public regulation of housing markets. STRs are a new target and element of this public intervention. In these cities, the market is on average more dispersed and less professionalised than in other cities: the share of multi-listings is lower than in cities of Worlds 1 and 3, as is the weight of the largest operators (with the exception of Vienna). However, Paris is close to London in terms of large operators due to the fact these are the two main touristic and STR markets in Europe: in 2023 the 10 largest hosts managed on average 277 properties.

Paris and Amsterdam were the most paradigmatic cases, very close to each other in many variables. They were both very touristic (respectively the second and the third city of our sample in terms of tourists and Airbnb listings per inhabitant in 2016, after Lisbon). Their housing stocks were characterised by a high share (>20%) of non-profit/social housing. Their governments put in place moderately stringent regulations without the presence of strong social movements initially advocating for it. As we will show in detail in Chapter 4, two mechanisms were at play here, linking these socio-economic features to STR regulation. On the one hand, the responsiveness of city governments to the intensity of tourism and STR saturation has led to its political salience within the local government and triggered a policy response. On the other hand, a strong tradition of public intervention in housing—indicated by the levels of non-profit/social rented housing and by the corporatist and social-democratic housing regimes to which these cities belong—has offered tools to deal with a phenomenon threatening housing affordability and availability. Paris is a good example, as detailed in Chapter 4: the politicisation of the STR issue has been driven by the city government, in particular by the Deputy Mayor for Housing, who argued that the dramatic increase in STRs contributed to a loss of residents in central districts and threatened the municipal efforts to increase the affordable housing stock in the city.

Vienna and Berlin also stood in this second world of regulation. Compared to Paris and Amsterdam, both cities had fewer tourists and STRs per inhabitant but shared *highly institutionalised housing policies*, especially in the rental sector. Vienna is the city with the highest share of social housing stock (more than 40%). Here, STR rules have been put in place to protect residential neighbourhoods and prevent, if possible, the misuse of this rental stock for STRs. In Berlin, a city of tenants (more than 80% of the dwelling stock is rented), the STR issue was taken up by the Senate Department for Housing of the city-state that initially passed very stringent STR rules (a quasi-ban was in place between 2014 and 2018 and was later softened into a middle-ground approach from 2018 onwards). However, while Berlin shares housing conditions and policies with the other cities from World 2, it differs from them because it is also a case of grassroots political mobilisation *prior* to new STR rules. Contrary to Amsterdam, Paris and Vienna, in Berlin existing residents' and tenants' organisations and movements made STRs a focus of grassroots campaigns pushing the ruling multi-party left-wing coalition to take action. This makes the city close to those of World 3, which is the world of social contention and responsive governments.

## World 3, 'The Spanish Apartment': Social Movements and City Governments Against STRs

The third world of STR regulation is *the world of cities regulating STRs with left-wing municipal politics influenced by social movements*. In our sample, in 2022 this world included Barcelona, Madrid and Lisbon. These cases shared a pattern combining middle-ground to stringent STR regulations (see Figure 14) and the presence, in 2015, of social movements and left-wing governments (new municipalist political forces at the city level in Barcelona and Madrid in 2015–2019; the left-wing anti-austerity national coalition *geringonça* in Portugal 2015–2019). Cities belonging to this world have housing tenure structures and institutions which are similar to cities from World 1 (a majority of homeowners, familistic welfare/housing regimes) and to a certain extent also exhibit some similarities in terms of STR market structure. As in cities from World 1, we find high concentrations of multi-listings (in

Lisbon and Barcelona those accounted for 69% and 66% of the total, respectively, at the end of 2023). It is also in these cities that the largest operators were among the strongest (share of STR units operated by the top hosts). Yet compared to cities in World 1, cities from World 3 had different political configurations, with the presence of grassroots movements and ruling left/new-left-wing parties in power at the time of regulations. Politics has been the main driver.

In Madrid and Barcelona, the STR issue has been taken up by new municipalist left-wing governments and social movements which were very actively (in Barcelona) or moderately actively (in Madrid) advocating for a better governance of tourism and housing. As suggested above, the two Spanish cities witnessed the arrival of new left-wing political forces into local power in power in 2015. These forces (Barcelona en Comú and Ahora Madrid) were rooted in the active social movements, in particular in the field of housing, that expanded in Spain in the aftermath of the 2008 economic crisis and austerity measures (Martínez and Wissink 2022; Rossini et al. 2023). The implementation of stringent STR regulations has become a political statement for these new municipalist governments, in particular in Barcelona, as detailed in Chapter 4.

This world also includes Lisbon, a case of *highly touristic, seemingly highly regulated city* where politics played an important role, but after years of laissez-faire and heavily driven at the national level, as detailed in Chapter 4. Due to the increasing tourism attractiveness of Portugal and a legacy of policies aimed at attracting visitors and investors (Mendes 2018; Cocola-Gant and Gago 2021; Marques Pereira 2022; Estevens et al. 2023), the pace of conversion of housing units into STRs has been dramatic. In 2016, the city had 3.1 STRs per inhabitants, against an average of 1.2 in our sample. In the five central districts of the city, Estevens et al. (2023) estimated that there was at least one STR in 50% of the buildings by 2020. Gradually, from the mid-2010s onwards, STRs have increasingly been framed as drivers of gentrification and evictions in the most touristic central districts and as an unfair competition to the hotel industry. Thanks to a national law voted in 2018, the city government of Lisbon passed, in 2019, the rather stringent rules analysed in this chapter. Those rules, however, were perceived as too little too late by activists who had denounced how a variety of public policies previously fuelled the conversion of housing units into STRs in historic neighbourhoods (Estevens et al. 2023:fig. 2). Moreover, as discussed in Chapter 5, these rules had, at the time of writing, been weakly applied, monitored and sanctioned—thus remaining rather ineffective.

Finally, a few words should be said about the Brussels case, whose specific combination of characteristics makes it an outlier in our threefold typology. It shares with the second and the third group a middleground/stringent STR regulatory intensity. Yet there have not been strongly visible social movements politicising the STR issue. It is a city of tenants with a low share of non-profit/social housing, but belonging to a liberal housing welfare cluster. It is not a highly touristic city in our sample, but is a city that hosts international institutions and is thus heavily used by temporary visitors using short-term rentals. It can be hypothesised that the protection of long-term rentals and/or of incumbent tourist accommodation operators might have played a role in Brussels, but we were not in a position to specify the policy mechanisms at this stage.

**CONCLUSION**

The regulation of STRs does not occur in a vacuum. Much of the literature dealing with STRs isolates the study of the instruments specifically dedicated to their regulation, without identifying the factors and mechanisms that underpin instrumentation processes. This chapter has therefore re-embedded the instruments regulating STRs into the different socio-economic, political and housing conditions of each city. In cities with an equivalent level of regulatory intensity (as captured by the IRI), the modes of regulation can be very different, depending on the housing system, the level of institutionalisation of housing policies and public intervention into the rental market and the forms of STR politicisation. The combination of these elements delineates different STR regulatory regimes, which we have categorised into three ideal-typical worlds of STR regulation: one of STR laissez-faire/supportive cities of homeowners; among cities where stringent rules were put in place, one of cities with robust housing institutions; and one of cities with social movements and responsive governments. We have looked at these worlds as synchronous arrangements: in the next chapter, we will study them as diachronic processes.

The construction of this ideal-typical typology was an objective in itself, to make sense of the diversity of regulations in a way that does not overlook its complexity. But it is also a starting point for the rest of the analysis: we must now pay attention to the *mechanisms* that explain regulations in their diversity. How has the STR issue been politicised and put on political agendas, and by whom? Why has it been the local or the national government that has taken action? Why have certain instruments been chosen and not others? These questions will now be answered through the in-depth analysis of the processes leading to specific regulations in key cases of each of the three worlds: Milan for the first, Paris for the second and Barcelona for the third.

# 4

## THE PATHS TO REGULATION

Emergence and Institutionalisation of Different
STR Rules in Barcelona, Paris and Milan

||||||||||||||||||||||||||||||||||||||||||||||||||||||||||||||||||||||||||||||||||||||||||||||||||||||||||||||||||||||||||||||||||||||||||||||||||||||||||||||||||||

IN THE PREVIOUS CHAPTER we identified three worlds of
STR regulation, within which cities share a number of characteristics and common approaches to STRs. These ideal
types give meaning to the diversity of regulatory regimes
but do not explain *how* the cities from our sample have
ended up in one 'world' or the other. To tackle this question,
we now consider the social and political processes through
which the global phenomenon of platform-mediated STRs
was met with very different political responses from one
city to the other. Based on extensive qualitative material, we
identify the main policy mechanisms that have led to different regulations in the three worlds.

The contribution of this chapter is twofold. First, considering that policy change results from the interplay of (collective and individual) actors within institutional frames
(Mahoney and Thelen 2010), we add *agency* and *historical
development* to the institutional analysis of STR regulation.

We start with an inductive process-tracing method that follows the history of regulations in three cities, one from each of the three worlds: Barcelona, Paris and Milan. We demonstrate that STR rules are the result of political initiatives and struggles between collective actors with conflicting interests, modes of action and narratives, embedded into pre-existing institutional arrangements. We show how, starting in the mid-2010s, local, regional and national administrations; platforms; the hotel industry; and citizens have given different meanings and levels of priority to the regulation of STRs. Their political agency has interplayed with socio-economic pressures and existing institutions, that is, established rules, instruments and worldviews in the fields of housing, planning, tourism and economic development, which have functioned as both constraints and opportunities for collective action. This also sheds light on the concrete nature of STR instrumentation, which we do not consider in isolation but as parts of broader policy sectors and administrations that activated and gave meanings to it.

Second, based on the cross-case analysis of Barcelona, Paris and Milan, this chapter identifies the main *policy mechanisms* that explain how and why different regulatory paths emerged in European cities.[1] They are (1) the *type of actors* who politicised the STR issue in the first place and *framed* it as part of broader *sectoral agendas*, (2) the availability and the reuse of *pre-existing policy instruments* and related *organisations* and (3) the distribution of *competencies* and *the political relations* between levels of government. Each mechanism articulates political agency with institutional and socio-economic arrangements, leading to different STR rules.

We then confront the cases of Barcelona, Paris and Milan with the other cities of our sample and show that these mechanisms have played out differently across the three worlds. In laissez-faire, homeowners' cities (World 1), politicisation has stemmed from governmental and economic actors producing light regulations mostly based on a limited number of pre-existing instruments that supported, at various levels of government, property-based revenues and tourism. In the world of touristic cities with robust housing policies (World 2), politici-sation has stemmed from within local governments, who activated and combined a range of well-established instruments from the multi-level housing field, leading to medium-high STR regulations. In the world of cities with social movements and intense STR regulation (World 3), grassroots organisations have allied with changing, responsive city gov-ernments who then produced new sets of instruments to intensively regulate STRs, often with limited support from the upper levels.

## A TALE OF THREE CITIES FACING STRs: POLITICISATION, AGENDA-SETTING AND NEW REGULATIONS

This first section follows the story of STR regulatory development in Barcelona, Paris and Milan. It traces the political processes that started with the emergence of STRs as a 'public problem', as the num-ber of STRs was increasing in each city (see Figure 16), and ended with the approval of new rules—and subsequent modifications of these rules—up to the end of 2023. For each city, we systematically iden-tify when and how specific groups of actors or coalitions at various levels of government have politicised STRs, put them on the politi-cal agenda, defined them as a problem belonging to a specific sector, proposed new regulations and passed or blocked specific regulatory instruments.

### Barcelona: Social Movements and a 'New Municipalist' Agenda

Barcelona is a case from World 3—cities regulating STRs with left-wing municipal governments influenced by social movements. It illus-trates in an emblematic way how grassroots mobilisations have been, in some cities, the main actor of the politicisation of STRs. Grow-ing civic activism around the negative effects of mass tourism even-tually filtered into the local political agenda in the run-up to the 2015

Barcelona, all Airbnb listings
June 2016

Barcelona, all Airbnb listings
December 2019

Barcelona, all Airbnb listings
June 2022

Paris, all Airbnb listings
June 2016

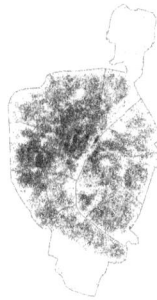

Paris, all Airbnb listings
December 2019

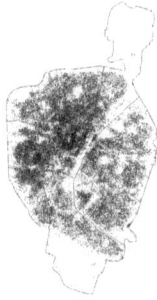

Paris, all Airbnb listings
June 2022

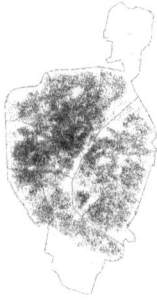

Milan, all Airbnb listings
June 2016

Milan, all Airbnb listings
December 2019

Milan, all Airbnb listings
June 2022

**Figure 16.** Concentration of Airbnb listings in the municipalities of Barcelona, Milan and Paris (2016–2022). *Source:* Produced by Murray Cox, based on Inside Airbnb data.

municipal elections, which brought to power a 'new municipalist' left-wing political force. The city government adopted a strict regulation of STRs that combined land use planning, zoning and licensing mechanisms to impose a cap on the growth of the market. It also invested significant resources into control and enforcement. In the Spanish context, this made the city one of the 'first movers' in terms of STR regulation: its approach inspired other (left-wing) city governments to take action, for example, in Madrid, Donostia-San Sebastian and Palma de Mallorca. But the Barcelona regulatory approach has been met with constant criticism and legal challenges from platforms, STR operators and associations of hosts. Political change following the 2023 municipal elections might put the approach in question.

---

**BOX 2: PROCEDURES TO OPERATE STRs IN BARCELONA IN 2022**

Under Catalan regional legislation, both the professional operation of a commercial STR (type i) and the occasional rental of a primary residence (type ii) fall under the category 'dwelling for touristic use' (rental of fewer than 31 consecutive days), for which the owner needs to *register* on the Tourism Register of Catalonia (the number must appear on all adverts), pay the *tourist tax*, and in the municipalities that have introduced a limitation on such STR via planning instruments, apply for a *licence*. In Barcelona, a Special Tourist Accommodation Plan (Plan Especial Urbanístico de Alojamiento Turístico, PEUAT) approved in 2017 (revised in 2021) froze the total number of licences for new STRs in the city to just under 10,000 and created a zoning system: it is impossible to obtain a licence for a new STR in central districts, but a very small number of licences can be granted in other districts. This effectively constrains entry into the STR market, even for occasional hosts.

For the rental of a room in a primary residence, a regional decree of 2020 created the legal category of 'shared home', leaving city governments to regulate this category further. In Barcelona, in August 2021 the city council decided to prohibit room rentals of fewer than 31 consecutive days.

Spain has since the mid-1950s been a major international tourist destination, a process encouraged by the democratisation of paid holidays in Europe and the promotion of 'sun-and-beach' tourism by the
Franco regime (Pack 2006). For decades, tourist flows were largely concentrated on Mediterranean coastal areas. From the 1990s onwards,
large Spanish cities started to receive increasing numbers of visitors,
attracted by culture, arts, food and entertainment. In Barcelona, the
1992 Olympic Games put the city on the international tourism map,
followed by sustained public investments in culture-led urban development and tourism marketing (Degen and García 2012; Palou i Rubio
2012). Between 1990 and 2010, tourist flows nearly quadrupled (from 1.7
to 7.1 million visitors and 3.8 to 14 million overnight stays).

Since the return of democracy in 1978, Spanish regions have, constitutionally, a wide range of competences. This includes tourism, in
particular the definition and classification of tourist accommodation
establishments. Property relations and tenancy law are a national competence, as are issues related to income and business taxation. The seasonal rental of holidays homes was a long-existing practice in Spain's
coastal regions. The growing number of *pisos turísticos* (as colloquially
known) in the centre of Spanish cities came on the radar of local residents before Airbnb appeared on the scene. In Barcelona in the early
2000s the residents' associations of the densely populated historical district of Ciutat Vella began to denounce the noise and nuisances caused
by visitors staying in holiday rentals. Residents' associations (known
in Catalan as *associacions de veïns i veïnes*, AVV) exist in many neighbourhoods of Barcelona and other large Spanish cities. They find their
roots in the urban social movements that emerged in the late 1960s—
the late years of the Franco regime—to demand improvements in

living conditions and public infrastructure (Borja 1977; Castells 1983). They played an important local role in the transition to democracy in the 1970s. Since 1978 these associations have maintained a strong role in many Spanish cities, channelling residents' demands, scrutinising local planning processes and keeping a critical eye on the actions of city governments (Calavita and Ferrer 2000; Andreu 2015). In Barcelona in 2008, a network of residents' associations and local activist groups joined forces to set up a new network, Xarxa Ciutat Vella, adopting the motto *Ciutat Vella no està en venta* (the Old City is not for sale). Its early campaigns denounced the corruption-ridden construction of a new luxury hotel and pressured the district government to regulate the proliferation of night-time economy and tourism-related establishments.

Shortly after Airbnb started operating in Europe, in Barcelona the growth of STRs was fuelled by a 2012 decree (159/2012) passed by the Catalan regional government that modified the Tourism Law (13/2002).[2] It created a new legal category of 'dwelling for touristic use' (i.e., the STR of a full unit for fewer than 31 consecutive days as a professional or occasional activity), subject to a registration and licence with relatively light requirements. Applications for licences are administered by local authorities. This effectively legalised an activity that had operated in a grey area so far. As a result, the number of licensed STRs in Barcelona jumped from 824 in 2011 to 9,606 in 2014, paralleled by an increase in unlicensed (and thus illegal) STRs (estimated at 6,275 in 2015) (Duhatis et al. 2016). This growth was heavily concentrated in the historical tourist district of Ciutat Vella, a socially and ethnically mixed area with a significant share of low-income households vulnerable to displacement. In the first half of the 2010s, the residents' associations of the district strengthened their mobilisation around the problems generated by STRs, through numerous public meetings, the lobbying of local councillors and the reporting of illegal STRs to local authorities—often with little effect.

At the city-wide level, until 2014 there was little political response by the city council to the issue of STRs. The demands of the residents' associations first found echoes at the district level. In the late 2000s the District Councillor of Ciutat Vella (a left-wing architect close to social movements) pushed for more stringent regulations through a so-called Pla d'Usos (Uses Plan). That councillor was subject to physical threats and intimidation after denouncing corruption practices related to the licensing of STRs in her district, and she resigned in 2009 in protest (Ríos 2010; Navarro 2014). A district-level Pla d'Usos, though, was approved in 2010, which regulated the opening of retail units, restaurants, bars, hotels and STRs. The plan recognised that the district had reached saturation point in terms of tourist accommodation and fixed a moratorium on new hotels and STRs.

The 2011–2015 years were a turbulent period of social protests and grassroots mobilisations in large Spanish cities (heralded by the Indignados and '15-M' movements), spearheaded by the brutal consequences of the 2008 Great Financial Crisis and drastic cuts and austerity measures for the Spanish population. In Barcelona, those 'years of discontent' (Mansilla 2023a) witnessed a wide range of social movements and local campaigns (Nel·lo 2015) that challenged the 'Barcelona model' of urban development that had prevailed since the 1990s. Their discontent was fuelled by the measures taken by the centre-right city government that had won the elections in 2011 (led by the Catalan conservative independentist party, then called Convergencia I Unió). In a context of recession, the government prioritised the attraction of external investments and visitors at all costs, through controversial measures such as the approval of a luxury yacht marina and the partial privatisation of the Park Güell (Russo and Arias Sans 2016). In 2013 the city council voted a modification of the Pla d'Usos of Ciutat Vella against the will of the district council, forcing a relaxation of restrictions on new hotels and restaurants. It maintained the ban on new STR licences and fixed a six-year deadline for the grouping of all STRs into single buildings, paying no attention to possible adverse effects.[3]

In that context, the Federation of Residents' Associations of Barcelona began to make the topic of tourism a key element of its campaigns (FAVB 2011). The issue of STRs became problematised by grassroots movements as part of a broader, articulated critique of the negative effects and externalities of mass tourism on the city (Querol Mayor and Santos Gordillo 2015; Holleran 2017). At that point, the residents' associations and grassroots movements of neighbourhoods further away from the historic city centre—in Poble Sec, Gràcia, Poble Nou and Sagrada Familia—had also started to campaign around those issues. This was the consequence of the increasing spread of visitor flows to 'everyday' neighbourhoods, a trend observed in many European cities (as mentioned in Chapter 1), encouraged by promotional policies promoting 'off the beaten track' neighbourhoods (Rius Ulldemolins 2014; Scarnato 2017; Mansilla and Milano 2022) and by the diffusion of platform-mediated STRs.

## THE 'POLITICISATION FROM BELOW' OF TOURISM (2014–2015)

In August 2014 a small incident received a lot of media attention and marked a turning point in the scale and visibility of citizen mobilisations around tourism. Three male tourists wandered around the streets and shops of the neighbourhood of La Barceloneta during the daytime, entirely naked. They were not stopped by the police, and their behaviour caused outrage, attracting attention from international newspapers such as the UK's *Guardian* (Kassam 2014). In the days that followed, the residents' associations of several neighbourhoods organised street demonstrations attended by several thousand people to demand the outright prohibition of STRs and a stronger regulation of the city's tourism economy. A prominent Barcelona-based housing activist who was a leading figure of the Spanish anti-eviction movement (the Plataforma de Afecta-dos por la Hipoteca, PAH, platform for mortgage-affected people), Ada Colau, published an opinion piece in the *Guardian* to explain to an inter-national audience why 'mass tourism can kill a city' (Colau 2014). She stressed that 'the answer is not to attack tourism' but 'to regulate the sec-tor, return to the traditions of local urban planning, and put the rights of residents before those of big business' (Colau 2014). A year later, following the May 2015 municipal elections, she became Barcelona's new mayor. What happened in between was the rise of the issue of tourism to the top of the local political agenda, as a symbol of what had gone 'wrong' with the city's urban development model after the 1992 Olympics.

Municipal elections were due to take place in May 2015: this created a window of opportunity seized by activists to shape the local politi-cal agenda, in a context where mass tourism had become a 'hot topic'. In the autumn of 2014, the FAVB prepared a list of key demands for the regulation of tourism that was sent to all political parties. Among those demands was a moratorium on new licences for all forms of tour-ist accommodation, including STRs. At that point, the centre-right city government felt compelled to make symbolic statements and take belated measures to appear to tackle the problem. It announced a freeze on the granting of new STR licences and a commitment to stronger enforcement by hiring 20 new inspectors. In February 2015 the city government organised a public debate on tourism, which attracted several hundreds of highly critical residents and activists who dis-played banners calling for the abolition of STRs. This position was not met with unanimity: professional STR property managers, small land-lords and residents favourable to STRs were also present in the room, defending their right to rent their property. At several public meetings on the issue of tourism and STRs observed by one of the authors dur-ing those years, tensions were highly visible.

The mediatisation and politicisation of the topic of tourism after the summer of 2014 eventually encouraged more collaboration between localised campaigns that had emerged in various neighbourhoods. In the spring of 2015, several residents' associations and grassroots campaigns formed a city-wide network called the Assembly of Neighbourhoods for a Sustainable Tourism (Assemblea de Barris per un Turisme Sostenible, ABTS), to counteract what they perceived as a 'hegemonic narrative' on the role of tourism in the city (Fernández Medrano and Pardo Rivacoba 2017). Its members were diverse in terms of age, socio-professional background, political leanings and cultures of activism—though many were involved in other campaigns around housing rights or anti-gentrification struggles (Mansilla 2023b). The Assembly was led by articulate activists who framed the tourism-related issues they were concerned with (e.g., proliferation of STRs, congestion and commodification of public space, loss of traditional retail, damaging impacts of cruise ships) within a broader critique of the city's urban development model—well aware that it was impossible to separate the effects of tourism from those of other processes driving neighbourhood change (e.g., speculative real estate practices). The Assembly later changed its name to Neighbourhoods for Tourism Degrowth (Assemblea de Barris pel Decreixement Turístic, ABDT), adopting a vocabulary that responded to the debates around 'overtourism' mentioned in Chapter 1 (Milano, Novelli, et al. 2019). It was also actively involved in the creation of an informal transnational network of citizens' collectives from Spain, Italy, Portugal and later Greece (Southern Europe against Touristification, SET), which has campaigned against the destruction of the socio-economic fabric and liveability of tourism-saturated Mediterranean cities.

The demand for a strict regulation of STRs has been a core element of the ABTS's campaigns. As the housing issue became central in social struggles across Spain after 2008 (Martínez and Gil 2024; Rossini et al. 2023), the framing of the 'problem' of STRs shifted—from their disruption of daily life to their structural impacts on housing markets and the resident population.[4] In some of streets of the Gothic Quarter of the historical district of Ciutat Vella, in the mid-2010s STRs amounted to up to 50% of the housing stock (Cocola-Gant 2016a). Those neighbourhoods with the largest presence of Airbnb listings were experiencing the greatest population loss (Arias Sans and Quaglieri Domínguez 2016). Correlation is not causation, but interviews with local activists revealed multiple cases of tenant evictions, non-renewal of rental contracts or heavy pressures on and intimidation of sitting tenants to make way for STRs. Those practices have been described as 'real estate harassment' in Spanish law (*acoso inmobiliario*) (Ajuntament de Barcelona 2020:23–29). In parallel, in areas with the highest number of Airbnb rentals, rents were estimated to have increased by 7% and purchase prices by 17% (Garcia-López et al. 2020). To attract media attention to the speculative processes behind the creation of new STRs and the role of platforms therein, in September 2016 the ABTS rented an unlicensed STR flat on Airbnb, owned by a landlord operating 12 unlicensed STRs in total. The flat was located in a building that had been emptied of its residents to make way for STRs (Cocola-Gant and Pardo 2017). Under the hashtag #Unfairbnb, the activists then hung a large banner from the balcony of the flat, which stated: 'This is an illegal hotel. Airbnb forces out local residents. Ciutat Vella is not for sale'.[5]

In their demands for strict STR regulation, activists found support from the local hotel industry, whose representatives (Gremi d'Hotels de Barcelona) were very vocal about the unfair competition that STRs represented (as in Paris and Milan). This produced an unlikely alignment between progressive social movements and an industry known to be rather politically conservative and economically liberal, something that has been witnessed in other European cities in the context of calls for more STR regulation.

Yet the arguments of the ABTS and other voices critical of the tourism economy have, in Barcelona, often been met with sharp rebuttal. Tourism was, until 2015, an undisputed, hegemonic component of the economic development strategies of successive municipal governments, even more so in the aftermath of the 2008 recession. Most local newspapers, politicians, business associations and the Chamber of Commerce argued that tourism was a unequivocally good thing for the city, with an economic weight estimated at 10–12% of the city's GDP (Garriga et al. 2015), amounting to an estimated 86,000–130,000 jobs (Consell Econòmic i Social 2016). Critics of tourism were accused of *turismofobia*, a term pejoratively used by actors supportive of the tourism industry to discredit discordant voices (Milano 2017). The actions of a minority of individuals were mediatised and decried, for example graffiti urging tourists to 'go home' or an act of vandalism on a tourist bus by masked individuals associated with a radical leftist independentist youth collective.[6] Yet the ABTS and other citizens' campaigns made it clear that their claims were not so much 'anti-tourists' as they were critical of the tourism industry and of the city government's approach to urban development more broadly (Colomb and Novy 2021).

## A NEW MUNICIPALIST GOVERNMENT AND A TOUGHER APPROACH TO STRs (2015–2020)

In June 2014 a progressive citizen platform called Guanyem Barcelona was founded as an alternative offer to existing political parties, in the run-up to the municipal elections of May 2015. It was rooted in a variety of local social movements that had stemmed from the 15-M mobilisations (Eizaguirre et al. 2017). Its programme was designed in a participatory manner through thematic working groups of volunteers, many of whom were involved in movements. The working group on tourism included representatives of residents' associations and activists mobilised on the issue. Many of the demands of the FAVB were thus included in the tourism section of the Guanyem Barcelona manifesto, including a moratorium on new licences for all forms of tourist accommodation while a special plan would be prepared, the promotion of B&B-style (home-sharing) approaches to STRs and the implementation of strict controls on commercial STRs.

In May 2015 that citizen platform—later renamed Barcelona en Comú—won a tight victory in the municipal elections (11 out of 41 seats). Its figurehead, the former anti-eviction activist Ada Colau, became Barcelona's new mayor. Barcelona en Comú promised to guarantee basic social rights (in particular access to housing); democratise local governance; and promote a change in the city's development model, including better regulation of tourism (Russo and Scarnato 2018). Unsurprisingly, the implementation of this agenda proved challenging, given the minority position of this new political force in a city council fragmented into seven political groups. But the pressures of social movements on the newly elected city council were high, and public opinion was clearly supportive of stronger public action in the field of tourism (Ajuntament de Barcelona 2017a).

A number of policy measures were taken early on by the city council to signal a change in tourism policy. The city's bid for the Winter Olympic Games 2016 was withdrawn. In July 2015 a one-year moratorium on new hotels and new STR licences was voted in, while a special plan would be prepared by the Department of Urban Planning. The freeze on new licences was controversial because it applied to all forms of tourist accommodation, not just STRs: it was fiercely contested by the hotel industry and several opposition parties. Two strategies were then prepared in parallel. The Tourism Department produced a Strategic Tourism Plan that marked, for the first time, an attempt at developing a cross-sectoral tourism policy seeking the conciliation between visitor and tourist practices with permanent living in the city (Ajuntament de Barcelona, Direcció de Turisme 2017). The Department of Urban Planning prepared a Special Plan for Tourist Accommodation (PEUAT), approved in January 2017, which has formed the core instrument for the regulation of STRs in Barcelona since. The PEUAT was presented as reconciling four rights: people's right to housing, to rest and privacy, to sustainable mobility (i.e., to tourism) and to a healthy environment (Ajuntament de Barcelona 2017b). It is a land use planning instrument that combines zoning with the licensing system for tourist accommodation enabled by regional legislation. The plan set the objective of zero growth in the total number of STRs in the city as a whole. It sought to rebalance the territorial distribution of STRs away from over-congested areas through a zoning system. In Zone 1 (the most central districts), no new tourist accommodation of any kind would be allowed.[7] In Zone 2, the existing number of STR licences would be maintained, with the possibility of replacing extinguished ones. In Zone 3, new STRs would be allowed within the city-wide limit on the number of licences.

Because the regional law that defines various forms of tourist accommodation does not distinguish between the professional, permanent operation of a STR and the occasional rental of someone's primary residence, the freeze on STR licences imposed by the PEUAT meant not only that it was impossible to legally start a new commercial, professional STR in central districts after that date, but also that residents were not allowed to rent out their homes for a few days if they did not already have a licence, effectively outlawing that practice for most people. The PEUAT virtually closed the entry of new actors into the STR market and created a privileged position for those who already had a licence (the market value of a flat with a valid licence to operate as 'dwelling for touristic use' in Barcelona was reported to be €100,000–150,000 higher).

Unsurprisingly, the PEUAT was met with polarised reactions from the diverse actors involved in the debates on STR regulation. In the first half of 2016, during the public consultation prior to the plan's approval, 700 written representations were submitted, and vociferous arguments took place in public meetings. After the PEUAT was approved, nearly 100 legal challenges were submitted against it in the Catalan Court of Justice. The PEUAT and associated enforcement measures were welcomed by residents' associations, the ABTS and part of the local population, although some deemed it too mild. The main organisation representing the hotel industry was unhappy with the strong restrictions put on new hotels and wanted a regulation that would force the concentration of STRs into single buildings and subject them to the same requirements as hotels. The professional association representing the professional managers of commercial holiday flats, Asociación de Apartamentos Turísticos de Barcelona (APARTUR), opposed the freezing of new STR licences. In parallel, newly created associations of hosts (Plataforma Pro-Vivienda Turística, representing small owners/operators of STR; Associació de Veïns i Amfitrions, representing hosts renting a room in their home) were very vocal against the PEUAT, which effectively outlawed their activities. The PEUAT was challenged for 'putting in the same bag' different types of STR actors and practices, as argued by ACABA, an association created in 2017 by individuals hit by fines and sanctions after sporadically renting their primary homes via Airbnb (see Chapter 5).

The strict regulation of STRs enacted through the PEUAT was accompanied by a 'shock plan' of control and inspections announced in June 2016 (Ajuntament de Barcelona 2016). It included measures analysed in detail in Chapter 5: an increase in street-level inspectors, a new team of 'digital visualisers' scrutinising online listings, tougher sanctions, negotiations with platforms and public communication campaigns. Between mid-2016 and mid-2023, according to the Inspection Service of the Department of Urban Planning, a total of 21,500 units were subject to inspection procedures, of which just over 10,000 were sanctioned (among which 9,000 ceased their STR activity). Those results were regularly publicised by the city government to show evidence of successful public action. In those years the relationship between the city government and large platforms oscillated between tension and collaboration, as detailed in Chapters 5 and 6. Concessions were gained from platforms after months of intense negotiations (e.g., requiring them to display the STR licence number on listings and to share detailed lists of STRs with the Inspection Department).

In addition, the Barcelona city government was, alongside Amsterdam, very proactive in initiating contacts with other Spanish and

European cities to exchange experiences on their approach to STR regulation. The mayor of Barcelona hosted a first international meeting on the topic in November 2016 with public officials and representatives (mayors or their deputies) from approximately 16 Spanish and European cities. Other meetings followed in Berlin and Amsterdam, which consolidated an informal network of European cities seeking to regulate STRs and eager to make their voices heard at the EU level (further discussed in Chapter 7).

## THE COVID-19 PANDEMIC, FURTHER REGULATION AND MOUNTING POLITICAL OPPOSITION (2020–2023)

The first version of the PEUAT did not include home-sharing in a strict sense (STR type iii), as the renting of a room in a primary residence was not captured in the categories of 'tourist accommodation' defined by the Catalan regional law. However, a proposal for an amended decree was drafted by the regional parliament in 2016–2017 to create a new legal category of 'shared home' (the STR of a room 'in the usual and permanent domicile of the tenant or owner-occupier'). This decree was passed in the summer of 2020 and gave municipal governments one year to develop their own regulation of this new type of STR if they so wished.[8] In Barcelona there were about 7,600 listings for rooms on Airbnb in Barcelona at the end of January 2021. There were intense debates within Barcelona en Comú and in the city council about whether to regulate the STR of rooms (Arias-Sans et al. 2022). Opinions were divided about a practice that was perceived by many as an economic necessity for the lower- and middle-class audience that forms the party's voter base. Associations of hosts (such as the Associació de Veïns i Amfitrions) fiercely opposed any restrictions. A proposed revision of the PEUAT published in January 2021 was, again, subject to many objections in the public consultation phase. A revised PEUAT was eventually approved in the autumn of 2021 and entered into force in January 2022. It prohibited the rental of rooms for fewer than 31 consecutive days (but room rentals of a longer period were allowed, to cater for students, temporary workers, etc.).

Visitor flows to Barcelona all but stopped during the pandemic but resumed rapidly afterwards. In 2022, 10.7 million overnight visitors were recorded, of which approximately 20% stayed in STRs; in 2023, this increased to 12.3 million visitors (Observatori del Turisme a Barcelona 2024). The tensions around the impacts of mass tourism that were so salient before the pandemic reappeared, but the social and political climate was less favourable to their critics. On the one hand, the second mandate of Ada Colau and Barcelona en Comú (2019–2023) was marked by sustained attacks and legal challenges against various policies by opposition parties, established business and economic elites. On the other, the adverse impacts of the COVID-19 pandemic on the city's economy and employment rate meant that the return of mass tourism was welcome to many stakeholders, making it difficult for social activists to reignite broad public interest in tourism-related issues in the immediate years after the pandemic. The limits of what the city government could do in its attempts to better govern tourism also became more apparent (Blázquez-Salom et al. 2019). In the municipal elections of May 2023, Ada Colau stood for a third mandate, but Barcelona en Comú came third. After weeks of negotiations, the centrist Catalan Socialist Party candidate Jaume Collboni was voted mayor by city councillors. In the absence of a majority in the city council, his party will have to gain the ad hoc support of other parties to govern. Whether the strong regulatory approach to STRs of the previous city government will be maintained remains to be seen.

After a change inside the regional government in 2022 (i.e., the withdrawal of the centre-right Junts per Catalunya party from the governing coalition), the centre-left party Esquerra Republicana de Catalunya put housing policy higher on the regional agenda, under pressure from housing movements. In November 2023 the regional government passed a decree law that gave more room for manoeuvre to municipal governments to restrict the growth of STRs.[9] It made STR licenses time-limited (five years, after which municipal governments can decide whether to renew them or not) and required municipal governments to respect a ratio of 10 STR licences per 100 inhabitants. Whether and how different local governments in Catalonia will take up this opportunity, and whether this will lead to much stricter local regulations of STRs, will be an interesting development to follow—including in the city of Barcelona.

During and after the pandemic, a growing topic of concern mobilised housing activists in Barcelona: the growing use by landlords of *medium-term* rental contracts (*de temporada*), of more than 31 days and less than one year (data from the Inside Airbnb website from early 2024 showed that 38% of all Airbnb listings in that city were on offer for 31 days or more). These have not only been used to respond to the demand of 'temporary city users', but also have been forced on local residents in search of long-term accommodation. Using such contracts allows landlords to avoid complying with the provisions of the national tenancy law (which requires rental contracts above one year to be granted for five or seven years minimum). In January 2024, those medium-term contracts were estimated to represent 30% of all rental contracts in Barcelona (Losada 2024), accompanied by often much higher rents. Housing activists and the tenants' movement have increasingly challenged this legal loophole and campaigned for a change in regional and national rental laws (Sindicat de Llogateres de Barcelona 2024), so far to no avail. As explained in Chapter 1, platforms have facilitated this shift (Sequera et al. 2022; Gil, Martínez, et al. 2023). The lack of regulation of medium-term rentals has thus become a key bone of contention in Barcelona and other Spanish cities, alongside the question of rent control (Gil, Vidal, et al. 2023) in the private rental sector as a whole. Figure 17 summarises the key milestones in the STR politicisation and regulation process in Barcelona.

**Main events**

| | 2012 | 2013 | 2014 | 2015 | 2016 | 2017 | 2018 | 2019 | 2020 | 2021 | 2022 | 2023 |
|---|---|---|---|---|---|---|---|---|---|---|---|---|
| National and European levels | | | | | | | | | | | | Spanish Tax Law 13/2023: platforms to declare host revenues to tax authorities |
| Regional level | Change in Catalan Tourism Law creating 'Dwelling for Touristic Use' | | | | | | | | Change in Catalan Tourism Law creating 'Room in Shared Home' | | | |
| Local level | | | | Municipal elections: arrival of BCN en Comú in power. Freeze on new STR licences | 'Shock Plan' for Enforcement and crackdown on illegal STRs | Approbation of PEUAT: special plan regulating STR | | | | Approbation of PEUAT II: prohibition of room rental <31 days | | Municipal elections: BCN en Comú lost power |
| **Dates** | 2012 | 2013 | 2014 | 2015 | 2016 | 2017 | 2018 | 2019 | 2020 | 2021 | 2022 | 2023 |

**Politics and contention**

City level:
- Grassroots movements against touristification and for strict STR regulation
- Freeze on new STR licences
- PEUAT—special plan regulating STR + intense control and enforcement measures on illegal STR
- Hosts, property owners and property managers challenge new STR regulations
- Difficult relationship with Airbnb: conflicts leading to some degree of collaboration
- Pressures and procedures from the hotel industry asking for regulation

Other actors/levels:
- STR as overtourism problem ·········· STR as a housing problem

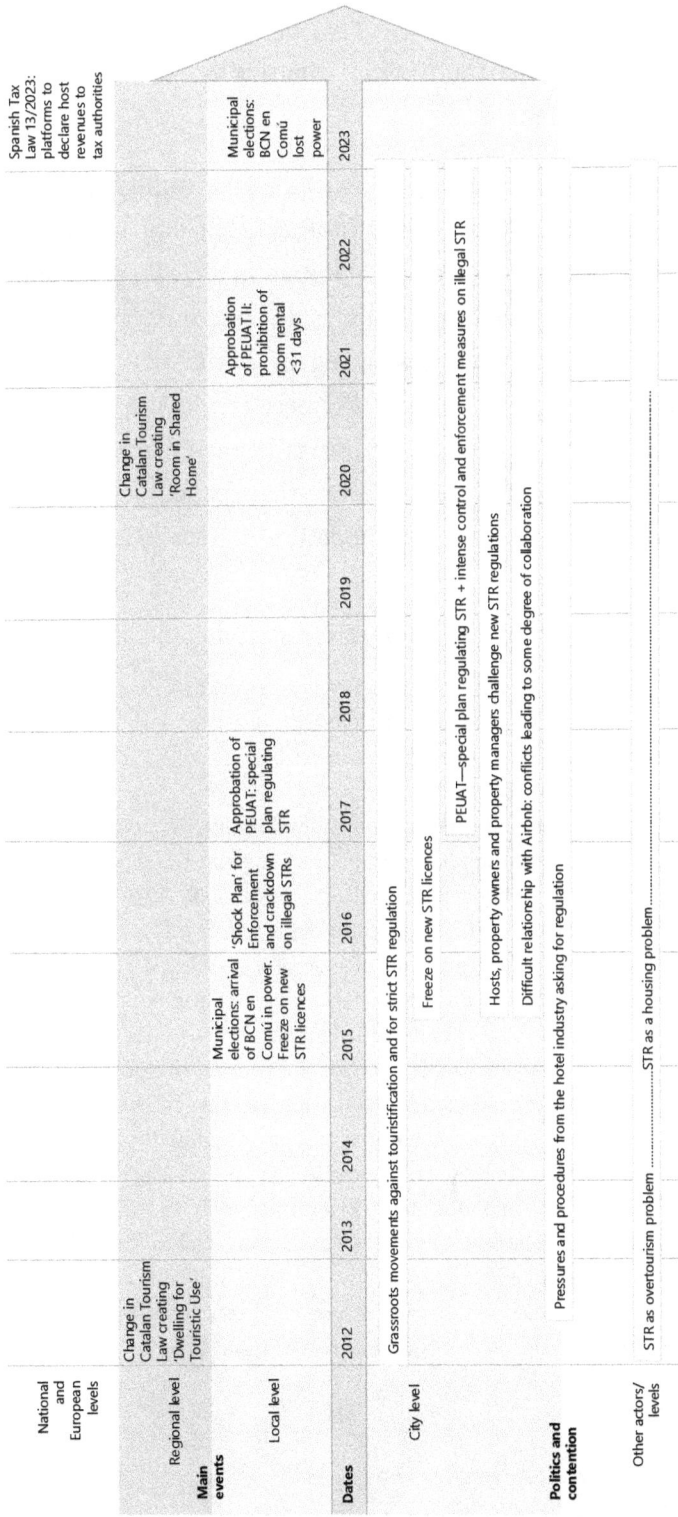

**Figure 17.** Timeline of STR regulation in Barcelona (2010–2022). *Source:* Authors.

## Paris: The Key Role of Local Officials—Housing Versus Tourism, City Versus Central State

Paris is part of World 2, that of tourist cities with highly institutionalised housing policies that protect affordable housing, and where local governments have been the political initiators of STR regulation. Paris is the most visited city in Europe alongside London. It has drawn much political and media attention with regard to the STR issue over the past decade, with a series of conflicts between its municipal government and the Airbnb platform. Additionally, the French capital hosted the Olympic Games in 2024, an event that fuelled political tensions around the issue of visitor accommodation, especially as Airbnb was a

---

**BOX 3: PROCEDURES TO OPERATE STRs IN PARIS IN 2022**

In Paris, it is possible to rent out a *primary residence as an STR for up to 120 days* a year, by registering with the City of Paris to obtain a unique registration number and paying the tourist tax, but without requesting a change of use.

For any rental *beyond 120 days, or for a dwelling that is not a primary residence*, the owner must apply for a change of use to the city's Office for the Protection of Residential Dwellings (Bureau de la Protection des Locaux d'Habitation, BPLH) and compensate for the loss of residential living space. This offsetting is usually done by buying a compensation voucher from a specialised company that converts non-residential premises into residential spaces of an equivalent floorspace in the same district (*arrondissement*), or even double or triple the amount of floorspace in the central districts most affected by STRs. The owner must then register online to obtain a registration number and pay the tourist tax.

To rent out furnished STRs in *premises that are not used for residential purposes* (e.g., offices or shops), the owner must apply to the city's Urban Planning Department for a change of destination, and to the BPLH for a change of use (a procedure governed by the Tourism Code and the Town Planning Code). Once the change of use has been accepted, the owner needs to register online to obtain a registration number and pay the tourist tax.

partner of the Paris 2024 Olympic and Paralympic Games International Organising Committee. In Paris, the politicisation process has taken place in a context of dense, pre-existing regulation of housing and tourist accommodation, characterised by two lines of tension: within the municipal administration (between the housing and tourism policy fields) and in a multi-level perspective, between the local and the national governments.

## THE REGULATION OF FURNISHED RENTALS BEFORE DIGITAL PLATFORMS: A LONG HISTORY OF HOUSING PROTECTION IN FRANCE AND PARIS (1960–2010)

The history of STR regulation in Paris must be understood within the context of a long-standing national legal framework of housing regulation in France, that included professional holiday lets in particular. In fact, since the 1960s both the French state and local authorities in Paris have been concerned with preserving the city's permanent housing stock in the face of STRs. Thus, the category of short-term 'furnished tourist rentals' (meublés de tourisme) (that belongs to type i as described in Box 1 in Chapter 3) has been regulated since the 1960s at the national level by different corpuses of law: the *Code of Tourism* regulates the diverse forms of professional tourist accommodation (like 'apart-hotel' [serviced apartments] or 'bed & breakfast') and tourist tax collection, the *Code on the Entry and Stay of Foreigners on the National Territory* regulates the inflows of visitors,[10] while the *Code of Construction and Housing* and the *Code of Urban Planning* regulate the transformation of a residential unit into a professional commercial rental. Three procedures are particularly important in this arsenal of rules: the definition of what constitutes a primary residence in France (including Paris), the process for a 'change of use', and the process for a 'change of destination'.

Since 2009 the City of Paris's Local Plan (Plan Local d'Urbanisme, PLU) considers short-term furnished rentals that are not a primary residence to be hotel residences, for which a change of destination and a change of use with compensation are required. This rule is the core of the Parisian regulatory regime because it distinguishes from the outset the occasional rental of a primary residence from the rental of furnished investment properties.[11] It is possible to rent out a home as furnished accommodation within a limit of 120 days per year; beyond this threshold, it is considered a secondary residence (or a hotel), and the owner has to apply for a change of use with compensation,[12] or for a change of destination if it is a non-residential commercial property.[13] Until 2009 these rules were enforced by the local representatives of the central state administration, but they were poorly enforced. In 2009 that responsibility was transferred to the city government of Paris, which took over existing cases and began to invest fully in this issue. Thus, while the number of STRs multiplied in the French capital in the 2010s, all the rules that would allow their control already existed long before the birth of corporate platforms, and they were routinely applied by the national, and subsequently the local, administration— namely the city's BPLH in the Department of Housing and the city's Department of Urban Planning. However, the rules were not always respected, nor were they publicised or politicised. The debates surrounding platforms brought these rules to light, as well as the flaws in their implementation.

## THE GRADUAL POLITICISATION OF STRs (2010–2015)

STRs were the object of a relatively gradual politicisation in Paris, but 2015 marked a sharp milestone in the trajectory of the issue. In 2010 this form of tourist accommodation was not debated much. The city's Department of Tourism and Economic Development was in charge of granting licences to professional tourist accommodation providers, checking compliance with standards and collecting tourist tax. Tourism is a key economic sector in France: the consensual political view is that it must be promoted. The only voices challenging the consequences of tourism in the city were those of middle- and upper-class residents' associations in central districts, complaining about the nuisances associated with café terraces and nightlife (Gravari-Barbas and Jacquot 2016). But the general perception was that the negative externalities of mass tourism could be regulated through standard local policies in the field of housing and public order, and through marketing campaigns encouraging the geographical deconcentration of tourism at a metropolitan scale (Gravari-Barbas and Fagnoni 2013).

However, in 2011, after observing a notable increase in the number of STRs, the city's Department of Housing and Habitat commissioned two reports. The reports highlighted the impact of a 2005 reform modifying tax on long-term furnished rentals and encouraging landlords to shift to short-term ones, but above all, they alerted officials to the risks posed by the development of digital platforms for permanent housing. They also pointed to a lack of implementation of existing rules, rather than a lack of rules (Ducarroz and Jankel 2011; Gadeix 2011).[14] Both reports called on local public authorities to enforce more strictly the existing procedures, particularly the rules for changing the use and destination of residential premises.[15] However, these two reports did not produce any major political impact. For their part, the city's office for the protection of residential dwellings (BPLH) was still doing its best to enforce change-of-use rules, with a small team of a dozen sworn enforcement agents knocking on apartment doors and taking legal action against offenders, notably multi-listing owners and real estate management companies.

However, in 2014–2015 two areas of tension intersected and led to a strong politicisation of the issue, both from outside and within the city government. On the one hand, professional organisations representing the hotel industry (UMIH, Union des Métiers et des Industries de l'Hôtellerie; AHTOP (later ATOP), Association pour un Hébergement et un Tourisme Professionnel) denounced unfair competition from

STRs in the media, in courts, and to Parisian elected officials.[16] Facing them, the National Union for the Promotion of Holiday Rentals (Union Nationale pour la Promotion de la Location de Vacances, UNPLV, created in 2013, at the time headed by the CEO of Abritel and bringing together French and multinational corporate platforms like Abritel, Airbnb, Homeway, TripAdvisor and Le Bon Coin) rapidly organised a counter-attack, highlighting the benefits of STRs for local economic development. The second area of tension, internal to the city administration, triggered the rise of STRs onto the political agenda. Between 2011 and 2014, tension developed between the Department of Tourism and Economic Development (that saw platform-mediated STRs as new opportunities for tourism development) and the Department of Housing (that saw STRs as a threat to housing). Between these two opposed framings of the issue, a middle-ground framing emerged: that the occasional or partial STR of one's home can allow permanent residents to raise extra income and be able to continue living in an expensive city such as Paris.

Three events tipped the balance towards a framing that would be more favourable to stricter regulation. On 5 April 2014, Ian Brossat (an elected official from the Communist Party with a strong commitment to housing issues) became deputy mayor in charge of housing. Quickly realising the scale of the phenomenon, he asked the BPLH to step up checks on platform-mediated STRs, particularly during the summer of 2014, in the central districts of Le Marais, Ile Saint-Louis, Montmartre and Saint-Germain-des-Prés. A few court cases against STRs began to attract media attention.[17] But a critical event happened on 26 February 2015: the deputy mayor in charge of cultural affairs (Bruno Julliard, centre-left Socialist Party) received Brian Chesky, the CEO of Airbnb, at the Paris City Hall, to celebrate the future agreement between the city government and the platform for the collection of the tourist tax. The city government officially announced that the meeting aimed at exchanging views with 'a platform that has become a key player in global tourism by proposing an offer that complements that of the hotel sector' (City of Paris press release, cited in Serafini 2015). However, this meeting took place without Deputy Mayor for Housing Ian Brossat, who, dissatisfied, set out on a campaign to re-establish the balance of power with the platform and convinced Mayor Anne Hidalgo (Socialist Party) to let him take the lead on the platform-mediated STR issue. Another event confirmed this politicisation: in November 2015, Airbnb rented the Grande Halle de la Villette of Paris (a large, publicly owned popular event venue in north-east Paris) to hold its second annual conference, Airbnb Open Paris,[18] for the first time outside the USA. The mayor of Paris was not invited, and elected officials were unable to attend. From that point onwards, the deputy mayor and the city's Department for Housing became the main political players in the campaign to regulate platform-mediated STRs in Paris, also influencing debates at the national and European levels, as discussed in Chapter 7. STRs became a *housing* problem, framed as producing excessive negative externalities on the already overstretched housing stock of Paris, a city in which the lower and middle classes, students and workers were no longer able to find accommodation easily. Elected officials and the city department in charge of tourism and economic development stepped aside, and the media-savvy deputy mayor for housing took the lead in the battle.

## PARIS VERSUS AIRBNB (2015–2020)

From 2015 onwards, policies around STRs emerged from the shadows and became publicised under the leadership of Ian Brossat. In his words, the platform economy is an 'economy of predation' that entails tax evasion and 'arrogant' lobbying (2018:29). By contrast, his argument on the effects of STRs on the housing stock in Paris was more moderate, to make it acceptable. He suggested that the 'Airbnb problem' was not that of tourists or individual homeowners (or tenants) who rent out their main residence from time to time (i.e., fewer than 120 days a year according to the law) to gain extra income. He maintained, instead, that it was a problem of professionalised landlords who rent out properties all year round, and of investors who own several STR properties and contribute to removing units from the long-term housing stock (between 20,000 and 30,000, according to his sources). Brossat thus distinguished between 'bad hosts' (STR type i) and 'good hosts' (STR types ii and iii). This narrative enabled the Paris city government to produce a coherent discourse that could be heard by both its upper-middle-class political clientele and those involved in economic development and tourism promotion: Paris needs tourism and STRs, but not at the expense of housing for its long-term inhabitants, and not for the benefit of the large corporations of platform capitalism.

In 2016 Brossat first sought to establish a dialogue with the director of public policy of Airbnb France, who announced in the press that she wanted to collaborate fully, in particular by validating the tourist tax collection and remittance agreement and potentially offering to flag 'illegal' listings on the platform. But on that second point, negotiations broke down when the city government proposed the introduction of a registration number for STR operators and requested the compulsory transfer of STR data from platforms to public authorities. A draft bill for new national legislation (the *Law on the Digital Republic*) also supported this proposal. Airbnb France closed the door on the negotiations, changed its director for France, and launched an intense lobbying campaign directed towards the national Ministry for Innovation and Digital Economy to undermine the law being drafted. The law was passed, nevertheless (explained further below).[19] On 1 December 2017, the procedure of a mandatory registration number attached to each STR listing (a measure voted unanimously by the Paris Council) came into force. Relations became tense, and a legal battle ensued between Airbnb and the city government. The latter subsequently developed a three-pronged public action.

The first and most visible aspect of the Parisian STR regulation (detailed in Chapter 5) has been the staged reinforcement of controls on suspected illegal STRs (i.e., those exceeding 120 days, or secondary residences with no permit for change of use). The BPLH stepped up its activities: a total of 15 sworn agents (among the 33 people who made up that office in the late 2010s) have been carrying out investigations on a daily basis or during 'hit operations', followed by legal action against the owners of suspected illegal STRs.

A second axis of political action has been the establishment of a different balance of power between the Paris city government and the hotel industry on the one hand, and Airbnb and the UNPLV on the other, via press releases but above all via an increasing judicialisation of the conflict (detailed in Chapter 6). Several court cases have gradually strengthened the case for the legitimacy of existing STR regulations. The most important one, in terms of its political effects, was initiated by two STR operators (Cali Apartments SCI and HX), whose STR properties were declared illegal under the City of Paris regulations. Their complaint was eventually referred by the Paris Court of Cassation (on behalf of the Paris Court of Appeal and City of Paris) to the Court of Justice of the European Union (CJEU). In September 2020 the CJEU ruled that the Parisian regulation complied with European law and was proportionate to the fight against the housing shortage, which is an 'overriding reason of general interest' (CJEU 2020a; see Chapter 7 for details of the ruling). In February 2021 the French Supreme Court (Cour de Cassation) also ruled that Parisian regulations were compliant and proportionate with national law.[20] The city government of Paris was able to resume the legal proceedings against 400 STR operators (for 420 listings without a registration number), which had been put on hold prior to this ruling, and thus recover €14 million in fines. In July 2021 the Judicial Court of Paris (Tribunal Judiciaire) ordered Airbnb to pay a fine of €8 million for maintaining 1,010 ads without registration numbers on its website.[21] In October

2021 the same court ordered Booking.com to pay a fine of €1.2 million for breaching the *French Tourism Code* (failure to provide the city government with detailed data on advertised listings).[22] This judicialisation reinforced the media coverage and politicisation of an issue that had hitherto been confined to the local administration. The media seized on the topic and relayed it on a massive scale, either celebrating unprecedented political voluntarism or criticising public action for its excessive rigor and for infringing on private property rights and tourism development.

## A LATE, TIMID BUT EFFECTIVE MOBILISATION
## OF GRASSROOTS MOVEMENTS IN THE 2020s

In contrast to the cities in World 3, the mobilisation of citizens and grassroots social movements has played a minor role in the initial politicisation of the issue in Paris. However, two types of mobilisation began to emerge timidly in 2016. The first were collectives of local residents in central Paris (in the Marais, for example, Les 4 Coins du 4) that had a relatively defensive discourse concerned with issues of quality of life, noise nuisances, the loss of traditional businesses and the decline in permanent population. Another collective (ParisVsBnb) was founded in 2017 by residents and activists from the second district of Paris who denounced the harmful effects of Airbnb and STRs on the disappearance of permanent housing units and local shops, unfair competition for tourism professionals, undeclared work and rise in crime. Starting out as a small group, the collective has practised 'web scraping' to produce data available online (see https://parisvsbnb.fr). But activists have complained that they have been disregarded, and have denounced the city government for its permissiveness, particularly on the issue of the conversion of non-residential properties: between 2015 and 2022, almost 90,000 square meters of office or retail space were converted into STRs in Paris. They acted as whistleblowers on this particular blind spot, prompting the Department of Housing to ask the Direction of Urban Planning, in 2020 and 2021, to step up its monitoring of changes of use, backed by a study that highlighted the 'blindness' of the local authorities to that issue (APUR 2020; de Frémont 2020). From January 2022 onwards, any change of use of retail or office premises is now subject to prior authorisation and strict conditions designed to preserve a balance between employment, housing, shops and tourist accommodation. It has now become hard to convert a ground-floor retail space into STR in the central districts of Paris.

Outside Paris, citizens' groups criticising overtourism in popular localities and calling for a greater regulation of STRs were set up in Saint-Malo, Douarnenez, Groix and Biarritz (on the Atlantic coast) and made contacts with ParisVsBnb and the Droit Au Logement (DAL) association (a well-known campaign group for the right to housing in France), holding joint press conferences and actions. This led to the creation of a national network of citizens' collectives in June 2023 (National Collective of Permanent Residents), helping to rescale the issue at the national level, taking it beyond Paris and the big cities.

## STABILISING THE PARISIAN REGULATORY SYSTEM AND OPENING UP A NATIONAL ARENA (2020–2022)

The last pillar of the politicisation of the STR issue has rested on the activities of the Paris city government to network with, and influence, local, national and European institutions to counter the lobbying of large platforms and to defend the legitimacy of its regulations at higher levels in the judicialised context mentioned above. The city government and the Paris mayor have become facilitators and active members of national and European networks for STR regulation (see Chapters 6 and 7). At the national level, since 2014 the Parisian BPLH has been in contact with the Ministry of Housing in an attempt to get nationally standardised procedures put in place through national legislation.

A breakthrough had been achieved by this ministry with the vote on the ALUR Law (*Law for the Access to Housing and Renovated Urbanism*)[23] that validated, in 2014, the principle of a change-of-use obligation (Art. 631–637 CCH) to use second homes as STRs. An interviewee from the Ministry of Housing (November 2017) explained, however, that the action of their ministry was partly curtailed by the Ministry of Economy and Finance, the latter more favourable to the platform economy, in particular when the minister in charge of that portfolio was Emmanuel Macron (2014–2016).

Later, the Paris city government tried to play a role in the drafting of the *Digital Republic Law* passed in October 2016,[24] drawing on a report that stressed the opportunities and risks of STRs (Terrasse 2016). This law allows large French cities (over 200,000 inhabitants) to require platforms to include a compulsory registration number in hosts' listings. However, the then national government (under the presidency of François Hollande) did not sign the enforcement decree for some of the law's provisions (particularly those asking platforms to share hosts' data with public authorities). This was the outcome of strong lobbying pressures by Airbnb and the European Holiday Home Association (EHHA) on the government, who feared potential judicial challenges in front of the CJEU. In 2018 the Law ELAN validated the possibility to implement the compulsory STR registration number and data sharing by platforms for all cities with more than 200,000 inhabitants that so wished,[25] or for cities with more than 50,000 inhabitants declared 'tense zones' (in terms of their housing markets). Finally, in 2019 the *Law of Engagement and Proximity* created an authorisation procedure for the rental of commercial real estate as STRs.[26] In 2022, the issue became truly national: the Ministry of Housing organised a consultation with local actors and published a *Practical Guide on the Regulation of [Short-Term] Furnished Accommodation for Municipalities*, which summarises all the national and local rules in place.[27] All major cities in France have, over the past few years, gradually taken steps to regulate

STRs. Outside of big cities, smaller but highly touristic localities have also developed fairly strict regulatory approaches or have positioned themselves on the battlefield against large platforms such as Airbnb.[28]

In line with this dynamic, and following a petition launched by citizens' collectives, in June 2023 members of the French Parliament from different and opposing political parties submitted a bill aiming at better regulating STRs 'to combat rental speculation and promote access to housing in areas under pressure',[29] but also to tighten taxation on hosts and platforms. This proposal was rebuffed by the presidency of the National Assembly, provoking widespread criticism from all political parties. This eventually prompted the minister for the economy and the prime minister in June 2023 to take a public stance in favour of opening up a debate on STR platform taxation. At the same time, the national government presented a national plan to address the issue of overtourism.[30] Figure 18 summarises the key milestones in the STR politicisation and regulation process in Paris.

## Milan: The Combination of a Pro-Visitor Agenda and a Liberalised Property Ownership Regime

In our clustering, Milan belongs to the World 1 of cities with laissez-faire STR regulations favourable to property ownership and policies for tourism attractiveness. Without being as popular as Rome, Venice or Florence, Milan attracts worldwide visitors (8 million visitors in 2019 in the metro area, 57% of which were international).[31] On top of globally known annual events such as the Fashion and Design Weeks, the city hosted the International Exhibition (World Expo, with 20 million visitors) in 2015 and will host the Winter Olympics Milano-Cortina in 2026. Milan was the first city in Italy where STRs became an object of political interest by the local government and then developed within a supportive regulatory environment: STRs have been treated as an economic activity based on residential property, to be made 'legal'

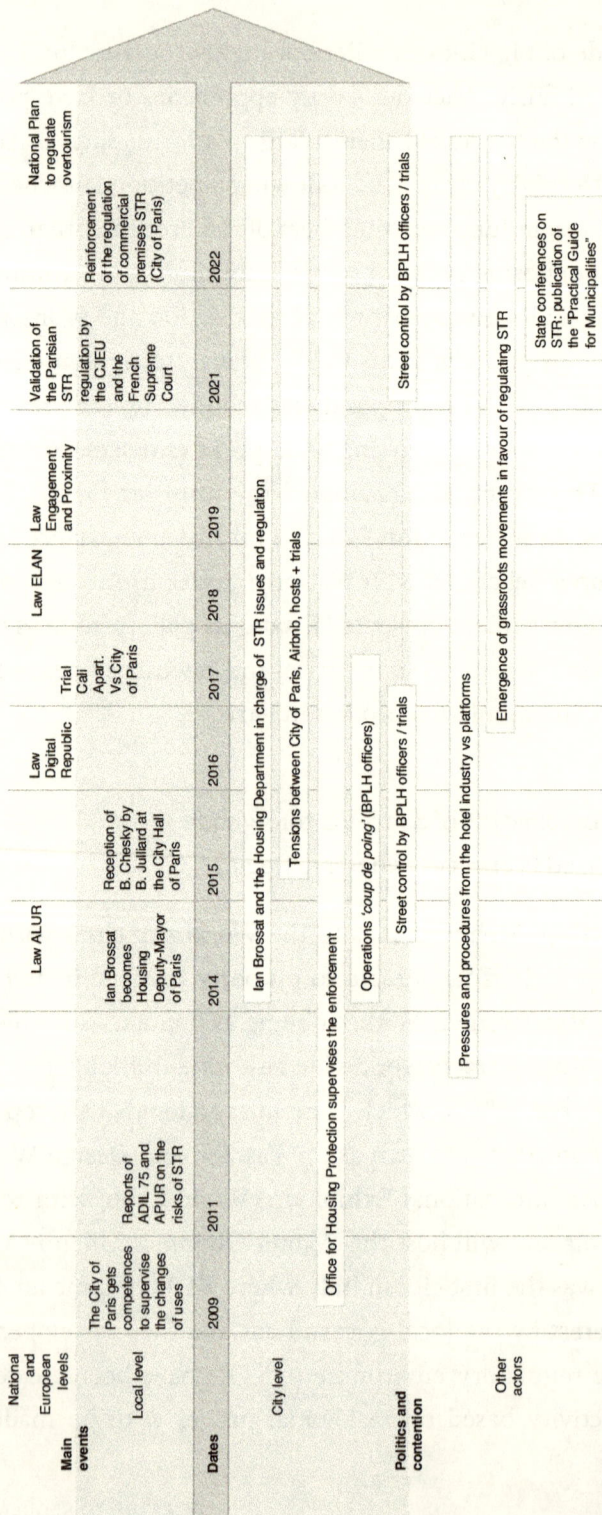

**Figure 18.** Timeline of STR regulation in Paris (2010–2022). *Source:* Authors.

and taxable and be brought out of informality—but not curbed. This case offers a perspective on the processes through which, in one of the countries with the largest STR market, this market has remained unrestricted. The Milan laissez-faire approach has emerged as a result of three complementary processes: a municipal, regional and national agenda supporting tourism; a national liberalised rental market and property-friendly regime; and multi-level political action that prevented the adoption of stricter STR rules, ignoring increasing social concerns around overtourism and the right to housing.

---

**BOX 4: PROCEDURES TO OPERATE STRs IN MILAN IN 2022**

In Milan, the rental of residential units to visitors staying for fewer than 30 consecutive days can be operated either as CAV (case e appartamenti per vacanze) under the regional tourism law if complementary services are offered (such as cleaning), or under the national rental law as LT (*locazioni turistiche*), when no such services are offered.

There are *no instruments that put up barriers to the use of a housing unit as CAV or LT, and thus to the growth of the STR offer* (STRs are only forbidden in the social housing stock).

Existing instruments simply regulate *how* to operate STRs: landlords starting/ending the activity have to *register* with the municipal government (Department for Commercial and Productive Activities), include a *regional identification number* (delivered by the metropolitan administration, Città Metropolitana di Milano) on online ads, pay the *tourist tax* to the city, communicate *data on guest flows* for statistical purposes to the region on a monthly basis, and communicate the *identity of guests* to the state police on a daily basis. According to the regional law, STR rented units must also comply with *quality standards* (e.g., ratio of guests per square metre, the obligation of two bathrooms above eight guests, minimum furniture and kitchenware).

The *distinction between professional and non-professional STRs is only fiscal* (CAVs are considered a professional activity if an operator rents out more than three units in the region, and LTs are considered a professional activity if an operator rents out more than four units in Italy during the fiscal year).

## THE WORLD EXPO 2015, THE MILANO SHARING CITY MUNICIPAL STRATEGY AND THE AGREEMENT WITH AIRBNB (2013–2015)

Milan was the first city in Italy where STRs became an object of political interest, from 2013 onwards, before the national state intervened in this matter several years later. The issue emerged in a specific political and economic context. First, it occurred during the preparation for the World Expo 2015, in the context of territorial policies and marketing strategies that, since the late 1990s, have aimed at fostering tourism and the city's attractiveness (Andreotti 2019; Anselmi and Vicari 2020; Conte and Anselmi 2022). The latter relies on business conferences, cultural offerings, trade fairs and seasonal events linked to the design and fashion industry (d'Ovidio and Pacetti 2020; Anselmi and Conte 2021). Second, the preparations for the World Expo 2015 took place in a moment of political renewal, as a centre-left majority led by Giuliano Pisapia had won the 2011 municipal elections after 18 years of right-wing governments (Andreotti 2019). The new majority's agenda was driven by the ambition to combine economic development with social inclusion through stakeholders' participation and co-production (Gascó et al. 2016; Armondi and Bruzzese 2017; Pais et al. 2019).

The first initiative to address STRs was the Milano Sharing City Strategy approved in 2014, under the leadership of Deputy Mayor in Charge of Employment and Economic Development Cristina Tajani. The strategy was first proposed by a group of 'sharing economy experts', consultants, academics and cultural workers who started the SharExpo project in November 2013.[32] They advocated for sharing economy services to be integrated into the World Expo, seen as an opportunity to upscale this (then) emerging economic model. Their project fed into the strategic document 'Milano Sharing City', approved by the municipality in December 2014.

This Sharing City strategy had three main characteristics. First, it saw the sharing economy as a new form of exchange that activates idle or underused resources and establishes new social relations, in line with its original optimistic theorisations, referred to in Chapter 1. It aimed at setting a 'collaborative institutional ecosystem' for a 'regulated', 'inclusive' and 'sustainable' sharing economy (Comune di Milano 2014). Second, this strategy was cross-sectoral: it involved the Deputy Mayors for Employment and Economic Development, Mobility and Commerce. STRs were seen as one among other manifestations of the sharing economy (e.g., car-sharing or bike-sharing). Finally, it relied on collaborative policy instruments: the local government's intervention did not seek to define the legal and fiscal rules applying to digitally mediated shared services, but instead consisted in mobilising a variety of actors (firms, associations, informal groups, etc.) to support the emergence of new services and initiatives. To do so, the city issued a public call for the creation of a city-wide network to sustain collaboration between sharing economy operators.

This municipal policy opened an important window of opportunity for Airbnb, which defined itself at the time as a home-sharing platform. Airbnb Italy, whose offices are based in Milan, responded to the city's public call: in February 2015 the company officially joined the 'network of sharing economy operators' coordinated by the municipality. In November 2015 (a few months after the contested Airbnb agreement in Paris), Airbnb Italy signed a widely publicised memorandum of understanding with the City of Milan (Comune di Milano 2016). This was the first one in Italy (yet part of a global strategy developed by the firm, based on striking agreements with local administrations, as analysed in Chapter 6). The agreement included shared initiatives to support the digital literacy of disadvantaged citizens; an economic impact assessment of Airbnb-listed STRs in the city; collaboration for increasing the accommodation offer during big events; and support for the implementation of rules, especially the tourist tax. The agreement gave the platform the benefit of visibility, legitimacy and public recognition, and marked the start of several years of political exchange with the city government.

## HOTEL INDUSTRY MOBILISATIONS AND NEW REGIONAL LAW ON TOURISM THAT 'LEGALISED STRS' (2015–2018)

The second form of politicisation of the STR issue in Milan took place during the same years at the regional level. It was also based on an approach favourable to the visitor economy in view of the upcoming World Expo 2015, but emerged in total disconnection from the municipal Sharing City strategy.

In early 2015 the Lombardy regional government, run by a centre-right coalition with a governor from the League Party, was preparing a new regional law on tourism (a field in which Italian regions have legislative power). The hotel industry jumped on the opportunity opened by the elaboration of the law to push the issue of STRs on the regional government agenda. At that time, the three main hotel organisations in Milan (Associazione Provinciale Albergatori Milano, Associazione Turismo e Ricettività and Assolombarda) were the sole vocal actors clamouring for stricter STR rules. They actively mobilised their well-established ties with politicians and administrations and organised actions in the public sphere—holding conferences, promoting pieces of research, setting up a 'hotelvsairbnb' website, and liaising with the media. They framed STRs as an 'illegal' market and as 'unfair' competition. They strongly criticised the use of the term *home-sharing* (and thus the municipal Sharing City strategy) for misrepresenting what was, in their view, a new, unregulated, accommodation industry.

In its law approved in 2015 and the subsequent implementation decree,[33] the regional government framed STRs as an opportunity for the growth of regional tourism, but one that needed a clearer legal framework, a better knowledge of the STR market for the administration and the collection of the tourist tax. The law establishes a legal category for STRs called *case e appartamenti per vacanze* (CAV), defined as accommodation and possibly services provided in a housing unit or part of it, with a bathroom and kitchen. This CAV typology already existed,[34] but was limited to rentals lasting 7 to 30 consecutive days. It was therefore stretched to cover the emerging STR market, where rentals are often shorter than seven days. Moreover, the law established a registration scheme: CAV operators must communicate the start—and eventually the end—of their STR activity to the municipality (Department for Commercial and Productive Activities). Becoming part of the regional tourist accommodation offer, they also owe the daily tourist tax to the municipal government, have to communicate data on guest flows for statistical purposes to the region and have to meet minimum quality standards. The operation of more than three CAVs in the region is defined as an entrepreneurial activity for registration and taxation purposes (of business revenues instead of rental revenues). In a 2018 law,[35] the registration scheme was updated to introduce a regional compulsory identification code for each STR. This code is delivered by the metropolitan authority,[36] and it has to be displayed by STR operators in all advertisements. All in all, the regional laws passed in 2015–2018 established the fundamentals of STR regulation in Milan, where STR is treated as a type of touristic accommodation, with no barriers to the growth of the market.

Airbnb, initially favourable to the regional law as it 'legalised' STRs, contested the 2016 implementation decree and the 2018 requirement for an identification code (Colombo 2018). The platform claimed that the procedures for STR operators were too complicated (e.g., online registration with a digital signature, online identification code) and too detailed (e.g., list of required furniture). In 2015, newly created STR property owners' organisations also began to argue that a regional law on tourism was interfering with their freedom to rent out their property—in contravention to the national law on rentals, in their view. This claim was at the origin of the referral, by the central government, of the Lombardy law to the Italian Constitutional Court in 2018 (see below).

## THE CENTRAL STATE: PROPERTY-FRIENDLY TAXATION AND TOURISM GROWTH MODEL (2017–2020)

While the Municipality of Milan and the Lombardy region were taking action on STRs, national governments remained silent until late 2016. Yet the central state has exclusive competences over the regulation of property rental relations, including touristic rentals. The 1998 national law on rentals,[37] which abolished the system of controlled rents in Italy (Storto 2018), defines a specific type of rental of a housing unit for touristic uses (*locazioni turistiche*, LT). These are rentals of fewer than 30 consecutive days with no additional services provided and that do not require a registered contract (contrary to long-term rentals). Starting in 2017, such a pre-existing legal category has been used by governments to tackle STRs from a very specific perspective: revenue taxation and the reduction of tax evasion. During the drafting of the annual *Finance Act for 2017*, both the Finance Committee of the Italian Chamber of Deputies and property managers organisations proposed to extend to STRs (*locazioni turistiche* as defined in the 1998 law) the property-friendly fiscal regime applying to rental revenues: a flat tax at a 21% rate for physical persons renting a property (so-called *cedolare secca*).[38] The extension of the 21% STR flat tax was proposed as an easily available policy instrument to reduce the risk of STR fiscal evasion while sustaining property owners' revenues. However, the parliamentary debates preceding the annual Finance Act and the then head of government Matteo Renzi (Democratic Party) rejected this proposal on the basis of a 'no to new taxes' promise.

A few months later, the new Gentiloni government (Democratic Party) eventually passed the decree that established the 21% flat tax as the 'tax regime for short-term rentals'.[39] Importantly, the decree also tried to strengthen the fiscal responsibilities of platforms: it established that platforms and other intermediaries should have a fiscal representative in the country, collect the flat tax and remit it to the Italian state, along with fiscal data of STR providers. While many Italian property agencies and managers started to collect and remit the flat tax, major international platforms refused to do so. Arguing that the law contravened the free provision of services within the EU, Airbnb Ireland (the European subsidiary of the USA-based platform) appealed to the Latium Administrative Court and then to the Italian Council of State, and the latter referred the case to the CJEU. This judicialisation process stalled Airbnb's fiscal compliance for six years (see Chapters 6 and 7). The Italian law was upheld by the CJEU in December 2022,[40] leading the Public Prosecutor to request a payment of €779 million to Airbnb in November 2023, which concluded with a €576 million payment from the company to the national Tax Agency to cover the non-collected taxes and sanctions (Bertolino 2023; Monaci 2023). A second, very specific state intervention came from the Ministry of the Interior, focused on security issues: it extended to STR operators the obligation to communicate the names of guests to the police,[41] a public order measure already in place for hotels and other types of tourist accommodation.

It was only in 2019 that STRs became increasingly seen not only as a fiscal problem but also as a national (over)tourism issue. Two distinct groups brought attention to the size of the STR market, particularly in the historic centres of touristic cities. First, grassroots movements—especially in Venice, Florence, Naples and Bologna—started to mobilise around STRs, claiming that the uncontrolled growth of tourism was emptying cities of their permanent inhabitants and turning them into visitor-oriented, standardised and commodified places. Established movements around touristification already existed in Venice (Vianello 2016) and to some extent Florence and Naples. Other groups were created in 2018 and 2019 and focused on STRs turning housing for inhabitants into tourist accommodation (mostly, Progetto Firenze in

Florence, Pensare Urbano in Bologna and OCIO in Venice) (see Tonetta et al. 2022). In 2018, some joined the already-mentioned international network SET (Southern Europe against Touristification) that gathered Spanish, Portuguese and Italian activists from various cities (Dinamopress 2018)—though not Milan (see below).[42] These local campaigns networked at the local and national levels to document, map, raise awareness and strike alliances with elected officials and tenants' organisations, supported by academics investigating the issue (research project Short-Term City, www.stcity.it) and journalists (Gainsforth 2019). They sometimes gained support from individual politicians from the centre-left, but with limited success in turning their claims into new, stricter STR regulations.

Second, in 2019–2020, the ministers of tourism (especially Franceschini, who was the minister in the Gentiloni and Conte II governments) and the mayors of touristic cities (mainly Florence, Venice, Naples, Rome) increasingly looked at STRs as a fully fledged and substantial share of the tourist accommodation offer that required a clearer framework. Yet their position remained anchored in a very ambiguous search for equilibrium between a pro-tourism and property-friendly agenda (both national and local) and the preservation of the liveability of historic city centres brought to light by increasing social debates around overtourism. This ambiguous equilibrium translated into a lack of action. In April 2019, during the Conte I government (Five-Stars/League coalition), the Ministry of Tourism created by decree a national registration system and database for tourist accommodation.[43] According to its proponents, it aimed at improving the quality of the STR offer, ensuring the protection of tourists and fighting against informal accommodation, also for tax purposes. It was also expected to centralise the various STR identification codes put in place by the regional governments. However, while a subsequent decree defined the precise content of the database,[44] and an agreement was drafted between the ministry and the regions in 2022, the measure was not yet operational four years later (end of 2023).

A few months later, in August 2019, two members of Parliament (from the Democratic Party, elected from Venice and Florence) from the opposition to the Conte I government presented a bill in the Chamber of Deputies aimed at regulating STRs and stopping the negative externalities of tourism in historic city centres (the Pellicani-Di Giorgi bill). Stemming from the overtourism debate pushed by grassroots movements in Venice and Florence, it proposed that municipalities be allowed to subject STRs to a licensing system, with a total number of granted licences, a time cap for occasional STRs and the exclusion of 'entrepreneurial STR operators' from the 21% flat tax benefit. The bill was submitted to a vote in January 2020 under the Conte II government (Five-Star/centre-left coalition). It was immediately rejected, including by members of the government party Italia Viva (Fossati 2020) and after strong mobilisations from host and property owners' organisations (Host+Host, Host Italia, Prolocatur, ABBAV, Confedilizia). Its failure was followed by an appeal from pro-regulation groups (Collective 2020). After the first COVID lockdown, only the fiscal part of this proposal was approved, leading to a limit on the favourable 21% flat tax to four apartments (beyond which the fiscal regime for business applies).[45]

During this 2012–2020 timespan, the national government also played an important role *against* regional laws trying to regulate STRs. As shown before, property rental contracts (including tourist leases) fall within the competence of the state as a civil law matter, while tourist accommodations are a regional matter. In 2017 and 2018 the national government took the view that the regional laws on tourism of Lombardy and Tuscany encroached on the state's exclusive competence in rental contracts and challenged them before the Constitutional Court. Property owners' organisations (especially Prolocatur and Confedilizia, according to our interviewees) played a role in pushing national politicians to take action against regional STR rules. In a landmark ruling in April 2019 (84/2019), the Constitutional Court upheld the Lombardy regional law. This made it clear that regions can act on STRs as part of their remit in the tourism field (through registration systems and identification codes, statistical requirements, etc.), but cannot interfere with rental relations (Menegus 2019, 2020).

All in all, through initial inaction, then followed by light taxation and litigation against regions, successive national governments have consolidated a liberalised STR market. This national framework rests on two complementary pillars. First is a national tourism-led growth model that has intensified since the 2008 crisis: tourism, and international tourism especially, has been seen as an engine of growth along with wage deflation and fiscal consolidation (Bürgisser and Di Carlo 2023). The second pillar is a housing system based on owner-occupation, multiple property ownership and a liberalised rental market (Fregolent and Torri 2018; Storto 2018; Filandri et al. 2020). Unrestricted STRs have come to occupy a nodal position between these two pillars, economically and politically: in the context of declining wages, owners and investors of all sizes have been left free to capitalise on residential assets by turning them into a source of revenue.

## MILAN AS A CITY OF STRs: ESTABLISHED OFFER, ASSOCIATIONS AND PLATFORMS (2015–2022)

STR rules in the city of Milan are embedded in this liberal national framework that sustains them. From the World Expo 2015 up to the time of writing (end of 2023), tourist flows and STR numbers have grown in the city. In 2016 the former executive director for Expo 2015, Giuseppe Sala, won the municipal elections, with a centre-left majority. In 2019 the city was selected to host the Winter Olympics Milano-Cortina 2026. Between 2010 and 2019 tourist arrivals to the metropolitan area increased by 41%, a rise significantly higher than that of large destinations such as Venice and Rome (Assolombarda 2023). STRs listed on Airbnb grew from 6,300 in January 2016 to 22,700 in January 2023. Over the same period, the share of multiple listings grew from 25% to 41%, which mostly reflects the consolidation of individuals and companies managing and commercialising STRs on behalf of owners.

During these years, four complementary regulatory activities have institutionalised STRs as a full-fledged economic sector in the city: (1) adjustments to the regional law, (2) the tourist tax collection and administrative implementation of the STR registration system and code, (3) a 'pragmatic' relationship with Airbnb and (4) the political recognition of associations of hosts and property managers. First, the regional government has maintained its tourism-oriented approach based on legalising the STR market. After the 2019 Constitutional Court decision, the regional government has clarified the differences between the two legal definitions of STRs coexisting in Lombardy, the local one (CAV) that includes the provision of services to visitors, and the national one (LT) that does not. It has stated that regional tourism requirements apply to both,[46] so that the market can operate legally, through communication of the start of the activity, regional identification code, reporting of tourist flows and tourist tax.

At the municipal level, most efforts have been put into improving the collection of the tourist tax. In 2016 the city modified the municipal fiscal regulation to allow platforms to collect the tax on behalf of the city's authorities. Airbnb started in March 2018. This was seen by the local government—mostly the taxation and the tourism departments, which pushed for this solution—as an important achievement and significant improvement to ensure STR fiscal compliance and the overall legality of the market. By contrast, the communication of the start/end of STR activity and the granting of the compulsory identification code to STR operators have received much less political attention. These rules have been implemented by public-facing local administrations (at the city and metropolitan levels) outnumbered and outpaced by the growth of STRs (see Chapter 5).

Third, since the 2015 agreement, the city government has claimed to have a pragmatic approach to platforms, seen as new and important economic players (interview, Department for Economic Development, April 2017). In 2018, aware that corporate platforms had shifted far away from the sharing economy ideal, the municipality revised its sharing city strategy to focus on smaller and local initiatives. This de facto took Airbnb out of this field of policy. On the other hand, however, the city government has continued to see Airbnb as contributing to the local agenda: the company supports the visitor economy, collects the tourist tax for the city, ensures a large accommodation offer during big events (annual Design Weeks, upcoming Winter Olympics, etc.), advertises medium-term rentals and offers corporate social responsibility initiatives such as the hosting of refugees or health workers during COVID. Good relationships and political exchanges between the city and the platform have never wavered (see Chapter 6).

Finally, interest groups representing STR hosts, property owners and property managers (mainly OspitaMI, Prolocatur, Property Managers Italia, Associazione Italiana Gestori di Affitti Brevi [AIGAB], Rescasa) have been recognised as key stakeholders in the governance of tourist accommodation (see Chapter 6). They have been participating in local meetings, round tables and consultations regarding the STR market, the improvement of STR quality and liability, the reduction of informality and the functioning of the rules in place. Starting in 2017, the local Chamber of Commerce has also become an arena for coordination between STR operators (including the drafting of an STR 'rental contract type' in 2019).[47]

Importantly, between 2015 and 2020, grassroots mobilisations against STRs were rather limited in Milan. Contrary to other cities, overtourism was not a politically salient issue; the groups mobilising around neighbourhood change or housing were not addressing STRs frontally. Neighbourhood associations voiced concerns about noise and disturbances brought on by the multiplication of bars, restaurants and visitors in previously residential areas (e.g., Isola). Tenants' organisations and housing and social movements focused on evictions in social housing and on maintaining public/common spaces in the city. One organisation of residents, academics and activists, called OffTopic, started to document and raise awareness around STRs, which nevertheless remained one area of concern among others.

All in all, the dominant local framing firmly treated STRs as a tourism economy matter. Neither the Deputy Mayor for Housing between 2016 and 2020 (Gabriele Rabaiotti) nor the local administration sought to intervene.[48] In February 2020, the Deputy Mayor for Tourism and colleagues from Naples, Rome, Bologna and Florence were signatories of a letter sent to Minister of Tourism Franceschini, demanding the implementation of the national identification code, the fiscal distinction of professional/non-professional STRs and the transformation of local planning tools to regulate non-hotel accommodation, yet also insisting (with implicit reference to the Milan situation) that not all Italian cities were facing overtourism (Pace 2020). In the same month, Deputy Mayor for Planning Pierfrancesco Maran provocatively posted on his Facebook page: 'Can we still afford Airbnb?' (La Repubblica 2020). He directly named STRs as part of the unaffordability problem in Milan. Yet the COVID-19 pandemic exploded in Lombardy a week later— dramatically stopping any debate on this issue for almost two years.

## THE SLOW EMERGENCE OF STRs AS A HOUSING PROBLEM (2021–2023)

The post-pandemic years have opened a timid bifurcation towards the framing of STRs from a tourism/overtourism issue to a housing one, but this view is still marginal in the Italian context: firmly opposed by the national government, STR operators and platforms, it has not led to regulatory changes. After the COVID-19 pandemic, large cities and smaller touristic cities have seen the concomitant return of tourists and the worsening of the housing crisis due to increasing rents, prices, interest rates and low-income households' liquidity. In Milan, the 'Milano euphoria' (Andreotti 2019) around a visitor-oriented strategy has been increasingly criticised for its negative effects on the city's liveability and affordability (Armondi et al. 2022; Bricocoli and Peverini 2024; Tozzi 2023). Milanese neighbourhoods and citizens' collectives have progressively politicised STRs as a threat to housing (e.g., OffTopic, Abitare in Via Padova, Chiediamo Casa). From the beginning of 2023 onwards, Deputy Mayor for Housing Pierfrancesco Maran (author of the above-mentioned 2020 Facebook post) started to politically frame STRs as a housing problem that needs some intervention. For the first time, the adverse effects of STRs on housing were mentioned in the new three-year Municipal Housing Strategy published in March 2023 (Comune di Milano 2023a). The deputy mayor opened the launching event (attended by one of the authors) with a speech requesting that the national government take stricter actions on STRs. In April 2023 he, along with the Deputy Mayors for Housing of 11 Italian cities ruled by centre-left governments, signed a 'municipalist alliance for a national housing policy'. These cities demanded, among five measures, a national STR law that would provide cities with regulatory tools.

Part of this shift in the Milanese government framing has exogenous sources. On the one hand, it heralds a return of housing being viewed as a matter requiring mobilisation from Italian social movements, student organisations and unions. On the other hand, it follows initiatives that had been developing in other cities since the end of the pandemic—Venice and Florence mostly. In November 2021, the pro-regulation movement in Venice (OCIO, part of the SET network) started the campaign 'Alta Tensione Abitativa' to support a national bill proposal. It is aimed at providing all Italian municipalities identified as 'under housing tension' (on the basis of an existing list of municipalities elaborated by the state) with the possibility of introducing a licensing scheme for STRs (type i) that can be adapted to different neighbourhoods, with a 'one host one licence' rule. It would give occasional operators (defined by a time cap) the possibility to rent short-term without a licence.

In July 2022 the Venetian member of Parliament, Pellicani (who was involved in the origin of the 2019 rejected bill), introduced an amendment for the City of Venice in a corrective financial law.[49] It created the possibility, for the Municipality of Venice only, to use planning instruments to limit STRs (with a system of change of use for STRs operating more than 120 days per year). In the summer of 2023 the implementing regulation had not yet been put in place by the Venice city government—a symptom of the ambiguous position of a mayor dependent on the tourism industry while publicly favourable to its regulation. By contrast, the municipality of Florence has been at the origin of an experimental STR restriction, the first in Italy, that attempts to stop STR growth. In June 2022 the mayor proposed a national bill 'for the preservation of historic centres' based on the aim of regulating tourism, that included the possibility for municipalities to put in place quantitative limits and change of use requirements for STRs. Yet this proposal faced the deadlock of the national legislative context described above. To circumvent this stalling, in October 2023 the Florence City Council passed a non-retroactive STR ban in buildings with residential uses that applies to the historic centre, in the area under UNESCO protection. This has been a highly symbolic political decision that however also carries strong legal uncertainties due to the absence of a national law.

Those mobilisations of Italian grassroots movements and centre-left mayors have emerged in a national political environment which remains unfavourable to stricter STR regulation. In May 2023 the central government, led by the far-right party Fratelli d'Italia (Brothers of Italy), drafted an STR bill proposal aimed at protecting hotels and legalising the STR market, while based on the dominant framing of STRs as a desirable tourist accommodation offer. The only measure taken so far has been to raise the flat tax on STR revenue from the 21% rate to 26%, a measure limited to those persons renting two to four units—signalling the continuity of a fiscal approach that protects property rentiership and the property owners' electorate. Figure 19

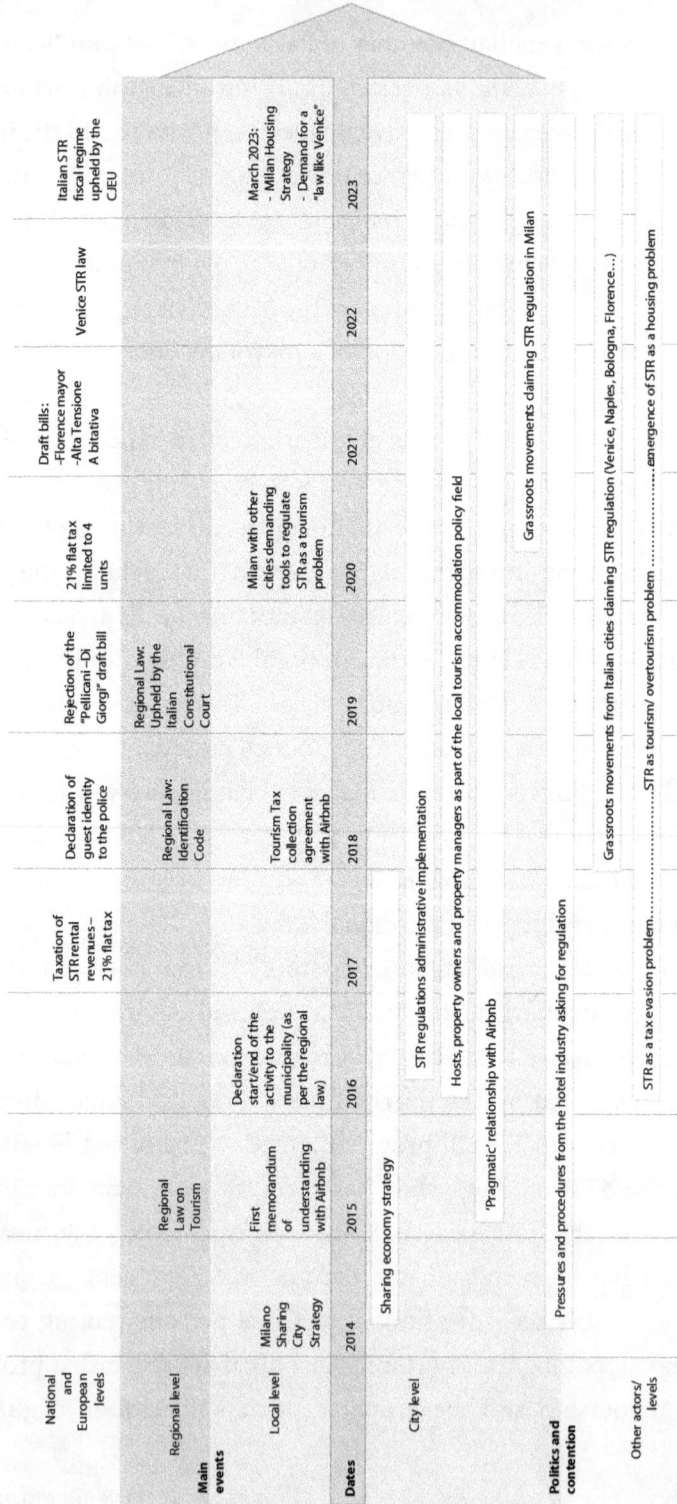

**Figure 19.** Timeline of STR regulation in Milan (2010–2022). *Source*: Authors.

| Main events | 2014 | 2015 | 2016 | 2017 | 2018 | 2019 | 2020 | 2021 | 2022 | 2023 |
|---|---|---|---|---|---|---|---|---|---|---|
| National and European levels | | | | Taxation of STR rental revenues – 21% flat tax | Declaration of guest identity to the police | Rejection of the "Pellicani–Di Giorgi" draft bill | 21% flat tax limited to 4 units | Draft bills: -Florence mayor -Alta Tensione A bitativa | Venice STR law | Italian STR fiscal regime upheld by the CJEU |
| Regional level | | Regional Law on Tourism | | | Regional Law: Identification Code | Regional Law: Upheld by the Italian Constitutional Court | | | | |
| Local level | Milano Sharing City Strategy | First memorandum of understanding with Airbnb | Declaration start/end of the activity to the municipality (as per the regional law) | | Tourism Tax collection agreement with Airbnb | | Milan with other cities demanding tools to regulate STR as a tourism problem | | | March 2023: - Milan Housing Strategy - Demand for a "law like Venice" |
| Dates | 2014 | 2015 | 2016 | 2017 | 2018 | 2019 | 2020 | 2021 | 2022 | 2023 |

**Politics and contention**

City level:
- Sharing economy strategy
- STR regulations administrative implementation
- Hosts, property owners and property managers as part of the local tourism accommodation policy field
- 'Pragmatic' relationship with Airbnb

Other actors/levels:
- Pressures and procedures from the hotel industry asking for regulation
- Grassroots movements from Italian cities claiming STR regulation (Venice, Naples, Bologna, Florence...)
- Grassroots movements claiming STR regulation in Milan
- STR as a tax evasion problem ............ STR as tourism/overtourism problem ............ emergence of STR as a housing problem

summarises the key milestones in the STR politicisation and regulation process in Milan.

## POLICY MECHANISMS LEADING TO DIFFERENT STR REGULATIONS

Through a cross-case comparison of Paris, Barcelona and Milan, we now analyse the three key policy mechanisms through which different paths to STR regulation emerged, took shape and were institutionalised in European cities. Those mechanisms produced regulatory diversity because of the differences in the type of first movers who mobilised and contributed to the issue framing, the type of pre-existing policy instruments and the multi-level relations between tiers of governments with different competences.

### 'First Movers' and Issue Framing: Connecting STRs to Broader Sectoral Agendas

The first differentiating mechanism has been the *type of actors* (or coalitions) who politicised the STR issue in the first place and discursively constructed it to justify some form of public intervention (see Aguilera et al. 2021:Table 2, p. 14 for a summary of these actors in the three cities). These actors and coalitions developed a particular policy framing to turn an emerging issue into an object of governmental intervention, connecting STRs with broader issues that were already high on political agendas. STRs were actively defined as a problem of 'something' (housing shortage, tourism or overtourism, sharing economy) and anchored to a set of emerging or institutionalised policy initiatives.

In their early years, platform-mediated STRs largely benefited from legal uncertainties, due to the speed of the STR growth and the 'wicked nature' of the phenomenon, as argued in Chapter 1. Before specific regulations were enacted, there were different narratives and claims concerning the definition of a local STR 'public problem', its scope, and its potential or actual effects. As they were dealing with a loose object, the first actors who constructed a public discourse around STRs sometimes benefited from the 'first movers' advantage'. They set the tone of local debates until the emergence of counter-narratives and mobilisations, which happened at different speeds from one city to the other. Since then, groups in favour of or against STR regulations have been actively mobilising resources to impose their own framing, in a dense political space analysed in detail in Chapter 6.

In Barcelona, STRs were framed as a *tourism problem* (and later as a housing issue) first by grassroots movements. Both long-standing residents' associations and new movements against touristification and for housing rights found a window of opportunity to put their demands on the political agenda in the run-up to the 2015 Spanish municipal elections. When the left-wing political force Barcelona en Comú came to power, they made tourism regulation and the 'right to housing' two central issues on the local agenda. STR regulation became one of the most visible, and contentious, symbols of the political change they intended to bring about. In Paris, STRs were framed mostly as a *housing problem*, starting from within the municipal government. With external support from the hotel industry, the issue was put on the political agenda by the Deputy Mayor for Housing, who wanted to take the leadership on this issue and managed to impose his framing, in opposition to the Deputy Mayor for Tourism. STR regulation was attached to an existing policy agenda around the protection and development of affordable housing in Paris, supported by the centre-left city government since the early 2000s. In Milan, STRs were first framed as a *tourism-related economic activity* by governmental and economic actors. Both the sharing economy advocates in alliance with the municipal government and the hotel industry in alliance with the regional government operated on the basis of a pro-tourism agenda. Anchored to the World Expo 2015, STR regulatory initiatives were aimed at promoting the sharing economy and updating tourist accommodation norms. Both local and regional governments shared the intention to address the informality and tax evasion that stemmed from this new activity, yet saw it as an economic opportunity.

The anchoring of the STR issue to a given policy sector thus played a crucial role: different types of instruments traditionally used in that sector, and existing public administrations and organisations (more or less well resourced), could then be mobilised. This connected locally defined STRs to the multi-level political-economic space of each sector, with its dominant administrations at different tiers, business actors and established agendas.

## Pre-Existing Instruments and Institutions

The processes that went from the initial framing and agenda-setting to the design of specific regulatory measures for STRs happened in a policy space of pre-existing institutions, organisations, policy programmes and instruments. This shaped, in part, the concrete options and choices available. The second policy mechanism leading to different regulations is thus the availability and the reuse of existing policy instruments and connected institutions. Established instruments were often quickly mobilised to deal with the new policy object of STRs: the instruments applying to similar classes of policy objects—such as other types of tourist accommodation, other uses of the housing stock, other types of rental revenues—helped fashion the ones crafted to deal with STRs. They also came with their connected administrations, routines and underlying administrative cultures. This is not to say that the choice of instrumentation was a linear process, or that there were no innovations in regulatory development. In the three cities, STR regulation has mixed existing and newly created instruments, yet in different proportions: more reuse in Paris and Milan (with opposite regulatory goals), more innovation in Barcelona. However, both new and existing instruments were often politically framed as 'new' to demonstrate proactive public action, and came with innovations in enforcement (see Chapter 5).

The case of Paris epitomises the *recycling of pre-existing instruments*, which mostly came from the arsenal of well-institutionalised housing policy tools, assembled with rules from other fields of action. The first measures taken to regulate STRs entailed a broadening of the objects targeted by existing instruments. Among them, the compensation rule—repeatedly presented by the Deputy Mayor for Housing as one of his flagship measures—was in fact at the heart of pre-existing French regulations. The existing city administration in charge of housing protection has been in charge of enforcing STR rules. Thus, few instruments were created from scratch. New instruments—in particular, the registration number created by a national law—were cobbled together with old ones by the agents of the municipal housing department, assembled in a corpus retroactively presented as coherent and innovative. No specific administrative department was created, and few dedicated recruitments were made. This shows how robust housing institutions, administrative departments and policies (as part of the French welfare/housing regime and the Parisian housing policy) were activated to tackle a new problem. The STR regulatory corpus became the object of a new, substantial political investment, through the publicisation of rules and the strengthening of enforcement efforts. The Deputy Mayor of Housing staged novelty as a political resource to take the lead on STRs in the city council, within the context of internal competition between different departments.

In Milan, too, most of the instruments used to regulate STRs already existed and were stretched to deal with the new phenomenon. By contrast to Paris, however, they came from the tourism, taxation and property sectors, de facto supporting STR development. The regional government extended an already existing type of non-hotel tourist accommodation (the CAV) to cover STRs and legalise them; subsequently, it stretched the requirements for CAV to the LT (as defined in the national law). Similarly, at the national level, governments used the 1998 rental law and the 2011 property-friendly flat tax system to define the STR fiscal regime. Additionally, in some cases these pre-existing favourable instruments have been used strategically to obstruct the passing of new STR rules. This was the case for the registration system in Milan and Lombardy, when the Italian national rental law from 1998 was used to challenge the 2018 regional law introducing the compulsory identification code in front of the Constitutional Court. Finally, even when new instruments strengthening STR regulation were passed, they have not always been implemented: while the regional identification code has been put in place, the national one has been under construction for several years; the 'Venice law' has not yet been implemented either. In this context, the multi-sectoral sharing economy strategy approved by the municipal government in 2014 came with some innovations in instruments, based on agreements with firms and operators. Those partnerships did not intend to regulate the STR market but to foster public–private relationships across a local ecosystem of service providers, including Airbnb.

By contrast with Paris and Milan, innovation in instruments was slightly more significant in Barcelona, for political and institutional reasons. First, political actors turned STR regulation into the symbol of their new political offer. The use of the municipal land use planning competence to limit the development of STRs spatially and quantitatively came with a new local planning document, the PEUAT. The latter was elaborated as a special tool that had a symbolic dimension, embodying the municipal willingness to act on the matter, while also having the advantage of avoiding the long procedure of modifying the General Metropolitan Plan. It also became the favourite target of property owners and hosts who mobilised against STR-stringent rules in the city (see Chapter 6). The choice of a regulatory instrument from land use planning was explained by the competence of the city government in that field. But it was also limited by the regional legislative framework: the PEUAT had to work with the definition of STRs inscribed in the Catalan regional law, which did not make a distinction between the professional and occasional STR of a full unit. This made the kind of regulatory differentiation set up in Paris between the two types of STR practices (through the 120 days rule) impossible. Nor did the regional law define *room rental* as a separate legal category until an amendment of 2020. This then allowed the city government of Barcelona to take restrictive measures for this category of STR.

## Multi-Level Governance, Institutional Competences and Political Relations

The third mechanism leading to different regulations is the distribution of competences and the political relations between levels of government. When compared to their respective national governments, the three cities have been forerunners in the politicisation of STRs (this is actually the case for most of the 12 cities we study in this book, except Lisbon and London, where national governments made the first move—as explained below). The story of Barcelona, Paris and Milan has been one of local actors putting an issue on the agenda when national governments were not active on this topic. Subsequently, the institutionalisation of STR regulations involved the upper levels of government, which hold legislative power over a range of relevant fields (rental housing, tourism, income taxation, national security and economic development). In our three cities, the very definition of STRs, from a legal point of view, falls outside municipal competences. In Barcelona, it is the regional government that has competence over the legal definition of *tourism-related establishments*, in Paris the national government, and in Milan both the regional and national governments (respectively through tourism and rental property laws). When national or regional legislation has been changed to give (more) scope for local governments to use land use planning tools or housing tools to regulate the change of use (e.g., in Paris, for STR type i) or the granting of new licences (e.g., in Barcelona, for STR types i and ii), this has facilitated the local regulation of STRs. In such multi-level contexts (the impacts of the supranational level of the EU are discussed in Chapter 7), the capacity of local politicians to influence legislative change at higher levels has been highly dependent on power relations, conflicts and the political alignment (or the lack thereof) between levels. Municipal regulations must therefore be understood in the context of those relationships and of differences in ideology and policy priorities between the local ruling majority and the upper levels of government.

Relying on upper levels for regulation, municipal officials from Paris (the Deputy Mayor for Housing) proactively pushed for national legislative changes. STR laws applying to France as a whole were drafted under pressure from the Paris city government. They gave other French municipalities (of above 200,000 inhabitants) the tools to limit the development of STR type i. This opportunity was rapidly seized by large cities such as Lyon and Bordeaux, and later by smaller yet extremely touristic coastal towns. Importantly, in the case of Paris, differences in policy priorities and political misalignment have played out both between levels and between policy sectors, which offered the city some allies within the central state. The French government led by Emmanuel Macron after 2017 was strongly supportive of both the quantitative growth of tourism and the digital platforms from the new start-up economy. The Ministry of Economy was highly reluctant to regulate digital platforms.[50] In the debates on new legislation on STR regulation (that included provisions applying to platforms), this part of the central state was therefore in disagreement with the city government of Paris. The latter, however, had the Ministry of Housing as an ally. Contrary to the cases of Milan and Barcelona, the existence within the central state of a relatively strong administration in charge of housing has been a source of support to the local governments of Paris and other French cities in STR regulatory development.

By contrast, in Milan, while the city government proudly advertised its early actions in dealing with platforms in 2015, it did not advocate for national legislative changes that would provide the city with the tools to control STRs until 2023. Italian central governments have played a crucial role in sustaining the unrestricted growth of STRs, with an agenda and legislative framework supportive of both tourism and the free use of real estate property. In this context, while the Lombardy regional law clarified what STR providers should do to operate STR accommodations in the city, it has not provided instruments that could allow the city to regulate this use of the housing stock. The Milan municipality has thus remained, for almost 10 years, without the legal capacity to govern the overall growth and spatial development of STRs.

In Barcelona, it is the regional government that can define the different categories of tourist accommodation that are subject to a registration and licensing process (in the *Tourism Law*). The city government has to work with those categories, using a special land use plan to set limits to the number of licences. Until the regional law created a new category for single rooms rented short-term in 2020, this particular form of STR could not be regulated at the local level and was in a legal vacuum. A new regional law passed in 2023 has opened the way for a stricter regulation of STRs by individual local governments, who can decide whether to renew existing STR licenses.

## HOW HAVE THESE MECHANISMS PLAYED OUT IN THE THREE WORLDS OF STR REGULATION?

Going back to our broader European comparison, we now embed Barcelona, Paris and Milan in their respective ideal-typical world of cities sharing similar socio-economic and political conditions, welfare/ housing regimes and STR regulatory intensities. We do not re-examine all the cities in our sample, but discuss here how the three key policy mechanisms presented above have played out in the three ideal-typical worlds. We highlight borderline cases in which some of these mechanisms have operated differently from the other cities belonging to the same world.

## World 1: The Political Production of STR Laissez-Faire

In the world of homeowners' laissez-faire cities (Milan, Rome, London, Prague), STRs were not, at first, framed as a threat to the long-term housing stock. Pushed both by governments and tourism/property interest groups, a business-oriented framing has prevailed and focused on issues connected to the fairness, competitiveness and legality of the tourist accommodation market. Actors trying to switch public attention towards the effects of STRs on the urban fabric and the housing stock have had limited room for manoeuvre. They have faced a lack of available instruments and policies for strong regulation of rental housing, in the context of a well-established and multi-level legal and fiscal arsenal that is favourable to property ownership. Importantly, unpacking those mechanisms shows that STR laissez-faire cannot be reduced to a *lack* of public intervention: in these cities, intense policy processes and rules have created and sustained a liberalised STR market as part of a tourism and property-friendly development model.

London is an interesting case in this respect: here, STRs have been an object of deliberate and targeted deregulation by the central state, against the will of some borough councils. The *Greater London Authority (General Powers) Act* of 1973 prohibited the rental of a property for fewer than 90 days a year without planning permission for a change of use. In 2015 this act was amended by the national government with the aim of promoting the sharing economy, self-entrepreneurship and the freedom to rent one's property (*Deregulation Act 2015*) (Department for Business, Innovation and Skills 2015; Department of Communities and Local Government 2015). In a global city where central and local government policies have prioritised economic attractiveness and competitiveness at all costs, several events led to this 'regulated deregulation' of STRs (Ferreri and Sanyal 2018). The 2012 Olympic Games served as a pretext to justify this. Large firms such as Google (that needed accommodation for their mobile employees) also influenced the favourable political reception to STRs (interview, Camden Council Cabinet member, February 2016). At the local level, however, the councillors and officials of some London boroughs that had witnessed a significant increase in STRs (Camden, Hackney, Tower Hamlets, Westminster) were not favourable to deregulation, as expressed in interviews in 2016. Yet their demands remained unheard.

## World 2: Local Governments Activating Housing Protection Instruments

By contrast, in the world of *touristic cities with robust housing policies* (Paris, Amsterdam, Vienna and Berlin), politicisation came from inside the local government (in Berlin, it was also influenced by housing activist movements). This specifically stemmed from departments and officials working on an everyday basis on the elaboration and implementation of interventionist housing strategies, who were witnessing the steep increase of STRs in key areas of their cities. The palette of pre-existing regulatory tools used by these administrations both facilitated the politicisation of the STR issue and offered some ready-to-use responses to be adapted to this new phenomenon. Established administrations were also entrusted with implementation. Therefore, in this cluster the processes of politicisation connected the STR issue to the existing institutions, tools and administrations of the socio-democratic and corporatist welfare/housing regimes of which these cities are part, which are characterised by public interventionism and partly decommodified housing. Importantly, in unitary countries (France, The Netherlands) this provided local actors willing to implement regulatory mechanisms with potential allies within central state administrations (e.g., ministries of housing), even when the ruling majorities in central government were unfavourable to STR regulation. In federal countries (Austria, Germany), rules against the misuse of housing were directly put in place by the governments and parliaments of the individual states (Vienna and Berlin both having the status of city-states).

Berlin was a border case between World 2 and World 3: politicisation did not come uniquely from within government and public administrations, but also from social movements that advocated for STR stringent rules. These movement could rely not just on political allies from within the ruling parties (as in World 3), but also on the established institutions and rules connected to the highly regulated rental housing market and its system of established actors (tenants' organisations, government housing departments, unions, etc.) (Bernt 2022). These actors and institutionalised rules were responsive to the emerging claims regarding the negative effects of STRs on the long-term rental market.

## World 3: Social Movements Allying with Responsive City Governments

In the world of left-wing politics with medium to dense STR regulations (Barcelona, Madrid, Lisbon), the agency that made STRs a public problem mainly came from social movements against gentrification, touristification and/or campaigns for housing rights and affordability, in alliance with elected and administrative officials, some of whom were coming from social movements themselves. Overall, STRs were framed as a channel for overtourism and for the (mis)use of the housing stock hampering long-term rental opportunities and inhabitants' lives. The issue was contentious, mediatised and politically salient at the local level. However, in Barcelona, Madrid and Lisbon, the actors willing to develop interventionist policies on STRs could not rely on a solid set of institutionalised policies for rental housing (as was the case in World 2). They relied on land use planning tools (more than housing protection ones) and had to recruit staff for policy implementation. In Barcelona and Madrid in 2015–2019, the distribution of competences across levels of government forced local actors demanding stronger regulation to work within the constraints of regional legislation, at a time when the regional parliaments were in the hands of parties on the opposite side of the political spectrum.

The case of Lisbon (the most stringent regulation in our sample) holds a special place in World 3. The adoption of a strict national law in 2018 shows the role played by the *national rescaling* of the STR issue on the one hand, and by coalition games between parties in the national and local governments on the other. Lisbon has a high ratio of tourists and STRs per inhabitant (see Chapter 3). While social movements calling for STR regulation gradually emerged in the second half of the 2010s (such as Morar em Lisboa), the agenda-setting for a new regulation has come from the national rather than the local government, and is done by a traditional social-democratic (Socialist) rather than a new municipalist party. This makes it a borderline case in our sample. At first, between 2010 and 2015 the STR market was seen by the then mayor F. Medina and some Lisbon residents as a positive contribution (Almeida 2016). Two national laws in 2014 and 2015 gave a legal framework to the STR market with minimal requirements, in order to support the activity (Estevens et al. 2023). However, from 2015 onwards, STRs were gradually seen as a major cause of rising rents and population displacement in the most popular tourist neighbourhoods of Lisbon (such as Alfama) (Cocola-Gant and Gago 2021). During the 2017 local election campaign, left-wing politicians, housing activists and hotel industry professionals mobilised to push the issue onto the agenda. The coalition government in power at the national level (Geringonça, 2015–2019: Socialist Party supported by Left parties) politicised the STR issue (Marques Pereira 2022) and passed a national law on STRs in 2018. It empowered municipal governments to set up their own local regulations with a territorialised approach (through complete or partial bans in specific neighbourhoods) and restrictive measures (e.g., compulsory licences with registration numbers). Armed with those options, the Lisbon city government, after a one-year moratorium on STRs, voted a restrictive regulation in 2019. This introduced *containment areas (zonas de contenção)*, in which no new registration of STR is allowed (or only under strict conditions). During the COVID-19 pandemic, the mayor previously favourable to STRs changed his mind in favour of stronger STR regulation to protect housing for residents (Medina 2020). There were, however, very few resources for enforcement of the new local STR regulations in Lisbon, so their effectiveness on the ground has been questionable to date.

## CONCLUSION

This chapter has shown that the same issue (the growth of STRs in major European tourist cities) has been grasped by actors in very diverse ways, leading to different modes of regulation. This diversity can be explained by looking at how three policy mechanisms unfolded in each city. Political framing games and social mobilisations matter: this is especially the case in World 3 cities, where the agenda was driven by social movements and local politics. But regulation was also guided by long-term policies in the states and cities concerned: STR rules have been constructed in dense political spaces with institutions, instruments and priorities already in place, notably on housing, urban planning and tourism. To put it more simply, the pre-existing world of public policies (before the emergence of platforms) is probably one of the factors that makes the biggest difference between our cases. This especially differentiates World 2 from the others: World 2 cities belong to socio-democratic or corporatist welfare/housing regimes, with a 50-plus-year history of robust multi-level housing policies intervening in the rental and private property market. These policies drove

STR regulatory interventions—which was not the case for World 1 and World 3 cities with more liberalised rental markets and less interventionist housing policies. In World 3, politicians developed instruments and regulatory change to curb STRs; by contrast they did not in World 1, where the STR market has been liberalised like the rest of the housing market.

By following detailed trajectories in three cities via process tracing, we have highlighted causal mechanisms and produced internal validity arguments about our cases. Using a cross-case analysis, we have checked those mechanisms by specifying them in relation to each other. Finally, by comparing the central cases in our ideal-typical worlds to the other cases in the same world, we have discussed how mechanisms have varied under certain combinations of conditions.

However, as the rest of the book will show, diversity is not the sole story. When trying to enforce rules over thousands of STRs, city governments have faced common challenges. STRs listed in the digital world have been hard to track down behind the building facades of European cities. Multinational digital platforms have tended to withhold data on listings and have actively pushed against market access restrictions. The next part of the book deals with three sets of dynamics: implementation and enforcement, interest group politics and judicialisation/transnational rescaling. While those dynamics could potentially push for convergence, they have not so far altered the significant differences in political and regulatory responses to platform-mediated STRs.

# PART III

# STRUGGLING WITH COMMON CHALLENGES

## Implementation, Judicialisation and Multi-Level Governance

# 5

# A CHALLENGING IMPLEMENTATION

## Regulatory Enforcement in the Digital Age

A REGULATION IS only as good as the possibility of the concrete implementation and enforcement of its instruments and procedures. This process involves three kinds of political activities: organising the coordination of individual and collective actors around the new rules and arbitrating the conflicts these rules give rise to (see Chapter 6); ensuring the new rules are properly applied to stabilise a regulated market; and detecting irregularities and sanctioning the operators and/or platforms who do not respect the rules. In this chapter we focus on the last two dimensions, by studying specifically what happens *after* new STR regulations have been adopted. We analyse the challenges shared by all public authorities in enforcing STR regulations in the physical and digital worlds of STR housing. How do public administrations identify, control and stop STRs deemed illegal? How do they cope with the strategies of the operators of illegal(ised) STRs who try to escape detection? What are the relationships between governments and digital platforms in the process of regulatory enforcement?

Everywhere, traditional zoning and planning instruments have faced significant difficulties with enforcement on the ground, and regulatory non-compliance is widespread in the STR market. While some of the enforcement difficulties reflect long-standing challenges associated with the control of illegalities in the built environment, others are specifically due to the digitally mediated nature of STRs. Platform intermediation has a paradoxical effect: it makes a local STR offer visible and instantaneously accessible to a global audience, but leaves the public authorities in charge of enforcement with limited knowledge about the providers of this offer. Their only public face is often 'an anonymous digital listing with an approximate location of the property and an unverified first name of the host' (Cox and Haar 2020:12). As data are at the heart of their business model (see Chapter 1), platform companies have usually refused to share detailed data on STR listings.

In this chapter, we dig into the paradoxical process of enforcing regulations over a phenomenon mediated by a data-driven business. We focus on the concrete means, strategies and activities deployed by local government managers and 'street-level bureaucrats' (Lipsky 2010) involved in regulatory enforcement. We do not seek to evaluate the quantitative outcomes and impacts of new regulations on the STR offer in each city as many scholars have done (see Chapter 2), but rather to complement their work by analysing the challenges of implementation. First, we show that there are significant differences in enforcement efforts between our 12 cities. Those differences are linked to the intensity and the logic of regulatory instrumentation (see Chapter 3), but also to political preferences and administrative capacities. Second, we demonstrate that when they do attempt to enforce, local administrations face very similar challenges due to the information gap between anonymous digital listings and real-world illegality. The chapter shows that local governments have attempted to reduce this gap through street-level inspections and through seeking access to platform data via formal means (laws and courts) or informal methods (do-it-yourself, DIY). In the process, local administrations have gradually acquired expertise and know-how to make their enforcement procedures more effective and strengthen their political impact in the face of platforms that still try to operate in the interstices of regulatory frameworks.

## ENFORCING NEW STR REGULATIONS, GRASPING NEW ILLEGALITIES

Implementation and enforcement efforts have not been the same across the three worlds of STR regulation analysed in Chapter 3. The process of implementing instruments and rules involves, in the first place, setting up standardised responses and procedures to allow STR operators to *comply with the new rules* (e.g., delivering registration numbers, processing requests for licences, etc.). Potential variation in implementation comes from the fact that the more instruments there are to implement (corresponding to a high IRI in Chapter 3), the more tasks the responsible authorities have to perform. Similarly, the more STR numbers grow, the more intensive those tasks become. This increased administrative workload can be tackled either by recruiting new agents in cities that already had services in charge of housing protection (World 2), or by mobilising existing administrations in other sectors (e.g., planning) or by creating new 'task forces' (World 3). If there are no new, or not enough, agents (World 1), existing administrations cope by applying the rules slowly or only partly.

A second mission (on which we focus in this chapter) is to detect and sanction those who *do not respect* the new rules, that is, illegal STR operators. From 2015 onwards, when measures began to be adopted in European cities, the public declarations of some political leaders and hotel industry representatives emphasised the 'illegality' of a large proportion of STR listings—an easy way to get political and moral credit.[1]

Yet the enforcement efforts to detect illegalities have not been the same across the three worlds of STR regulation. Rather unsurprisingly, they depend on the logic and intensity of each regulatory regime and are, in general, more intense in those cities with regulations that seek to limit STR market development and negative externalities (Worlds 2 and 3). However, this is not the only explanation. Enforcement is also significantly influenced by political will and by the availability of financial and human resources dedicated to the task. Even when public officials or political leaders have been keen to crack down on illegal STRs, there have been substantial differences in the resources that they have been able to deploy to enforce STR rules (for a larger discussion, see McKay 2003; Alterman and Calor 2020). Stringent regulations can be a dead letter without enforcement means (as the case of Lisbon partially demonstrates; see below).

## World 1: Enforcing Regulations with Limited Staffing and Little Political Support

In World 1 cities, regulations have been supportive of STR practices. They rely on a limited number of instruments, mostly dealing with how the STR market *operates* (e.g,. registration systems and identification codes, obligation to communicate the identity of the hosts). In Prague, Milan and Rome (and Lisbon before 2018), fiscal, tourism or trade licencing inspectors have performed some controls in order to verify tourist tax compliance; facilitate market competition; and ensure minimum standards of health, safety and security. However, those controls have often been limited and have not sought to detect 'illegal' STRs in order to curb the market, but rather to ensure its 'legalised' functioning.

STR rules have been implemented by administrations that were already in place, without increases in their staffing to cope with STRs. In Milan, there are two main enforcement branches in the local government,[2] which have limited exchanges with one another. First, since 2016 the Department for Commercial and Productive Activities has received and stored the declaration of the start/end of the STR activity from STR providers (for CAV since 2016, and for *locazioni turistiche* since 2019). Since 2018 this department has then transferred these declarations to the metropolitan authority that delivers the compulsory identification code to STR providers. The three people who work in the relevant department's office (interviewed in July 2022) struggle to cope with the number of queries and have been overwhelmed by phone calls from STR operators asking for information that is often beyond their remit (e.g., on the taxation of STR revenue). They do not physically welcome users, but the number of phone calls forces them to arbitrate between answering the phone and processing new STR registrations. To limit phone calls, they try to maintain an updated website with detailed instructions for hosts who wish to register the start of their activity.

Furthermore, between 2015 and 2018 (when the regional identification code was put in place), their office did not record in a systematised database the declarations of the start of an STR activity that they received from STR providers. According to one member of the unit:

> [Between 2015 and 2018] physical and legal persons managing STRs sent to the municipality lists of dozens of flats with simple addresses and no exact cadastral identification of the properties. And those people who were present in our office during those years (2015–2016–2017) would take these paper communications, and file them. If we are lucky, they kept track of them on a computer application. . . . [L]ater they put in place a certified email address . . . but there was no real monitoring nor reasoning on the fact that the phenomenon was becoming really important in the city. (interview, Department for Commercial and Productive Activities, July 2022)

In 2018 the introduction of a compulsory identification code and more formalised communication system between STR operators and the city administration brought clarity for newly started STRs but did not entirely solve the opacity regarding the ones that had started before 2018. The number of defunct STRs is not certain either, since, according to interviewees, a significant but unknown number of providers do not declare the termination of their STR activity. As a result, huge uncertainties have remained regarding the exact list of *registered* and *active* STRs. Similar difficulties in coping with the exponential growth of STRs can be observed at the metropolitan level. Due to a lack of staff and technological challenges, the delivery of the STR identification code by the metropolitan authority has been slow, sometimes taking up to six or even nine months (interviews, senior officers in the Regional Tourism Department, January 2020, and the Municipal Department for Commercial and Productive Activities, July 2022).

In this first area of implementation and enforcement, the control of non-compliant STR operators is carried out by a department of the local police (*polizia annonaria*), in which about 10 inspectors are in charge of the control of STR registration and safety and quality standards, but also of hotels, bars, restaurants, grocery stores, and so on. According to our interviews with the local administration and Milanese associations of STR hosts, there are *some* controls, but not very many. They are focused on verifying that registered STRs comply with safety and quality rules, similar to checks on hotels. This means that there is no targeted, intentional strategy to detect illegal STRs (contrary to cities in Worlds 2 and 3). Unlike the enforcement of the tourist tax collection (described below), the enforcement of the registration system has been considered a purely administrative issue, with limited interest in or support from local politicians for its enforcement. In July 2022, there were about 9,700 *registered STRs* with an identification code in Milan (interview, Department for Commercial and Productive Activities, July 2022);[3] at the same point in time, the website of Inside Airbnb recorded 19,032 listings—double the number. In July 2023, the ratio was the same: there were about 11,700 registered STRs in Milan (Lombardy

Open Data portal),[4] against 22,673 listings recorded by Inside Airbnb (in May 2023). While these numbers are not entirely comparable,[5] they do give a rough indication about the huge size of the unregistered STR offer in the context of rather limited enforcement activities.

The second main implementation and enforcement branch within the local government is the Tax Department that deals with physical/legal STR operators who must pay the tourist tax through a dedicated online system (interviews, Tax Department, April 2017 and January 2020). A tax evasion and collection team (of about 10 people) controls this fiscal compliance as part of the enforcement of local taxation. In this context, the tourist tax collection and remittance agreement with the platform Airbnb (2018c) has been a highly publicised political decision, presented both by the platform and by city officials as a fundamental step towards fiscal compliance and STR legality (Airbnb 2018c; La Repubblica 2018). From this perspective, Airbnb is a single legal person that collects the tax from thousands of STR operators. It is thus seen by the Tax Department as a 'complying actor' and a facilitator of fiscal enforcement. Therefore, municipal controls do not focus on the platform but rather on tracking tourist tax evasion from STR operators *outside* Airbnb (interview, senior officer in the Tax Department, January 2020).

Altogether, in Milan, pre-existing administrations have been in charge of regulatory implementation and enforcement with no or limited additional staffing. As of mid-2023, the implementation of the registration scheme was only partially applied. While the tourist tax collection by Airbnb has been one way of dealing with limited staff while enforcing taxation rules, it has also implied delegating fiscal powers from public authorities to a corporation over which the city has limited oversight (see Chapter 6). Furthermore, the enforcement of tourist tax, and of safety and quality standards and registration rules, operated separately—with no unifying political agenda around the detection of illegal STRs.

In terms of enforcement, London differed from the other three cities in World 1 (Milan, Rome and Prague), as there is an access type of instrument meant to protect the housing stock. The rule requires an STR operator to obtain planning consent if a housing unit is used as a STR more than 90 days per year. However, the enforcement of this rule falls under the remit of the planning departments of the borough councils, which have been understaffed and under-resourced (due to central government cuts to the funding of English local authorities since 2010). An officer from an inner London borough explained that in 2018 they only had four staff members to control all types of suspected breaches of planning regulations, leading to virtually no 'planning contravention notices' being served in relation to STR (see also Ferreri and Sanyal 2018). He additionally reported that as of September 2018, the planning department had not received any application for change of use from 'residential' to 'short-term letting' over the previous three years, although many full units were on offer on Airbnb for more than 90 days in the borough. He was therefore facing extensive STR illegalities, but with very little enforcement capacity to do anything about it.

### Worlds 2 and 3: Politics, Path Dependence and the Symbolic Power of Implementation

By contrast, other city governments from Worlds 2 and 3 have been trying to control the overall growth, quantity and/or location of STRs through stricter regulations. They have used instruments from planning and housing policy (e.g., licences, change of use authorisation, zoning) that limit the access to the STR market, in order to protect the long-term residential stock and prevent its conversion into STRs. In those cities, the enforcement agents and mechanisms used to address STRs have usually been an extension of the existing framework in place for other types of housing and planning illegalities. However, there were considerable differences in the resourcing of their inspection teams. As of mid-2018 (see Colomb and Moreira de Souza 2021:66–92), there were approximately 70 agents in charge of STR regulatory enforcement in Amsterdam, 63 in Berlin (mostly at district level), 33 in Paris, 30 in Barcelona (supplemented by 40 office-based online 'visualisers'), and 22 in Madrid. Importantly, in many cities street-level inspectors have to deal with other types of illegalities besides STRs: for instance, in Barcelona they are also in charge of monitoring the compliance by bar/restaurant operators of rules about outdoor terraces.

Those differences in the resourcing of enforcement services reflect the financial capacity of local governments, but only partially. They also depend on existing housing policies and on the importance assigned to the issue of controlling STRs in the local political agenda. In some cases (notably the cities of World 2), the existence of institutionalised policies protecting housing for residential uses explains the investment in administrative enforcement. As shown in Chapter 4, the City of Paris was able to tackle the STR issue proactively because it already had an office for the Protection of Residential Dwellings, the BPLH, a powerful administrative unit in charge of controlling the use of housing and related illegalities under the political supervision of the Deputy Mayor for Housing and the Department of Housing. This office has been politically mandated to develop and steer STR regulatory enforcement. As a consequence, the BPLH has grown from 29 agents in 2016 to 33 in 2022 (among them 15 solely dedicated to the enforcement of STR regulation),[6] and it has benefitted from strong political, financial and administrative support (including from lawyers from the municipality). This office carries out four types of mission. The first is to examine all the applications for change of use submitted by STR operators who want to normalise their situation. The huge growth in STR numbers has made this task more time-consuming and complex and has required a degree of flexibility in the interpretation of rules to make them applicable (interview, BPLH officer, April 2017). The other missions entail the coercive side of enforcement: finding and sanctioning illegalities by processing listings, physically controlling STRs (door-to-door) and sending cases to court.

Political variables also shape enforcement (Short 2021) and explain the level of investment in implementation: showing a strong bureaucratic investment in implementation means demonstrating political voluntarism to get credit from public opinion. In some cities—notably Amsterdam, Barcelona and Paris—from the mid-2010s onwards there has been a clear drive for the local governments to invest in the expansion and strengthening of enforcement teams. But this political variable can play different roles. In Barcelona, following the victory of a new political force (Barcelona en Comú) in 2015, the city council launched a specific 'shock plan' for STR detection and enforcement costing €1.35 million per year (Ajuntament de Barcelona 2016). Resources were invested to supplement the 30 inspectors attached to the Department of Urban Planning with up to 40 office-based investigators, temporarily contracted to perform online searches on platform websites. The results of the 'enforcement offensive' launched in 2015 have been visible and staged as efficient through public communication.[7] In Paris, political leadership has intensified, politicised and publicised an already well-established enforcement instrumentation, rather than creating a new one. This implies a stronger anchoring of STR regulatory enforcement in administrative practice and less dependence on politics than is the case for cities in World 3.

In some cities, we observed a lack of alignment between the strict nature of new STR regulations and the lack of capacity for, or political will to invest resources in, enforcing them. As of the end of 2023, Lisbon appeared to be an example of such a situation. While the city government has enacted strict regulatory measures that prohibit new STRs in certain neighbourhoods (high IRI; see Chapter 3), a strict enforcement of the new rules at municipal level does not seem to have followed so far. Enforcement is entrusted to police teams from the national Food and Economic Security Authority (ASAE) and to a team from the municipality. Although the national government announced an increase in the number of physical inspections and amount of online monitoring planned by the ASAE (to 4,800 by 2023) (TPN/Lusa 2022), the reality has been very different: just under a hundred STRs were shut down by the agency over a seven-year period (Cristino 2024), with only 20 units closed in Lisbon in 2023.

In the following two sections, we focus on cities belonging to the second and third worlds of STR regulation—more specifically Barcelona and Paris—where significant enforcement efforts have faced equally substantial challenges. The local administrations have progressively institutionalised their enforcement procedures, from the DIY identification of illegalities to the strengthening of judicial procedures.

## FINDING AND SANCTIONING ILLEGAL STR OPERATORS: POLITICISING AND INSTITUTIONALISING ADMINISTRATIVE ENFORCEMENT WORK

### Street-Level Strategies of Inspection

In May 2018 in Barcelona, a young man in plain clothes, only armed with an identification card indicating his status as an employee of the city council, patiently rang the bells of a series of flats listed on a piece of paper in the streets of the Old City of Barcelona. Sometimes, a voice answered, and the inspector managed to make it to the door of the flat. A young British tourist, woken up from his sleep, angrily responded behind the closed door that the inspector had no warrant to enter the property and that he would not open the door. On another occasion, the occupant stated they were friends of the legal long-term occupier of the flat, just staying for a few days. On another, a long-term rental contract was produced. More often than not, no one answered the bell, even when signs of presence could be spotted, such as bath towels hanging from the balcony. (Fieldwork notes: observation of an inspector by one of the authors, Barcelona, May 2018)

This has been the daily routine of the inspectors who, in Barcelona, Paris and other cities, have been tasked with checking STRs suspected of lacking proper authorisation (i.e., a licence in Barcelona, an authorisation for change of use in Paris). Part of the enforcement work involves identifying the allegedly illegal units from thousands of online advertisements posted on STR platforms and identifying the physical or legal persons renting out those STR units (the hosts), as well as the owners of such units (who could be the same or different persons). Additionally, in densely built continental European cities, STRs often take place in apartment blocks, which make them even more difficult to identify. A simple address is not enough, as a building may contain dozens of apartments. Considering the lack of individualised platform data (or the huge limitations of the data provided by platforms; see below), this identification work has required specific intelligence and the creative combination of different sources, particularly at the beginning of the battle against illegal listings in the second half of the 2010s.

The first source of information can come from cross-referencing several national registers with online advertisements. In Paris, the housing database of the INSEE (French National Institute for Statistical Studies) allows the inspector to know, if they have a precise address, whether the property is a primary or secondary residence, which allows agents to operate a first filter:

> We look at the ads. If it's a second home and we can't find any change of use, then it's easy—it's illegal from day one! So we start a 'file' and we organise a visit to prove that the advert refers to a real apartment. (interview, BPLH inspector 1, April 2017)

National fiscal and tax databases shared with the Department of Housing can also be used to identify illegal STRs when STR operators declare their rental income to the national fiscal authorities but have not taken the necessary steps to apply for a change of use. However, these sources of information are only useful if the inspectors manage to match the ads with a precise and accurate address for the apartment, which is not always the case:

Even with a precise address, a floor and an ad, you can't be sure of finding the right apartment because you have four or more apartments on each floor. (interview, BPLH inspector 1, April 2017)

To remediate those uncertainties, the local administrations (and their inspectors) have developed other strategies. The second source of information stems from complaints by local residents. The Barcelona and Paris city governments have created phone and online channels for third parties to report suspected illegal STRs (as in Amsterdam and Berlin). In Barcelona, a communication campaign in three languages was launched in 2016, accompanied by a letter sent to the city's residents, urging them to help combat illegal tourist accommodation by reporting suspected STRs. In Paris, a reporting platform was opened on the City of Paris website dedicated to STRs: while complaints have mainly been about noise and nuisances, they did allow some illegal STRs to be identified. However, this reporting platform was criticised for encouraging snitching, so it was quickly closed to avoid political blame (interview, vice-chief of the BPLH, April 2017). Another channel was set up: the BPLH distributed a letter to condominium managers specifying the rules for STRs and the risks incurred in case of illegality, to discourage potential offenders and encourage citizens to report those addresses where changes of use had not been made (providing a link to a public database and map for verification).[8] On average, the BPLH received 600 reports every year (BPLH during fieldwork, May 2017).

In Barcelona and Madrid, where citizens have been actively mobilised around the STR issue, city authorities have been helped by residents' associations and activist networks who have proactively reported suspected illegalities.[9] In Paris, the ParisVSBnB citizen collective came very close to implementing this type of collaboration in 2019: the collective developed a web scraping code and offered to make it freely available to the BPLH and the cabinet of the Deputy Mayor for Housing (interview, co-founder of ParisVSBnB, autumn 2019). The latter did not follow up because of concerns with legal issues, considering that the battle and hunt for data had to be played out elsewhere—at the level of the platform itself (interview, BPLH officers, 2020).

The third source of information came later: in those cities that have put in place a registration and/or licencing system, online listings with a reference number could be checked against the relevant register, though this has been a time-consuming process. But STR hosts often voluntarily or involuntarily failed to display the compulsory number in the advertisement. This was a visible form of non-compliance that provided public officials with a rough measure of the degree of illegality of the local STR market (in respect to the registration rule). It also provided intelligence for physical controls, though with limits. In Paris, until Airbnb withdrew the listings without a registration number in 2021 (see section below and Chapter 6), about half of the STRs advertised on the platform did not display the compulsory registration number—way too many to be scrutinised by the 15 officers in charge of STR inspections. Even after the withdrawal of unregistered listings from the platform, a significant share still displayed a fake registration number, as reported by Parisian municipal employees in charge of the matter (interview, BPLH officer, July 2022).

The fourth source of intelligence has been online advertisements specifically flagged by employees tasked with screening individual listings on platforms (detailed in the next section). As explained by Parisian inspectors (spring 2017), scrutinising the photographs included in STR listings helps them understand whether a place looks like 'somebody's home' or whether it looks like an anonymous apartment, with standardised decoration and no personal items (thus possibly an unauthorised full-time STR). Furthermore, as explained by the Parisian BPLH inspectors (spring 2017) and the Barcelona inspector (May 2018), online listings do not show the exact address of a property, but only an approximate location with a pin on a map. Inspectors consequently have to walk around in the streets to search for visual clues that appear in online photographs to identify a possible STR (e.g., window shape, curtain colour, appearance of the entrance). As with other fields of inspection (Van de Walle and Raaphorst 2019), this informal search is helped by tacit knowledge, experience and tricks: for example, in Barcelona, inspectors looked for swimming suits and large beach towels drying on the balconies on a weekday, which may be a sign that tourists occupy a dwelling. As we observed with the Parisian BPLH inspectors during one of their rounds (spring 2017), one tactic has been to set up a stake-out in a café opposite a building containing a suspected STR in the early hours of the morning and await the arrival and departure of tourists with their suitcases. Once a tourist has been spotted, the agent will run and get to the entrance of the building just as the door opens. In this way, inspection agents have developed an informal know-how closely modelled on 'investigative police work' (interview, BPLH inspector 1, April 2017).

Control visits to a suspected STR unit are not announced in advance. As witnessed in Barcelona and Paris, once at the foot of a building, an inspector presses the buzzer of the flat to be visited, hoping that the occupants will reply. If the inspector manages to reach the apartment, and if the occupants do open the door, the plain-clothed inspector displays an identification card before asking them about the conditions under which they arrived at the property: Which platform or real estate agency was used to rent the property? What contact was made with the operator? How long is their stay? How much did the booking cost? Do they know the owner? In what capacity are they occupying the flat? Finally, they ask if they can take photographs of the premises, to prove to a judge later on that the targeted ad does indeed correspond to the visited accommodation. Occupants are invited to produce evidence to support their claims (e.g., a booking/financial transaction if they claim to be short-term visitors, a long-term rental contract if they purport to be tenants).

Often, there might be no answer or a refusal by the occupants to open the door. In Barcelona, inspectors do not have a warrant to enter a private property and have to stay at the door, which is not the case in Paris, where the agents are allowed to enter.[10] But as we have observed during fieldwork with BPLH officers (spring 2017), they have to bargain, by explaining to occupants that they are not themselves the target of the inspection and do not risk any fine. The inspectors explained to us that the simple fact of being inspected early in the morning, by an agent brandishing an official card from the municipal administration with legal provisions written on it, generally provoked a rather cooperative reaction. But some visitors who might have been briefed by the host would often close the door quickly, sometimes with a threatening tone.[11] This has made the inspectors' work quite hard, and in Paris, it is compulsory for them to go in pairs for safety reasons.

In some cities, housing/planning inspectors do benefit from the collaboration of other agencies with more powers: in Amsterdam, the fire brigade has the power to enter any premise and immediately shut down a housing unit if it does not comply with fire safety regulations, a technique that has been used to crack down on 'illegal hostels' (residential flats crammed with bunk beds for STRs to groups of travellers). The cooperation between different agencies or administrative departments was mentioned by several local authority interviewees (e.g., in Amsterdam, London, Milan and Paris) as an important ingredient in the effective enforcement of STR regulations. They noted, however, that achieving coordination between the services in charge of local tax, housing, business licencing, planning, environmental health, fire protection or the police is often difficult to organise in practice.

### 'If You Can't Find Us, You Can't Fine Us'

The heading, a sentence from Cox and Haar (2020:12), illustrates how the chances of success for street-level inspectors are made harder by the multiple tactics devised by the operators of illegal STRs to avoid detection or to make the burden of proof very difficult. As with other kinds of illegal uses of housing, these tactics include the informal management of guests; physical concealment (Kelling 2021; Shrestha et al. 2021;

Gurran et al. 2022); and in the context of platform intermediation, digital concealment (Leshinsky and Schatz 2018; Mermet 2021; Richon 2024).

The operators of STRs (hosts or their representative as conciergeries) may typically ask guests, when welcoming them into a flat, to *not* answer the bell or to tell inquisitive neighbours that they are friends visiting the host—behaviours that we witnessed during our observations of inspectors' rounds in Paris (spring 2017) and Barcelona (spring 2018). Additionally, over the past years, STR operators have removed the small key safe boxes that were once visibly present near the street-level entrance of apartment blocks and have started using less visible mechanisms for the handover of keys to guests (e.g., leaving them at a nearby café). Some also deliberately choose to rent out flats with less scrutiny, with no balcony or building manager (Richon 2024).

Furthermore, physical concealment overlaps with digital concealment. In cities where a time limit has been set up to cap occasional, non-professional STRs (type ii), like Paris or London, some operators of professional STRs (type i) seek to appear as type ii, deactivating a listing when bookings have reached the time limit, then recreating a new listing with slightly different photographs under a different name, on the same platform or another. To disguise their activity, hosts use false names, addresses and registration numbers; create several adverts for each flat rented out (to 'escape' the 120-day limit in Paris); temporarily block the advert when the political debate around STR is tense; or use platforms in combination with other booking channels that are less visible and leave no trace (Richon 2024). They also prepare for the event of an inspection by creating several separate STR accounts or false supporting documents (e.g., rental leases) or by using different types of rental leases that allow temporary rentals. In France, two types of rental contracts—the mobility lease (*bail mobilité*) and the civil lease (*bail civil*)—make it possible to rent short-term accommodation legally and without many constraints.[12] Such contracts are promoted by platforms and platform-friendly legal consultancy experts (i.e., LegalPlace) who provide guidance and templates, and they represent a legal loophole in the French STR regulation model. This is also the case in Barcelona, with medium-term rental contracts of less than a year. In other cases, a flat illegally rented out as an STR may be advertised as a series of independent rooms via different ads (in a city where individual room rental is allowed). This was a typical disguise strategy in Barcelona, where the city government estimated that at the end of 2020, 445 rooms advertised on digital platforms were in fact unlicenced STR flats.

Consequently, inspection efforts are painstaking: it takes tenacity, repeated visits, thorough observations and the accumulation of administrative forms to obtain the necessary evidence that will be accepted by courts as a valid proof of illegality. That evidence needs to demonstrate the repeated presence of fee-paying, short-term guests in a housing unit, in non-compliance with extant rules. Even in cities like Amsterdam, Paris or Barcelona that had comparatively well-resourced teams, interviewees stated that human resources were never going to be sufficient to comprehensively monitor such large numbers of STRs. Some of them preferred to insist on the symbolic and political role of enforcement activities in the hunt for illegal STRs: inspections and court cases have become a strong political weapon not only to enforce the rules, but to steer political debates and incentivise compliant behaviour. One interviewee, importantly, stressed that 'we're not in the same league as Airbnb, we're in a parallel world. We spend all our time controlling the hosts, but in fact we should be hitting the platform directly' (interview, vice-chief of BPLH, April 2017).

## The Pragmatic Politics of Court Trials and Sanctions: From Bricolage to the Institutionalisation of a Political Mode of Action

In the mid-2010s, the legal and juridical processes applied to suspected illegal STRs were more a matter of bricolage than a truly institutionalised policy. Because of the above-mentioned complexity of the enforcement tasks, some compromises had to be made at the political and administrative levels in order to prioritise the inspectors' work, with sometimes different perspectives that can generate tensions in their daily tasks. In Paris, elected officials and the directors of inspection departments have tended to steer their teams towards the search for 'big fish', that is, seemingly more problematic and morally reprehensible cases. This allows them to strongly denounce the dark side of STRs (and thus get political credit), while avoiding openly tackling small hosts looking for extra income. Foreign professional investors, real estate agencies and timeshare owners thus often made the headlines in the first court proceedings in 2015 and 2016.[13] Gradually, more sinister cases appeared: agents discovered some STRs hosting prostitution networks or slum landlords housing precarious families and illegal migrants, some of them organised by mafia-like networks. Those kinds of cases were given a high priority (interview and observations, BPLH officers, spring 2017).

In that sense, enforcement activities are at times used for public relation purposes when local governments want to be visibly seen to address the problem. Since 2015 the Parisian administration has put in place recurrent *opérations coups de poing* ('punch operations') targeting the most touristic areas (Montmartre, Marais, Les Halles) while inviting journalists to cover the events. During such inspection stints, municipal agents systematically verify all the apartments, knocking on all the doors in one delimited area to detect STRs and verify if they are legal. The goal is primarily symbolic, first to show the magnitude of the phenomenon. In 2016, six such operations were organised, 200 buildings visited, 4,500 dwellings inspected and 264 offences recorded, which meant that 6% of the inspected housing stock was identified as STRs (BPLH during fieldwork, May 2017). Second, those operations aim to send a message to illegal STR operators and to local residents, voters and the national government, that the City of Paris is strongly determined to enforce STR rules:

Here it's more quantitative work, for the politicians to show numbers, this is for television. The elected representatives wanted us to do it every month, but our boss refused, to organise things better. (interview, BPLH inspector 1, April 2017)

For us, the goal is to get the illegal hosts condemned at the trial, to set an example and show that the city government is addressing the issue. It's not the money from fines that motivates us. (interview, vice-chief of the BPLH, April 2017)

As political scientists and sociologists have shown, there are always 'pragmatic politics' involved in regulatory enforcement (Coslovsky et al. 2011), including room for exceptions and discretion. In the field, inspectors are confronted with uncertainty and constraints. They have to mobilise their moral judgement sensitively, to distinguish cases where the violation seems less morally reprehensible from cases where there is blatant evidence of repeated violations of the rules or of serious harm to people. This can lead to moral dilemmas:

An unemployed, divorced woman with a child to support. She and her sister inherited a large apartment. Her sister said, 'We'll rent it out'. This would enable her to finance her studies. She was in breach of the law, so I reported the matter to my boss, who told me we had to go to court. It made me sick. (interview, BPLH inspector 1, April 2017)

Once enforcement teams have gathered evidence that specific STRs violate some rules, it may take months or even years for the administrative or legal proceedings to be concluded, leading to a cessation order and/or a fine. But a judge can reject the case if the evidence is considered weak. Knowing that—and wary of the risk of appeals—public agents exercise discretion in deciding whether to pursue legal action based on the severity of the offence, the robustness of the gathered evidence, and the perceived chance of winning. Paris provides a powerful illustration of this. Since 2016 the local administration has sent between 100 and 200 cases to court per year against STR operators deemed illegal,[14] with a significant increase in 2022. In that year, 420 pending cases were processed, following the three-year suspension of hearings due to the Cali Apartments court case (see Chapter 4),[15] leading to a total of €14 million in fines. Most cases deal with STR providers operating more than 120 days per year without the proper authorisation of change of use. But the provision of evidence that will be accepted by judges has become increasingly difficult.

By law, a unit is considered used for residential purposes if it was used for this purpose on 1 January 1970 (the date of the last comprehensive national property survey in France),[16] unless a change of use has been recorded after that date (Wallut 2015:70). To prove a housing misuse, the municipal administration must bring proof that the unit in question was residential in 1970, based on a form (H2) that property owners completed in 1970. This apparently trivial administrative requirement has become the basis for a substantial number of lost court cases. Since 2019–2020, courts have upheld an increasingly strict interpretation of the validity of that form: the presence of a date after 1970, the lack of date or of rental values and the illegibility of part of the content have been cited as reasons to dismiss its validity. As reported by one of the officers of the BPLH: 'Before, we used to present clues of the residential use, a few years before . . . like in 1969, a little bit later . . . like in 1973' (interview, BPLH officer, July 2022). The new, stricter interpretation has opened a huge legal loophole, since the Paris administration estimates that one-third of the H2 forms for Parisian properties is in conformity, one-third is not, and one-third went missing before the forms were digitalised (Richon 2022). Between 2020 and 2022, almost 50% of the court cases were lost by the municipality because of non-conformity of the H2 property form (Richon 2022). As a result, officials now carefully examine their cases, based on the robustness of the form and sometimes refrain from sending a case to court.

If an STR is judged to be illegal, the fines imposed on individual hosts vary hugely (in our sample, as of 2022 the fines applied to individual operators per listing ranged from approximately €2,500–4,000 in Lisbon, €20,000 in Amsterdam, €30,000 in Barcelona, and €50,000 in Paris—€80,000 in case of dissimulation—up to €500,000 in Berlin). The judges in charge of assessing STR-related cases can also exercise a degree of discretion in the application of rules, based on the circumstances of the suspect and whether non-compliance is 'justifiable' or 'non-justifiable' (Alterman and Calor 2020). Our observation of various hearings conducted in May 2018 at the responsible court in Paris showed that judges do take individual circumstances into account when assessing the good faith of hosts (fieldwork observations, Tribunal de Grande Instance, Paris, May 2017).

After a few years of trial and error, the legal and judicial actions described above have become institutionalised on two levels. Internally, procedures have become more routinised, and the expertise acquired by public agents has made it possible to achieve a high level of efficiency in identifying and checking properties and compiling cases for submission to the relevant court. In Paris, while in 2015 the Public Prosecutor and judges were unable to keep up with the influx of cases (interview, vice-chief of BPLH, April 2017), the processing of BPLH cases has now reached its cruising speed. Procedures have also become institutionalised, and the City of Paris is now a stakeholder in the court trial:

> In the past, we gave the file to the Prosecutor but the City was not involved. Now, since 2016, it's the City directly that puts together and defends the case. We [BPLH] put together the case, we show it to the Legal Affairs Department [of the City of Paris], which checks it, and the City's lawyers come and defend the cases. . . . We go and attend the sessions at the Tribunal. (interview, vice-chief of BPLH, April 2017)

On the other side, STR owners or operators often appeal against such decisions with the help of specialised lawyers.[17] For some non-professional individual hosts, fines have had a devastating impact. In Barcelona, an association named Citizens Affected by the Conflict between the City Council and Airbnb was created to represent 300 individuals who received fines of up to €60,000 for occasionally renting out their primary homes on Airbnb. They have campaigned against such sanctions on the following grounds:

> We are not mafia. We are not speculators. We are not 'vulture funds'. We are not big property owners. We are not companies. . . . We are residents of Barcelona, individuals, who rented their home (usual residence) sporadically, and in some cases, only placed an ad. We did it out of economic necessity and not for speculative purposes. . . . [We] have been disproportionately sanctioned as a result of the conflict between Barcelona City Council and Airbnb. (ACABA 2022)

Unusually, this association has not just fought against the city council's decision to fine them but has also criticised Airbnb for misleading 'normal citizens' by not making it clear to them, at the stage of setting up an online listing, that they needed to comply with local rules. In an unprecedented move in Europe, they have lodged a legal challenge against Airbnb, accusing it of 'let[ting] citizens publish their flat without a license' (ACABA 2022).

Interviewees from local authorities reported that for a minority of operators, fines were not always a deterrent. As noted by Gurran et al. (2022:26), because of the high profits to be made from short-term (as opposed to long-term) rental arrangements, 'unscrupulous operators familiar with regulatory frameworks . . . were known to continually reoffend, preferring to pay a fine and resume operations'. According to interviewees from the Barcelona city administration, by 2021, small-scale STR operators or individual hosts who rented their home occasionally without a licence had mostly been scared off by the first waves of fines in 2016–2017, but a small minority of multi-property operators had come up with cunning strategies of concealment and fraud to continue operating illegal STRs (estimated to represent a few hundred illegal units). The same observation was made by the Parisian BPLH officers we interviewed in 2022. In both cities, inspectors noted that unsurprisingly, any toughening of the rules and accompanying processes of regulatory enforcement led to more 'creativity' from those determined to flaunt them. An example from Barcelona included people posing as tenants (sometimes connected with organised criminal networks) who signed several long-term rental contracts and, unbeknownst to the landlords, fraudulently turned the dwellings into intensive STRs. This led the Barcelona city government to modify the system of fines, lowering those for minor infractions and increasing those for severe cases of 'multi-infractions'. In the same vein, Parisian BPLH agents explained that they were not always able to trace the true identity of STR hosts, or at least to establish responsibility and bring the (real) offenders to trial. This was particularly the case when it came to suspected 'slum landlords', as we were able to observe during the inspection of shabby flats in Belleville (spring 2017), crowded with migrant workers who did not know exactly who owned the dwellings.

While most enforcement efforts have targeted the provider's side, some local governments have also tried to heighten awareness among consumers. The glossy design, ubiquity and user rating systems of platforms give a varnish of trust and apparent legality, which means unsuspecting consumers do not ask themselves whether the existence of, or access to, the service they are about to purchase is 'legal'. In Barcelona, this was vividly illustrated by a slogan written on posters displayed by the city government in touristic neighbourhoods in 2016: 'Just because this bed has 2,519 positive reviews doesn't mean it's legal'. This was part of a communication campaign to alert visitors to the illegal nature of many STRs and caution them to verify the status of their holiday accommodation via an online official register.[18] This attempt by a local government to address the consumers of platform-mediated STRs was, at the time of writing, a rather unique one within our sample of cities—though awareness-raising actions by activists had attempted to do the same.

## 'DATA WARS', PLATFORM COMPLIANCE AND DIY PRACTICES OF DATA PRODUCTION

### The Contentious Release of Individualised Data by Platforms

Local government interviewees all stated that in order to tackle the difficulties with the detection of illegal STRs in the physical world, some form of action, if not full cooperation, from platforms is essential for effective enforcement. First in the USA and then in Europe,[19] data have been one of the major bones of contention between platforms and cities and the object of intense negotiations, new legislation and lawsuits.

First, the data held by digital platforms are a key source that would allow local governments to assess whether operators comply with extant regulations. Until recently, most platforms did not agree to supply public authorities with listings of non-anonymised data without a court decision, though aggregate data have sometimes been released—not helpful for enforcement purposes.[20] In Europe, pressures on platforms for data sharing have come first from *tax authorities*, both national and/or local (Spain, Belgium, Italy, the Czech Republic) and increasingly from the EU (see Chapter 7). In Brussels, a regional ordinance of 2016 requires intermediaries (platforms) to communicate detailed data on individual operators and bookings to the regional tax office. Airbnb received several €10,000 fines for not transferring the required data and lodged a court case against the regional ordinance in front of the Belgian Constitutional Court, which turned to the Court of Justice of the EU (CJEU) in November 2020 to ask about compliance with EU law. In Italy, Decree 50/2017 requires intermediaries (platforms) to communicate data on individual (non-business) STR operators and their activities to national tax authorities and to automatically deduct (and transmit), via the platform, a 21%

flat tax on the rental income generated. Airbnb refused to comply and started legal proceedings to contest the law. In September 2019 the Italian Council of State referred the matter to the CJEU. In both cases, the European Court (respectively in April and December 2022) ruled in favour of the transmission of fiscal data (but rebutted the obligation for Airbnb to establish a fiscal representative in Italy). However, it should be noted that EU data protection legislation prohibits the transfer of data obtained for one purpose by one public administration to another for another purpose: data obtained by tax authorities usually cannot be transferred to urban planning or housing departments.

Several city governments have explicitly requested platforms to give them individualised data listings for the implementation of their STR regulations, through negotiations (a working group negotiating with platforms in Barcelona), formal legal requests in court (Berlin) or the backing of a new national law that requires platforms to release such data to local governments (Paris). In several cities like Vienna or Berlin, the legal requests made by city governments for systematic data sharing had not succeeded yet at the time of writing—hindered by strict requirements from Airbnb as a precondition for releasing any data.[21] Interviewed city representatives explained that the national Airbnb office, when contacted, referred them back to the company's European headquarters in Dublin and invoked the EU *E-Commerce Directive* and *General Data Protection Regulation* (GDPR) as impediments to data sharing, though the latter need not prevent such sharing (see Chapter 7).

Eventually, only two city governments in our sample managed to secure an agreement to obtain regular, detailed listings from platforms, after several years of negotiations. In Barcelona, in May 2018 Airbnb agreed to supply a monthly list of detailed host data (Ajuntament de Barcelona 2018), but interviewees from the Department of Urban Planning explained that a significant portion of the data was incomplete and reported that in 2020 approximately 60–70% of listings displayed missing or incorrect addresses. In France, since December 2019 and according to a national law (ELAN, voted in 2018), all platforms have to supply, on an annual basis, detailed data for 'full unit' STRs (types i and ii) in cities that have introduced a registration scheme, including Paris. The list should include the host's name, address and status of the property (primary or secondary home), STR registration number, and number of days during which the unit was rented out. According to an interviewee at the French Ministry of Housing in 2017, the law was opposed by Airbnb and other platforms, who later lobbied to postpone its implementing decree. While the first version of the decree included the obligation for platforms to communicate the uniform resource locator (URL) of each listing, such key information had disappeared in the final version (APUR 2020:9).

Since then, platforms' compliance with data transmission has been variable. At the beginning, several of them simply did not comply (detailed in Chapter 6). In Paris, nine platforms, including large ones such as Abritel (HomeAway), Trip Advisor and Booking, initially failed to transfer data, or transferred data of extremely poor quality, leading the city government to sue them. Booking was condemned to a €1.2 million fine in October 2021 (Ville de Paris 2021) but Abritel (HomeAway) was acquitted in November 2023, revealing once again the key role of courts in the enforcement process. As we observed in the office of BPLH in January 2020, Airbnb-supplied data were initially rather incomplete but have improved over time, especially after the platform was fined in 2021 for displaying illegal ads (interview, officers from BPLH, July 2022). To improve the overall quality of data transmitted by platforms and facilitate data exchange, in 2022 the French Ministries of Economy and Housing implemented a six-month pilot project to test an application programming interface (API) with five French cities and five large platforms (Direction Générale des Entreprises 2022). The City of Paris, however, did not join the pilot due to its contentious relationship with platforms (interview, officers from BPLH, July 2022). Nationally, the pilot was deemed successful; in July 2023, a generalisation of the tested API was integrated into a draft national bill dealing with digital security and regulation (Le Monde 2023).

In the European context, the French law was perceived as a milestone regarding the transmission of platform data to local governments for STR regulation. However, BPLH officials also underlined its practical limitations for enforcement (interview, January 2020). In particular, the lack of a URL and of a verified name for the host significantly complicates the cross-checking of platform data with the municipal STR register and with real-world apartments. This points to one of the major drawbacks of platform data: they are based on self-declarations from each host at the moment of posting an STR advertisement, with no official documents required (e.g., proof of property ownership).

## Turning the Platform into an Enforcement Tool

As an alternative or an addition to the transfer of individualised data, governments have tried to use the corporate platforms' central position in the market as an enforcement tool. This means convincing or constraining private companies to participate in regulatory enforcement by deleting illegal STRs, introducing specific requirements in the online form (e.g., a compulsory field for the registration number) and blocking the listings rented for longer than authorised (in those cities with a time cap).

In several cities of our sample, interviewees reported that platforms have sometimes agreed to remove a *limited number of listings* about which public authorities have provided evidence of an illegality, though not always.[22] The removal of large numbers of listings was a much more contentious matter. The city of Vienna prohibits STRs in its municipal housing stock: while most platforms removed public housing units from their websites after they were requested to, it took until the autumn of 2021 for Airbnb to commit to do so (The Local AT 2021). In Barcelona, in 2017 the city government made an agreement with Booking, Homeaway, Tripadvisor and Rentalia, which committed to remove unlicenced STR listings from their websites. Following intense negotiations, on 29 May 2018 the Deputy Mayor for Urban Planning announced that an agreement had been made with Airbnb involving the removal of 2,577 illegal ads from its website, as well as a commitment to require hosts to include their STR licence number in the online listing and to accept that their personal data may be communicated to public authorities (Rodríguez 2018).[23] Yet in December 2020, the city government still identified more than a thousand illegal listings on Airbnb and formally requested the platform to remove them (La Vanguardia 2020).

In the cities where an STR registration or authorisation scheme has been set up, authorities have asked platforms to include an online field requiring hosts to enter their registration number. Some platforms agreed to implement that measure rapidly; others took time to do so or did not. In November 2016 the Barcelona city government started proceedings to fine Airbnb and Homeaway €600,000 each for repeatedly advertising STR listings without a licence number. But the process to enforce those fines is complex, long and uncertain if the platforms' headquarters are located in another country. Both platforms subsequently introduced a field for the registration number a few years later. In Paris, between 2017 and 2021 Airbnb disregarded the obligation for listings to display a compulsory registration number: at the end of 2020, Cox and Haar (2020) estimated that 60% of the Airbnb offer in Paris (and 80% in Berlin, which had a similar requirement) did not display the required registration number. To force platform compliance, in 2019 the Paris city government started legal proceedings to fine Airbnb an unprecedented €12.5 million for advertising 1,010 unregistered listings. In February 2021, under increasing pressure, the company announced its intention to suspend listings without a registration number (Airbnb 2021a). This happened a few months later, in July 2021, on the day on which the Paris Court of Justice fined Airbnb €8 million

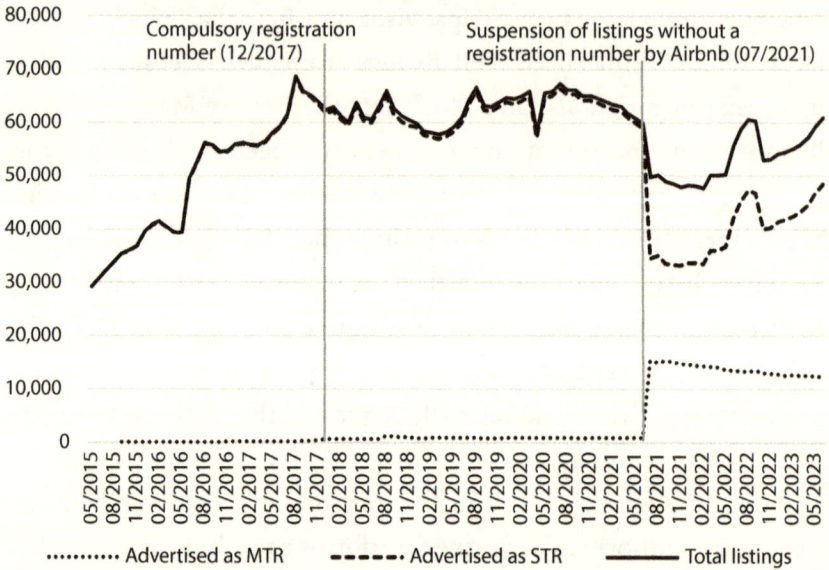

**Figure 20.** Paris, number of Airbnb listings (2015–2023): total, short-term rentals and medium-term rentals. *Source:* Authors' calculations based on data from Inside Airbnb (2023).

for having displayed illegal listings online for four years. This led to an unprecedented drop in the total number of listings advertised in the city, as shown in Figure 20 (−17%, around 10,000 listings removed in one day). We can assume that part of the remaining listings were converted from STRs into medium-term rentals. Since the latter do not fall under STR restrictions, these listings became 'legal' online ads, which has created a huge uncertainty about the real nature of the rentals behind their online facade.

Where a time cap has been set up to distinguish between occasional home-sharing and professional STRs, some city governments have managed to secure an agreement with large platforms, such as Airbnb and Homeaway, to automatically suspend listings that exceed the threshold—of 120 days in Paris, 90 days in London and 60 days in Amsterdam until 2019. However, after the Amsterdam city government voted to reduce the cap from 60 to 30 days in 2018, Airbnb (2019) refused to apply the new limit of 30 days per year, which led to the suspension of the agreement previously signed between the company and the city government. By contrast, in Berlin platforms do not enforce the 90-day cap for the STR of second homes, nor do they provide any data on the corresponding listings to the city authorities.

These various episodes show the central role of platforms as both a *vehicle* for enforcement and the *object* of enforcement, in the implementation of STR regulations. In the EU legal context, in line with the provisions of the 2000 *E-Commerce Directive* and 2022 *Digital Services Act*, platforms do not have an obligation to monitor the content of the listings they publish (see Chapter 7) and therefore do not verify the validity of the registration numbers supplied by hosts. There is no integrated 'pass-through registration' system in place (unlike a few rare cases in the USA).[24] Platforms merely encourage hosts to comply with local rules—Airbnb has, for instance, set up dedicated web pages on 'responsible hosting' that give an overview of the regulations applying to STRs in specific countries, regions and cities, with a disclaimer.[25] However, platform representatives argue that they cannot be held liable for illegal listings and that hosts are legally responsible for understanding and complying with applicable rules. This explains why platforms continue to publish illegal listings with invalid registration numbers. Cross-checks have to be carried out by the responsible public administration against the relevant register. A platform can only be held liable for illegal content if it fails to remove listings after being presented with evidence of illegality.

## 'Datactivism' for, and from, Local Governments

To circumvent the lack of access to platform-owned data as well as the limitation on platform-enforced rules, interviewees mentioned a number of DIY strategies that local authorities have deployed to get a better sense of the overall quantity, geography and typology of the STR supply.

The relevance of such data is not just for enforcement: data are a crucial political resource for claiming legitimacy to govern the phenomenon at stake. Data also help governments whose regulation has been contested in court to prove the size and scope of the STR phenomenon in a given place and therefore to justify that their regulation was 'legitimate' and 'proportional', which are two key criteria under EU law (see Chapter 7).

DIY data collection mainly relies on *web scraping*, the process of automatically extracting mass data from a platform website. This can be done manually, but more often is done through the use of software or of a custom-made script/program that harvests the data in an automated way.[26] A few notable 'data activists' are behind the origin of STR data scraping. In 2013 and 2014, in particular, Tom Slee (http://tomslee .net), an activist based in Canada, and Murray Cox (founder of Inside Airbnb, https://insideairbnb.com/), a community and data activist based in New York City, independently started to compile data on the growth of Airbnb-mediated STRs in their respective areas. They aimed to reveal the extent of a phenomenon they considered harmful to cities, and to help citizens, campaigners and researchers who do not have access to the data owned by the platforms. The two activists quickly expanded their data analytics activities to many other cities, helped by others who have used their open-source code and open data. Over the years, Inside Airbnb has become a key source of reference for many campaigners interested in STR regulation, as well as for governments.[27] Murray Cox, its founder, was in contact with half of the local governments covered in this book (Amsterdam, Barcelona, some London boroughs, Paris, Vienna). His data were published in reports by public administrations (London, Paris), used internally by teams of the city administration to compare with the data scraped in-house (Barcelona), to assess the effects of specific events (Vienna) or to prepare for court test cases (Berlin).

A few city governments (e.g., in Amsterdam and Barcelona) have done web scraping in-house or have contracted employees to scrutinise each listing to find details that would help inspectors localise a dwelling used as an STR. In 2016 the Barcelona City Council temporarily hired 40 'visualisers' to perform such detailed online searches, who scanned 17,000 ads on 140 websites in three years (Ajuntament de Barcelona 2019). A few years later, the Inspection Department reported that in-house scraping of data on large platforms had been routinised, carried out once a month. The team developed an internal protocol to sift through, analyse, sort and set aside the ads that could potentially be illegal, as well as an elaborate system of mapping and inspection follow-up. By contrast, some local authorities have commissioned commercial firms to do web scraping and analyse the data for them. AirDNA is one of the largest data analytics companies that scrape data available on the Airbnb and VRBO (HomeAway) websites for a variety of clients. Smaller European start-up companies have also offered STR data scraping and monitoring services to city governments (e.g., the now defunct Spanish company Talk and Code, commissioned by some London boroughs). Other scholars working on the regulatory responses to STRs in the USA have shown that some city governments have turned to hiring new private companies, such as Host Compliance, now part of Granicus to locate illegal STRs using tailored software that monitors listings (see also Gurran and Sadowski 2019 on Australia). In our fieldwork, we have not heard (yet) of such a strategy being used in European cities, though this could change given the increasing trend towards the contracting of private data analytics companies by local governments for enforcement purposes (Barry Born 2021).

## CONCLUSION

The analysis of regulatory enforcement activities in the European cities under study shows that many of the practical challenges met by city authorities in seeking to grasp and legalise a regulated STR market, on the one hand, and to control STRs to detect illegalities, on the other, are similar to those they face for other types of building and housing uses. Insufficient resources for the control of suspected illegalities are compounded by various informal practices of evasion by operators of illegal units (guest behaviour management, physical and sometimes digital concealment). While some of them bluntly operate illegally, others have found and exploited regulatory blind spots, grey zones and loopholes.

New challenges have also arisen from the *digitally mediated* nature of STR practices: for almost 10 years, platforms have been withholding STR data that are crucial for the development of informed public policy choices, the design of new regulations, and the monitoring of compliance. This has led some critics to argue that 'it's not a stretch to say that the business model of STR platforms . . . rely on shielding illegal listings' (Cox and Haar 2020:12). While some European governments (national or local), after years of negotiations and legal battles, have succeeded in getting platforms to partially transfer individualised data, suspend some illegal listings and include STR registration numbers, the relationships between cities and platforms remain fraught, oscillating between collaboration and conflict. Contention around access to platform data is one of the key elements in the complex relationships between platforms and (local) governments (see Chapter 6). Some city authorities have thus relied on a variety of more or less formal, imperfect, time-consuming DIY processes of digital data assembly (Colomb and Moreira de Souza 2024).

While there is still a notable degree of experimentation and bricolage in regulatory enforcement in the digital age, and many shared challenges between cities, we have shown significant differences between European cities. Thanks to a combination of financial and human resource availability, political will and court decisions, *some* governments have significantly increased their control and enforcement capacity and have managed to reduce the illegal STR offer, though at a high cost. When implemented, regulations have produced effects (presented in Chapter 2), as a result of hosts removing their listings, or of the withdrawal of illegal listings by platforms and sanctions on illegal hosts. These are not insignificant achievements in cities marked by an acute housing availability and affordability crisis. They are, above all, important symbolic results for city governments trying to signal pro-active policies and show that they can fight against transnational plat-forms. However, for many critics of STRs (such as grassroots campaigns and the hotel industry), those enforcement efforts are not enough, either because an illegal offer subsists or because the legal offer is deemed too big due to laissez-faire and even supportive regulations.

Regulatory approaches and their enforcement outcomes have become a matter of mobilisation from all kinds of STR-related interest groups, to which we turn in the next chapter. There is more at stake than just 'solving' the STR problem itself and implementing rules effec-tively. Enforcement is also about the staging of political power over property owners and over private firms—the political capacity to push forward symbolic decisions that embody the political regulation of multinational corporations in Europe. Conversely, on the platforms' side, what is at stake is not just the transfer of data on STR listings to public authorities, but also challenges to their power based on data ownership and information asymmetry.

# 6

# PLATFORM POWER, GRASSROOTS MOBILISATIONS AND POLITICAL CLIENTELES

<hr>

THIS CHAPTER SHIFTS from the emergence and enforcement of STR regulations to the interest group politics around those rules. For almost a decade now, corporate platforms, hosts' associations, organisations of property owners and property managers, residents' associations, social movements and the hotel industry have engaged with governments and courts to (re)shape the STR regulatory environment in directions favourable to their own interests and values. This chapter deals with these actors, their alliances and conflicts, their political activities, and the effects of these activities on STR regulations and on urban governance more broadly. Moving from regulations to governance, it highlights what happens 'around' national and local governments, which are not the sole masters of the game. What impact has the introduction of STR regulations had on business and grassroots actors and their relationships? Have new groups emerged and contributed to shaping STR market regulation in the long run?

What has been the political relevance of corporate platforms, given their quasi-monopolistic economic position?

The answer is threefold. First, we demonstrate that platforms have, in fact, been part of a broader, fragmented, but networked and highly contentious political space. Interest groups have been mobilising on the opposite sides of the STR struggle, lobbying regulators and challenging them in courts. This has nurtured legal instability and continues to do so. Second, this instability has especially been fuelled by and beneficial to corporate platforms and 'short-term rentiers' organisations which have become powerful actors in European cities. They have operated as multi-level policy entrepreneurs attempting to shape their regulatory environment while ignoring or contesting unwanted rules. Third, however, the political strength of platforms and their connected groups, as well as their strategies, has differed in European cities, thus shaping different types of power relationships between regulators and markets, leaving urban governments with uneven political capacity to advance their own agenda and steer STRs.

The chapter shows that platforms have been able to establish relatively collaborative relationships with the governments of cities from World 1 (including Milan)—where homeowners and property managers have an important economic and political weight and where the STR market seems dominated by large operators—while organising part of civil society in their favour. This has not been the case in the cities from World 2 (including Paris), where the market was more dispersed and where local governments have remained relatively autonomous from other stakeholders (platforms, homeowners, grassroots movements), nor in cities from World 3 (including Barcelona), where grassroots movements have played a more important role (despite the fact that the market is mainly shaped by large and important multi-listings operators). The comparative systematisation of this result supports the idea that platform capitalism has not produced the same political effects everywhere, depending on institutions, organisations and market structures, at the local and national levels, as described in Chapter 3.

More broadly, the chapter looks at the reconfiguration of the social, economic and political space around STRs and housing. In relation to the general argument of the book and our model of regulation, it allows us to grasp the *political effects of the adopted regulations* on the positioning and the relationships of the actors involved (as an outcome of the processes studied in Chapters 4 and 5). It also specifies how, in turn, the relationships between actors affect the processes of *politicisation*, *agenda-setting* (Chapter 4) and *implementation* (Chapter 5). In addition, although the question of the quantitative effects of regulations on the STR and housing markets is not directly investigated in the book, it is touched upon here to the extent that the actors (both governments and STR operators) themselves think about, exploit and communicate about the potential or perceived effects of regulations, presented as positive or negative. The chapter thus broadens our understanding of regulation, which concerns not only regulatory tools, their political justification and their enforcement, but also their effects on the strategic fields of action of economic, political and social stakeholders.

## A MULTI-LEVEL, CONTENTIOUS AND INCREASINGLY CONNECTED POLITICAL SPACE

STR interest groups are understood here as all the formal and informal organisations who have mobilised to influence the public debate and the policy-making process around STR regulation—from a quasi-monopolistic multinational company such as Airbnb (which operates 84% of the listings in our sample)[1] to a small and informal association of neighbours. While a number of studies have focused on platform companies and host groups and their repertoires of collective action (Ferreri and Sanyal 2018; van Doorn 2020; Yates 2023, 2025), we contend that regulation must be understood by considering the whole space of political action and contentious politics around STR rules in a comparative perspective (see Boon et al. 2019 and McNeill 2016 for a similar argument). Figure 21 illustrates the spaces of contention in Barcelona, Paris and Milan between 2015 (when the first rules were elaborated) and 2022.

In addition to state actors at various tiers of government, two broad sets of actors have confronted each other on opposite sides of the STR regulatory struggle. They have pushed for, or against, stricter rules; they have produced opposed narratives, made claims about 'rights' and even contested 'truths' regarding STRs. These actors are numbered in Figure 21, and their coalitions are circled in grey. On one side, the hotel industry (3), residents' groups and housing and tourism-related social movements (4) were at the origin of the politicisation of STRs and have contributed to the adoption of stricter rules in a number of cities (as demonstrated in Chapters 3 and 4). Sometimes they have joined forces in an 'unlikely alliance' (identified by dark grey circles in the figure), to which we will return later in this chapter. But STR politicisation has not ended there and has subsequently been reshaped through a backlash from what we call the *platform-rentiers bloc* (light grey circles) of actors extracting land rent and value from STRs. This bloc includes corporate platforms (5) along with various kinds of short-term rentiers organisations,[2] namely professional STR operators and property managers (1), hosts' associations and home-sharing clubs (2). When city and regional governments passed new rules or planned to do so, those groups directed their efforts to oppose stricter public regulation. Since then, every regulatory change, or prospective change, has triggered rounds of mobilisations from both opponents and supporters of the limitations put on the STR market. By contrast, pro-sharing organisations (6) have played a more limited role: while they were present in the STR debate in the early 2010s, they withdrew from it to the extent that the market shifted away from the sharing economy ideal they defended in the first place (e.g., in Milan; see Chapter 4). The exception to this

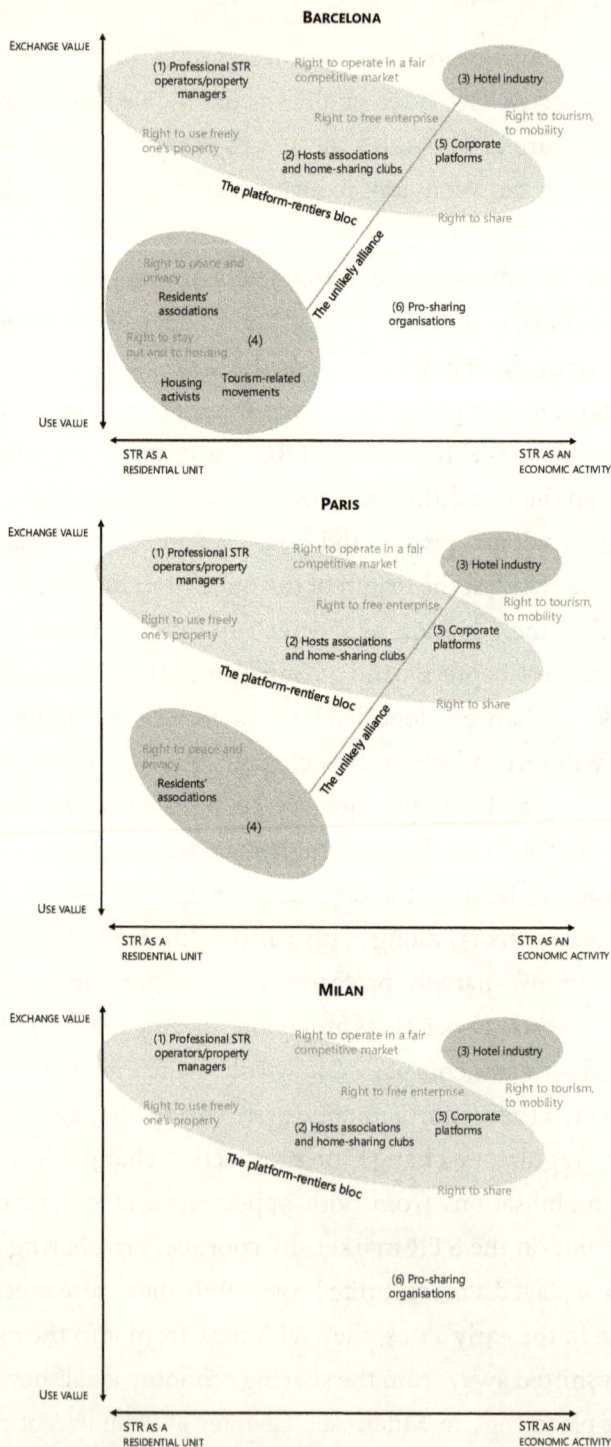

**BARCELONA**

EXCHANGE VALUE

(1) Professional STR operators/property managers

Right to operate in a fair competitive market

(3) Hotel industry

Right to tourism, to mobility

Right to use freely one's property

Right to free enterprise

(2) Hosts associations and home-sharing clubs

(5) Corporate platforms

*The platform-rentiers bloc*

Right to share

Right to peace and privacy

Residents' associations

*The unlikely alliance*

(6) Pro-sharing organisations

Right to stay put and to housing

(4)

Housing activists

Tourism-related movements

USE VALUE

STR AS A RESIDENTIAL UNIT

STR AS AN ECONOMIC ACTIVITY

**PARIS**

EXCHANGE VALUE

(1) Professional STR operators/property managers

Right to operate in a fair competitive market

(3) Hotel industry

Right to tourism, to mobility

Right to use freely one's property

Right to free enterprise

(2) Hosts associations and home-sharing clubs

(5) Corporate platforms

*The platform-rentiers bloc*

Right to share

Right to peace and privacy

Residents' associations

*The unlikely alliance*

(4)

USE VALUE

STR AS A RESIDENTIAL UNIT

STR AS AN ECONOMIC ACTIVITY

**MILAN**

EXCHANGE VALUE

(1) Professional STR operators/property managers

Right to operate in a fair competitive market

(3) Hotel industry

Right to free enterprise

Right to tourism, to mobility

Right to use freely one's property

(2) Hosts associations and home-sharing clubs

(5) Corporate platforms

*The platform-rentiers bloc*

Right to share

(6) Pro-sharing organisations

USE VALUE

STR AS A RESIDENTIAL UNIT

STR AS AN ECONOMIC ACTIVITY

**Figure 21.** Local spaces of contention in Barcelona, Paris and Milan in the second half of the 2010s. *Source*: Authors.

are small initiatives that have emerged to develop new forms of *platform cooperativism,* as a response to the transformation of the sharing economy into platform capitalism explored in Chapter 1 (Scholz and Schneider 2016), the most well-known in the field of STRs in Europe being Fairbnb (https://fairbnb.coop/).[3]

The contentious political space of STRs is characterised by clashing material interests, values and narratives everywhere, but their configuration differs depending on the city. STR struggles have remained highly embedded in local jurisdictions and configurations of actors, as well as in housing and STR market structures that influence the economic and political weight of the various stakeholders. As a result, the political space around the STR market and its regulation has remained locally differentiated from city to city, or rather between Worlds 1, 2 and 3 in our typology. Figure 21 shows the sharp differences in the presence and strength of pro-STR restriction voices (introduced in Chapter 4). In Barcelona, they have brought together the hotel industry with housing and tourism-related social movements and residents' associations. In Paris, residents' associations have been moderately present, along with a vocal hotel industry. Finally, in Milan, the hotel sector has for a long time been the only organised group asking for limitations on the STR market. Similar differences were observed between the three cities when considering the discourses, narratives and claims present in the public sphere. While in Barcelona and Paris, the protection of housing and residents' rights have been defended in the public arena and somehow supported by the municipal governments, this has been largely absent from the Milanese debate (until the recent changes in 2022–2023 described in Chapter 4). By contrast, in all three cities, the platform-rentiers bloc has been present, partially fuelled by corporate platforms and their strategies of mobilisation of hosts.

Differences in the types of actors present (or not) in each city, as well as in the intensity of regulation, help us understand the uneven levels of contention between cities, as well as the power relations between these groups and between them and governmental actors. Conflicts have been more intense in Barcelona and, to a lesser extent, in Paris, where interest groups have pushed regulations in opposite directions. Disagreements have been much softer in Milan, where a light regulatory system and the absence of strong housing and residents' movements around STRs have left the platform-rentiers bloc with limited opposition apart from the hotel industry. Similarly, local government political agendas (see Chapter 4) were more inclined to support some groups and grievances at the expense of others: this has shaped the room for manoeuvre and political strength of different actors to influence policy-making.

Notwithstanding their differences, these contentious local political spaces have, in recent years, become more *interconnected* (between cities, levels, groups and countries in Europe), as well as more *homogeneous in terms of dominant clashing narratives, claims, and repertoires of action*. This has been due to two major processes: the rescaling of political action and multi-level judicialisation. First, interest groups have increasingly been mobilising simultaneously at multiple levels of government. Corporate platforms have been extremely agile at navigating jurisdictions, but STR operators, hotel industry representatives and city governments themselves have also created or strengthened regional, national and European networks to lobby around STR regulation. The professional associations of the hotel industry have used their pre-existing multi-level networks, while new groups representing STR operators have created links from scratch. Starting from the local and going towards the national and the European levels (the latter analysed in detail in Chapter 7), interest groups have developed similar narratives and claims, repertoires of action and sometimes alliances.

Second, contention has partially shifted from the political to the judicial terrain, from the world of elected politicians and public officials to that of courts, lawyers and judges. Interest groups have engaged in litigation against both regulations and each other; have dragged out court cases over time and have appealed to all possible levels. Journalists have at times referred to an STR 'legal guerrilla' (Schwyter 2018) of overlapping and mutually influencing court cases. To provide an example, in Paris between 2017 and 2019 there were three major legal actions: by the hotel association (at the time called AHTOP) against Airbnb for non-compliance with the French real estate intermediation law; by two operators of STRs declared illegal (Cali Apartments) against regulation by the City of Paris; and from the City of Paris against Airbnb for non-compliance with the compulsory municipal STR registration scheme. All of these actions lasted for years and went through several court jurisdictions, and several of them were referred to the Court of Justice of the EU for a final verdict (see Chapter 7). Judicialisation has, everywhere, brought about delays and uncertainties in the implementation of regulations. Along with the enforcement difficulties described in Chapter 5, this has formed the second common challenge to the implementation of STR rules, despite the regulatory variety across cities and countries. As demonstrated in Chapter 7, judicialisation at the EU level has also set important precedents for local regulatory initiatives.

In the remainder of the chapter, we explore the political and legal activities of each type of interest group in more detail.

## CORPORATE PLATFORMS AS MULTI-LEVEL POLICY ENTREPRENEURS

### The Growth of a (Differential) Platform 'Infrastructural Power'

In the platform-rentiers bloc, corporate platforms have occupied a nodal position backed by billionaire investors, skilled lobbyists and global policy strategists, as analysed by a number of researchers (McNeill 2016; Pollman and Barry 2017; Stabrowski 2017; Sharp 2018; Ferreri and Sanyal 2018; Boon et al. 2019; van Doorn 2020; Artioli 2020; Aguilera et al. 2021; Yates 2023, 2025). Altogether, as noted by legal scholars Pollman and Barry (2017), corporate platforms have operated since their emergence as 'regulatory entrepreneurs'—a concept that reminds us that platforms are not against regulation per se. They know that regulation is inevitable on the one hand, and necessary on the other: state regulation ensures market stability through the allocation and protection of property rights, the coordination of competition and the establishment of trust procedures (Beckert 2009). In an interview given in 2014 to *The Atlantic* magazine, Airbnb CEO Brian Chesky emphasised the stunning growth of a global STR 'community' and then stated: 'We want to be regulated—because to regulate us would be to recognize us'. He also made it clear that the company would resist market bans, but was prompt to offer guidance to regulators: 'What we don't want is a blanket prohibition. What we do not want is people regulating us without even understanding what we are' (Friedman 2014). In March 2017, during a public talk we attended in Paris,[4] the head of global policy and public affairs of Airbnb, Chris Lehane, argued that governments 'were not prepared' for the changes brought about by digital technologies to cities and were 'to be helped' by platforms to make their laws evolve.

These quotes illustrate how, in times of market emergence, as was the case with STRs in the 2010s, firms attempt to participate in the settlement of rules in order to establish themselves, if possible, in a hierarchical position—to be able to close off access to potential new incumbents on the one hand and absorb competitors on the other (Fligstein 1996)—before regulation coalesces. The rapid conquest of the market is also an important variable for the 'primitive accumulation' of platforms' *political* power (Mazur and Serafin 2023; see Chapter 1). Once a near-monopoly is acquired (as has been the case for Airbnb in Europe), a platform is in a position to shape future rules in order to dominate a market where it has previously contributed to the setting of market regulations (Mazur and Serafin 2023; see Chapter 1).

This process that connects market expansion, regulatory control and power accumulation has been based on five main interrelated strategies from corporate platforms, which we consider in turn:

offering self-regulation and pre-crafted regulatory solutions for operate rules (i.e., tax collection); fighting against legal barriers to 'market access' (e.g., STR licensing and authorisation systems, overall quantitative limits, spatial restrictions); using litigation and user-base mobilisation to buy time and influence unwanted rules; organising public campaigning to shape public opinion; and investing in classic lobbying over the drafting of legislation. However, these activities have taken different forms, and have been more or less contentious, from place to place and over time. Platforms have adapted their tactics according to the STR market and regulatory initiatives of each city and country. Similarly, they have not acquired the same power everywhere.

The sources of platform power over policy-making have been highlighted by scholars of platform capitalism, discussed in Chapter 1. First, they have argued that, while direct lobbying is important, corporate platforms also benefit politically from the privileged relationship with their user base: the latter is a clientele that can be mobilised against governments, or whose opposition to platform regulation is anticipated by politicians (Culpepper and Thelen 2020). As analysed in depth by Yates (2021, 2023, 2025) for Airbnb, the active mobilisation of hosts is central to the platform's political strategies of 'grassroots lobbying' and has been deployed on a global scale. Our European comparison confirms this observation, but it also shows that hosts' mobilisation has not materialised in the same way everywhere, nor has it produced the same effects, because platforms' *economic clienteles* (property owners as potential hosts) on the one hand, and governments' *political clienteles* (voters) on the other hand, are not always aligned in the same ways. Later in this chapter we show that differences in the share of homeowners in cities (who are both potential hosts and voters) seem to account for a large part of the differences in local government reactions to the mobilisations of hosts and their platform strategies. To put it briefly, where the share of property owners is higher (World 1), their interests—which coincide with those of platforms—carry more weight in local politics: governments must satisfy this political clientele and must concur with the platforms, unless they manage to impose a different politicisation that makes them more autonomous (World 3). Where the share of property owners is low (World 2), they have less influence on local governance, and governments can pursue an agenda that is closer to their political clientele (not tied to homeownership) and more autonomous from platforms.

Second, beyond user-based political strength, scholars have argued that platforms have gained a broader 'infrastructural power' from their mediating position in the economy (see Chapter 1). Over time, platform intermediation creates multiple dependencies that become sources of political strength. In the case of the STR market, dependencies include not only hosts but also the large world of connected STR operators and intermediaries that depend on platform infrastructure (property managers and 'conciergeries', rental and tourist service providers, cleaning companies, etc.). When these operators mobilise against regulations limiting STRs, they serve both platform interests and their own at the same time. Importantly, the dependency created by platform intermediation also relates to governments themselves, which have been drawn to the platform ecosystem. As we will show below, state actors have delegated some public functions to corporate platforms, especially the collection of tourist/city taxes and data. This has given platforms an 'institutional business power', based on the private delivery of public functions (Busemeyer and Thelen 2020). Over time, through lock-in effects and policy feedback, it has created an asymmetrical dependence of both private and public actors on the continued existence of platforms and their commitment to operate. Yet, again, this asymmetry is not the same everywhere: it has been reduced when city governments (especially in Worlds 2 and 3) have been actively gathering data, intelligence and oversight capacity over both platforms and the STR market.

## The Corporate Offer for Self-Regulation and Its Pitfalls

Among corporate platforms, Airbnb has been a global influential player whose political action shall be analysed in itself. In several cities, it was the only platform engaged, since the beginning, in proactive and intense political activities and in challenging STR-related policy-making and restrictions. These activities have comprised standardised approaches adapted to local political contexts. Other platforms have, by contrast, tended to operate through joining organisations with other professional STR operators, like the UNPLV in France (to which we will turn later in the chapter) or the EHHA at the EU level (see Chapter 7).

The company has developed both a proactive and reactive strategy to keep control of the STR regulatory environment. On the proactive side, Airbnb has rolled out a strategy to shape the regulatory debate by proposing to governments a selected and limited set of standardised policy solutions that could, in the company's view, be used to regulate STRs everywhere (Ferreri and Sanyal 2018; Gurran 2018; Artioli 2020; van Doorn 2020; Colomb and Moreira de Souza 2021). These solutions were presented as proof of the corporate willingness to collaborate with governments while advancing the 'right to share'. The Airbnb Community Compact (Airbnb 2015) first set out these principles, later formalised in a public policy guidance document entitled *Airbnb Policy Tool Chest* (Airbnb 2016a; updated in 2017). The latter was explicitly presented as 'a resource for governments to consider as they draft or amend these rules' (2016a:2). It offered four policy interventions that the company was prepared to accept (Airbnb 2016a:3): facilitating tourist tax collection via the platform through voluntary collection agreements; offering tools and good practices to 'help ensure that hosts and guests are respectful of the neighbourhoods in which they share space'; fostering accountability through collaboration with authorities on 'practical, enforceable rules for home sharing'; and combining transparency and privacy by providing some data to local policy-makers 'to enable smarter decision-making about home sharing rules without compromising hosts' or guests' privacy rights'. In 2020 the platform launched a new website—called City Portal (www.airbnb.com /cityportal)—specifically dedicated to both local governments and tourism organisations presented as Airbnb 'partners'. From the portal, the latter could access aggregate data regarding visitor flows and STR offer (but not individualised data for enforcement, as analysed in Chapter 5), find information regarding the tourist tax collection and make contact with Airbnb policy staff.

These self-defined and self-selected policy solutions are mainly about operate rules and not about access rules (according to the typology of Chapter 3), so do not seek to limit the growth of the STR market but to shape its functioning. Among them, *tourist tax collection agreements* have undoubtedly been the most popular. Thanks to its intermediation role, Airbnb was indeed well positioned to collect part of the money that constantly flows through the platform and transfer it to city governments. In 2019 the company stated that it was engaged in more than 400 voluntary collection agreements worldwide, through which it collected and remitted the city tax or tourist tax on behalf of governments. Among the 12 European cities considered in Chapter 3, by 2022, 5 were involved in such an agreement with Airbnb: Amsterdam since 2014 (updated in 2016), Paris since 2015, Lisbon since 2016, Milan since 2018 (after a first memorandum of understanding signed in 2015) and Rome since 2020.

These agreements have not been without effects. They have brought substantial revenues to local governments. In Italy, in 2019 the platform transferred to 24 local governments with whom it had an agreement a total €22 million (Aquaro and dell'Oste 2022). In Milan, platform-collected revenues amounted to €7.2 million out of a total of €56.2 million from the tourist tax (Facchini 2021). Since 2022 the platform has collected and remitted the tourist tax in more than 1,100 Italian localities that have such a tax in place, scaling up from the existing city-based agreements to a nationwide tax collection scheme in partnership with the communication company of the National Association of Italian municipalities (ANCI Comunicare). All the other Italian local administrations can now join the programme through a dedicated website (https://tassadisoggiorno-airbnb.it/). In Paris, Airbnb remitted €15.3 million to the city in 2019, €9.4 in 2021 and €24.3 in 2022 (Charpantier 2023). This represented roughly between 16% and 26% of the total tourist tax revenues for the city—not an insignificant share.[5] Additionally, in France in the early 2020s, while Airbnb and its hosts were under legal attack from several city governments (such as Paris, Oléron, Saint-Malo and la Rochelle, notably over a failure to collect the tourist tax in Oléron),[6] Airbnb presented itself as a promoter of local economic development via the payment of €148 million in tourist tax to 23,000 French municipalities. Through skilful public communication, the platform has tried to divert attention from the Parisian issues by highlighting its contribution to local development in other territories (see below). As stated by the director of Airbnb France in a press release: 'The tourist tax paid by Airbnb is becoming a growing source of revenue for neighbouring cities [located in the periphery of large cities] that are well served by transportation networks, offering opportunities for less expensive, quiet stays that make it easy to reach the centre of the agglomeration'.[7]

However, such tax agreements have also strengthened the platform's corporate power and legitimised its position as a 'government partner' in shaping regulations. Though bringing in significant income, they have made governments dependent both on the company commitment to transfer money and on its honesty in reporting the correct amount of collected tax, which is often handed in to city governments at regular intervals as an aggregate sum. They have enhanced the platform's 'institutional power' (Busemeyer and Thelen 2020), where governments rely on business to perform vital operations such as tax collection. Furthermore, in most cities where there is no agreed transfer of individualised STR data (as discussed in Chapter 5), it has been impossible to control whether the transferred amount was consistent with the exact number of overnight stays and therefore the due tax. In Rome, after the agreement was established in 2020, Airbnb started transferring lump-sum payments without a detailed list of guests and bookings. When, in 2022, the new deputy mayor in charge of tourism filed a complaint against Airbnb in the National Court of Auditors, the platform declared a miscalculation and transferred to the city an additional €70,000. Still, this case brought to light that tax collection, which is one of the most defining features of state action and its governing and redistribution capacity, had been delegated to a corporation with limited accountability, and on which the city government had almost no oversight.

The platform's ability to influence local governments with self-defined policies has varied greatly according to the local regulatory approach and overall housing/tourism agendas. Milan has offered Airbnb a rather unique structure of opportunity to deploy its offer of 'self-regulation' and social responsibility: a series of initiatives running from 2014 to 2022 made the city the corporation's Italian testbed for its global strategies. They were almost systematically met with municipal support, based on a liberalised approach to the use of property and a local agenda to promote visitors' attractiveness. This led to a loose, uninterrupted and non-contentious relationship between the platform and the local government, something very different from what was observed in cities with stringent STR rules. This relationship began with the platform participation in the call for partners in the Milano Sharing City Strategy (in 2014; see Chapter 4). The company took stock of the overall municipal agenda based on innovation and collaboration with the private and non-governmental sectors to gain recognition at the local level. According to a former Airbnb executive:

Everything started in November 2015 when the Municipality of Milan launched a consultation on the sharing economy. . . . And the Municipality of Milan did not recognise Uber as part of the sharing economy, which made Airbnb the biggest player in the room. (interview, Airbnb executive, April 2017)

As analysed in Chapter 4, the first memorandum of understanding between Airbnb and the city government was signed in 2015 and included initiatives to support digital literacy, economic impact assessments of Airbnb-listed STRs (as part of the impact studies commissioned by Airbnb worldwide; see below), collaboration during big events (e.g., the Design Week and Fashion Week) and tourist tax collection. In 2017 Airbnb financially supported an intensive workshop addressed to unemployed citizens, to whom STR services were presented as an opportunity for micro-entrepreneurship, which took place in a venue provided by the city government (Degoli 2017). Between 2016 and 2020 the platform's corporate social responsibility initiative, called Open Homes, was deployed in Milan, involving Italian non-profit organisations: STRs were offered for free or at a discounted price to the families of hospital patients in 2016 (Airbnb 2016b), to refugees in 2017 (De Vito 2017) and to medical staff during the first year of the COVID-19 pandemic (Airbnb 2020b). In 2018 the platform started the collection and remittance of the tourist tax. In 2021 the municipal government was looking to enrol real estate agents and property owners in offering medium-term 'controlled rents' (namely rentals offered by owners at lower prices, in exchange for public guarantee and a significant tax relief)[8] as a response to the acute housing crisis faced by students and temporary workers. In reaction, Airbnb created a webpage dedicated to medium-term rentals in Milan (https://www.airbnb.it/d/milanoalungotermine). While this was part of the platform's global strategy targeting the new medium-term rental post-pandemic market (Airbnb 2022a; Colomb and Gallent 2022), its initiative was publicised and supported by the city government (Comune di Milano 2021). Finally, in 2023 Airbnb was invited among other 'big players' to the Housing Forum organised by the city government to present its views regarding STR regulations, along with host and pro-regulation groups (Comune di Milano 2023b; attended by the authors).

During those years, Airbnb has been able to grow an unrestricted market only subject to operate rules (tourist tax, identification code, etc.) and has gained recognition as a legitimate actor in the city. Its above-mentioned corporate social responsibility initiatives have brought limited policy outputs to the city (due to the limited duration, size and effective content of these initiatives), yet they have increased the platform's political legitimacy locally. For the municipality, a stable relationship with Airbnb has drawn on the role played by the platform in contributing to boosting the local accommodation offer and attractiveness for visitors, while allowing property owners (who are also a political clientele) to gain revenues. Building on this, politicians have also showcased their capacity to collaborate with large corporations, from the sharing economy strategy of 2014 up to today.

## Regulatory Non-Compliance, Court Stalling and Contentious Relations

Beyond offering pre-crafted policy solutions, platforms (and short-term rentiers organisations, analysed below) have also reacted to unwanted regulations through non-compliance and litigation. This has led to contentious relationships with local, and sometimes national, governments that initiated restrictive policies. All in all, in those cities where STR regulations were more intense (in our Worlds 2 and 3, as defined in Chapter 3), the relationships between governments and platforms have also been much more contentious and judicialised compared to cities with less intense STR restrictions (in World 1).

Platforms and short-term rentiers organisations (to which we will turn later in the chapter) have legally challenged unwanted restrictions in courts. Litigation can be analysed as a strategy to overturn political decisions, but also as a stalling technique (as argued by Mazur and Serafin 2023 about Uber). Proceedings have been dragged from one jurisdiction to the other. While waiting for courts' decisions, which usually have come a few years later, especially when referred to the EU level (see Chapter 7), the contested local regulations have been ignored. The market has kept on expanding along with platform power and its connected short-term rentiers interest groups. For instance, as discussed in Chapter 5, Airbnb challenged the Italian fiscal law passed in 2017—which compelled the platform to collect and remit the 21% flat tax on rental revenues and transfer data to the state—in front of the Regional Administrative Court and the Council of State. In 2019 the latter referred the case to the Court of Justice of the EU to establish whether obligations introduced by Italian law were compatible with EU legislation. The CJEU made its decision in December 2022 (favourable to the Italian law). The decision was then received by the Italian courts, leading to both financial sanctions for Airbnb and the collection of the flat tax by the platform starting in 2024. Yet over six years Airbnb did not comply, and the STR market grew from about 480,000 listings in 2017 (Milone et al. 2022) to about 640,000 in 2023 (Cicognani 2023).

These judicial actions have also come from short-term rentiers groups, at times supported by platforms. The role of the latter in 'indirectly' encouraging litigation aimed at contesting and suspending STR rules is hard to establish. It can be said, however, that platforms have frequently formed alliances with existing groups (in this case, short-term rentiers organisations) and supported them financially (a repertoire of action also studied by Yates 2023, 2025). Court cases against new STR regulations have been filed by local short-term rentiers organisations and some specialised law firms (as has been the case for firms focusing on the defence of STR operators sanctioned for illegal rentals;

see Chapter 5). In Barcelona, for example, in the early 2020s nearly 100 cases against the STR regulation plan (PEUAT) had been lodged in front of the Regional Court. In Paris, in 2017 two landlords started a legal case against the municipal regulation (see Chapter 4). After being found guilty of having rented out (via a property company called SCI Cali Apartments) accommodation units on Airbnb on a full-time basis without the municipal authorisation of change of use, they appealed in front of the French Court of Cassation, which referred the matter to the Court of Justice of the EU in November 2018. The latter made a decision in September 2020. While waiting for the CJEU ruling (a milestone analysed in Chapter 7), several proceedings on the disputes between STR owners and the city government of Paris were postponed. All cases were 'frozen', which stalled regulatory enforcement for several years. When proceedings were finally resumed, there were about 400 cases on hold (interview, BPLH officers, July 2022). Interestingly, the lawyers who represented SCI Cali Apartments against the city government of Paris at all stages of the legal challenge (up to the CJEU) have since then specialised in litigation against STR regulations. They have been involved in most of the legal actions initiated by French short-term rentiers organisations against restrictions passed by local governments: in the Disneyland Paris area (Val d'Europe), in two coastal localities on the Atlantic Ocean (La Rochelle and Pays Basque) and in Obernai (close to Strasbourg). When successful, litigation has led to the new local regulations being revoked or postponed, which has strongly benefitted the platform-rentiers bloc as a whole, from digital corporations to STR operators of all kinds.

A slightly different stalling technique has consisted in platforms bluntly ignoring unwanted regulations. We have provided evidence, in Chapter 5, about how the obligation to transfer individualised data and the obligation to display a registration number have been disregarded or postponed by various platforms for several years. These delays have triggered new responses by city governments—which often consisted in prosecuting platforms, as the Paris and Barcelona city governments did—thus making the relationship between platforms and local governments even more contentious and judicialised. While court cases were going on, political negotiations have been often interrupted. In Paris, the relationships between Airbnb and the deputy mayor for housing and his team became much cooler after the episode of 2016 (described in Chapter 4), when the French head of Airbnb public policy slammed the door on negotiations around data transfer. Dialogue with politicians had never really been re-established in the years that followed, according to the deputy mayor's cabinet (interview, director of the Cabinet of the Deputy Mayor for Housing, Paris, March 2020).

Eventually, when losing a regulatory battle platforms have adjusted by turning compliance into a communication asset: the compelled conformity with the law, often enforced by a court decision, has been presented as corporate goodwill and self-regulation. This was particularly visible in several responses by Airbnb to the Parisian and French regulations: starting in December 2019, a legislative decree obliged online platforms to transfer to the City of Paris (and other French municipalities) individual data regarding short-term renters and the number of rented days, to verify that the 120-day limit was respected (see Chapter 5). Beforehand, Airbnb had fiercely opposed such an obligation, but once the decree passed, the company reversed the narrative and started to abundantly communicate about its willingness to transfer data. In December 2019 Emmanuel Marill, director of Airbnb France, declared:

We want to work with authorities to promote the responsible and sustainable rental of tourist accommodations. That's why we have been working with the French government on measures to help hosts in several major French cities to rent out their accommodation on Airbnb in accordance with local regulations. The data we are publishing today illustrates the good results of this collaboration, and we hope to continue this fruitful work with all the players involved. (Airbnb 2019b)

Data sharing has since then been showcased in the list of the company's 'commitments to sustainable tourism' in the country (Airbnb 2021a).

## Public Campaigning, User-Base Mobilisation and Direct Lobbying

Finally, Airbnb's interests have been voiced through extensive campaigning about the platform's benefits and through the direct mobilisation of hosts, based on the platform's user-based power (Culpepper and Thelen 2020; Yates 2023, 2025). First, the platform has built on tacit consumer loyalty to engage in 'broad-based political communication pitting its popularity against its critics or opponents' (Culpepper and Thelen 2020:301). Public campaigning was first experimented with in 2015 in San Francisco to resist a local regulatory initiative (Proposition F) and then generalised as one of the company's repertoires of action. In November 2015 Airbnb launched an advertising campaign in the Parisian metro and public spaces. Huge billboards pictured a young man saying, 'My flat is helping me to launch my start-up', or a young woman saying, 'My flat is helping me to finance my first movie'. The campaign aimed at demonstrating the advantages of STR activities, painted as beneficial for young middle-class urban dwellers who, thanks to the platform, could fully realise their innovative and self-entrepreneurial dreams. The timing of the campaign was not anecdotal: the STR market was quickly expanding in the city, but its adverse effects on local housing were increasingly under political scrutiny.

Airbnb has campaigned since then to divert attention from the negative externalities of STRs in Paris and other large cities towards other kinds of territories, particularly rural areas, where some local authorities have been more supportive of STRs as a channel of economic development in declining or peripheral areas. Airbnb and the Association of Rural Mayors of France (AMRF) signed an agreement in 2021 (see https://www.amrf.fr/2021/08/20/airbnb/) to 'boost tourism' with the aim of developing 15,000 listings and promoting remote working in less visited rural towns and villages (Airbnb 2022b). According to this agreement, Airbnb will pay €100 to the AMRF for each new listing advertised on the platform, and a new fund (*Campagnes d'avenir*; see https://www .airbnb.fr/d/campagnesdavenir) will finance tourism-related projects and training activities to help future hosts develop their STR activity:

> At Airbnb, we have been aware for a long time of the enormous tourism potential of rural France. . . . [W]e believe that this vast program . . . will help to develop a long-term economic model for rural territories and their inhabitants, to better disperse stays beyond the big cities and thus give a more sustainable horizon to the tourism economy in France. (Emmanuel Marill, director of Airbnb France, Belgium, Netherlands, AMRF website)

Airbnb has also tried to show that it helps promote historic heritage to 'support the development of meaningful and attractive tourism for rural areas'. In France, the platform has financially supported (with €5.6 million in 2022) the rehabilitation of heritage sites via one of the major foundations operating in the country, Fondation du Patrimoine,[9] boasting that Airbnb was the 'main sponsor of its Heritage and Local Tourism program'.[10] A very similar strategy has been witnessed in Italy, where in 2017 the platform signed a partnership with the Ministry of Tourism and Culture and the National Association of Italian municipalities (ANCI) aimed at supporting 40 'Italian Villages'. The plan sought to boost STRs in rural areas, through a dedicated platform targeting an international clientele, while the platform co-funded the refurbishment of one iconic building in four of these villages (Airbnb 2017a, 2017b).

To feed into public campaigning, an intense political effort has also been dedicated to demonstrating the many positive impacts of STRs. Airbnb has commissioned hundreds of studies all over the world. In summary (Airbnb 2018a), those reports have argued that in popular urban destinations, the increase in STRs has contributed to a better territorial spread of tourist accommodation across neighbourhoods and has generated sizable trickle-down effects on local economies—claiming that 42% of guests' spending 'stays local'. The reports have emphasised positive impacts for consumers and the tourism industry, for neighbourhoods and local businesses and for resident households. The claim of beneficial effects—whose reality has been discussed in Chapter 2—has been connected to a second line of argument typical of the 'Californian ideology' (Barbrook and Cameron 1996), which mixes determinism regarding the beneficial effects of technology with the defence of individual freedom and criticism of state intervention. Following this rhetoric, the platform has framed itself as a channel of technological and social progress, in front of which legal norms appear fatally outdated and destined to be overtaken. This worldwide claim has been adapted to specific regulatory controversies. For instance, when the national law for the taxation of STR rental incomes was discussed in the Italian Parliament in 2017, the platform combined this general argument with the recurrent criticism of Italian bureaucracy in order to capitalise on the 'limited trust' Italian citizens had in their state (Cassese 2011) and therefore oppose regulation. The law was depicted in media campaigning as a bureaucratic maze suffocating individual enterprises and rights, as much as depriving consumers of an innovative accommodation service. An online host mobilisation was launched in May 2017 under the title 'I am a host and I stand for home-sharing'. Slogans spelled out: 'These amendments stop innovation. They look at the past, not to the future' and 'You [the government] are suffocating us with bureaucracy'.[11]

This case also illustrates how the platform's user base has been actively mobilised against regulations through the direct creation of host groups and temporary mobilisations (strategies studied in depth in Yates 2021, 2023, 2025). Yates defines this 'corporate grassroots lobbying' as the 'selection, mobilization, resourcing and coordination of ordinary users and grassroots allies to influence the public and policy-making process' (Yates 2023:1). Users have been framed as 'Airbnb citizens', 'a community of entrepreneurial middle-class citizens looking to supplement their income in a climate of economic insecurity and tech-enabled opportunity' (van Doorn 2020:1808). In 2015 the company began to roll out a global strategy of mobilisation of individual users who have been encouraged to form local advocacy groups called Home Sharing Clubs (https://www.airbnbcitizen.com/clubs/), helped by Airbnb's Public Policy Teams, in order to 'share best practices' but above all to push for favourable regulation in their own country and city.[12] These clubs were mainly composed of landlords who rented their own homes short-term and not the 59% of 'professional landlords' who advertise units on Airbnb (Yates 2021). In 2017 Airbnb counted 'more than 120' clubs in the world, according to the then head of global policy, Chris Lehane, at the above-mentioned Paris public lecture; in 2021, the number of these groups had reached 350–400 globally (Yates 2021). In 2016 Airbnb also created a dedicated website (airbnbcitizen.com) aimed at supporting 'a global network . . . working to create fair, responsible laws to bring the benefits of home sharing to communities everywhere' (the site is no longer active).[13] It included country-specific sections on local legislation, corporate social responsibility initiatives and local home-sharing clubs. Other large platforms, such as VRBO, also encouraged their user base to engage in advocacy activities to influence public debates about regulation, through guidance to hosts about how to do so.[14]

Home-sharing clubs have been the frontline groups that have mobilised during the phases of policy conflict and in response to regulatory threats. Yet in the most contentious times, Airbnb has also directly reached out to all local hosts and invited them to join temporary mobilisations (through petitioning). For instance, in 2017 in Barcelona, the company organised a 'mail-bombing' campaign to 'stop restrictions in the home-sharing sector' (Iborra 2017). Hosts were asked by email to send a letter to city authorities by clicking on a user-friendly interface provided on the platform. On these occasions, the platform itself turned from a market infrastructure into an infrastructure for political action.

Finally, the company has also used classical forms of lobbying at different levels of scale, which entail closely following the drafting of new regulations and voicing the company's interests through various channels. Initially relying on policy consultancy firms such as Political Intelligence at the EU level (Corporate Europe Observatory 2018), Airbnb then included in-house lobbying teams in its regional offices by hiring experienced public relations professionals, who sometimes had previously worked for governments. In 2017 Airbnb France recruited the communication manager of the Secretary of State in Charge of the Digital Economy, who went from one post to the other, giving rise to heated debates. In 2016 the company recruited the former mayors of Rome (Italy), Houston and Philadelphia (USA), and Adelaide (Australia) to join its Mayoral Advisory Board that advises the company on how to collaborate with municipal authorities. In those EU countries that publish 'transparency registers' of the interest groups that have access to parliamentary and governmental institutions, Airbnb has been listed as an interest group in its own name, not just as a member of other STR business associations. According to the French register, for instance, Airbnb France dedicated in 2022 between €200,000 and €300,000 to lobbying the French Parliament and the national government, with 10 people working on that task (against 2 in 2017, the year of the first available data).[15] Comparatively, the French platform/property managers association UNPLV (see below) spent much less, between €50,000 and €75,000, with two dedicated staff members in 2021. Airbnb and other large platforms have also, alone and as part of the European Holiday Home Association, lobbied EU institutions (see below and Chapter 7).

## THE NEW SHORT-TERM RENTIERS GROUPS
## IN EUROPEAN CITIES: A POLITICAL CLIENTELE

### The Privileged Position of STR Property Interests
### in Cities of Homeowners

On the same side of the STR regulatory battle, short-term rentiers have acquired significant power in European cities. The last 10 years have seen the consolidation of STR landed property interests and operators (as explained in Chapter 1). They are hosts and 'home-sharers', property managers and professional/corporate STR operators and their representative associations. Despite their differences, these actors share a patrimonial position in the STR market from which they extract revenues and rents. They have gained visibility and legitimacy in the public arena and embody, in alliance with corporate platforms themselves, the most extensive opposition to stricter STR regulations.

These groups have three main sources of power. First, as demonstrated above, they have benefitted from the support of platforms, especially Airbnb. They have relied on platform intermediation not just to grow their business at an unprecedented scale, but also to gain political influence. Airbnb has sometimes directly orchestrated and often backed the creation of their associations; has supported court actions against regulations on their behalf; and importantly, has contributed to shaping the narratives around STRs at a global level. These narratives have set a favourable ground for claims coming from landed property interests and operators.

Second, these groups have benefitted from the strength of numbers and the size of the market, which have given short-term rentiers a form of structural power. The latter is the political strength that does not flow from direct lobbying but from the 'privileged position' of business actors (Lindblom 1977), and that influences politicians' minds in anticipatory ways. Since the STR offer has been largely in short-term rentiers' hands, they have drawn political strength from their position and operation in the urban property and accommodation markets. As the STR market expanded, new wealth was extracted from it; individual and corporate property owners turned apartments into STRs and invested money in the market; new attendant economic services and companies were created; and more and more travellers stayed in STRs. It thus became increasingly difficult for politicians to curb the market or shut it down. In some ways this situation renewed the privileged position of landed capital and property owners in urban policies—already identified by Logan and Molotch (1987)—and put these actors in an advantageous position compared to other interest groups.

Third, in connection to the last point, the strength of these groups has grown from the political, legal and sometimes constitutional protection of individual property rights on which they have based their business. Along with the right to free enterprise, property rights are enshrined in the legal apparatuses of most European countries. Their protection has been held in high consideration during STR regulatory debates.

Importantly, however, the political strength of short-term rentiers has varied according to local and national political agendas regarding STRs, the local STR market structures and the local weight of the property-owning electorate (as discussed in Chapters 3 and 4). Where these political agendas were based on tourism attractiveness and/or on the protection of individual property ownership, as was the case in Milan, politicians were much more reactive to the threat of real estate disinvestment, diminishing STR revenues, decreasing tourism accommodation offer, and alienation of the property-owning electorate. The political strength of short-term rentiers was therefore more significant there (as in London, and in Lisbon until 2017, before the issue framing shifted; see Chapter 4), compared to those cities where the political agendas, and their supporting electorates, were or became less oriented towards a tourism- and property-based growth model, as in cities from World 2 (i.e., Paris) or World 3 (i.e., Barcelona).

The role and weight of short-term rentiers in local politics also differs depending on the STR market structure. In some cities of World 1, where the market is quite concentrated and professionalised (with high rates of multi-listings; see Figure 10 in Chapter 3 and Table 3 in the Appendix), one could expect large operators (institutional investors, owners or intermediaries such as property managers) to seek to weigh in more on the local politics of STR regulation. In World 3 cities, where the weight of multi-listings and professional operators is also high, one could expect strong conflicts between large operators and left-wing municipal governments. In World 2 cities, where the STR market is less dominated by large multi-listings operators (even if the weight in absolute numbers of a few large operators is notable, as in Paris), one may expect local governments to be more autonomous in terms of their local agenda.

Taking this argument further, we can say that when and where the political clienteles (property owners as voters) and the economic clientele (property owners as STR operators) are aligned, governments are more dependent on STR rentiers, platforms and their intermediation. This is the case in World 1 cities that have a high proportion of homeowners (on average between 50% and 80%), who are potentially interested in renting their properties as STRs and have a strong influence on local governance and politics. In World 3 cities with high homeownership rates (between 50% and 65% in Barcelona, Madrid and Lisbon), the political and economic clienteles are also potentially aligned. However, governments have managed to distance themselves from owners/STR operators (whatever their type and size) through a process of politicisation that addressed their specific left-wing electorate—in particular younger generations unable to access property ownership—sometimes directly blaming property owners. This shows a different facet of the strength of politicisation processes at play in World 3, that produces a very different outcome in terms of regulation compared to World 1. The question that remains is whether this mechanism of politicisation would be sufficient to maintain the political distance between regulators and STR operators if the political majority shifts to the right or to more market-oriented political parties.

In the cities of World 2 (Paris, Amsterdam, Vienna, Berlin), the power of STR rentiers and platforms is even less obvious, as the weight of homeowners in urban politics is low (homeownership amounts to between 10% and 30% of the housing stock). Also, the political clientele of governments is favourable to public housing and tenant protection: in those cities, which have been ruled by left-wing coalitions over the past decade, 20–40% of the housing stock is social or public (Paris, Amsterdam and Vienna), while Berlin has a comparatively strongly regulated private rental market. In World 2, governments are therefore relatively more autonomous—in terms of their political agenda—from the influence of STR rentiers and platforms.

At a broader level, differences in the political strength of STR rentiers can also be connected to variations in the social and political acceptance of state intervention in property rights and housing markets (e.g., through planning and housing laws). These broader institutional arrangements and connected ideologies frame the room for manoeuvre and the 'legitimacy' of public intervention in STRs (as discussed in Chapters 2 and 3). This also helps us to understand the positioning of certain national governments, for example, the Czech Republic (in the case of Prague), where the post-communist legacy has created a context unfavourable to public intervention in private property.

## The Differential Weight and Organisation of Short-Term Rentiers in European Cities

Everywhere, short-term rentiers have been represented mainly by two types of organisations: associations of hosts and individual property

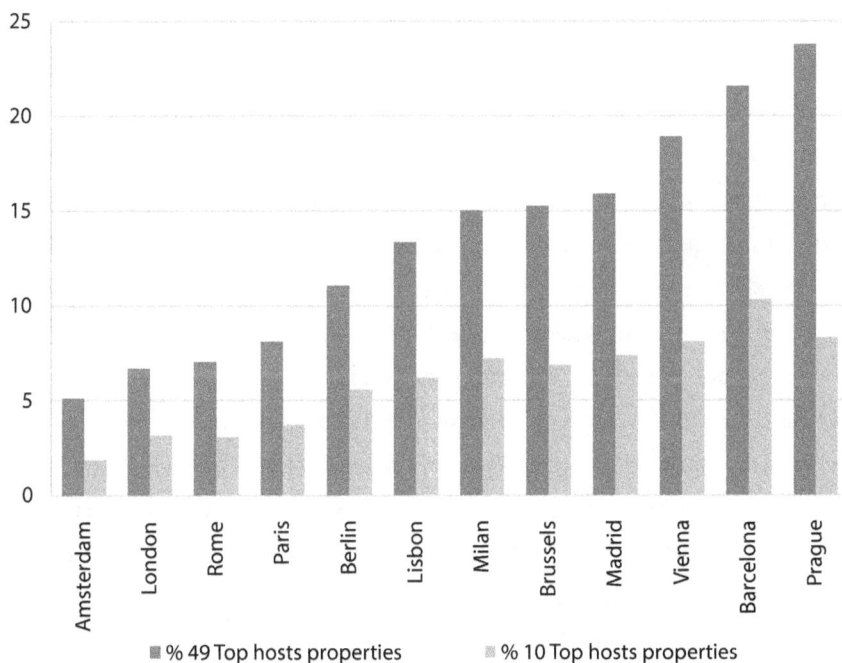

**Figure 22.** Weight of the top hosts (% of properties on STR markets offered by 49 top hosts and 10 top hosts). The graph reads as follow: in Barcelona, the 10 top hosts operate 10.3% of the total STR market stock in the city; the 49 top hosts operate 22% of the market. *Source*: Authors' calculations based on data from Inside Airbnb (2023).

owners (called *clubs* by Airbnb) on the one hand, and professional property managers and intermediaries (sometimes called *conciergeries*), on the other. But these organisations do not have the same weight and political role in each city. Figure 22 represents the weight of the top hosts in each city as an indicator of the professionalisation of the market.

## ASSOCIATIONS OF HOSTS

Associations of hosts, individual STR owners and home-sharing clubs have been created by volunteers in several cities all over Europe since mid-2010: we can mention OspitaMi in Milan, Homesharing Berlin, Associació de Veïns i Amfitrions in Barcelona, Gastvrij Amsterdam or later, Collectif Entr'hotes in Paris. Most of them have initially started informally via Facebook groups and other social media, then often built formal associations. They have also scaled up from local groups to national networks, such as Host+Host and Host Italiani in Italy. These groups have intended to represent small-scale operators, distinct from management companies. Some of them purport to represent 'home-sharers' only in a strict sense. For instance, according to one of its coordinators, Homesharing Berlin has gathered 'students, freelance workers, academics, creatives, employees and retired people', who rent a room in their flat or their whole flat occasionally when they are travelling for work or holidays (interview, 2019). This self-distinction from the capitalist 'investor host' has been witnessed in other contexts, for example, the USA (Medvedeva 2023). Others have represented small individual operators more broadly. Gastvrij Amsterdam, for instance, presents itself as an organisation that runs 'entirely on volunteers' and 'stands up for . . . ordinary Amsterdammers who like to receive tourists hospitably in their own homes—according to the legal rules—in the city's tradition of freedom and tolerance' (Amsterdam Gastvrij 2023). The Parisian Collectif Entr'hotes wrote in an open letter to Mayor Anne Hidalgo: 'We're Parisians, just like you. We rent out our apartment occasionally on platforms whose names everyone knows. . . . [W]e are not, and have no desire to become, STR professionals. . . . [O]ur situations are diverse, but many of us actually need the money to stay in Paris'.[16] The Home Sharing Club of Milan, later renamed OspitaMI, consists of people whose involvement in the short-stay accommodation sector started on a small scale by renting an apartment (e.g., inherited from parents or grandparents); yet some of them have turned this into a full-time activity by investing in several STR properties. They still present themselves as a group representing 'normal people' and not companies (interviews, 2017 and 2020).

While many associations of hosts have been created with Airbnb support and have been in contact with the platform (Sharp 2018; Boon et al. 2019; van Doorn 2020; Yates 2023, 2025), others have preferred to remain independent (and at times critical) of it, like Homesharing Berlin (interview, 2019). The Home Sharing Club of Milan has been an interesting case of the ambivalent relationship between the platform and host clubs. The Milanese club was set up by Airbnb in 2016: according to one of the founders, a 'community organiser' from the platform was in charge of 'organising meetings where they offered us [the hosts] an "aperitivo" while we talked to each other' (interview, Home Sharing Club Milano, April 2017). At the time the Home Sharing Club had no direct access to local governmental actors: according to our interviews, Airbnb acted as a gatekeeper between public authorities and 'its' club, leaving to the latter the role of petitioning and campaigning while reserving in-house lobbyists for negotiations with governments. Starting in 2017, this Home Sharing Club decided to turn from an informal group into a legal association funded by membership fees and with an official status; in 2018, it joined the national network of associations Host+Host, which is now the major Italian host organisation. These two shifts were aimed at gaining independence from Airbnb and directly engaging with governments, even if OspitaMi has continued to receive support from the platform.

Local governments have also often played an important role in recognising and consolidating short-term rentiers organisations. Indeed, at the beginning of the regulatory wave of the mid-2010s, public officials were searching for ways to engage with the STR market stakeholders, in an attempt to reduce their uncertainty around this emerging and wicked problem. While they usually knew quite well who the representatives of the hotel industry were, they searched for representatives from the hosts' ranks and, by doing so, contributed to their recognition and institutionalisation. Although totally new, relatively small and not necessarily representative, in those early years all these host/property owners organisations quickly become identified as stakeholders by policy-makers, which in turn fuelled the legitimacy and representativeness of these groups. They have benefitted from a firstcomer's advantage in their lobbying activities.

Again, new groups in Milan have been an interesting case (Artioli 2020). Besides the Home Sharing Club, Milan has been home to two other groups among the first organisations of Italian hosts: Host Italiani—Ospitalità in Regola, born in April 2015, first as a mere Facebook group, and Prolocatur, created in March 2016 by two notaries. Unlike informal host groups, Prolocatur was legally constituted in March 2016, with the goal of establishing a new 'union of property owners' defending their right to freely rent on a short-term basis'. As stated by one of the founding members: 'There was a Facebook group. But . . . myself and another notary from Genoa were convinced that if we wanted to have representative power, we needed to create an organisation. We are property owners and landlords, we are not "hosts"!' (interview, Prolocatur president, April 2017). Although a new and small group, Prolocatur quickly became highly visible in the STR debate, sat in consultations with public actors and established an alliance with the main national association of property owners, Confedilizia. This was due not only to the social and political capital of its founders—all professionals in the real estate sector—but also to the fact that Prolocatur, along with the Airbnb-founded Home Sharing Club, was one of the visible political faces of short-term rentiers in Milan.

In cities from World 2 such as Paris, the role of these clubs has remained much more modest; local authorities have had less need to organise spaces of interest representation, not needing them to build STR restrictive regulations that these clubs have systematically opposed. In Paris there is little evidence of meetings between local authorities and such clubs (interview, cabinet director of the Housing Deputy Mayor, City of Paris, March 2020). Representatives of the Collectif Entre'hotes were heard at the national level along with the Accor Group, Airbnb and the National Chamber of Property Owners as part of the preparation of a report to the Senate in April 2018 (Sénat 2018).

Yet the effect of the presence of host groups remains small compared to the other stakeholders.

## PROPERTY MANAGERS AND CONCIERGERIES

Short-term rentiers groups include associations of property managers and large professional STR operators, for example, the Asociación de Apartamentos Turísticos de Barcelona (APARTUR) and the Associação do Alojamento Local em Portugal (ALEP) in Lisbon; Property Managers Italia and the Associazione Italiana Gestori di Affitti Brevi (AIGAB) in Milan; the Short-Term Accommodation Association in London; and French conciergeries such as WeHost, Conciergerie BNB and Tranquille Emile. Property managers associations are most of the time made up of companies that manage STR units owned by others, even if sometimes they are also open to individual hosts and thus locally represent the whole sector, from small hosts to large property managers. Sometimes they also include corporate platforms among their members. In France the UNPLV, created in 2013, has involved platforms (Abritel, Airbnb, Booking, Trip Advisor, Leboncoin) and national property managers (e.g., FonciaVacances). Many of these groups have organised at multiple levels. To mention one of the most visible groups, APARTUR in Barcelona is also part of Federación Española de Asociaciones de Viviendas y Apartamentos Turísticos (FEVITUR, the Spanish Federation of Holiday Rentals Associations), and of the EHHA. At the European level, the EHHA, founded in 2013, included, in 2022, 6 individual corporations (Airbnb, Expedia Group-VRBO, Awaze, Lomarengas, Oyo Vacation Homes, Schibsted Media Group-Leboncoin) and 15 national federations of platforms/professional operators. Among the latter are the above-mentioned AIGAB (Italy), FEVITUR (Spain) and UNPLV (France).

In some cities from Worlds 1 and 3 (such as Milan and Barcelona), these organisations have tended to be formalised, financially supported by members and connected to other interest groups in the property and tourism industries, as well as to formal instances of business representation (e.g., Chambers of Commerce). Some were large, well-established and predated the emergence of platforms (e.g., associations of holiday property rentals in highly tourism-dependent countries); others have been created anew; but all have grown and strengthened along with the growth of the STR market and in response to STR regulations or other threats. The Italian AIGAB, for instance, was created at the beginning of the COVID-19 pandemic by major property managers operating in the country—Altido, CleanBnB House (that operates 226 listings in Milan in 2024), ItalianWay (518 listings in Milan), SweetGuest and Wonderful Italy—or specifically in Milan (Easylife House that operates around 270 listings) to negotiate public subsidies and favourable conditions with the national government during the COVID-related restrictions.[17] AIGAB is now one of the largest organisations in defence of STR interests. In Barcelona a few big international operators like Ukio, Enter Apartments and SweetInn operate more than 200 listings (the 10 biggest hosts operate more than 20% of the STR market).[18]

In other cities, such as Paris, we also find large property management organisations that operate among the largest portfolios of STR listings. The 10 largest operators run an average of 277 listings: Blueground (628 listings), WeHost (424 listings) and Veeve (300 listings).[19] But until the 2020s, these property managers had remained less vocal in the public arena compared to the cities mentioned above. It would even appear that they have sought to remain in the shadow of major regulatory controversies, letting large platforms and their organisations do the lobbying work while developing tools and techniques for circumventing and bending the rules to further develop the market. For instance, the Airbnb French conciergerie Tranquille Emile, created in 2015, has openly encouraged the transformation of commercial units into STRs,[20] in the midst of the debate over the regulation of such units in Paris in 2022. Conciergerie BB (https://www.conciergebb.fr/)

works closely with Airbnb and promotes its strategy of working with corporate visitors in 'off-peak periods', claiming therefore to not contribute to overtourism.

## Mobilising for the Protection of Property Rights and Free Enterprise

Despite their huge differences, short-term rentiers organisations have mobilised in parallel, when not in alliance. They have lobbied for the lightest possible barriers to the expansion of the STR market. Interviews with representatives of such organisations and the analysis of their public statements showed that, on the whole, they have declared themselves favourable to some 'light' forms of regulation (of the operate kind), accompanied by effective enforcement measures that would distinguish and shelter them from competition from their 'illegal' STR-operating counterparts. In their view, the STR legal framework should protect, but not limit, the rights 'to share', 'to rent', to 'free enterprise' and to the 'free use of one's property'. As a result, they have tended to be critical of, or opposed to, permit or licencing schemes and other instruments that limit access to the market and its quantitative, temporal or spatial expansion. In Barcelona, after the suspension of new STR licences in 2015 and the adoption of the restrictive Special Plan for Tourist Accommodation in January 2017, the director of the professional association representing the professional managers of commercial holiday flats, APARTUR (interview, 2018), argued that the freezing of new STR licences was 'the worse way to combat illegality'. According to him, this approach ignored the growing demand for STRs (and could therefore foster even more illegalities), was arbitrary and unjust (new hotels were allowed to open in some zones, but not STRs), and even possibly illegal under the EU *Services Directive* (an argument discussed in Chapter 7). At the same time, he acknowledged the problem of over-concentration of STRs in certain areas and the safety issues caused by illegal STRs, remaining open to the possibility of enacting *some* degree of restrictions in congested areas if necessary. In other cities, other kinds of regulatory instruments have also been contested by small-scale operators when perceived as too complex or not proportionate to the size of their business. OspitaMi in Milan did not oppose the creation of a legal definition of STRs by regional law, but objected to the complexity of the procedure which required a digital signature and, in their words, the 'meaningless standard requirements' (interview, April 2017) imposed on STRs, such as the obligation to display rental prices in the house.

In order to contest STR regulations, these organisations have met politicians, attended public consultations, petitioned and liaised with the media. They have both contested and proactively engaged with public authorities. This has, for example, been the case in Lisbon, where ALEP contributed ideas and technical knowledge to the drafting of the national law on tourist accommodation that was in the process of being discussed in the Portuguese Parliament in the summer of 2018, and in Barcelona, where APARTUR has systematically participated in round tables, public consultations and meetings with the city government.

Short-term rentiers have, along with platforms, highlighted the benefits brought by STRs to the city (e.g., tourist expenditure and reinvestment in property and building renovations). They have rejected the existence of a correlation between the rise of STRs and the increase in rents and house prices and have presented themselves as scapegoats for a housing crisis that, they have contended, is not of their own making and has much broader causes. On the contrary, they have argued, individuals (and companies and localities) need the extra income provided by STRs to survive financially. This argument has been particularly present in the countries heavily affected by the post-2008 recession and its consequences in terms of unemployment, decreasing wages and decreasing pensions, for example, in Southern Europe, as mentioned in Chapter 1 (Semi and Tonetta 2021). Individual strategies of rent-based micro-entrepreneurship have been glorified as a revenue solution that policy-makers ought to protect. When inflation started to rise in Europe in 2022, this argument was revived in the context of a cost-of-living crisis.

On their side, property managers organisations have also insisted on the 'quality' of their professionalised STR offer, which has developed complementary to hotels and should, in their view, be demarcated from illegal and unsafe DIY STR operators. Additionally, such organisations have often expressed scepticism about the data used by public authorities (or by citizens movements) to demonstrate the adverse impacts of STRs on the housing supply and rent levels in their cities. Some of them (e.g., APARTUR in Barcelona) have produced their own alternative studies of the impact of STRs, usually concluding that these are less significant than their detractors' claims.

All in all, activities from these diverse associations have included not only lobbying the governments at various levels but also supporting their members and offering legal advice to cope with regulations. For instance, OspitaMi in Milan was organised into neighbourhood-level sub-groups offering a forum for mutual advice between hosts having, most of the time, no or limited professional background in tourist accommodation. It aimed at fostering STR growth through networking and partnership with local restaurants or shops. The association also provided its members with legal advice targeted at small/medium-sized operators, something which was perceived as missing. In 2016, in a context of huge legal uncertainty, they collected information for a step-by-step regularisation of someone's STR activity, summed up in a 25-page document entitled 'The Host Gymkhana'. Finally, in response to increasing criticism about STRs, these associations have also promoted guidance and best practices on 'sustainable' and 'responsible' STR. They have made proposals to improve the co-existence of STR uses with neighbouring residents and improve the public image and legitimacy of their activity. Acknowledging the problems and disturbances that STR guests can cause neighbours in residential buildings, the Catalan organisation APARTUR has, for example, been promoting the use of noise meters in STR properties (devices linked to the operator's/landlord's phone, which send an alert if the noise level goes above a certain threshold, prompting immediate contact with the guests).

## DEMANDING AND DEFENDING STR RESTRICTIONS: THE UNLIKELY ALLIANCE OF HOTELIERS AND SOCIAL MOVEMENTS

### Hotels Going Global

The actors who supported new, or stronger, STR regulations include the hotel industry, citizens movements and those elected officials and administrators who elaborated restrictions in the first place. They have formed what we call an *unlikely alliance* of groups with radically different resources, repertoires of actions, political values and norms. While joining forces only sporadically, they have nevertheless pushed in the same direction, asking for restrictions to the STR market, as well as defending the rules in place against the backlash from platforms and rentiers.

Everywhere in Europe, the hotel sector, in particular, has been one of the most stable and vocal interest groups since the early 2010s, as we have shown in detail for Barcelona, Paris and Milan (Chapter 4). The hotel industry's market response to the rise of STRs varied from ignoring the phenomenon (as was initially the case with Hilton Hotels, IHG and Marriott) from embracing it (e.g., AccorHotels' acquisition of Onefinestay and Marriott's subsequent launch of an STR offer of luxury 'Homes and Villas') (Marvel 2017). By contrast, in terms of regulation, in all cities and countries, representatives from the hotel industry have systematically advocated a tougher approach to STRs which they perceived as unfair competition. They have demanded that operators of STRs be subject to the same set of rules that apply to hotels, and that the principles of a *level playing field* be upheld (a term recurrent in their public statements). These demands have been channelled through well-established local, regional and national hotel federations or professional organisations: for example, Federalberghi in Italy, the Dutch Association of Hotels (Koninklijke Horeca Nederland), UKHospitality in the UK (formerly the British Hospitality Association) and ATOP in France (Association for a Professional Tourism, formerly AHTOP, a think-tank of French tourism entrepreneurs born in 2015 and fighting unfair competition from platforms in order to promote 'quality tourism'). Many of these hotel organisations existed before the growth of platform-mediated STRs. They possess a large amount of resources and benefit from established access to the public and private actors operating in the tourism sector and regulating it. Sometimes these associations include other hospitality-related sectors besides traditional hotels (such as restaurants and bars in France with the UMIH, Union des Métiers et de l'Industrie de l'Hôtellerie, the main employers' organisation in the sector).

The position of these organisations, as expressed in their public statements, has been similar across cities and countries and even at the global level. This is a strong point of convergence in the cases of our sample. While they have tended to view occasional home-sharing (in the strict sense of a room rental, STR type iii) as an acceptable phenomenon, they have stressed that a large part of the STR offer is composed of full units managed by professional landlords or multi-property owners who do not have to comply with the same rules that apply to hotels. They have argued that 'properties with high levels of short-term use are "hotels/ guesthouses" in all but name, and thus traditional business models are placed in a position of unfair competitive disadvantage' (BHA 2016:3). On this ground, the main areas of concern recurrently mentioned by hotel industry representatives have been health and safety (fire/gas/food); tax (corporation tax, VAT, income tax, tourist tax); insurance; registration, permits and licencing; reporting obligations for public order and statistical purposes; consumers' rights; zoning/land use category in urban planning; and labour law, employees' rights and protection. Additionally, hospitality industry organisations have been particularly critical of the platforms' perceived lack of cooperation with public authorities, seeing them as providing 'a "loophole" (albeit legal) for "pseudo-hotels" to circumvent . . . regulations' (BHA 2016:1). Sometimes they have also been concerned by the lack of accommodation for seasonal workers in tourist areas (compounded by the growth of STRs), as stated by the UMIH president in 2023:

> Today there is a rental housing stock that completely escapes the state and is not taxed, which is unfair competition, totally unfair for people whose job it is to do hotel and restaurant business. . . . In tourist areas, you no longer have rentals for your seasonal workers. . . . And that's becoming a real problem, with things being rented out practically under the table and without protection, but with health and safety risks. (Thierry Marx, Michelin-starred chef, UMIH president, 2023, cited in Vignon 2023)

To support their claims, hotel associations have been active producers of studies demonstrating the size, nature and unregulated comparative advantage of the STR market. In Italy in 2016, Federalberghi commissioned one of the first nationwide studies about the size of the STR market, whose vivid title was *Tourism Informal Economy and Short-Term Rentals: The Lies of the Sharing Economy*, to stress its view of an unfair competition from professional STRs disguised as hosts (Federalberghi and Incipit Consulting 2016). In France, hotel industry professional organisations have been leading the fight on the legal front against STR actors, both hosts and platforms, since 2013 (Chapter 4). The UMIH took the owners of allegedly illegal STRs to court in 2013 (Caldini 2013), and then Airbnb itself in 2018 for unfair competition (Errard and Visseyrias 2018). The AHTOP filed a complaint in 2017 against Airbnb for 'illegally exercising the profession of real estate agent' (dismissed by the CJEU, which ruled in 2019 that Airbnb was an information society service company; see Chapter 7).

Hotel associations have also employed themselves to lobby at multiple levels. At the European scale, the umbrella Association of Hotels, Restaurants, Pubs and Cafes (HOTREC) and similar establishments was founded in 2007 as a not-for-profit association under Belgian law, bringing together 44 national associations from 32 countries. It has represented and championed the interest of the established hospitality industry before EU institutions and other relevant stakeholders, and acted as a platform for knowledge sharing and best practices among its members. After analysing the implications of STR and the 'collaborative economy' on its industry (HOTREC 2015), in 2017 HOTREC published a list of policy priorities under five key themes: STR registration schemes; yearly and quantitative limits; taxation; health, safety and security; and liability (HOTREC 2017). They argued that 'an equilibrium should emerge thanks to a clear distinction between private and professional activities, ensuring that it truly reflects the principles of fair competition promoted at the supranational level by the European Commission' (HOTREC 2017:1). Eventually, hotels started a global movement for the regulation of STRs, with the unambiguous name Global ReformBnB (https://globalreformbnb.com/). Such an umbrella network sought to achieve 'the goals that it would be very difficult for the hotel associations of the world to achieve individually' (Global Reformbnb 2023). It organised annual gatherings (the first of which was held in New York City in 2018) and global campaigning. This has made hotels, along with corporate platforms, the only interest group with 'global' representation, although much more fragmented than its platform counterpart.

While the hotel industry lobbied to protect the material interests of their business, one of the most interesting dimensions of their campaigning has been its occasional convergence with both citizen movements and left-wing local politicians. They have occasionally met and mutually supported each other in ways that would have been unexpected before the rise of the STR market. In May 2022 we attended the 4th Global ReformBnB conference, held in Paris.[21] It gathered an unlikely combination of deputy mayors and representatives from Paris, Barcelona, Lyon, Amsterdam and Brussels, coming from Social-Democratic, Communist, Green and New Municipalist parties, but also from other cities led by right-wing and conservative mayors; with top hotel lobbyists from the USA, Spain, Argentina and Japan—all of them spending two days together to discuss how to effectively achieve more stringent STR regulations. Hotel industry representatives also reused arguments developed by both social activists and regulators. Appealing to a common interest, not just to their business interest, they stressed the adverse effects of STR on housing markets and residents' quality of life, which they argued hotels did not cause.

## Re-Scaling Grassroots Movements

The above-mentioned arguments were, of course, at the core of grassroots campaigns by residents' associations and citizens' movements. The role that these have played in some cities in framing STRs as a policy problem and in putting it on the policy agenda has been analysed in Chapters 3 and 4, especially in the cases of Barcelona, Madrid, Berlin and Lisbon. In general, however, few cities actually witnessed the emergence of dedicated grassroots campaigns against STRs per se during the 2010s: rather, the issue of STR regulation became integrated into the demands of broader movements, such as anti-touristification movements in Barcelona (Novy and Colomb 2019; Chapter 4), housing rights collectives in Lisbon (Marques Pereira 2022) and Madrid (Wilson et al. 2021). In Prague, while the depopulation of the historic centre through touristification and the nuisances caused by STRs had been issues of concern for local residents and district councillors for many years (Pixová and Sládek 2016; Pixová 2020), it is only since the second half of the 2010s that residents' campaigns and grassroots mobilisations actually focused on the issue of STR have emerged (e.g., Stop Airbnb,

At Home in Prague—Regulate Airbnb, and the association for a Tolerable Living in the Centre of Prague) (Kafkadesk 2020). In Milan as well, existing grassroots and citizens movements active on housing and planning issues have started directing their claims to STRs in 2020–2021.

The grievances from residents and housing movements include the immediate, daily disturbance that STRs may create in the buildings and neighbourhoods where they are located (noise, uncivil behaviour, litter, damage to communal spaces), and the structural impacts they have on the housing stock and retail fabric, described in Chapter 1. They have demanded stricter forms of regulation, greater control or even prohibition of STRs. They have implicitly or explicitly grounded their claims in the individual right to 'peace' and 'privacy', and in the collective rights 'to housing' and 'to stay put'. These rights are, contrary to property rights, weakly institutionalised, often not protected legally and constitutionally.

Furthermore, despite a rising awareness about the global housing affordability crisis (Wetzstein 2017), in Europe citizens and housing movements have mostly remained organised and mobilised at the local and, sometimes, regional or national scales. They have only rarely lobbied in multi-level settings (with the exception of existing transnational networks, such as the International Union of Tenants; see Chapter 7). The informal network SET (Southern Europe against Touristification), mentioned in Chapter 4, has been an exception in this respect. While having played a fundamental role in framing the STR problem in their cities, the interests and demands of local grassroots mobilisations have in fact been mediated by local and national government representatives or Members of Parliament (and sometimes Members of the European Parliament; see Chapter 7). They have rarely been directly invited to participate in decision-making and to negotiate the scope and content of STR regulation, though have often been present at local public meetings or consultations on those regulations.

In one attempt to foster direct public participation, the city government of Paris organised in January 2021 a 'citizens' conference on short-term rentals'. Randomly selected Parisian residents were called as volunteers to work together and elaborate recommendations about the possible evolution of local STR regulations, after sitting in intensive training and information sessions listening to a variety of voices and interest groups (we were invited to present evidence in one of these sessions as researchers). Their conclusions were presented to the city council, but the role of the citizens' conference remained limited to that consultation exercise.[22] In Paris, as discussed in Chapter 4, grassroots movements have played a relatively minor role in the first half of the 2010s, though later, smaller collectives such as ParisVsBnB have taken up the issue from 2017 onwards (Chapter 4). Interestingly, however, ParisVsBnb has also been consolidated by emergent mobilisations in other French cities, for example, in Saint-Malo (Brittany), where residents and hotels set up the Saint-Malo, j'y suis j'y reste collective, which joined forces with ParisVsBnb and some 30 other collectives in France to create the Collectif National des Habitants Permanents in June 2023. A similar process of consolidation of citizens' collectives under the impetus of other movements from outside the city has also been witnessed in Milan. As argued in Chapter 4, anti-STR groups originated first in other Italian cities (Venice, Florence, Naples, Bologna), then fed into the activities of Milanese groups mobilised to (re)frame STRs as a housing problem in their local context.

## CONCLUSION

In the 2010s, a variety of interest groups were involved in, and affected by, the design and implementation of STR regulations. On the one hand, some actors attempted to intervene in the debates to soften the access type regulations that were blocking the market or to propose operate rules that better fitted their interests: platforms, of course, but also hosts and property managers. Their political strategies have considerably slowed down the conception and implementation of regulatory measures, adding to the difficulties inherent in enforcement discussed in Chapter 5. On the other hand, other interest groups have been whistleblowers or have urged local and national governments to step up and enact stronger regulation: hotel organisations and housing activists and other citizen mobilisations. In less than 10 years, all these actors have contributed to the construction of a contentious socio-political and economic space. This is a classic conflict between 'disruptive' firms that seek to dominate a market through shaping the rules, incumbent businesses who are being overtaken, governments who seek to coordinate economic relations and control them, and possibly citizens who are harmed by the produced externalities.

But these actors and processes have gone beyond the sole STR issue. They have contributed to transforming urban governance more broadly in the fields of housing, real estate, tourism and planning. From this perspective, this chapter brings three additional innovative results. First, we outline a new dimension in the power relations and politics of housing and real estate in European cities: the presence and political strength of a platform-rentiers bloc comprising corporate platforms and short-term rentiers, both extracting a new form of land rent from the digitally intermediated uses of the housing stock. This chapter demonstrates that the political strength of these actors stands on two mutually reinforcing legs. On the one hand, platforms have consolidated their role as individual political players through lobbying, an advantageous infrastructural position (with the control of data, transactions and tax collection linked to that position), and the mobilisation of their user base. Yet the political strength of STR platforms cannot be understood without looking at housing tenure and markets on the one hand, and the STR market structure on the other. The platform-rentiers bloc rests on a second leg: the political strength of (both small and large) property owners in European cities. They are STR market operators but also form a share of the electorate benefitting from a new use of property as a source of revenue. Politicians are not indifferent to them, above all in the cities from World 1. This shows that while scholars of platform capitalism have tended to consider different kinds of corporate platforms alike (Srnicek 2016; Culpepper and Thelen 2020), the user base that gives strength to STR platforms should be analysed from a sectoral (housing/real estate) and political perspective. This is necessary to make sense of differences in platform power between places and between types of platforms.

Second, the chapter provides a comparative argument by showing that the weight and the strategies of these various players in the governance of European cities differ significantly depending on the regulatory regime of each city. This plays out through two major variables: the housing regime (that also shapes the STR market structure) and the type/intensity of STR regulation. First, the weight of property owners in a given city establishes a specific relationship between the political clientele of local governments and the economic clientele of platforms. In World 1 cities (such as Milan), the two clienteles overlap: the share of homeowners is high, making local governments dependent on their interests, which are partly in line with those of the platforms (as explained above), and favour fewer limitations to the STR market growth. This large share of homeowners seems to be correlated with high rates of multi-listings, which tend to shape markets where large investors or operators can influence both the market and the local politics. In World 2 cities (such as Paris), the two clienteles are very distinct: property owners do not represent a major political weight, and city governments (from centre-left parties or coalitions) have been more interested in satisfying their larger political clientele—the tenants of private or social housing—making them more autonomous vis-à-vis the interests of the short-term rentier bloc and the platforms. In World 3 cities (such as Barcelona), the situation is hybrid: the share and weight of owners is potentially strong, platforms are trying to capitalise on it and large STR operators shape the markets, but recent governments led by a new political force have tried to make strong political choices that keep them at bay. This is possibly a fragile position, which may be challenged in subsequent elections, as we saw in the spring of 2023 in Spain, when all new municipalist governments lost the big cities that they had won in 2015 and/or 2019, including Barcelona. Second, the type of STR regulation adopted differentiates *how* all these actors mobilise and the relationships between them: when regulations are intense (Worlds 2 and 3), they are attacked in courts and produce a strong judicialisation. This is the case in Paris, for example, where the number of lawsuits between hosts, property managers, platforms, hotels and governments has been very large, and they are a major driver of policy development at the local and national level.

Finally, the chapter shows that all these relationships unfold in a multi-level political-economic space. At the national level, after focusing their efforts on the major cities studied in this book, many players have deployed strategies targeting other cities and rural areas: platforms have been diverting attention from the negative externalities evident in major cities while seeking to open up new market opportunities elsewhere (the cost of relocating platform activities is very low since platforms do not *own* what they commercialise). Social movements have formed in various localities and have strengthened their networking at the national level in an attempt to push national governments to act. Local governments have attempted alliances with other cities in their own countries and in Europe. Finally, these strategies are making the STR political space increasingly interconnected in a multilevel Europe, in terms of organisations, claims and narratives and court decisions. Here, the EU has become a new battleground, something to which we turn in detail in the next chapter.

# 7

## THE JUDICIALISATION AND TRANSNATIONALISATION OF LOCAL CONFLICTS

### The European Union as a Regulatory Battleground

LOCAL STR REGULATIONS have been the object of intense political mobilisation by various organised interests and actors. Opponents have often filed legal cases against the regulations in regional or national courts. In the context of the EU—a political construct characterised by a body of law that applies to all its member states—the process of judicialisation and the contentious politics of STR regulation have shifted upwards towards the supranational scale. This chapter shows two interrelated processes of political rescaling at the European level: on the one hand, the strategic use of existing EU law by corporate platforms and short-term rentiers *against* local and national STR regulations, and on the other hand, the mobilisation of city governments and all types of interest groups to influence EU regulatory change in directions favourable to their interests.

The EU integration project is built on the construction of a common market across the EU territory, the Single

Market. A complex body of EU laws supports the functioning of the Single Market, among which two pieces are of central relevance to the operation of digital platforms and the services they mediate (such as STRs): the 2000 *E-Commerce Directive* and the 2006 *Services Directive*. These two directives have been mobilised by the actors opposed to strict regulations of platform-mediated STRs. The EU level has consequently become a key battleground for the future of STR regulation and the governance of platforms more broadly. Large platforms, and some of the professional organisations that represent STR operators at various levels (presented in the previous chapter), have invested in intensive communication and lobbying activities at the EU level to push for a strict interpretation of existing EU rules or to influence the debates about proposed reforms to EU law. In parallel, the governments of large European cities have started to network with each other to exchange expertise, speak with a common voice and exert political influence at the European level to counterweigh that of platforms and STR rentier organisations.[1] In the second part of the chapter we analyse the rescaling of collective action and political mobilisation of the key actors discussed in Chapter 6 towards the transnational scale of EU institutions,[2] in the context of the preparation of two new sets of EU legislation between 2020 and 2024: the *Digital Services* and *Digital Market Acts* on the one hand, and a new EU regulation on data collection and sharing relating to STR services on the other.

Going back to the general puzzle underlying this book—the diversity of local STR regulatory regimes—this chapter shows that this 10-year process of political rescaling at the EU level has not led to a convergence in local regulatory approaches, despite attempts by specific actors to use the EU legislative framework to push in that direction to restrict regulatory interventions to the minimum. The new EU regulation on STR data sharing approved in early 2024 offers some resources to local governments willing to regulate, but does not affect local regulatory approaches in place, as long as the latter are deemed compatible with the *Services Directive* by relevant courts.

## THE JUDICIALISATION OF LOCAL REGULATORY CONFLICTS IN THE CONTEXT OF THE EU SINGLE MARKET

The EU is a political construct of 27 nation-states (as of 2023) that combines supranational and intergovernmental features. Since the mid-1980s, one of the main aspects of the EU project has been the construction of a single market based on the free movement of goods, persons, capital and services within the EU territory. That Single Market has been gradually constructed through political decisions backed by the development of an extensive body of EU legislation in multiple fields, in order to remove legal, technical and bureaucratic barriers. This includes EU competition law (e.g., antitrust and cartel policy, 'state aid' rules), but also the regulation of e-commerce and the exchange of services within the EU. The overall functioning of the Single Market is overseen by the European Commission's Directorate-General (DG) for Internal Market, Industry, Entrepreneurship and SMEs (DG GROW) and its DG for Competition.

In the framework of the Single Market, the European Commission and the European Parliament have, since the mid-2010s, promoted the growth of the 'collaborative economy' (European Commission 2016a, 2016b, n.d.-a) and the development of a 'digital single market'.[3] Until 2020, the European Commission took the view that the existing EU legal framework was fit for purpose to deal with the growth of that sector, supplemented by 'soft' guidance (European Commission 2016a, 2018). As stated above, two key pieces of EU law have formed the basis of the regulatory framework that applies to, respectively, digital platforms and the providers of the services they mediate: the 2000 *E-Commerce Directive* and the 2006 *Services Directive*. These were supplemented by the new *Digital Services Act* and *Digital Market Act* approved in the autumn of 2022.

As shown in Chapters 4 and 6, new local, regional or national STR regulations have been the object of intense opposition and legal challenges filed by corporate platforms, professional STR operators and associations of hosts in front of regional or national courts (in Amsterdam, Paris, Berlin, Barcelona, Brussels and Madrid, among others). Courts evaluate the cases presented to them against regional and national laws (that are often the result of a transposition of EU law into domestic law), and ultimately, against EU law itself, which prevails over domestic law in case of conflict. The *E-Commerce* and *Services Directives* have been explicitly referred to by the actors opposed to new forms of STR regulation, alongside the *General Data Protection Regulation* (the EU's privacy law).[4] In a situation of uncertainty, regional or national courts can refer a case to the Court of Justice of the EU. The CJEU will then issue a ruling over the correct interpretation of EU law in that particular case, which is then transposed by the competent national court. The CJEU ruling becomes binding jurisprudence on all courts in the EU dealing with a similar case in the future.

Consequently, the interpretation of the *E-Commerce* and *Services Directives* by regional, national and EU courts ultimately defines the possibility—and acceptable forms—of regulation of both online platforms and STR operators by public authorities in the EU. Two main issues have been the object of fierce legal debates. First, should platforms be considered mere digital intermediaries or service providers? Second, what are the 'overriding reasons relating to the public interest' that the courts will recognise as valid (i.e., compliant with EU law) when assessing specific STR regulations passed by local, regional and national authorities, and what types of regulatory interventions/instruments will be deemed acceptable?

## The Ambiguous Nature of Digital Platforms in EU Law: Service Providers or Mere Intermediaries?

Regarding the first area of debate, on the *nature* of digital platforms, should they be treated as mere intermediaries between suppliers and consumers, as providers of the underlying services (e.g., transport or STR), or both? Some platforms act as 'pure notice boards' that simply match supply and demand, while others intervene in the configuration of the product or service or may even provide it (Martínez Mata 2017). This distinction is essential, because it determines which pieces and provisions of EU law apply to particular platforms. If a platform is considered a pure noticeboard, only the provisions of the *E-Commerce Directive* apply to it,[5] which significantly limits the potential for local or national regulations of its activities across the EU, as explained below. If a platform is considered a provider of the underlying service, then the local, regional or national regulations relevant to that sector will apply too, provided the latter are in accordance with the EU *Services Directive*.

Whether a platform is considered a pure intermediary (an *information society service* [ISS] in the jargon of the *E-Commerce Directive*) or a provider of the underlying service has to be established on a case-by-case basis. In 2017, following the referral of a case initially submitted by a Barcelona-based taxi drivers' association to a Spanish court, the CJEU (C-434/15) ruled that the service offered by the Uber platform went beyond that of an 'information society service' and qualified as a 'transport service'. This 'Uber ruling' means that the company should be treated like a taxi operator and thus is subject to national transport regulations in EU countries. However, the CJEU took the opposite view with regard to Airbnb. In a ruling in December 2019, the CJEU (C-390/18) stated that Airbnb, as an intermediation service, should be classified as an information society service under the *E-Commerce Directive* (i.e., a pure intermediary). This ruling responded to a case referred by the Tribunal de Grande Instance (administrative court) of Paris in June 2018. The French professional hotel association AHTOP (introduced in Chapters 4 and 6) had started legal proceedings against Airbnb Ireland (the European subsidiary of the platform), arguing that the platform operates like a real estate agent and that it should therefore be subject to the same licensing, accounting, insurance and financial obligations as traditional brokers of rental accommodation: 'Airbnb not only creates relationships between two people, it creates a STR market, helps fix the prices, centralizes payments, provides insurance services, publishes and advertises it. . . . All these elements show that they are much more than just an intermediation service' (Chee 2018). Airbnb replied that it 'doesn't intervene in the transaction' (Chee 2018).

This CJEU ruling on Airbnb limits the capacity of public authorities to take measures restricting the market access and operations of Airbnb in the EU,[6] as the company is now considered a mere intermediary (information society service) under the *E-Commerce Directive*. As such, according to the directive (Section 4, Articles 12 to 15), the platform is liable *only* for the electronic intermediation service it offers, *not* for the possibly illegal content or service it advertises—unless it has actual knowledge, in factual terms, of the illegal content or activity. The *E-Commerce Directive* does not place a general obligation on platforms to monitor content systematically or to actively detect illegal activity.[7] While several public authorities have asked for a 'general obligation' on platforms to systematically check every listing they publish to monitor compliance with domestic laws, platforms have refused to do so. But if a platform *does* know that there is illegal content (e.g., because a city government has notified it of individual cases of illegal STRs), the platform is obliged to remove the illegal listings. However, the 'notice-and-takedown' provisions of the *E-Commerce Directive* are not always very effective: several city governments, such as Vienna or Paris, have asked Airbnb to remove listings that were in breach of local rules, but the company either has not done so or has taken a long time to do so (Cox and Haar 2020), as reported by interviewees in those cities (see Chapter 5).

Second, according to the *E-Commerce Directive*'s 'country of origin principle' (Article 3(2)), only the regulations of the EU country where an ISS company is established should normally apply to that company (in the case of Airbnb, Ireland, where its European headquarter is based). Elsewhere in the EU, 'nothing can be adopted that can be seen as an obstacle to the company's day-to-day business'. That general rule can be derogated from in order to protect specific legal interests (e.g., public security, health and consumer protection), but any measure taken by a public authority needs to be *necessary* and *proportionate*, and notified in advance to the European Commission and the country of establishment. This restricts the market access requirements that can be imposed on Airbnb by a public authority outside of Ireland. The obligation to include an STR registration number in all published listings, for example (a key request by several city governments, as explained in Chapter 5), has to be justified under the above-mentioned derogation. So far, the municipal, regional or national governments that have filed legal cases against Airbnb in front of domestic courts to gain access to platform-held data have often lost those cases on the basis of the *E-Commerce Directive* principles (e.g., in Berlin, Munich, Vienna and the Balearic Islands—see Cox and Haar 2020). Some European city governments appealed to Irish courts for the right to request host data from Airbnb or for the right to impose a fine on the platform for publishing illegal listings (Cox and Haar 2020). As reported by an interviewee from Berlin in 2019, this is a costly and lengthy process, which requires legal skills and resources that are not always available to local authorities. Altogether, the above-mentioned CJEU ruling is likely to pave the way for more legal challenges by platforms (and associations of STR operators) against local, regional or national regulatory measures.

## The Services Directive: Can Limits on Short-Term Rental Activities Be Imposed by Public Authorities?

The second area of debate in the context of the EU legal framework concerns the application of the *Services Directive* and the conditions that it spells out for public authorities to be able to regulate a service (such as STR accommodation). The *Services Directive* aims to support the creation of a single European market for 'services provided for economic return', by removing barriers to trade and creating a level playing field for businesses and consumers across the EU.[8] The provisions of the directive thus apply to STR operators/hosts as providers of accommodation services (rather than platforms, as explained above). These operators are subject to the relevant local, regional or national regulations that apply to the sector of the service they offer.

Under the directive, any measure taken by a public authority to regulate the exercise of, or access to, a service may be considered a barrier to the Single Market and deemed incompatible with EU law. Public authorities can only set up a 'market access requirement' (e.g., an authorisation or licensing scheme for STRs) provided that it is *necessary* to attain a clearly identified overriding reason of public interest, *non-discriminatory* (i.e., not favouring one business model over another), and *proportionate* to achieving this interest (i.e., not replaceable by less restrictive means). These conditions make it harder for public authorities to enact and maintain restrictive regulations of STRs. Any measure taken by a public authority, if challenged in court, needs justification, through a clear identification of the problem that will determine the possible 'overriding reason of public interest'. Two challenges thus arise from the *Services Directive*: the scope of the overriding reasons relating to the public interest that are recognised as legitimate by courts to justify regulatory interventions by public authorities, and the types of regulatory interventions that are deemed acceptable.

The *Services Directive* contains an open list of overriding reasons relating to the public interest that may justify national measures restricting the freedom to provide services. But public interest objectives cannot all be decided ex ante. National authorities have the possibility to advance other reasons than those listed. In the field of STRs, the public interest reasons mentioned by city governments to justify regulatory intervention have varied: protecting consumers, ensuring public safety, combating tax evasion, safeguarding public health or remedying the scarcity of affordable housing (European Commission 2016a:3). The city government of Barcelona, for example, invoked the need to 'protect the city environment' when it asked the Spanish government to expand the list of public interest reasons that may justify regulatory interventions in the relevant national law (Martínez Mata 2017).

Ultimately, it will be case-law from the CJEU that will clarify what are considered acceptable 'reasons of public interest' justifying a particular regulation of STRs in specific circumstances, and what regulatory measures are deemed to be adequate and proportional. In previous decisions unrelated to STRs, the CJEU has recognised reasons related to the 'right to housing' (Martínez Mata 2017). In October 2020 the CJEU made a significant ruling that could potentially help European city governments uphold some of their STR regulations in the name of housing protection. The context for that ruling was a legal dispute in Paris mentioned in Chapters 5 and 6: two STR owners were fined by the Tribunal de Grande Instance for illegally renting their property without the necessary authorisation and were ordered to return the properties back to residential use. The two owners appealed against that decision by claiming that the authorisation scheme breached the *Services Directive* (for not being proportional or justified by an overriding public interest reason). The French Court of Appeal turned to the CJEU to ask whether the relevant regulations (i.e., an authorisation scheme rooted in national legislation but implemented by the City of Paris) complied with the EU *Services Directive* (Cases C-724/18 and C-727/18).

In April 2020, in an advisory opinion that preceded the final CJEU ruling, Advocate General Michal Bobek stated that

> combating a housing shortage and seeking to ensure the availability of sufficient and affordable (long-term) housing (in particular in large cities), as well as the protection of the urban environment, are valid justifications for the establishment of authorisation schemes broadly based on social policy. (CJEU 2020b:19)

On 22 September 2020, the CJEU confirmed that the objective of combating the long-term rental housing shortage constitutes an over-riding reason relating to the public interest (CJEU 2020b), which justifies the regulatory measures taken by the French national government and the City of Paris. These were deemed compliant with EU law (CJEU 2020a).

This ruling was a landmark in the context of public debates on the regulation of STRs, legitimising the use of authorisation schemes for STR (type i) under certain conditions. The CJEU, however, leaves it up to national or regional courts to decide on the proportionality of specific measures, in light of contextual evidence.[9] In February 2021 the French Cour de Cassation ruled that the regime applicable in Paris was proportional to the objective pursued.[10] This allowed the Paris city government to resume their legal proceedings against 400 STR operators suspected of illegal 'change of usage', which had been put on hold (see Chapter 4).

There is one important caveat to this CJEU ruling: it concerns only *one* type of regulatory instrument used by city governments in Europe (namely a prior authorisation scheme for change of use), not the other types exposed in Chapter 3—all of which can potentially be challenged in front of the courts by actors opposed to them. This has indeed been the case for the bans or freezes on STR type i declared in some cities or parts thereof (e.g., in Barcelona and Berlin), which have been legally challenged in front of domestic courts, and on which there is yet no

EU case-law. Article 15 of the *Services Directive* stipulates that absolute bans or 'quantitative restrictions' of an activity should be a measure of last resort. According to the European Commission, such bans have to be justified with very solid evidence and used only 'where other policy measures . . . have failed to address the shortage in the availability and affordability of local housing' (European Commission 2018:3). It is on those grounds that in March 2021, the Court of Amsterdam overturned the STR ban in three central districts that had previously been established by the city government.

The evaluation of any given STR regulatory measure against the EU *Services Directive* by regional or national courts and the CJEU has to be undertaken on a case-by-case basis. Its outcome will depend on the justifications presented by a public authority in terms of the public interest objectives that are pursued through STR regulation. For city governments, this means having to collate solid evidence of the impacts of STRs on housing markets, among other impacts. The CJEU ruling of September 2020 defers to national courts the responsibility to 'verify, in the light of all the evidence available to it . . . whether that option is an effective response to the shortage of long-term rental housing that has been observed in the territories concerned'. The legitimacy of public intervention is therefore grounded in the capacity of public authorities to demonstrate a 'serious and grave risk' to the availability of affordable housing causally linked with the proliferation of STRs in a particular city.

Yet as we have seen in Chapters 1 and 5, it is difficult to prove that there is such a serious and grave risk, for two main reasons—methodological (other factors intervene in creating a crisis of supply and affordability in housing markets), and practical (one needs precise data on the STR offer, which platforms have often refused to supply). Data, therefore, are not only important for local authorities to locate STRs and enforce any potential STR regulation. They are also, in the EU context, essential to convince courts of the necessity and proportionality of regulatory measures by demonstrating negative housing market (or other) impacts. Consequently, courts are likely to only accept evidence of *significant* adverse impacts as a condition to uphold a strict STR regulation: this means that the identified problem (the proliferation of STRs) is already at an advanced stage in the territory concerned. This logic has been contested by city governments, who have argued that it prevents them from taking a *preventative* regulatory approach to protect the housing stock and urban environment before the problem becomes too big.

This brings us back to the thorny question of access to, and production of, data that are necessary for public policy formation, implementation and enforcement (discussed in Chapter 5). Until 2022, the position of the European Commission was that according to existing EU law, platforms did not have an obligation to communicate detailed data about individual listings to public authorities.[11] But the question of access to platform data and, more broadly, the relationship between public authorities and platforms, took centre stage in the debates around two new sets of EU legislation that unfolded between 2020 and 2023.

## THE BATTLE AROUND THE REFORM OF THE EU REGULATORY FRAMEWORK: TRANSNATIONAL ADVOCACY AND LOBBYING

Since the mid-2010s, large platforms, the EHHA, the ETTSA (European Technology & Travel Services Association), and some of the largest professional organisations representing STR operators and the hotel industry (presented in the previous chapter), have invested in intensive communication and lobbying activities at the EU level. The EHHA, Booking, Airbnb Ireland and the Expedia Group (that owns VRBO and HomeAway) have been registered in the EU Transparency Register under the category 'In-house lobbyists and trade/business/professional associations' since 2013, 2014, 2015 and 2017 respectively.[12] In 2021 these companies reported, respectively, 1, 3, 4.25 and

1.25 full-time equivalent lobbyists, as well as relatively modest though increasing sums of money spent on lobbying activities. Such activities include networking, meetings with Commission officials and Members of the European Parliament (MEPs)[13] and preparing reports and official responses to public consultations (see Corporate Europe Observatory 2018 for a critical assessment of the early lobbying activities of platforms in the mid-2010s). Up to the late 2010s, those activities were aimed at advocating a strict interpretation of the above-mentioned EU directives, which, as we have seen, constrain the room for manoeuvre of public authorities in their demands on platforms and in their regulation of STR activities. From 2020 onwards, those activities focused on influencing the debates about proposed reforms to EU law in ways that were favourable to platforms' and STR operators' interests.

The complexity of the jargon used in EU documents, the required understanding of the competences of EU institutions, the intricacies of EU law and the workings of the policy process within and between EU institutions and member states have meant that ordinary citizens or grassroots movements have not been very involved in the debates and processes outlined below, with some exceptions: individual hosts often briefed by 'host clubs', platforms or other STR professional associations (as described in Chapter 6); a small number of European-wide advocacy networks or NGOs (e.g., the International Union of Tenants and the Housing Europe network of national/regional federations of social and public housing providers); and individual researchers close to local social movements fighting for housing rights or against touristification.

### Pushing for, or Resisting, the Strict Interpretation and Application of EU Law

At the EU level, in 2016 the EHHA filed a complaint with the European Commission's department in charge of monitoring the compliance of national laws with the Single Market principles,[14] which targeted the city governments of Berlin, Barcelona, Brussels and Paris. The EHHA criticised them for 'some of the most over-zealous rules and restrictions/bans which are not consistent with EU law' (EHHA 2016:1), referring to the *E-Commerce* and the *Services Directives*. It specifically challenged three actions: the request to platforms to hand over data about hosts or to monitor the legality of listings, the requirement for hosts to go through registration and authorisation schemes and the quantitative restrictions on STRs imposed by particular authorities. According to the EHHA's Secretary General, those restrictions 'infringe the EU's fundamental freedom to provide services across Europe', and 'the EU must intervene to put an end to the unnecessary patchwork of restrictive and contradictory municipal rules and red-tape' (EHHA 2016: 2). In response to the EHHA complaint,[15] the European Commission has to date taken action with regard to the case of Brussels, sending a letter of formal notice to the Belgian government in January 2019 to seek explanations of the authorisation procedure and requirements set by the Brussels Capital Region (whose government set very strict requirements on STR types ii and iii) (European Commission 2019). The then minister-president of the Brussels Capital Region, Rudi Vervoort, stated in the press that he did not intend in the first instance to modify the regulations, but instead to explain their rationale to the Commission (Sente 2019).

In 2018 the EHHA and the ETTSA jointly published a 'roadmap' document that adopted a more conciliatory tone, clarifying the actions to which its member platforms would agree. It stated that the STR sector was 'ready to exchange with the relevant authorities on the impact of STR services in their locality, including statistics relating to STR accommodation providers when in line with GDPR rules'. It claimed that online platforms would 'provide tools to STR accommodation providers to assist them in their compliance with local laws', for example, through a field for registration numbers; would 'take down any property where they have received effective knowledge of illegality from the enforcement authorities'; and would 'cooperate with public authorities in order to facilitate compliance by STR accommodation providers' on issues of taxation (EHHA and ETTSA 2018:3).

Mirroring the activities of the EHHA and large platforms, European city governments gradually began to mobilise collectively to make their voice heard at the EU level. From 2016 onwards, initially under the impulse of public officials and elected representatives from Barcelona, and later on from Berlin and Amsterdam, a number of large city governments started to meet regularly to compare their experiences, approaches and difficulties in regulating STRs and dealing with large platforms. In January 2018 eight city representatives sent a letter to the European Commission asking for a legal initiative that would allow public authorities to obtain access to individualised data from platforms (Boztas 2018). In June 2019, 10 city governments—mostly led by left-of-centre mayors or coalitions (Amsterdam, Barcelona, Berlin, Bordeaux, Brussels, Krakow, Munich, Paris, Valencia and Vienna)—published an open letter to the European Commission and European Parliament (reproduced in Henley 2019), which argued that the protection of the local housing stock is a public interest objective that must be allowed to override the restrictions of the *Services* and *E-Commerce Directives*. The public policy director of Airbnb explicitly replied to the cities' letter through another public letter addressed to 'European governments and regulators', stating: 'We want to work with governments to embrace regulations that leverage the best of the collaborative economy, which is why we were disappointed to read comments from a small number of cities to the Commission'. Airbnb's response rebutted some of the cities' statements by mentioning its own evidence on the benefits of STRs and on the company's recent goodwill in working with city governments such as Amsterdam and Barcelona.

## Towards a New EU Digital Services Act:
## Cities Versus Platforms

Following the above-mentioned CJEU ruling of March 2020 that qualified Airbnb as a digital intermediary, the governments of 22 cities (including, from our sample, Amsterdam, Barcelona, Berlin, Brussels, London, Milan, Paris, Prague and Vienna) publicly called for a new EU legislative framework to supersede the *E-Commerce Directive* (Eurocities 2020b). Their demands were spelled out in a policy paper published by the Eurocities (2020a) association in response to the European Commission's announcement of the preparation of a new *Digital Services Act* that would modernise the *E-Commerce Directive*. The 22 city governments argued that new EU legislation should require platforms to share relevant data with city administrations, to publish STR registration numbers on listings where applicable and to be liable for fulfilling their obligations according to national and local legislation. In September 2020 public officials from Paris, Amsterdam and Berlin, among other cities, met with European Commission Executive Vice-President Margrethe Vestager to reiterate those demands (Eurocities 2020c). While this network of cities published its first declarations under the umbrella of the existing Eurocities network, it later made public statements on its own, steered by strong leadership from the Amsterdam city government. The choice of setting up an informal network between city governments working on an ad hoc basis was partly explained by the limits of existing modes of participation of city governments into formal EU decision-making processes and channels (Heinelt 2017; Vidal 2019).

However, in parallel, the European Committee of the Regions (CoR), an advisory EU body that represents the voice of regional and local governments in the EU policy-making processes, published an opinion (European Committee of the Regions 2020) advocating a new 'European framework for regulatory responses' to what it still called the 'collaborative economy'. It noted that 'many of the sectors in which digital platforms are active, from accommodation, urban transport, delivery services to the use of public spaces, are regulated or taxed at the local and regional level'. It stressed that some provisions of the *E-Commerce Directive*—enacted before the age of platforms—were outdated and problematic for cities and regions. It called for a future European framework 'to strengthen the capacity of public authorities to take action to regulate . . . according to their national, regional or local situation, in full respect of the principle of subsidiarity', by making platforms 'liable for illegal actions or dissemination of illegal content (e.g. social housing offers on short-term rental platforms)' and requiring them to 'provide public authorities with the data necessary to enforce the rules applicable to the platform and/or its sector of activity on a legal basis'. Altogether, the position of local and regional authorities in Europe was made clear to the European Commission through various channels.

On 15 December 2020 the European Commission published draft proposals for two legislative initiatives: the *Digital Markets Act* (DMA) and the *Digital Services Act* (DSA). The former focuses 'on the market power of big platforms and stipulating obligations of conduct', and the latter aims at 'minimally controlling provision of digital services' (Martínez Mata 2021:1). The Commission's proposals aimed 'to create a safer digital space where the fundamental rights of users are protected and to establish a level playing field for businesses'.[16] This responded to 'growing concerns about enforceability of national laws, market domination by USA tech platforms, algorithmic amplification of disinformation, and the partial success of the General Data Protection Regulation' (McCourt Institute 2023:3). Both proposals were subject to intense scrutiny and lobbying by large digital technology companies such as Google, Apple, Facebook, Amazon and Twitter, and other actors with a stake in the regulation of the digitally mediated economy in Europe, including STR platforms.

The DSA was meant to update the *E-Commerce Directive* and harmonise the rules on the provision of digital services in the EU Single

Market.[17] In the first published draft of the DSA, three key principles enshrined in the *E-Commerce Directive* were maintained: (1) the 'country of origin' principle, through which platforms should in general abide only by the laws of the member state in which they are established; (2) the absence of obligation for platforms to monitor the content they advertise; and 3) the limited liability of platforms in relation to illegal content, activities and services provided by third parties. The draft, however, contained some changes (for a summary, see Martínez Mata 2021) that strengthened the requirements on platforms to act upon orders by judicial or administrative authorities to remove illegal content or to provide information.

Between 2020 and 2022 the preparation of the DSA was accompanied by an intense collective mobilisation of the stakeholders concerned. During the consultations and parliamentary debates that are part of the EU policy-making process, several interest groups analysed in Chapter 6 actively lobbied EU institutions to convey their policy preferences. Platforms were unsurprisingly very active. In the two years of debates, Airbnb reported that its staff held six meetings with high-level Commission officials, participated in three workshops organised by committees of the European Parliament, and accompanied two delegations of MEPs to the Airbnb HQ in San Francisco and Airbnb office in Washington, D.C.[18] For the company, the existence of an EU-wide regulatory framework is a positive thing: if EU law continues to support smooth access to the STR market, it makes it easier for the platform to operate in 27 countries, some of which are its biggest markets outside of the USA. In its official statement in response to the public consultation on the DSA that closed in September 2020 (Airbnb 2020c), the company emphasised some of the actions it had taken in terms of self-regulation (in relation to safety and consumer trust) and broadly supported the provisions of the draft act. However, the company requested more clarity on data-sharing obligations with public authorities.

From the point of view of local governments, however, the first draft of the DSA did not deliver the necessary provisions for cities to regulate STRs adequately, because it did not meet any of their above-mentioned key demands (Eurocities 2020a; see Cox and Haar 2020:72–73 for a summary). The DSA was eventually approved by the European Parliament and the EU Council of Ministers and came into force in November 2022.[19] The final version of the act did not respond to the concerns expressed by city governments over the previous years and fell short of their demands in terms of platform accountability and data disclosure. It maintains the principles that limit the regulatory power of public authorities (i.e., the 'country of origin' principle, the limited liability of platforms in relation to illegal content and the non-obligation for 'general monitoring').

In parallel, however, in a different policy area—that of taxation—a change in EU legislation strengthened the obligation on platforms to share data with public authorities. In 2020 the European Commission proposed a revision of Directive 2011/16 on administrative cooperation in the field of taxation, which frames the exchange of information between the national tax authorities of EU member states. The Amending Directive (2021/514, known as DAC7), approved in March 2021, entered into force on 1 January 2023. It introduced a new reporting obligation on digital platforms, which are required to share with national tax authorities detailed information about the revenue received by the sellers of goods and services they advertise, that is, hosts in the case of STRs. This was the first step in a process of strengthening of EU requirements on platforms for data release.

### Harmonisation Versus Diversity of Local STR Regulations in the European Single Market Logic

Under pressure from various sides to delve further into the issue of platform-mediated STRs, in the autumn of 2021 the European

Commission's directorate general responsible for the Internal Market (DG GROW—more specifically its unit on digital transformation) published a series of scoping documents for public consultation under the title *Tourist Services—Short-Term Rental Initiative*.[20] Those documents discussed why, and to what extent, EU action might be needed to address the concerns that had emerged in previous years—those raised by platforms and STR operators on the one hand and by city governments on the other. DG GROW organised two public workshops and ran a consultation to collect 'feedback from all stakeholders on the current situation and the potential impacts of possible measures relating to the provision of STR' (European Commission, DG GROW 2021). A total of just under 5,700 valid responses were received, of which 85% were submitted by individual citizens (many of them STR hosts), and the rest by private companies, business associations and public authorities. Over half of the responses came from the three biggest STR markets in Europe (France, Italy and Spain). The diversity of responses submitted during the consultation process, and our observation of the exchanges in two public online workshops attended by dozens of stakeholders, reveal a clash between different positions and rationalities.

The problems that the initiative sought to tackle were framed by DG GROW as twofold. First, the lack of STR data was identified as a major challenge for effective policy-making and implementation: 'Without consistent access to data on STR, public authorities will continue to find it difficult to design justified, effective and proportionate policy responses and enforce the rules' (European Commission, DG GROW 2021:3). However, in the text that introduced the online questionnaire of the public consultation, it was stated that 'this is often due to, amongst others, uncertainty regarding the applicable rules, lack of consistent and systematic requests from public authorities and privacy concerns'. This does not match the arguments put forward by the local authority representatives we interviewed, who consistently requested platforms to share individualised data and, in most cases bar a few exceptions discussed in Chapter 5, faced a lack of response or a rejection.

Second, the diversity of local, regional and national STR regulations was recurrently presented, in the documents and statements of DG GROW, as a problem: 'fragmented', burdensome on market players, creating market access barriers for STR service providers and resulting in a 'lack of level playing field situation' at the European level (European Commission, DG GROW 2021). This was used to justify the need for an EU initiative to 'clarify and streamline the rules and requirements public authorities can impose on hosts and online platforms' (European Commission, DG GROW 2021). This view of STR regulations is shaped by an economic, 'free-trade' rationality that seeks, first and foremost, to improve conditions for STR players and remove 'unnecessary market access barriers'—unsurprisingly, given that this is the remit of this specific DG in the European Commission.[21]

The EHHA, in its response to the DG GROW documents (2021), welcomed 'the EU-level intervention to help reduce regulatory fragmentation and increase legal certainty for all' and outlined its policy preferences: creating a standardised EU STR registration (notification) scheme at a national level (which cities can opt into or not); 'specifying the EU rules public authorities should always respect when deciding to impose market access requirements to STR services'; and 'creating [a] common and consistent approach for online STR platforms to share and report data, in line with GDPR, and clarifying what additional data should be shared (if any) which is not already covered by the EU legal framework'. It reiterated its critique of 'stricter, unjustified, disproportionate and discriminative STR rules (such as change of use of a property, consent of neighbors, night caps, hotel like requirements for individual hosts and bans)', and again asked the European Commission to ensure the proper enforcement of the *Services Directive*. It concluded that 'avoiding the regulatory fragmentation of rules for STR services and improving its functioning can only be achieved at EU level (such as Proposal for a Regulation)'.

Airbnb published its own response and policy proposals (2021b) for what an EU intervention should look like in a document entitled *The EU Host Action Plan*. The proposals were explicitly phrased to appear to respond to the key concerns of city governments:

> Airbnb has . . . committed to support authorities as they enforce new responsible and harmonized EU rules that get tough on property speculators, while making it easier for everyday Europeans to welcome guests into their homes. Providing a solution to outdated and fragmented rules that vary greatly across the bloc, Airbnb's proposal would unlock the benefits of hosting for millions of EU citizens and help address challenges associated with property speculators and overtourism.

The reference to these latter two challenges was relatively new in the public narrative of the company. One can hypothesise that the issues of real estate speculation and overtourism had become too central in European debates (see Chapters 1 and 4) for the company to ignore. In any case, this illustrates the continuation of the company's strategy outlined in the previous chapter, through which it seeks to present itself as amenable to regulation and willingly helping policy-makers. Interestingly, it pitted the 'everyday host' against the 'speculators', coopting a language and distinction used by the advocates of strict STR regulation (e.g., in Paris; see Chapter 4).

In its *Action Plan*, Airbnb made five proposals. First, it wanted to see an EU-wide host register that would replace local registration schemes, which the company would support 'by ensuring only those hosts with an EU registration number are allowed to publish listings on the platform'. Second, it insisted on the necessity of 'clarifying local rules and introducing safeguards for everyday hosts' 'to create more economic opportunities for everyday Europeans to participate in the travel economy'. The language here was vague, recognising the possibility 'for local governments to take action to limit property speculators . . . to the extent these local rules are reasonable and proportionate . . .

whilst safeguarding everyday hosts from excessive restrictions'. Third, it promised to support enforcement by removing listings that do not show the EU registration number and 'expanding access to the City Portal' (https://www.airbnb.com/cityportal), described as a 'purpose-built tool to support public sector regulation by providing insights on Airbnb's presence in neighborhoods, tools to help enforce laws, and better access to Airbnb when needed'. Fourth, it committed 'to ensure that local and national authorities have the necessary data to manage effective enforcement'—a commitment that had not been clearly expressed before. Finally, it pledged to 'support local communities' by helping address problems of incivility (e.g., noise), expanding the tourist tax collection and helping 'disperse the concentration of travelers' outside of congested areas (Airbnb 2021b). Overall, the proposals displayed a more amenable and collaborative tone than was the case a few years before.

In contrast to the positions of the EHHA and Airbnb, for the network of European city governments seeking to regulate STRs, the framing of the issues in the documents published by the European Commission's DG GROW was highly problematic. For those city governments, the variation in local, regional and national STR regulations is not a *problem*—a 'market barrier'—to be overcome, but is the legitimate result of a diversity of local situations in terms of housing markets and tourism pressures, as well as of choices made by democratically elected local governments. The response submitted by the European Cities Alliance on Short-Term Holiday Rentals on 14 October 2021 made this clear:

> Local authorities assume their responsibilities to find a reasonable regulatory balance in ensuring a sufficient supply of decent and affordable long-term rental housing for all who wish to live and work in our cities, whilst also accommodating tourism and related economic interests, and as well as safeguarding the liveability and public safety in our cities. . . . The interests in this balance are, however, not interchangeable. For it is clear that we as local public authorities have a primary responsibility for ensuring

affordable housing for all as well as for the liveability and public safety in our communities.

While the DG GROW document acknowledged the need to 'fully respect the principle of subsidiarity [of cities], for example in relation to urban planning rules' (European Commission, DG GROW 2021), it did not explain how to resolve the tension between that principle and the Single Market objectives. From the point of view of local governments, STRs are not just a 'service' to be governed to serve the logic of the Single Market. They are a specific type of land use that is subject to urban planning, housing and security/safety regulations, which according to the subsidiarity principle are within the remit of lower tiers of government.[22] As extensively discussed in Chapters 3 and 4, STRs are a hybrid object of regulation: they are both an economic activity (a service) and a land use. In practice, any EU regulation that would seek to define ex ante how this economic activity should or should not be regulated would most likely impinge on the competences that are in the hands of local, regional and national authorities in fields such as taxation, housing and urban planning regulations. For city governments, any harmonisation of STR rules at EU level would thus run against the core EU principle of subsidiarity.[23]

## Towards an EU-Wide Framework for Data Sharing Between Platforms and Public Authorities

After processing the thousands of pages of feedback it received in the public consultation of 2021, the European Commission took a year to prepare a more concrete legislative proposal. In July 2022 a coalition of MEPs (mainly from Green and left-wing parties) led by Kim van Sparrentak (Greens/European Free Alliance) wrote a letter to EU Commissioners M. Vestager and T. Breton, respectively in charge of competition (including digital services) and the internal market, to insist on the urgency of regulatory action at the EU level, stressing the negative impacts of STRs on local housing markets and liveability. The letter was co-signed by some members of the European Cities Alliance for Short-Term Rentals, including the mayors of seven cities in our sample (Amsterdam, Barcelona, Berlin, Brussels, Paris, Prague, Vienna). It encouraged the Commission to 'present a legislative proposal giving clear authorisation and discretion to authorities to regulate holiday rental in the general public interest' (Eurocities 2022).

In November 2022 the European Commission published its proposal for a *Regulation on Data Collection and Sharing Relating to Short-Term Accommodation Rental Services* (hereafter rSTR Data Regulation). Its stated objectives were 'to harmonise and improve the framework for data generation and data sharing on STRs across the EU, and to enhance transparency in the STR sector'. The main proposals included

- a harmonised approach to STR registration schemes via a central national website, which would issue a unique identification number to identify hosts and properties;
- for those member states that have set up a registration scheme, the possibility to obtain detailed data from platforms for policy-making and enforcement purposes;
- the obligation for platforms to enable hosts to display registration numbers and to 'make reasonable efforts to randomly check the declaration' of the hosts;
- the obligation for platforms to share data about hosts' activities and their listings with public authorities on a monthly basis in an automated way through a national single entry point (digital gateway); and
- the requirement for member states to maintain a one-stop national information website that would list areas where authorisation schemes are in place and the areas where STRs are banned. (European Commission 2022)

The Commission argued that the draft regulation would benefit all the actors involved: public authorities, hosts,[24] online platforms, local communities, tourists and the tourism sector. The proposal represented a compromise between *some* demands of the platforms (a harmonised approach to registration schemes) and *some* demands of city governments (registration number display on listings; obligation for platforms to share individualised STR data). Its provisions actually went further than what would have been possible with only the *E-Commerce Directive* and *Digital Services Act*. The draft regulation represented, to an extent, a partial success for the EU cities that had campaigned for such outcomes since the late 2010s. Notably, it restricted itself to proposing a harmonisation of national registration schemes and a framework for data sharing by platforms, with no provisions that would regulate market access for STR activities—a possibility that had been hinted at in the 2021 consultation documents described above. The draft regulation specified that it was without prejudice to 'national, regional or local rules regulating access to, or the provision of, short-term accommodation rental services by hosts' and 'regulating the development or use of land, town and country planning or building standards' (European Commission 2022). The text thus steered clear of referring to particular local instruments of STR regulation (as this could infringe on the subsidiarity principle, and is in any case covered by the existing *Services Directive*). The International Union of Tenants (IUT), one of the few NGOs that responded to the draft regulation, noted the proposal was 'a step in the right direction', but criticised it for not going far enough to stop the 'professional profit-oriented exploitation of the housing market' which exacerbates the 'affordable housing shortage in Europe and beyond' (IUT 2023).

Airbnb welcomed the proposed regulation but immediately stated that 'the EU can go further' in terms of coordination and harmonisation at EU level 'through an independent body or Tourism Agency or other': 'our ultimate objective is to ensure that the final text actually delivers on harmonised and proportionate rules, in particular for STR Hosts' (Airbnb 2022c). The company made three proposals that built on its EU Host Action Plan: an EU-wide (rather than national) Single Data Entry point to streamline the data-sharing process; a clearer role for the European Commission in assessing and verifying the proportionality of registration and other STR rules established by public authorities; and a better enforcement of the *Services Directive* in instances of 'disproportionate' STR rules. Those demands combined, again, both a collaborative and an adversarial attitude to European cities' regulatory choices.

The draft regulation was agreed by the EU Council of Ministers in March 2023 and was subsequently scrutinised by the Internal Market and Consumer Protection Committee of the European Parliament. The parliamentary rapporteur for the regulation, MEP Kim Van Sparrentak (Greens/European Free Alliance), submitted amendments to make the proposals more stringent on platforms and more empowering for public authorities (Bertuzzi 2023). The European Parliament and the Council reached a provisional agreement on a draft regulation in November 2023, with some amendments to the Commission's initial proposal (for an overview of the preparation and debates on the regulation, see European Parliamentary Research Service 2024). The final text of the regulation was approved by the Parliament on 29 February 2024. It broadly maintains the main proposals contained in the Commission's initial draft of 2022. Regulation (EU) 2024/1028 of 11 April 2024 will apply from 20 May 2026 to all EU member states. The countries that wish to require STR platforms to share data with competent public authorities will have to set up an online registration procedure for STR operators via a single, national registration system that requires standardised information about each unit. Online platforms will make 'reasonable efforts' to check if the host registration information provided is correct. Member states will then have to set up a single digital entry point (interoperable and compliant with data protection law) to receive host activity data from platforms on a monthly basis (or every three months for micro and small platforms).

## CONCLUSION

The political conflicts at the local (and sometimes regional and national) levels that we have extensively analysed in previous chapters have become both judicialised and transnationalised at the EU level. Due to the unique existence of a supranational body of law that underpins the existence of a single market among the 27 members of the EU, EU law has been strategically mobilised by the stakeholders opposed to new forms of regulation of platform-mediated STRs, in particular the 2000 *E-Commerce Directive* and the 2006 *Services Directive*. The former limits what public authorities can demand from platforms. The latter limits the interventions that public authorities can make in the market access and operation of any commercial service provider in the EU (e.g., an STR operator). Rulings from the EU Court of Justice have provided important clarifications about the interpretation of those directives, sending a mixed picture with respect to platform-mediated STRs. On the one hand, the CJEU ruled that Airbnb should be classified as a mere digital intermediary whose operations cannot easily be restricted outside of Ireland. On the other, the court upheld that efforts to combat a long-term rental housing shortage constitute an 'overriding reason relating to the public interest' which can justify specific regulatory measures by local authorities.

This judicialisation has come with the rescaling of collective action by platforms, professional organisations of hosts and city governments towards the EU level. This has opened a contested field of demands placed on the European Commission, and later on the Council of EU Ministers and European Parliament, for the reform of EU law. Those contradictory demands played out in the debates around the *Digital Services Act* that modernised the *E-Commerce Directive*, and around the new regulation on data sharing between STR platforms and public authorities. In those debates, a 'market harmonisation' logic driven by the construction of the EU Single Market for services clashed with the defence of the subsidiarity principle and the competences of local authorities.

Importantly, in the multi-level governance game analysed in this book, the rescaling of the regulatory conflict at the EU level gives national governments a more important role to play, as it is with them that EU institutions negotiate (through the Council of the EU, which brings together the government ministers from each EU country in the specific policy field under discussion). But at the same time, city governments have also mobilised to strengthen their voice at the EU level—autonomously through an informal network, and by engaging with formal EU institutions known to be more receptive to their concerns: the Committee of the Regions and the European Parliament. They have organised to face up to the lobbying activities of platforms and to defend their interests and agendas—which, as we have demonstrated, are sometimes different from those of their national governments.

Altogether, recent developments are pointing to a limited European standardisation in some aspects of STR regulation, in the form of national STR registration systems and a data sharing framework between platforms and public authorities (yet to be put in place at the time of writing). This is a potentially important evolution since, as demonstrated in Chapters 5 and 6, governmental access to individualised STR data is absolutely key for the effective implementation of STR rules and for the public oversight of corporate platforms that derive part of their power from information asymmetry and data monopoly. In this sense, the implementation of an EU regulation over platform data sharing adds an important layer to the multi-level landscape of regulatory instruments analysed in this book. It would encourage the generalisation of STR registration schemes—which are not present everywhere (see Chapter 3)—and offer new data resources for regulatory enforcement. How quickly and effectively the new EU regulation will be implemented remains to be seen.

But this should not be seen as a form of convergence between the different STR regulatory regimes of European cities, nor as a shift towards a more stringent approach to STRs in Europe. Data sharing and registration systems are *operate* types of instruments that regulate the transparency of the STR market: they may, or may not, be used by local authorities to control, limit and curb the growth of the STR market. As the book has shown, this depends on local and multi-level agendas and politics, on the combination with other available instruments that seek to restrict market access and on the intensity of implementation efforts. In this respect, while cities from our second and third worlds of STR regulation might use new EU instruments to enhance their capacity to protect the housing stock for long-term residents by limiting the growth of STR, cities from the first world of regulation might just use them to improve the taxation and the transparency of STR markets within visitor-oriented and property-friendly urban regimes and agendas.

# CONCLUSION

## Urban Platform Capitalism, Governability and Democracy

IN THE EARLY 2010s, initial observations and research on platform-mediated STRs viewed the phenomenon as a disruptive innovation that would escape existing regulatory frameworks. The offer of STRs grew in digital spaces that were complex to grasp, mediated by transnational platforms. These platforms—born, in some cases, on the other side of the world—were not easily governed and taxed by the public authorities of the countries they operate in. By contrast, this book shows that in European cities, governments have developed instruments and procedures that have made the STR market legal, and that they have governed some of its dimensions. Public authorities at different scales have, in a short period of time, developed modes of regulation, often based on their existing competences. To an extent, European local governments have been able to assert their political, social and economic interests, that is, to retain some control of their own agendas and not be completely subject to the pace imposed by digital platforms. They have made political choices regarding whether to steer or stifle the growth of the STR market. At a broader level, this book thus confirms that European public authorities, particularly at the city level, still have some political capacity to organise societies, markets and territories (Le Galès 2002).

Yet the question remains, for whom and in which direction. Indeed, not all local governments have made the same political choices: some have chosen to regulate in order to limit the growth of STRs, others to support this growth. By adopting a comparative approach at the crossroads of the sociology of public policies, multi-level urban governance and the political economy of urban capitalism, the book has explained *why* the political work of making the field of platform-mediated STRs governable has been carried out in very different ways; *how* local governments have implemented regulatory policies; and how a decade of conflicts and negotiations over STR regulations have transformed the relationships between business interests, grassroots movements and public authorities in urban governance more broadly.

## THE THREE WORLDS OF STR REGULATION: POLITICS, INSTITUTIONALISATION AND URBAN RENT EXTRACTION

The overall line of argumentation of our book has combined four explanatory strands to explain the diversity of STR regulations in Europe: the roles of politics; of socio-economic and urban conditions; of welfare/ housing regimes; and of multi-level relations between cities, states and the EU. Four main results make contributions to the literature on platform-mediated STR regulation and, more generally, on the comparative urban governance of platform capitalism, tourism and housing:

· There are three types of STR regulatory regimes in European cities, each characterised by institutional, political and socio-economic conditions and different intensities and types of STR rules. These regimes not only make sense of the diversity of STR regulations, but help us to understand their implementation and, potentially, their effects.

- The diversity of STR regulations is largely explained by conditions and mechanisms that do not depend solely on the STR issue, but also on pre-existing institutional arrangements and instruments on the one hand and the multi-level organisation of different policy sectors (tourism, housing, land use planning, economic development, etc.) on the other.

- The role of politics is important, but not so much in terms of partisan preferences (most cities in our sample were governed by centre-left coalitions that have taken different approaches to regulation), as in terms of the political role played by platforms and short-term rentiers in local politics and policies (as business groups and political clienteles), as well as by grassroots mobilisations.

- Taken together, those three results make it possible to develop a comparative argument on the diversity of urban rent extraction mechanisms. While platform-mediated STRs and, more generally, platform capitalism are present at a transnational scale in relatively similar ways, the mechanisms, types and intensity of rent extraction are not the same everywhere: this depends on the institutional arrangements of welfare/housing regimes, socioeconomic contexts and political strategies that affect them. This is the second face of what we call the varieties of STR regulatory regimes, which tie into a variety of STR rent extraction regimes.

As discussed in Chapter 2, the issue of the diversity of STR regulations was not absent from the existing scholarly literature. Our book can be read as a step forward from previous attempts to objectify regulatory diversity: it does so through an ideal-typical typology that takes into account not only the types of regulatory instruments but also, more broadly, the characteristics of cities and states in which STR markets have rapidly expanded. To do this, first, we have shown that it is not just the intensity of tourism flows, the concentration of STRs, the presence of social movements, protests from incumbent actors (the hotel industry) or the political colour of the local government in a given period that explain the differences in STR regulations, but rather sets of combinations of these conditions. To explain the modes of regulation of STRs, the book goes *beyond* the STR issue: it takes into account broader policies, agendas and administrations in the fields of housing, tourism, economic development, planning and taxation. Although STRs are presented as a wicked issue at the crossroads of different dynamics and sectors (Chapter 1), the book shows that STR regulation is firmly rooted in sectoral logics that tackle STRs from their own perspective, and sometimes compete or collide with each other.

Second, we have shown that the way cities and states regulate STRs depends on existing institutions and previous political choices, sometimes reversed by political-electoral changes (as in Barcelona and Madrid after 2015). This path dependence leads to a certain consistency between types of cities regulating STRs, which we have classified according to a quantitative index of STR regulatory intensity combined with socio-economic (intensity of tourism, STR market structures) and political (partisan alignment, competition) variables, welfare/housing regimes and the distribution of competencies between levels of government. The new 'public problem' of platform-mediated STRs has been captured in these political-institutional spaces. In cities from World 2 (Paris, Amsterdam, Vienna and Berlin), STRs have been grasped via housing policies and, in particular, housing protection instruments, which are highly institutionalised and interventionist, unlike cities from World 1 (Milan, Rome, London, Prague), whose STR regulations are rooted in a logic of tourism development and a liberalised approach to homeownership (yet increasingly contested). In cities from World 3 (Lisbon, Barcelona, Madrid), the intensity of regulation is linked to a strong politicisation of the issue, partly shaped by grassroots movements (which were also strong in Berlin, a borderline case between Worlds 2 and 3).

The differences in the scope and the degree of institutionalisation of public intervention in the property/housing markets have potential implications for the durability of regulations that have sought to limit STR growth. Anchoring these new rules in a highly institutionalised field is more likely to ensure they withstand economic and political changes. While our analysis of STR regulations in this book was valid as of 2023, subsequent local, regional or national political changes might affect the evolution of such regulations in one direction or the other in our case study cities. As discussed in the Italian case, in the cities of World 1 there have been increasing demands from social movements and some left-wing politicians for more regulation. New national legislation paving the way for stronger regulation has been enacted (e.g., the UK *Levelling Up and Regeneration Act* in the autumn of 2023) or proposed (e.g., in the Czech Republic). By contrast, in World 3 there is a risk that local, regional or national political change might lead to a weakening of the stricter regulations that had been enacted since the mid-2010s.

The third contribution of the book has been to test the role of local politics, partisan preferences and alignments and ideological choices: with few exceptions, in big European cities it was the local governments led by left-wing parties or coalitions that *first* pushed for a stricter regulation of STRs. But this was not the central political mechanism. Politics matter more in terms of political and economic clienteles. As shown in Chapter 6, the balance of power in European cities revolves around the importance of the platforms' economic clienteles (short-term rentiers) in local politics and urban governance. When this economic clientele is aligned with the political clientele of the ruling parties, then the balance tips towards the interests of platforms, short-term rentiers, and the multiple organisations and operators of this ecosystem. In World 1 cities (as clearly shown in Italian cities and in London), the share of homeowners and potential short-term rentiers is high, and their weight is significant in the electorate, pushing local governments to align and develop regulations that sustain this electorate and thus platforms. In World 2 cities, the political weight of the platforms' economic clientele is weaker; this leaves the space for governments to develop more autonomous political agendas that talk to their political clientele favourable to a stricter STR regulation. In World 3 cities, the political weight of the economic clientele of potential short-term rentiers is relatively strong, but local governments have demonstrated political voluntarism, in some cases under the influence of strong bottom-up social movements (Barcelona) in the context of an acute housing crisis compounded by touristification processes. They have gone against part of their electorate (or have convinced them) and taken the risk of developing stricter STR regulations with a possibly fragile long-term support—though the changing tenure split in those cities (manifested by an increasing share of tenants) may maintain the balance in their favour. This analysis also makes it possible to understand the relevance of our distinction between the access type of regulatory instruments (that put barriers to entry into the STR market) and the operate type (that simply establish market operating rules). In cities where the platforms' economic clientele has more weight, regulations tend to be based on operate rules, whereas they are more focused on the access type in Worlds 2 and 3, with the exception of London, where pre-existing access-type urban planning instruments had been maintained while being made more flexible (as explained in Chapters 3 and 4).

The fourth contribution of the book lays the ground for a future, more advanced analysis that would investigate the comparative political economy of STR *rent extraction regimes*. One would expect that the rent produced through the exploitation of data and transactions (for platforms) and through the STR of accommodation units (for operators) will not be extracted in the same way, by the same players, with the same benefits and to the same extent in all countries and cities.

This variety could be explained (at least partially) by institutional, socio-economic and political factors and mechanisms, which shape the strategies of firms (platforms), their clients (hosts and all kinds of STR operators) or social movements, who can in turn, under certain conditions, push to change the rules and institutional frameworks. These interactions between institutions, contexts and actors form a system that will stabilise over time, constituting *rent extraction regimes* whose variety can only be understood and explained by explaining the variety of *regulatory regimes* that we developed in this book. These two types of regime are linked and influence each other. We have shown that the structure of the STR markets (in terms of volume of listings, size and weight of operators, concentration of supply and ratio of multi-listings) was (in part) constitutive of both our types of regulatory regimes (Chapter 3) and of the relationships between market operators and regulators (Chapter 6). Moreover, the adjustment of the regulatory and rent extraction regimes probably also explains some of the differentiated effects of STR regulations on STR markets. Existing studies on those effects (presented in Chapter 2) do not take this sufficiently into account and could be elaborated upon. Thus, in our sample of European cities, while the hierarchy measured in terms of the share of multi-listings in each local STR market has not evolved much (see Figure 10 in Chapter 3), this share has evolved at different rates: a strong increase in the cities of Worlds 1 and 3 and a less pronounced one in the cities of World 2 (with the exception of Vienna which has a smaller STR market). This result would be in line with our typology—a high level of institutionalisation of housing protection policies would produce more solid and durable effects on STR markets—and with our approach—it is not just the intensity of STR regulations alone that explains the effect of regulatory instruments, but the institutions and politics that surround these instruments.

In this book, we have mainly studied the institutionalisation of regulatory regimes. In future research, it would be worth furthering our understanding of the worlds of STR platforms and markets in order to strengthen the analytical link between regulatory regimes and rent extraction regimes. This requires digging deeper into the platforms' economic preferences and strategies, as well as into the nature, variety and motivations of STR operators and investors. On both aspects, though, access to qualitative and quantitative data has been, and will remain, challenging. This also requires a longer-term perspective to really assess and explain the effects of modes of regulation on the STR market in each city (size, structure, actors, location), now that a decade has passed since the first regulations of STRs in the mid-2010s.

## RETHINKING THE DIVERSITY OF REGULATIONS THROUGH THEIR LIMITS

At a broader level, we can consider the implications of our findings for the question of the governability of (European) urban societies and economies in a world of platform capitalism, changing patterns of human mobilities and transnational housing investments. In this book we study the constituent activities of a market in the process of institutionalisation, which has emerged in spaces of a-legality and not-yet-(il)legalised practices (Smart and Zerilli 2014). We also explore the capacity of city (and other tiers of) governments to govern powerful multinational corporations that have sought to escape existing regulations and to turn emerging rules to their advantage. In this sense, the book contributes to the comparative analysis of the governability of twenty-first-century urban societies (Borraz and Le Galès 2010; Le Galès and Vitale 2013).

As summarised in Chapter 2, an important stream of research has questioned the governability of platform-mediated STRs by quantitatively evaluating the effects of STR regulations following their implementation. That research shows that regulations seeking to limit the expansion of the STR market, its professionalisation (i.e., shares of

multi-listings) or its negative externalities (i.e., effects on rents or primary residences) have, in some cases, succeeded in doing so—though
often to a moderate extent—but in other cases have not. Altogether,
restrictive STR regulations have had some effect on STR markets in cities, notably by limiting their development before the COVID pandemic.

Our book complements those quantitative studies of regulatory
impacts by throwing light on the mechanisms and the limits of regulation. In terms of mechanisms, the three worlds model helps to understand and explain the differential effects of regulatory instruments.
In addition, it shows that what could appear as 'limits' of regulatory
instruments shall not be considered as mere insufficiencies or failures of the regulatory tools (meaning that a change in the instrument
would not necessarily lead to a more effective outcome). On the contrary, we see regulatory limits as the results of the socio-political processes and power struggles around the institutionalisation of the STR
market: they reflect less the lack of effectiveness of a political intervention in a developing market than the balance of power, preferences
and strategies between different actors that have mobilised around
the institutionalisation of this market. In this sense, the limits of regulations also reflect 'who gets what, when and how?' (Lasswell 1936)
from STR markets, once institutionalised differently in different cities. These limits are also often exploited on the one hand by platforms,
STR operator associations or some of the media, who like to highlight
the 'perverse effects' of regulations, or on the other by social activists
and hotel industry representatives who deem regulations ineffective.

The approach taken in this book helps us to understand regulatory
limits in three ways. First, it shows that STR regulatory instruments are
not isolated tools: they form part of a system with other instruments—
their use in the STR market is attached to administrations in charge of
other issues, which are more or less resourced and legitimate. Thus, the
same instrument in different regulatory regimes will not produce the
same effects. To give an example, both Paris and London have a 'time

cap' instrument that limits the number of days per year one can operate an STR without having to apply for planning permission (90 days in London) or for change of use (120 days in Paris). The book has shown that this instrument, in Paris, has been much more politically invested, becoming one of the pillars of the Parisian approach, enforced through a housing policy administration specifically dedicated to its implementation. This was not the case in London, where local planning departments in charge of enforcing planning rules have been understaffed and dealing with a multiplicity of issues beyond STRs.

Second, STR regulatory limits depend on the politics of the targets of regulation. We have analysed the different types of STR tackled by regulatory instruments (professional rentals, occasional rentals of a primary or secondary residence and room rentals). The book has shown the interplay between, on the one hand, these categories established by policy-makers to make sense of the STR world, restrict some activities while allowing others in politically acceptable ways, and, on the other hand, the variety of STR operators and their political activities around these distinctions. In some cases, like Paris, city governments have distinguished between occasional (the 'good STR') or professional (the 'bad STR') operators. In others, like Barcelona, the city government has considered all types of STR activities to be harmful in neighbourhoods under pressure. In other cases, like Italian cities, different types of STRs have been targeted by similar operate rules, yet there is a differential fiscal treatment for 'small' property owners and for 'big/professional' STR operators (the threshold between the two being four rented units, a number that can be politically contested). Due to these distinctions, the same STR regulatory instrument that exists in two cities can target, in fact, different types of STRs and will therefore have different effects on the market—and trigger different political responses. As shown by other scholars and by our own data, there has been a steady trend towards the professionalisation of the STR offer (visible through multi-listings), via the ousting of small hosts operating independently who have had more difficulties in coping with legal constraints, plat-form pressures or changes in demand (e.g., in a pandemic) compared to large owners, investors or property managers. The study of the politics of regulatory targets (Chapter 6) also complements existing research, by showing that hosts, corporate landlords, property managers and legal advisors have developed strategies for neutralising, bypassing or contesting the rules with which they are supposed to comply. We have shown that these strategies are not the same in all cities, because the spaces for negotiation and rule evasion are not the same (there are fewer rules to circumvent in World 1, unlike in World 2 and World 3).

Third, the book sheds light on the limits of regulating platforms themselves. The underlying question is whether regulations that bend local STR markets also influence the digital intermediaries and reg-ulatory entrepreneurs of those markets, which are transnational cor-porations. Two platforms have managed to establish themselves as a duopoly (Airbnb constitutes 84% of the market in our sample, and Abritel-VRBO 14%, according to AirDNA in2024). They have diversi-fied their activities and anticipated the opening up of new, as yet unreg-ulated markets (e.g., medium-term rentals). Our book shows that the instruments that make up regulatory regimes in European cities pri-marily regulate the activities and the actors intermediated by platforms (hosts, property owners and managers, etc.). Many of these rules do not really affect platforms as organisations, and city governments are usually not legally competent to directly constrain them. City govern-ments have, however, negotiated with platforms to get them involved in regulatory enforcement, sometimes fought with their represen-tatives and sometimes accepted their policy offer (tax collection and remittance agreements). But local governments need the support of national governments and, in the context of Europe, of EU institutions to be able to tackle platforms as corporations, as explained in Chapter 7.

We have also shown that platforms (especially Airbnb) have deployed intense political action to influence regulations and prevent restrictions, applying to them as firms and to the STR market as a whole. On a broader scale, pessimistic observers could thus argue that, after 15 years of political action, European cities, states and the EU have partially failed (or been unwilling) to 'govern' multinational corporate platforms. However, such a pessimistic assessment of the power relationships between platforms and governments is too simplistic. Our book shows that governments have controlled some corporate platform activities, at some moments in time, under some conditions, in some places, depending on the regulatory regime. After initial years of inaction, European nation-states have developed instruments and policies to impose rules on platforms regarding taxation and data sharing, something that has been confirmed—albeit timidly—by new legislation from the EU institutions (see Chapter 7). In the world of platform capitalism, no actor can claim to be able to exert successful pressure on all scales of political power: multi-level governance limits the ability of both large firms and their clienteles to fully capture political power and democratic institutions.

Altogether, while the book began by observing that local governments have, since the mid-2010s, been confronted with a similar, globally spreading phenomenon, we can now conclude by highlighting the *variety of urban platform capitalism*: it takes diverse forms—regimes of accumulation and rent extraction—depending on the constraints and opportunities in different cities, that is, in different regulatory regimes (see Figure 23). On this basis, we can move beyond the question of whether platform-mediated STRs can be *governed*—understood as the exercise of unilateral power actions by governments over a field. Rather, we can think about their *governability* by scrutinising how the relationships between a plurality of political actors claiming to rule at various scales (local, regional, national, European), and a plurality of actors seeking to develop their activities or contesting the established order (platforms, short-term rentiers, grassroots movements, the hotel industry), have stabilised a field (Aguilera 2017:594). In this book, we

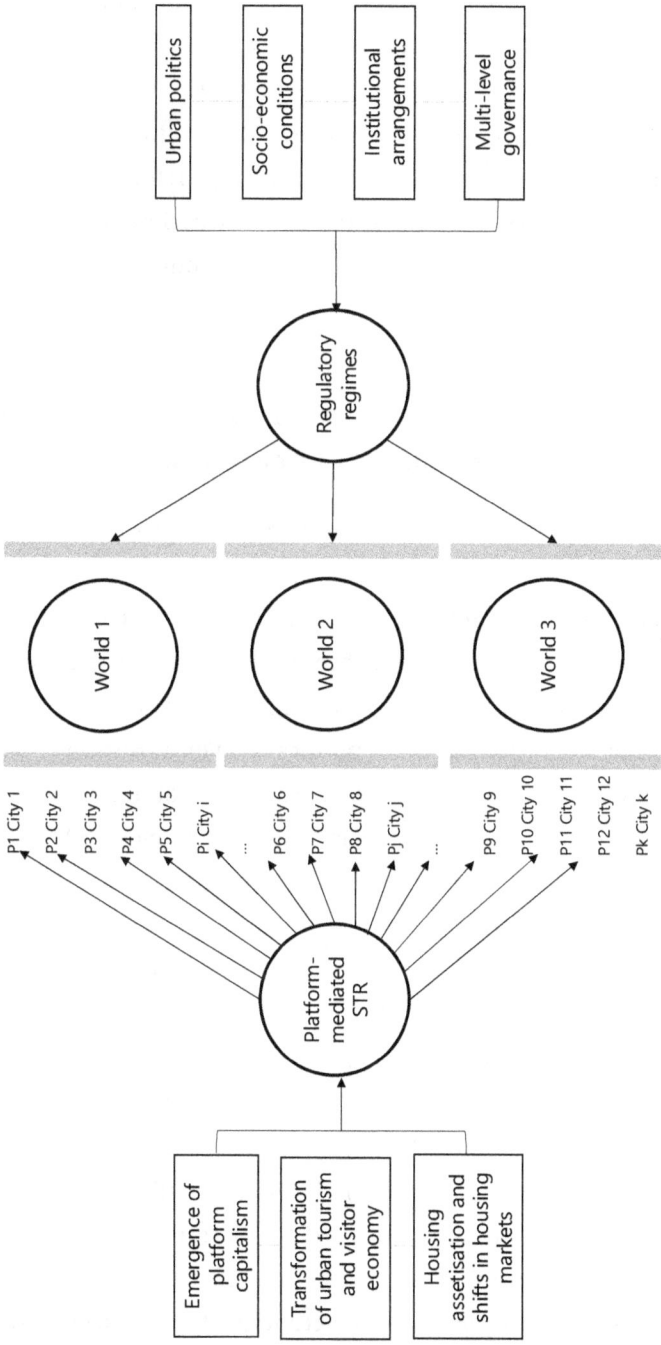

**Figure 23.** A model of regulation: the interface between regulatory regimes and platform-mediated STRs. Pi City i = configuration of the platform-mediated STR world in city number i. *Source:* Authors.

have demonstrated and conceptualised this through different *regulatory regimes* (or 'worlds of regulation') that give meaning to the diverse ways in which actors form and stabilise institutional systems, work in coordination, but also clash—sometimes challenging existing institutions to propose new ones. Each of these regulatory regimes corresponds to regimes of accumulation and extraction of urban rent that vary: in that sense, there is not one world, but several *worlds* of platform-mediated STRs.

## PLATFORM CAPITALISM, LOCAL POLITICS AND DEMOCRATIC GOVERNANCE IN EUROPE AND BEYOND

Beyond public policy problems, the issue of governability raises the question of democracy (urban or otherwise) in a globalised world shaped by transnational flows of technology, people and capital. Ultimately, the book addresses larger questions that are fundamental for the social sciences and for public debates: Does platform capitalism call into question the democratic organisation of political power in European societies and beyond? Can (city) governments exert control in the face of the power of Silicon Valley corporations and globalised investors?

In a comment made in 2017 about the decision by the Berlin city-state government to soften the quasi-prohibition against STRs that had been enacted a year before, Arun Sundararajan, professor of entrepreneurship and technology at New York University and author of a book about 'crowd-based capitalism' (2017), stated that 'cities have to let go of the dream that they have control over these platforms, because that's not the world we live in anymore' (quoted in Beck 2018). This statement, infused with techno-economic 'inevitabilism' (Zuboff 2019), is interesting. It is also often put forward by platforms and short-term rentier groups (Chapter 6). While it captures the fact that city governments are struggling to regulate the activities of transnational digital tech corporations, it also carries two strong assumptions that can be empirically and normatively challenged, drawing on the analysis of this book. First, this view implies that the world of platform capitalism is no longer governable as 'old' forms of capitalism used to be, and that governments should mourn the loss of their usual modes of government and governance: big data and algorithms would replace politics in the regulation of societies. Second, it implies that platform-led forms of socio-economic organisation based on the unrestricted assetisation and commodification of things (here, housing and urban space) are the only possible political direction.

But we have shown two main results that stand against techno-economic inevitabilism and could inspire public policy-makers and practitioners. First, governments have mostly used twentieth-century political tools that predate platforms and have evolved gradually: by layering, recycling and improving existing policy instruments, they have innovated on that basis. And when willing to do so, they have managed to steer STRs, in part, through these instruments. This does not entirely solve what most analysts of platform capitalism have conceived as one of its problematic aspects in relation to democracy: the asymmetrical power that the appropriation, accumulation and analytics of proprietary data give to platforms. Yet as demonstrated in this book, local governments, even in the absence of data, have been able to limit, somewhat, the extension of STR markets, and sometimes bend the platforms, through the sheer force of the symbolic and the political. And more directly, they have obtained platform data, in a few cases through stubborn negotiations, in others by putting pressure (alongside other actors) on national governments (e.g., in France) and on EU institutions. Strong forms of coordination, cooperation and political will by national and transnational public authorities and organisations (e.g., the EU) are absolutely crucial for the future regulation of platform capitalism, and more broadly, of digital technology companies.

Second, the book shows that governments that wish to limit or curb the STR market and its negative effects have to regulate far beyond

STRs per se. As shown in Chapter 1, STRs have been fuelled by, and contributed to, overtourism and the housing crisis. The latter has become structural in many large European cities, compounded by other dynamics that produce socio-spatial inequalities. It is thus impossible to seek to limit STRs and their negative externalities by regulating STRs alone. This means choosing for whom to regulate and to arbitrate between diverging interests. Housing can be protected for long-term residents, and particularly for the most disadvantaged, only by adopting bold and strong public housing policies and forms of regulation of the private rental sector (as also concluded, in this book series, by Arbaci 2019 and Bernt 2022). Strategies can be put in place to regulate tourism, tackle overtourism and generally encourage less damaging forms of human mobility and place consumption in the face of a global energy and climate crisis. This means building models of local economic development that are less dependent on the visitor economy and speculative real estate dynamics.

While much published scholarship has analysed the dynamics of platform-mediated STRs in the Global North, and our own empirical investigation has focused on Europe, we hope that this book can help other scholars to study the socio-political and policy responses to urban platform capitalism (and to platform-mediated STRs in particular) in other contexts, for example in South America, where the urban impacts of, and regulatory responses to, the phenomenon have been underresearched until now (Lerena Rongvaux and Rodriguez 2024). Like the internal diversity of responses uncovered within Europe, one can expect a great diversity of responses elsewhere. The potential for comparison within, and between, large world regions should be explored, and the four explanatory strands that we proposed in the book should be operationalised, refined, tested and critiqued in other contexts.

While state capacity, multi-level governance frameworks, local government competences and welfare/housing regimes vary hugely, the challenges posed by the intersection of platform capitalism, global mobilities and housing assetisation are becoming extremely salient in many places around the globe. In that regard, differences between cities of the global North, South and East (themselves contested categories) are not ontological (Marques 2021:8–10): there may be 'commonalities in processes and actors, but also particularities that must be considered' (9). Beyond Europe, 'familistic' forms of welfare capitalism are also widespread in Latin American and Asian societies, where family and inheritance play central roles in sustaining national political economies and in delivering welfare (Arbaci 2019:13). Therefore, in those geographical contexts, the growing use of real estate property as a source of rent extraction via platform-mediated STRs, fuelled by a sustained demand by tourists, transnational elites and other 'temporary city users', is not surprising. There too, as witnessed in the European cities considered in this book, one may expect that the role of different political clienteles (e.g., local real estate-owning elites, or impoverished workers or residents who might find sources of income through engaging with platform capitalism), and of transnational actors like platforms, will be key to understanding the different modes of politicisation and regulation of the phenomenon. At the same time, the entanglement of platform capitalism with multiple, prevalent forms of urban informality will have to be given particular attention. In the context of intense debates on the possibility and desirability of international comparisons in global urban studies (Le Galès and Robinson 2023), investigating the collective capacity of multiple actors to govern and regulate transnational, digital technology-driven platform capitalism, human mobilities and housing market transformations matter hugely for more equitable urban futures.

# Note on Methods and Data Sources

THE EMPIRICAL MATERIALS presented in this book come from in-depth fieldwork carried out by the three authors between 2016 and 2023, covering 12 cities in 10 European countries: Amsterdam, Barcelona, Berlin, Brussels, Lisbon, London, Madrid, Milan, Paris, Prague, Rome and Vienna (with a period of research assistance in 2018 from Dr. Tatiana Moreira de Souza for the Lisbon, Amsterdam and London cases). Some preliminary results based on those materials were previously published (Aguilera et al. 2021; Artioli 2020; Colomb and Moreira de Souza 2021, 2024). We developed, updated, and reworked the materials completely for this book, which combines quantitative and qualitative data. Additional materials, data and updates related to the book's core topic can be found at the companion website produced by the authors: https://strpolitics.hypotheses.org.

## DOCUMENTARY ANALYSIS OF WRITTEN SOURCES

We collected and analysed three main types of written sources. First, governmental, administrative and legal documents were crucial to study the regulatory process and build our detailed database of STR rules. We reviewed hundreds of documents, in particular regional, national and EU laws, decrees and jurisprudence, as well as municipal by-laws, regulations, land use plans and urban policy strategies. The press statements and public reports commissioned by public authorities helped us understand how public actors defined and problematised the STR issue and defended their regulatory approaches. During our ethnographic fieldwork (see below), we also had access to several unpublished working documents produced by public administrations.

Second, the documentation produced by STR operators and intermediaries (e.g., associations of hosts and property managers, corporate platforms) was crucial to understanding the behaviour of these economic agents and their claims. We consulted the numerous public reports and press statements published by Airbnb about the impacts of STRs and about STR regulations. Similarly, our analysis of citizen mobilisations and hotel industry strategies drew on publicly available reports, petitions, social media statements and press releases.

Finally, the written local, regional and national press was an important source of information to scrutinise regulatory developments in our cities and countries, to understand how the STR 'public problem' was framed in different places and to follow the evolution of its salience in public debates over the years.

## ETHNOGRAPHIC OBSERVATION
## AND SEMI-STRUCTURED INTERVIEWS

Between 2016 and 2023 we conducted short episodes of ethnographic observation and 86 semi-structured interviews aimed at exploring collective action, material interests, discourses, social conflict and collaboration in the making of STR regulations, as well as in their implementation on the ground. The three case study cities at the core of our qualitative analysis were the object of extensive, repeated rounds of interviews with multiple actors, accompanied by participant and non-participant observation of social mobilisations, the work of public authorities and public events around STRs: in Barcelona, this was conducted by Claire Colomb; in Paris, by Thomas Aguilera and Francesca Artioli; and in Milan, by Francesca Artioli. Shorter visits were conducted in the other nine cities to do semi-structured interviews.

We carried out ethnographic observations of a wide range of settings. These included visits to the neighbourhoods most affected by STRs (to detect signs of opposition to STRs such as posters and have informal discussions in-situ with shopkeepers, residents or activists). In Paris, Milan and Barcelona, we spent time with staff of the local, regional and/or national administrations, whom we met for semi-structured interviews and informal discussions, sometimes on several occasions over the years (e.g., the team of the Paris BPLH). In Paris and Barcelona, we did a short ethnographic observation of the inspectors responsible for monitoring STR listings and enforcing STR regulations, following them for a day in their street-level work (Aguilera in Paris in the spring of 2017 and Colomb in Barcelona in the spring of 2018). We also attended the court trials of property owners whose STRs had been deemed illegal (Aguilera in Paris in the spring of 2017). Finally, we attended some 25 events about STR regulation organised by different actors: policy- and industry-focused conferences or workshops, public consultation meetings and grassroots or activist-led events, in France, Italy, Spain and the UK and at the EU level. Such events were often attended by a variety of stakeholders and were important settings for observing the contentious debates and opposing interests at play around platforms and STRs. Sometimes we were asked to participate as experts to present our research.

We conducted 86 semi-structured interviews (listed in Table 2) with public actors in different tiers and sectors of government and public administration (elected officials, officers and enforcement teams in the fields of housing, planning, tourism, economic development, culture and the digital economy); with members of professional STR property management organisations and host clubs; with local residents' associations, social movement activists and researchers; and with tourism, hotel and hospitality industry professionals. This enabled us to understand how actors grasped the issue of STRs and what their claims and strategies about STR regulation were, in order to explain regulatory conflicts, change or inertia. We were able to conduct only one interview with representatives from the largest STR platform, Airbnb (with Airbnb Italy, in 2017), as the company either declined or did not respond to our requests for interviews. Consequently, we mainly relied on the company's publications, statements and reports, as well as on the public statements made by some of its representatives in public lectures, conferences or news articles, for our analysis.

TABLE 2
Interviews

| Organisation | Position of the Interviewee(s) | Category of Actor | Date |
|---|---|---|---|
| *Amsterdam (n = 6)* | | | |
| Association of B&B and Short-term Lets Amsterdam Gastvrij | Representative | Professional organisation, STR operators | July 2018 |
| Dutch Association of Hotels Koninklijke Horeca Nederland | Representative | Professional organisation, hotel & hospitality industry | July 2018 |
| Amsterdam in Progress Independent think-tank on tourism | Founder | Think-tank | July 2018 |
| Friends of Amsterdam City Centre Vereniging Vrienden van de Amsterdamse Binnenstad | Member (volunteer) | Residents' association or citizens movement | July 2018 |
| Amsterdam city government Gemeente Amsterdam | Elected Alderman Laurens Ivens, Deputy Mayor for Housing | City government | July 2018 |
| Amsterdam city government | Two senior policy advisors on housing and STR | City government | July 2018 |
| *Barcelona (n = 7)* | | | |
| Barcelona city government Ajuntament de Barcelona | Senior official from Department of Tourism | City government | May/June 2018 |
| Barcelona city government | Senior official from Department of Urban Planning | City government | May/June 2018 and July 2021 |

| | | | |
|---|---|---|---|
| Barcelona city government | Senior official from Department of Urban Planning (inspection service) | City government | May/June 2018 |
| Regional government of Catalonia Generalitat de Catalunya | Three senior officials from Department of Tourism | Regional government | May/June 2018 |
| Barcelona Association of Tourist Apartments Asociación de Apartamentos Turísticos de Barcelona (APARTUR) | Senior representative | Professional organisation, STR operators | May/June 2018 |
| Assembly of Neighbourhoods for a Sustainable Tourism Assemblea de Barris per un Turisme Sostenible (ABTS) | Member (volunteer) | Residents' association or citizens movement | May/June 2018 |
| Barcelona city government | Two officials from Department of Urban Planning (inspection service) | City government | May 2021 |
| *Berlin (n = 3)* | | | |
| Berlin Senate Department for Urban Development and Housing Berlin Senatsverwaltung für Stadtentwicklung und Wohnen | Official from Housing and Rental Law Unit | City government | March/April 2019 |
| HomeSharing Berlin | Member (volunteer) | Association of hosts/ home-sharers | March/April 2019 |
| Apartment Allianz Berlin | Two representatives | Professional organisation, STR operators | March/April 2019 |

*(continued)*

TABLE 2
*(continued)*

| Organisation | Position of the Interviewee(s) | Category of Actor | Date |
|---|---|---|---|
| *Lisbon (n = 6)* | | | |
| Lisbon city government<br>Câmara Municipal de Lisboa | Senior official from Department of Urban Planning | City government | June 2018 |
| National Parliament of the Republic of Portugal<br>Assembleia da República | Two elected members of Parliament involved in working group on holiday rentals active in 2018 | National parliament | June 2018 |
| Association of Holiday Rentals in Portugal<br>Associação do Alojamento Local em Portugal (ALEP) | Senior representative | Professional organisation, STR operators | June 2018 |
| University of Lisbon<br>Universidade de Lisboa | Two researchers (geographers) | University | June 2018 |
| Portuguese Association of Hotels, Restaurants and Similar Establishments<br>Associação da Hotelaria, Restauração e Similares de Portugal (AHRESP) | Representative | Professional organisation, hotel and hospitality industry | June 2018 |
| Living in Lisbon<br>Morar em Lisboa | Member (volunteer) | Residents' association or citizens movement | June 2018 |

**TABLE 2**
*(continued)*

| Organisation | Position of the Interviewee(s) | Category of Actor | Date |
|---|---|---|---|
| UK Short-Term Accommodation Association (STAA) | Two representatives | Professional organisation, STR operators | September 2018 |
| *Madrid (n = 3)* | | | |
| Madrid city government Ayuntamiento de Madrid | Two senior officials from Urban Planning Department | City government | June 2018 |
| National Distance Education University Universidad Nacional de Educación a Distancia | Researcher (sociologist) | University | June 2018 |
| Residents' Association of Sol y Barrio de las Letras Asociación Vecinal de Sol y Barrio de las Letras | Member (voluntary) | Residents' association or citizens movement | June 2018 |
| *Milan (n = 27)* | | | |
| Milan city government Comune di Milano | Senior official, Department for Economic Innovation, Smart City and University | City government | April 2017 |
| Milan city government | Senior official, Department of Finance and Taxation Cabinet member of the Deputy Mayor in Charge of Tourism | City government | April 2017 |

| | | | |
|---|---|---|---|
| Lombardy regional government Regione Lombardia | Senior official, Regional Direction for Tourism, Territorial Marketing and Fashion | Regional government | April 2017 |
| Collaboriamo | Founder | Sharing economy organisation and expert | April 2017 |
| Università Cattolica | Academic | Sharing economy organisation and expert | April 2017 |
| Assoedilizia | President and senior member (two people) | Property owners organisation | April 2017 |
| Prolocatur | President | Property owners/STR operators organisation | April 2017 |
| Rescasa Lombardia | General secretary | Professional STR operators organisation | April 2017 |
| Associazione Provinciale Albergatori Milano (APAM), Confcommercio | Three senior representatives | Professional organisation of the hotel industry | April 2017 |
| Cooperativa I Sei Petali | Representative | NGO (involved in Airbnb social responsibility initiative) | April 2017 |
| Associazione Turismo e Ricettività (ATR), Confesercenti | President | Professional organisation of the hotel industry | April 2017 |
| Airbnb Italy | Public policy manager | Corporate platform | April 2017 |

*(continued)*

**TABLE 2**
*(continued)*

| Organisation | Position of the Interviewee(s) | Category of Actor | Date |
|---|---|---|---|
| Home Sharing Club Milan (later renamed OspitaMI) | Founding member | Host association | April 2017 |
| Milan city government | Two officials from the Department of Finance and Taxation, cabinet member of the Deputy Mayor in Charge of Tourism | City government | January 2020 |
| Lombardy regional government | Two senior officials from the Department for Tourism, Territorial Marketing and Fashion | Regional government | January 2020 |
| Property Managers Italia | General secretary | Property managers association | January 2020 |
| Milan city government | Elected member | Politician | January 2020 |
| Hospres/Ospitare in Regola | President and CEO | STR operators organisation | January 2020 |
| Host Italia (association) | Secretary/Treasurer | Host association | January 2020 |
| OspitaMI and Host+Host (association) | OspitaMI President Host+Host Vice-President | Host association | January 2020 |
| Chamber of Commerce Milano Monza Brianza Lodi | Chamber councillor and president FIMAA MiLoMB (real estate intermediators) | Functionally independent public body carrying business services and interests | January 2020 |

| | | | |
|---|---|---|---|
| Milan city government | Three officials, Project Directorate Economic Innovation and Business Support | City government | January 2020 |
| AIGAB—Associazione Italiana Gestori Affitti Brevi | President | Property managers association | March 2022 |
| OffTopic Lab | Two members | Citizen group | April 2022 |
| Milan city government | Deputy Mayor for Housing | City government | July 2022 |
| Milan city government | Senior official, Housing Directorate | City government | July 2022 |
| Milan city government | Three officials, Department for Commercial and Productive Activities | City government | July 2022 |

*Paris (n = 17)*

| | | | |
|---|---|---|---|
| Association 4 coins du 4 | Two members of 4 coins du 4 (neighbourhood association, 4th District of Paris) | NGO (grassroots, tourism issues) | November 2016 |
| Paris city government Mairie de Paris | Deputy Mayor for Housing | City government | April 2017 |
| Paris city government | Office for Housing Protection, inspector 1 (Department of Housing) | City government | April 2017 |
| Paris city government | PhD student intern at the Department of Attractiveness and Employment | City government | April 2017 |

(continued)

TABLE 2
(continued)

| Organisation | Position of the Interviewee(s) | Category of Actor | Date |
|---|---|---|---|
| Paris city government | Vice-chief of the Office for Housing Protection, inspector (Department of Housing) | City government | April 2017 |
| Paris city government | Office for Housing Protection, inspector 1 (Department of Housing) | City government | May 2017 |
| Paris city government | Office for Housing Protection, inspector 2 (Department of Housing) | City government | May 2017 |
| Paris city government | Vice-director of the Office for Housing Protection, inspector (Department of Housing) | City government | May 2017 |
| Paris city government | Team Office for Housing Protection (collective interview) | City government | May 2017 |
| Paris district government Mairie du 4ème arrondissement | Mayor | City government | May 2017 |
| Departmental Association for Housing Information (Paris) Association Départementale d'Information sur le Logement | Director of ADIL 75 | NGO (Housing Right) | May 2017 |

| | | | |
|---|---|---|---|
| Collective Saint-Malo j'y suis j'y reste | Activist 1 and 2 | NGO (grassroots, pro-STR regulation) | July 2019 |
| ParisVsBnB | Activist 1 | NGO (grassroots, anti-STR/ pro-regulation) | November 2019 |
| ParisVsBnB | Activist 2 | NGO (grassroots, anti-STR/ pro-regulation) | November 2019 |
| Paris city government | Chief of the Office for Housing Protection | City government | January 2020 |
| | Chief of the Office for Municipal Real Estate Assets | | |
| | PhD student intern at the Housing Department | | |
| Paris city government | Vice-director of the Cabinet of Deputy Mayor for Housing | City government | March 2020 |
| Paris city government | Vice-chief of the OPH (Housing Department) | City government | July 2022 |
| | Chief of the Office for Municipal Real Estate Assets | | |
| | Researcher working for the Housing Department | | |
| *Prague (n = 3)* | | | |
| Prague 1 district government Městská Část Praha 1 | Elected district councillor Pavel Nazarský | City government (district) | April 2019 |

*(continued)*

TABLE 2
*(continued)*

| Organisation | Position of the Interviewee(s) | Category of Actor | Date |
|---|---|---|---|
| Prague city government Magistrát hlavního města Prahy | Elected city councillor Adam Zábranský, in charge of housing and transparency | City government | April 2019 |
| Housing rights campaign: Housing-living Bydlet-Žít! | Three members (voluntary) | Residents' association or citizens movement | April 2019 |
| *Rome (n = 1)* | | | |
| Journalist | Independent journalist | STR expert | May 2022 |
| *Vienna (n = 3)* | | | |
| Vienna city government Stadt Wien | Two senior officials from Department for Economic Affairs | City government | April 2019 |
| Vienna University of Technology TU Wien | Two researchers (sociology/ geography) | University | April 2019 |
| Viennese Apartment Manager Association Wiener Apartmentvermieter Vereinigung | Representative | Professional organisation, STR operators | April 2019 |

SOURCE: Authors.

This variety of interviews and ethnographic observations repeated over seven years, conducted in the local languages, enabled us to collect a wealth of qualitative materials to understand the contentious processes of STR politicisation, regulatory change, implementation and governance (mainly analysed in Chapters 4, 5 and 6).

## THE STR REGULATORY DATABASE AND THE INTENSITY OF REGULATION INDEX (IRI)

The book additionally relies on two original databases that we produced to define and qualify the three worlds of STR regulation discussed in Chapter 3. To empirically show and compare the diversity of STR regulations in European cities, we first built an *STR regulatory database*, from which we derived an aggregate score, the Intensity of Regulation Index (IRI). The STR regulatory database cannot be reproduced here, but an earlier version is available in an online report (Colomb and Moreira de Souza 2021:Tables 5.1. to 5.12) and on a companion website. We compiled the rules that applied to the three main types of STR (see Box 1) in each city (as of May 2022) in 12 tables, using a comparable analytical template containing data on 12 indicators. The latter correspond to all the existing policy instrument options that we identified in the European STR regulatory landscape as of the end of 2023.

We subsequently coded the qualitative content of the tables to count the *type* and *number* of instruments applying to each type of STR in each city. We coded the data with the values of 0 and 1 (0 indicates the absence of a specific instrument and 1 its presence). We then produced an aggregate score of regulatory intensity (the IRI), based on a simple addition (without weighting) of the scores obtained for the 12 indicators for each type of STR (scores ranging from min = 0 to max = 36). The scores were converted into a scale of 0 to 1 to allow an easier synchronic comparison. The higher the value of the IRI, the more restrictions on the STR market have been put in place in a city.

The definition of this IRI is a compromise between parsimony and complexity. We did not perform a time-series analysis, as we sought to explain the processes that have led to the first wave of regulatory arrangements at one point in time. The IRI is the outcome of socio-political developments that we explain through qualitative methods and materials in the rest of the book. Moreover, while the IRI integrates a qualitative dimension through a distinction between access and operate types of instruments (explained in Chapter 3), it does not capture the tiers and sectors of regulation, because these aspects cannot be coded in a binary way.

Two possible misinterpretations of our index must be mentioned. First, it aggregates policy instruments that are not of the same nature, that do not necessarily regulate in the same direction or produce the same effects depending on their combination. The index simply reflects the presence or absence of instruments that were mobilised during the 2010s in many European cities, and often in the rest of the world. Second, the value of the indicator does not in itself say anything about the *effectiveness* of regulations. It characterises a 'regulatory thickness' that indicates the level of institutionalisation of STR policies and, from the perspective of an STR operator, the series of conditions necessary to start an activity in a given city. The actual implementation, enforcement and socio-political effects of the regulations were investigated qualitatively in Chapters 5 and 6 of the book. A high IRI does not automatically mean an effective regulation that will limit the number of STRs (Lisbon being a case in point, as discussed in the book), but it does indicate that a lot of requirements are to be met in order to develop an STR activity legally, more than in another city with a lower IRI.

To explain the differences in IRI between our 12 cities, we applied a descriptive statistical and classificatory treatment (Chapter 3), followed by a qualitative one aimed at unpacking causation (Chapter 4).

## THE COMPARATIVE DATABASE ABOUT EUROPEAN CITIES AND STR MARKETS (INPUTS TABLE)

The second database (see Table 3) contains variables that grasp key socio-economic, tourism, housing and STR-related indicators, and political-institutional features, for each city. This enabled us to characterise and compare the cities in our sample, to test correlations between these variables and the IRI and subsequently to draw up an ideal-typical typology of the three worlds of STR regulation.

Finding comparable data related to large European cities for the construction of this second database proved a challenge. It required the mobilisation

## TABLE 3

### Inputs for 12 European Cities: Housing, Tourism, Short-Term Rentals and Political-Institutional Indicators

| | Amsterdam | Barcelona | Berlin | Brussels | Lisbon | London | Madrid | Milan | Paris | Prague | Rome | Vienna |
|---|---|---|---|---|---|---|---|---|---|---|---|---|
| **Population (municipal level)[1]** | | | | | | | | | | | | |
| Population, millions (2019) | 0.9 | 1.6 | 3.6 | 1.2 | 0.5 | 8.9 | 3.3 | 1.4 | 2.2 | 1.3 | 2.8 | 1.9 |
| Population (2019) | 860,000 | 1,640,000 | 3,640,000 | 1,220,000 | 510,000 | 8,900,000 | 3,270,000 | 1,400,000 | 2,210,000 | 1,320,000 | 2,820,000 | 1,900,000 |
| Area, km2 | 219 | 102 | 892 | 161 (region) | 100 | 1 572 | 604 | 182 | 105 | 496 | 1 285 | 415 |
| **Housing (municipal level)** | | | | | | | | | | | | |
| Total number of housing units | 449,982 | 774,190 | 1,982,825 | 592,942 | 325,887 | 3,607,800 | 1,530,955 | 645,833 | 1,386,846 | 587,832 | 1,259,649 | 983,840 |
| % of social/public housing (out of the total number of dwellings) | 40.6 | 1.0 | 4.8 | 6.8 | 8.2 | 21.7 | 1.8 | 9.0 | 21.8 | 5.0 | 6.1 | 43.0 |
| % of homeownership (out of the total number of dwellings) | 28.7 | 61.3 | 11.1 | 38.8 | 50.4 | 50.9 | 63.0 | 64.1 | 27.3 | 52.4 | 69.3 | 20.0 |
| % of privately rented housing (out of the total number of dwellings) | 30.7 | 35.0 | 84.1 | 54.2 | 42.3 | 27.4 | 20.0 | 18.2 | 51.0 | 34.0 | 13.1 | 34.0 |

*(continued)*

1. Sources for population and housing (latest available data as of 2021, unless otherwise specified): Data Amsterdam (Amsterdam, NL); INE (Barcelona, ES); IBB, Berlin Senatsverwaltung für Stadtentwicklung, Bauen und Wohnen (Berlin, DE); STATBEL, Institut Bruxellois de statistique et d'analyse, Bruxelles Logemenr, Commission Communautaire Commune (Brussels, BE); INE-Statistics Portugal, LXHABIDATA-ISCTE-Instituto Universitário de Lisboa (Lisbon, PT); LondonDataStore, ONS (London, UK); INE (Madrid, ES); Comune di Milano-Sistema Statistico Integrato, Osservatorio Regionale sulla Condizione Abitativa, ISTAT 2011 Census (Milan, IT); INSEE, ADIL (Paris, FR); CZSO, Prague Housing Strategy (Prague, CZ); Roma Capitale, Osservatorio Casa Roma, ISTAT 2011 Census (Rome, IT); Statistisches Jahrbuch Stadt Wien (Vienna, AT).

TABLE 3
(continued)

| | Amsterdam | Barcelona | Berlin | Brussels | Lisbon | London | Madrid | Milan | Paris | Prague | Rome | Vienna |
|---|---|---|---|---|---|---|---|---|---|---|---|---|
| % of vacant housing (out of the total number of dwellings) | 2.4 | 3.5 | 3.5 | 3.7 | 15.6 | 2.4 | 5.4 | 5.8 | 8.5 | 8.0 | 9.7 | 3.0 |
| Average rent in private sector per m2[2] | 20.7 | 19.3 | 9.1 | 11.8 | 11.8 | 27.0 | 18.6 | 12.5 | 28.3 | 12.3 | 13.3 | 9.9 |
| Average sale price for an apartment per m2[3] | 5,315 | 5,763 | 5,478 | 3,350 | 3,908 | 7,699 | 4,394 | 3,729 | 12,863 | 3,395 | 3,259 | 4,868 |
| Affordability of the rental market (square metres of an apartment that can be rented with the average monthly net salary) | 172 | 90 | 330 | 221 | 89 | 142 | 96 | 143 | 92 | 121 | 111 | 222 |
| Affordability of the property market (square metres of an apartment that can be bought with the average monthly net salary) | 0.7 | 0.3 | 0.5 | 0.8 | 0.3 | 0.5 | 0.4 | 0.5 | 0.2 | 0.4 | 0.5 | 0.5 |
| Tenure profile of the city | Mixed | Home-owners | Tenants | Tenants | Home-owners | Mixed | Home-owners | Home-owners | Mixed | Home-owners | Home-owners | Mixed |

*GDP and income (EU NUTS 2—regional, EU NUTS 3—subregional and municipal levels)[4]*

| | | | | | | | | | | | | |
|---|---|---|---|---|---|---|---|---|---|---|---|---|
| GDP at current market prices by NUTS 2, euros per inhabitant (2019, Greater London 2017) | 62,600 | 31,200 | 42,900 | 71,800 | 27,100 | 63,700 | 36,000 | 39,700 | 61,500 | 46,800 | 35,000 | 52,600 |
| GDP at current market prices by NUTS 3, euros per inhabitant (2019, Greater London 2017) | 92,300 | 31,700 | 42,900 | 71,800 | 27,100 | 63,700 | 36,000 | 55,600 | 116,000 | 46,800 | 39,300 | 52,600 |
| Households' net disposable income by NUTS 2 regions, euros per inhabitant (2019) | 22,500 | 17,600 | 20,600 | 20,200 | 14,800 | na | 19,500 | 22,000 | 23,800 | 14,000 | 19,000 | 22,600 |
| Rate of unemployment by NUTS 2 (% of labour force aged 15–74, 2019) | 3.2 | 11.0 | 5.3 | 12.6 | 7.2 | 4.3 | 10.6 | 5.6 | 7.9 | 1.3 | 9.9 | 9.3 |
| Average monthly net salary after tax, euros (2021, municipal level)[5] | 3,551 | 1,730 | 3,004 | 2,604 | 1,051 | 3,841 | 1,791 | 1,791 | 2,603 | 1,490 | 1,473 | 2,193 |

*(continued)*

2. Deloitte (2020).
3. Deloitte (2020).
4. Source for GDP and income (excluding average monthly net salary): Eurostat (n.d.-a).
5. Numbeo (2021).

## TABLE 3
### (continued)

| | Amsterdam | Barcelona | Berlin | Brussels | Lisbon | London | Madrid | Milan | Paris | Prague | Rome | Vienna |
|---|---|---|---|---|---|---|---|---|---|---|---|---|
| *Visitor economy (municipal level)* | | | | | | | | | | | | |
| Tourist arrivals, millions p/y (overnight international visitors, 2016)[6] | 8.0 | 8.2 | 4.9 | 2.7 | 3.6 | 19.9 | 5.3 | 7.7 | 18.0 | 5.8 | 7.1 | 6.7 |
| Tourist arrivals per inhabitant (2016) | 9.3 | 5.0 | 1.4 | 2.2 | 7.1 | 2.2 | 1.6 | 5.5 | 8.2 | 4.4 | 2.5 | 3.5 |
| Tourist arrivals, millions p/y (overnight national and international visitors, 2019)[7] | 9.2 | 9.5 | 14.0 | 3.9 | 5.9 | 22.5 | 9.9 | 8.0 | 25.0 | 80 | 9.2 | 8.6 |
| Tourist arrivals per inhabitant (2019) | 10.7 | 5.8 | 3.8 | 3.2 | 11.5 | 2.5 | 3.0 | 5.7 | 113 | 6.1 | 3.3 | 4.5 |
| Bednights, millions p/y (2019)[8] | 18.4 | 19.9 | 34.1 | 7.8 | 13.8 | 85.1 | 20.7 | 13.0 | 52.5 | 18.5 | 29.1 | 18.6 |
| Cultural and Creative Cities Index (2019)[9] | 39.2 | 31.2 | 34.0 | 24.6 | 46.3 | 36.1 | 27.9 | 35.3 | 66.0 | 32.7 | 26.3 | 33.4 |
| *Short-term rental offer in 2016 (Airbnb listings, municipal level)[10]* | | | | | | | | | | | | |
| Peak number of Airbnb listings (yearly, 2016) | 15,258 | 20,031 | 18,373 | 6,640 | 15,949 | 52,143 | 12,293 | 12,721 | 56,177 | 12,911 | 24,046 | 7,612 |
| Average number of Airbnb listings (yearly, 2016) | 13,233 | 17,013 | 16,405 | 6,204 | 11,941 | 42,867 | 10,814 | 11,166 | 49,133 | 12,911 | 20,836 | 6,743 |

| | | | | | | | | | | | | |
|---|---|---|---|---|---|---|---|---|---|---|---|---|
| Share of entire units (% of the total number of listings, 2016) | 81 | 51 | 53 | 65 | 71 | 51 | 59 | 64 | 85 | 77 | 59 | 66 |
| Share of multi-listings (% of the total number of listings, 2016) | 17 | 42 | 13 | 24 | 54 | 27 | 40 | 27 | 16 | 56 | 46 | 33 |
| Average booked nights/year (2016) | 102 | 97 | 103 | 73 | 97 | 89 | 96 | 76 | 96 | 78 | 80 | 82 |
| Share of entire apartments available > 60 days/year (% of entire apartments, 2016) | 55 | 52 | 56 | 40 | 57 | 49 | 55 | 44 | 52 | 54 | 50 | 44 |
| Average price/night for an entire apartment, euros (2016, converted when needed) | 145 | 122 | 76 | 81 | 87 | 161 | 88 | 100 | 104 | 92 | 100 | 81 |
| Peak number of Airbnb per 100 inhabitants (yearly, 2016) | 1.8 | 1.2 | 0.5 | 0.5 | 3.1 | 0.6 | 0.4 | 0.9 | 2.5 | 1.0 | 0.9 | 0.4 |
| Peak number of Airbnb per 100 housing units (yearly, 2016) | 3.4 | 2.6 | 0.9 | 1.1 | 4.9 | 1.4 | 0.8 | 2.0 | 4.1 | 2.2 | 1.9 | 0.8 |

*(continued)*

6. MasterCard (2016).

7. European Cities Marketing (2019) and Tourmis (n.d.).

8. European Cities Marketing (2019).

9. European Union Joint Research Centre (2019).

10. Inside Airbnb (n.d.-c), our elaboration (for Prague, we have taken the first available data set, December 2017).

## TABLE 3
### (continued)

*Short-term rental offer 2023 (Airbnb listings, municipal level)[11]*

| | Amsterdam | Barcelona | Berlin | Brussels | Lisbon | London | Madrid | Milan | Paris | Prague | Rome | Vienna |
|---|---|---|---|---|---|---|---|---|---|---|---|---|
| Peak number of Airbnb listings (yearly, 2023) | 8,739 | 18,321 | 15,543 | 6,902 | 22,751 | 91,778 | 25,543 | 24,936 | 74,329 | 9,388 | 29,357 | 14,697 |
| Average number of Airbnb listings (yearly, 2023) | 7,781 | 17,185 | 13,185 | 6,452 | 21,465 | 82,663 | 23,409 | 22,580 | 63,623 | 8,524 | 26,775 | 13,371 |
| Share of entire units (% of the total number of listings, 2023) | 76 | 59 | 64 | 73 | 75 | 61 | 64 | 81 | 86 | 80 | 69 | 79 |
| Share of multi-listings (% of the total number of listings, 2023) | 13 | 65 | 30 | 41 | 69 | 39 | 54 | 42 | 28 | 73 | 55 | 56 |
| Average booked nights/year (2023) | 62 | 88 | 105 | 81 | 90 | 46 | 77 | 54 | 78 | 90 | 82 | 67 |
| Share of entire apartments available > 60 days/year (% of entire apartments, 2023) | 17 | 56 | 41 | 42 | 53 | 25 | 46 | 29 | 36 | 50 | 48 | 39 |
| Average price/night for an entire apartment, euros (2023, converted when needed) | 270 | 188 | 132 | 137 | 168 | 268 | 162 | 201 | 197 | 135 | 228 | 115 |

| | | | | | | | | | | | | |
|---|---|---|---|---|---|---|---|---|---|---|---|---|
| Peak number of Airbnb per 100 inhabitants (yearly, 2023)[11] | 1.0 | 1.1 | 0.4 | 0.6 | 4.5 | 1.0 | 0.8 | 1.8 | 3.4 | 0.7 | 1.0 | 0.8 |
| Peak number of Airbnb per 100 housing units (yearly, 2023) | 1.9 | 2.4 | 0.8 | 1.2 | 7.0 | 2.5 | 1.7 | 3.9 | 5.4 | 1.6 | 2.3 | 1.5 |
| Evolution of the number of listings (2016–2023, %) | −41 | 1 | −20 | 4 | 80 | 93 | 116 | 102 | 29 | −34 | 29 | 98 |
| *Short-term rental offer 2023 (various platforms)* | | | | | | | | | | | | |
| Airbnb market share (2023, % of the sum of Airbnb and VRBO listings)[12] | 92 | 75 | 87 | 93 | 74 | 82 | 83 | 87 | 83 | 91 | 77 | 87 |
| Short-stay accommodation offered via Airbnb, Booking.com, Tripadvisor and Expedia Group (nights spent, EU Local Administrative Unit–City, 2022)[13] | 924,663 | 8,553,840 | 2,593,192 | 1,665,742 | 8,522,158 | n.a. | 6,671,388 | 3,992,459 | 13,523,206 | 3,102,705 | 8,020,662 | 3,796,797 |

*(continued)*

11. Inside Airbnb (n.d.–c), our elaboration.
12. AirDNA (2024).
13. Eurostat (n.d.-b).

## TABLE 3
### (continued)

|  | Amsterdam | Barcelona | Berlin | Brussels | Lisbon | London | Madrid | Milan | Paris | Prague | Rome | Vienna |
|---|---|---|---|---|---|---|---|---|---|---|---|---|
| *Institutional arrangements (national level)* | | | | | | | | | | | | |
| Welfare/housing regime (Arbaci 2019) | social-democratic | familistic | corporatist | liberal | familistic | liberal | familistic | familistic | corporatist | post-socialist | familistic | corporatist |
| Variety of capitalism (Hall and Soskice 2001; Schmidt 2016) | coordinated market economy | state-influenced market economy | coordinated market economy | coordinated market economy | state-influenced market economy | liberal market economy | state-influenced market economy | state-influenced market economy | state-influenced market economy | dependent market economy | state-influenced market economy | coordinated market economy |
| Territorial organisation | unitary | regionalised/federal | regionalised/federal | regionalised/federal | unitary | unitary (England) | regionalised/federal | regionalised/federal | unitary | unitary | regionalised/federal | regionalised/federal |
| *Politics (municipal level)* | | | | | | | | | | | | |
| Ruling majority at time of first STR rules (2015) | centre-left | new municipalist | centre-left | centre-left | centre-left | centre-left | new municipalist | centre-left | centre-left | other | other | centre-left |
| Social movements advocating STR regulation (prior to the first STR rules) | absent | strongly present | moderately present | absent | moderately present | absent | moderately present | absent | absent | moderately present | absent | absent |
| Hotel industry advocating STR regulation (prior to the first STR rules) | yes | yes | yes | yes | yes | yes | yes | yes | yes | yes | yes | yes |

| | Short-term rental regulation | | | | | | | | | | | |
|---|---|---|---|---|---|---|---|---|---|---|---|---|
| Intensity of Regulations Index (2022, municipal level) | 0.7 | 0.7 | 0.4 | 0.6 | 0.8 | 0.2 | 0.5 | 0.3 | 0.5 | 0.2 | 0.3 | 0.5 |
| World of STR Regulation (2022, municipal level) | World 2 | World 3 | World 2 | - | World 3 | World 1 | World 3 | World 1 | World 2 | World 1 | World 1 | World 2 |

*Source:* Compiled by authors based on various sources cited in table notes.

of multiple and only partially standardised sources. As a result of the EU integration process, there is now a wealth of European statistical and geographical data sources that can support cross-national comparative research, though mostly at the national and regional levels. Comparable city-level data is still patchy and scant (Colomb and Kazepov 2023), in particular on housing tenure, housing markets and income levels. We had to compile such data from national and local statistics. Comparison based on those sources is not perfect, as statistical bodies may use different definitions, protocols and dates of collection. For housing market conditions, we used data produced by the private firm Deloitte (often used in official reports by international organisations and EU institutions). We faced a similar challenge regarding STR data, given the reluctance by platforms to release detailed data. Following other scholars, we used data on our 12 cities from the non-profit initiative Inside Airbnb (www.insideairbnb.com), in collaboration with Murray Cox, its founder (for a discussion of this data source and its limits, see the section '"Datactivism" for, and from, Local Governments' in Chapter 5).

# Notes

## INTRODUCTION

1. Airbnb (2024).

2. In journalistic and common language, including that of politicians and researchers, the ubiquitous company's name Airbnb is often used as a shorthand to refer to STRs themselves, somewhat incorrectly. We have avoided this pitfall throughout the book: we use the company's name only when referring to its activities, publications, or the STR listings advertised specifically on that platform.

## CHAPTER 1. THE RISE OF SHORT-TERM RENTALS

1. We subsequently noted that Alessandra Esposito, in her work on the touristification of Naples, defines her object of study at the intersection of three similar fields (Esposito 2023a).

2. Online marketplaces offering vacation rentals existed before Airbnb. Vacation Rental By Owner (VRBO) was created in 1995 in the USA, initially for second-home owners, followed by Perfectplaces (1996) or UK companies Owners Direct (1997) and

HolidayLettings (1999). Online notice boards such as CraigsList also advertised STR opportunities, as well as websites for home exchanges such as Couchsurfing. Airbnb was created in 2008 and was the first platform to offer an online credit card payment system. New platforms with an international offer were set up in the 2010s, for example, Housetrip (2009) or Homestay (2013). Some disappeared after a few years (i.e., the Germany-based Wimdu, 2011–2018). Others were bought by larger platforms or online travel firms. HomeAway (2005) quickly became one of the giants in the sector after buying VRBO, the French Abritel, the British OwnersDirect.co.uk, the German FeWo-direkt and the Spanish TopRural. It now operates as VRBO, offering all types of STR accommodation in 190 countries. It was bought in 2015 by Expedia, an American travel technology company. Other online travel companies originally set up as travel fare aggregators for hotel accommodation, like Booking.com, Trivago.com and Hotels.com (the latter two owned by Expedia), have recently expanded their offerings to include serviced apartments and STRs. The travel guidance platform TripAdvisor expanded its activities to STRs (Tripadvisor Rentals) by acquiring HolidayLettings and Flipkey and partnering with Housetrip. Finally, 'aggregators' have emerged (e.g., Tripping.com, 2009) to allow users to search STRs across different platforms. Hotel companies such as Marriott, Hyatt and Accor have also set up STR services for luxury holiday accommodation. In some countries, residential property rental platforms have also started to advertise STRs, alongside long-term rentals.

3. Corporate platforms encompass a variety of organisational forms. Srnicek (2016) distinguishes four types: (1) advertising and social media platforms like Facebook that rely on advertising and sales of personalised data; (2) cloud platforms like Google that provide IT infrastructure; (3) product platforms like Netflix that offer goods or services on demand; and (4) lean platforms that allow the exchange of goods, services, or information owned by others, like Uber and Airbnb (the latter can be P2P or B2C). The majority are for-profit, taking a commission for the intermediation between supply and demand.

4. For example, Amnesty International (2019) has denounced the role of Airbnb, Booking, Expedia and TripAdvisor in advertising STR units and other tourist attractions in Israeli settlements (that are illegal under international law) in the occupied Palestinian Territories.

5. Tourism statistics based on this definition rely on specific sources of data (e.g., hotel or airport arrivals) that do not necessarily capture other forms of 'tourism' such as day-trippers, people visiting friends or relatives, or those staying in STRs (Novy and Colomb 2016).

6. The notion of the 'tourist' as a distinguishable sociological entity was called into question three decades ago in tourism sociology and geography, in debates about the 'de-differentiation' of tourism and everyday life (e.g., Urry 1990; McCabe 2005).

7. The Schengen Area guarantees free movement to more than 425 million EU citizens who can travel, work and live in participating EU countries without specific formalities.

8. In the spring of 2020, when the first lockdowns were implemented, Airbnb announced measures to reimburse travellers and compensate affected hosts. The firm also opened a channel offering STR accommodation to healthcare staff. In early May 2020, the company dismissed 25% of its workforce (1,900 employees), reduced its marketing budget by one billion dollars and paused some of its planned new activities. In 2021 and 2022, however, it launched a raft of new initiatives to rebound from the COVID-19 crisis.

9. It is worth noting that Airbnb has developed expansion and marketing strategies beyond Europe and North America, for example in African countries (Reuters 2018), adapting its narrative to espouse context-specific developmental goals.

10. In the Global South, studies have noted the emergence of STRs in low-income neighbourhoods *not* traditionally associated with the visitor economy, for example as part of a growing trend of 'favela tourism' in Brazil (Törnberg and Uitermark 2022) or 'township tourism' in South Africa (Hofäcker and Gebauer 2021).

11. This research project (2018–2023), led by Niels Van Doorn and a team of researchers, was funded by the European Research Council (see https://platformlabor.net).

12. STRs have also been discussed in relation to broader processes of 'transnational gentrification' beyond Europe, in particular in South and Central America, where scholars have emphasised the role of the state in encouraging inflows of transnational tourists, 'expats', 'digital nomads' and investors

(Alexandri and Janoschka 2020; Hayes and Zaban 2020; Navarrete Escobedo 2020; Sigler and Wachsmuth 2020).

## CHAPTER 2. THEORISING AND RESEARCHING THE REGULATION OF PLATFORM-MEDIATED SHORT-TERM RENTAL HOUSING

1. These are registration requirement, authorisation requirement, time cap, residence obligation, zonal restrictions, authorisation from other parties, cooperation with/obligation for platforms and other measures. One of the sources used by those authors is the publicly available report produced by Claire Colomb and Tatiana Moreira (2021), whose detailed tables of regulation in 12 cities formed the basis of our own empirical materials. This explains some of the similarities between our respective indicators.

2. In this book, we use the term *STR regulation* (singular) when referring to this abstract conceptual definition. We use *STR regulations* (plural) to designate the specific set of instruments and institutional arrangements that characterise each city.

3. Until the 2000s, European countries fell into five ideal-typical clusters of welfare/housing regimes (Arbaci 2019): the *social-democratic* cluster (Scandinavian countries and the Netherlands), the *corporatist* cluster (Central Europe), the *familistic* cluster (Southern Europe), the *liberal* cluster (UK and Ireland since the 1980s and Belgium) and a fifth *post-socialist* cluster added in the 1990s (Stephens et al. 2015). The regimes differed from each other first by their tenure split (balanced split with predominance of social rental sector in social-democratic systems, balanced split with predominance of private rental sector in corporatists systems, polarised split with predominance of owner occupation in liberal and familistic systems). Second, they differed by the organisation of the rental market (unitary systems in which social and private renting are integrated into a single market, and dualist systems in which social renting is residualised to protect private renting from competition). And finally, they varied in terms of state intervention (from the active promotion of rented and cooperative housing in social-democratic systems, to 'market correction' measures in corporatist systems, to limited intervention in liberal and familistic systems). The *post-socialist* cluster and familistic systems shared high levels of homeownership, informal housing provision

and low household debt, but was not a variant of the Italian, Spanish or Greek systems (Stephens et al. 2015).

## CHAPTER 3. THE THREE WORLDS OF SHORT-TERM RENTAL REGULATION IN EUROPEAN CITIES

1. In some cases, however, such requirements—when very stringent—were in fact used to try to limit the proliferation of STRs (hence, they can also be considered 'market access' instruments). This argument was used by critics of the STR regulatory requirements enacted in Brussels, for example (see Chapter 7).

2. In several cities, in land use planning terms, the STR of a housing unit on a commercial basis (type i) does not entail a change of use from residential to commercial (as in Lisbon, Milan or Rome).

3. See Câmara Municipal de Lisboa (2023).

4. The ban was challenged by a professional organisation representing STR operators (Amsterdam Gastvrij). The court argued that a system of permits cannot contain a total prohibition, which infringes on the right to property and the freedom of establishment under the EU *Services Directive* (Lomas 2021), as discussed in Chapter 7.

5. Unsurprisingly, the numbers of tourists and STRs are strongly correlated, both in absolute numbers and per inhabitant.

6. On the basis of the data we had access to, it was not possible to say who the actors behind these multi-listings are. These operators can be financial investors or family offices, but also second-tier platforms or property managers and conciergeries that manage STRs on behalf of smaller owners. However, it is important to take into account this diversity of STR market structures to explain the differences in the mobilisation of STR market players, as we do in Chapter 6.

7. This share is positively correlated with the share of homeownership.

8. Scholarly arguments regarding housing vacancy and shortage are also contradictory. Housing vacancy seems to have a parabolic effect: below a certain threshold, the more vacancies there are, the less regulation there is, with governments letting the market benefit investors and owners; above a certain vacancy threshold, governments regulate strongly (Furukawa and Onuki

2022). A high level of housing shortage seems to push governments to take strong measures, as was the case in Lisbon (Marques Pereira 2022).

## CHAPTER 4. THE PATHS TO REGULATION

1. These mechanisms have been identified and discussed briefly in a previous article; see Aguilera et al. (2021).

2. Decree 159/2012 d'establiments d'allotjament turístic i d'habitatges d'ús turístic; and Law 13/2002 de Turisme de Catalunya.

3. The concentration of STRs in single buildings has been a controversial proposal: while it can limit the impact of disturbances on neighbouring residents, activists argue that it can encourage evictions of long-term tenants by investors.

4. Besides complaints about noise nuisances, residents reported stories of law-breaking or criminal activities taking place in STR units (drug dealing, prostitution or parties during the COVID-19 lockdowns).

5. ABDT (2016).

6. Masked individuals sprayed the slogan 'tourism is killing neighbourhoods' on the front screen of the bus without causing harm to passengers (Hughes 2018).

7. A study commissioned by the city government (Duhatis et al. 2016) estimated that the total STR offer amounted to roughly 6% of the rental housing stock (1% of the total housing stock), with much higher concentrations in certain districts popular with visitors.

8. Decree 75/2020 de turisme de Catalunya.

9. Decree Law 3/2023 de mesures urgents sobre el règim urbanístic dels habitatges d'ús turístic.

10. Article R.611-42: obligation to transmit the names of visitors to the public administration for surveillance and statistical purposes.

11. A primary residence, under French law, refers to a place in which a person lives for at least eight months a year. This means that the property cannot be unoccupied, or rented out, for more than four months (120 days) a year; otherwise it is considered by law to be a secondary residence.

12. When an owner wants to change the use of a residential property to make it a commercial STR, they must submit a request for change of use to the office for the protection of residential dwellings (BPLH) (Article L. 631-7

of the *Code of Construction and Housing*). In some areas of France (*zones tendues* where the housing market is tight; in cities of more than 200,000 inhabitants; or because the municipal council has so voted), like Paris, the change of use of a property which was defined as residential as of 1 January 1970 must be accompanied by a compensation measure for the loss of residential living space: the owner must buy back the equivalent floorspace (or double or even triple the amount in Paris) of commercial space to convert it into residential space in the same district. In practice, owners do not necessarily buy commercial properties themselves but buy financial shares managed by companies that then resell them to other operators for delivery of residential real estate.

13. Any request for a *change of use* with compensation (Decree of 5 January 2007; Article R. 421-17-b of the French *Code of Urban Planning*) must be accompanied by a request for a *change of destination* to the Department of Urban Planning (in this case, the request is attached to a property and not to a person). The *destination* of a property (governed by Article R. 123-9 of the *Code of Urban Planning*, and by the urban plan at the local level) establishes the destination of all built properties (e.g., housing, hotel, office, shop, public facilities).

14. The Atelier Parisien d'Urbanisme (APUR) is a non-profit association created by the Paris City Council, which produces studies and data for the City of Paris and the Greater Paris Metropolis. In close contact with researchers, it has been a major player in public debates on the development and planning of the Paris region, in particular on the issue of STRs.

15. The APUR report estimated that STRs had contributed to the disappearance of 20,000 units from the permanent residential rental stock (APUR 2011).

16. The Union des Métiers et des Industries de l'Hôtellerie (UMIH, the main professional organisation of hotels) went as far as taking allegedly illegal B&B and STR owners to court in 2013 (Caldini 2013), and even Airbnb itself in 2018, for unfair competition (Errard and Visseyrias 2018). The AHTOP, later ATOP (Association pour un Hébergement et un Tourisme Professionnel—an organisation of French tourism entrepreneurs) has made it one of its primary missions to fight unfair competition from platforms in order to promote 'quality tourism'.

17. In 2014 a Civil Real Estate Company (SCI) was fined €130,000 by the city government, a multi-property operator €100,000, and other owners €10,000 to 40,000 (Serafini 2015).

18. Airbnb (n.d.-a).

19. Law 2016-1321, République Numérique.

20. Court de Cassation, Ruling no. 195 of 18 February 2021 (17-26.156).

21. Tribunal Judiciaire (hereafter TJ Paris), 1 July 2021, 19/54288.

22. TJ Paris, 18 October 2021, 21/52480.

23. Law No. 2014-366, *Accès au Logement et Urbanisme Rénové*.

24. Law No. 2016-1321, *République Numérique*.

25. Law No. 2018-1021, *Evolution du Logement, de l'Aménagement et du Numérique*.

26. Law No. 2020-634, *Engagement et Proximité*.

27. See Ministère Chargé du Logement (2022).

28. For instance, the small city of Oléron (an island) has begun to sue Airbnb for non-payment of the tourist tax, demanding 30 million euros.

29. The bill recommended expanding existing requirements—change of use and registration number—to the entire country, to lower the maximum rental threshold from 120 to 60 days for occasional STRs and to apply to STRs the new regulations on the energy performance of residential buildings.

30. France Info and AFP (2023).

31. Assolombarda (2023).

32. Sharexpo (2014).

33. Lombardia Regional Law 27/2015, Politiche regionali in materia di turismo e attrattività del territorio lombardo, and Regional Regulation 7/2016, Definizione dei servizi, degli standard qualitativi e delle dotazioni minime obbligatorie degli ostelli per la gioventù, delle case e appartamenti per vacanze, delle foresterie lombarde, delle locande e dei bed and breakfast e requisiti strutturali ed igienico-sanitari dei rifugi alpinistici ed escursionistici.

34. Lombardia Regional Law 15/2007, Testo unico delle leggi regionali in materia di turismo.

35. Lombardia Regional Law, 7/2018, Integrazione alla legge regionale 1 ottobre 2015, n. 27 (Politiche regionali in materia di turismo e attrattività del territorio lombardo). Istituzione del codice identificativo da assegnare a case e appartamenti per vacanze.

36. The *città metropolitana* is an administrative division of Italy created in 2015 as a special type of provincial authority for large agglomerations. It has responsibilities in the field of tourism (e.g., the classification of tourist

accommodations), which is why the Lombardy regional law assigned the delivery of the compulsory identification code to the metropolitan authority.

37. Law 431/1998, Disciplina delle locazioni e del rilascio degli immobili adibiti ad uso abitativo.

38. Otherwise, according to the law, the revenues earned from renting accommodation—including STRs—should be declared under the normal income tax regime for both individuals (IRPEF, which is an incremental tax) and companies (IRES, which is a flat rate tax).

39. Decree Law 50/2017, Disposizioni urgenti in materia finanziaria, iniziative a favore degli enti territoriali, ulteriori interventi per le zone colpite da eventi sismici e misure per lo sviluppo.

40. The CJEU ruled that EU law does not preclude the requirement to collect information or to withhold tax under a national tax regime, but that the obligation to appoint a tax representative is a disproportionate restriction on the free provision of services.

41. Decree Law 113/2018, Disposizioni urgenti in materia di protezione internazionale e immigrazione, sicurezza pubblica.

42. SET (2021).

43. Decree Law 34/2019, Misure urgenti di crescita economica e per la risoluzione di specifiche situazioni di crisi.

44. Ministry of Tourism Decree, 29/09/2021, no. 161, Regolamento recante modalità di realizzazione e di gestione della banca di dati delle strutture ricettive e degli immobili destinati alle locazioni brevi.

45. Law 178/2020, Bilancio di previsione dello Stato per l'anno finanziario 2021 e bilancio pluriennale per il triennio 2021-2023.

46. Lombardia Regional Decree 13056, 17/09/2019, Approvazione degli schemi di comunicazione per chi offre alloggio o parti di esso, per finalità turistiche, in regime di locazione.

47. Camera di Commercio Milano Monza Brianza Lodi (n.d.).

48. In 2020, we wrote to the Deputy Mayor for Housing to ask for an interview about STRs, and he replied that it was a matter of responsibility of the Deputy Mayor for Tourism. The municipal government's planning and housing priorities in the 2010s were focused on new private residential development programmes and on the management of the existing public housing stock, rather than on the private rental sector.

49. Law 91/2022, Conversione in legge, con modificazioni, del decreto-legge 17 maggio 2022, n. 50, recante misure urgenti in materia di politiche energetiche nazionali, produttività' delle imprese e attrazione degli investimenti, nonché in materia di politiche sociali e di crisi Ucraina.

50. The 'Uber Files' scandal in 2022 showed the extent to which E. Macron (when Minister of Economy and Finance, 2014–2016) and his team were supportive of Uber's activities and its economic model and thus advocated the deregulation of the market (Leloup 2022).

## CHAPTER 5. A CHALLENGING IMPLEMENTATION

1. *Illegality* refers to the non-compliance of the STR operator with one or more provisions among the multiple instruments and layers of regulation in force in a given city. Because STR regulations have emanated from various tiers of government, policy fields and instruments, the illegality of STR can manifest itself in different ways: lack of registration, lack of licence for an economic activity, lack of permit for a change of use, lack of compliance with particular conditions or tax evasion. In any of the three categories of STRs, an operator might comply with *some* aspects of regulation (e.g., have the right authorisation) but not others (e.g., not declare the income to the relevant tax authorities). This can be due to a lack of awareness of the rules or to a deliberate choice based on the perceived high cost of compliance or low risk of penalties (Durst and Wegmann 2017; Harris 2018). The meaning of *illegality* also changed over time. As new regulations were passed by city governments, this has produced situations in which a formerly legal STR became illegal overnight: in Berlin, a change of rules in 2014 turned small holiday rental businesses that had legally operated for years into an illegal activity, a retroactivity condemned by the representative of an STR professional association as a 'criminalisation' of their activities. Different regulatory regimes have therefore produced new demarcations of what *legal* or *illegal* STR accommodation means from one city to the other. They have also shaped the practical nature of, and the distribution of responsibilities in, enforcement activities: the agents potentially in charge of controlling illegality can thus be located in different public authorities and departments: business licensing, tourism, taxation, planning or housing.

2. We do not deal here with the implementation of national rules by the central state, namely the taxation of rental revenues and the obligation to declare guests' names to the police.

3. 8,210 CAV and 1,513 *locazioni turistiche* (interview, Department for Commercial and Productive activities, July 2022).

4. 8,365 CAV and 3,341 *locazioni turistiche* (Regione Lombardia n.d.).

5. This is due to the fact that Inside Airbnb data include single rooms that can be in the same property, as well as other types of tourist accommodation (such as traditional B&Bs) that use the Airbnb platform for advertisement.

6. Eleven agents work on the change-of-use procedure; fifteen agents control STR listings and properties, and there are four directors and two secretaries (interview with BPLH Team, July 2022).

7. According to the city government, between July 2016 and July 2018, 2,355 STRs were closed down; steps were taken to close a further 1,800, 10,635 proceedings were opened and 5,503 fines were imposed. The number of illegal STRs identified on platforms was cut from 5,875 in 2016 to 1,714 in June 2018, a reduction of 70% (Ajuntament de Barcelona 2018). A total of 2,176 flats were deemed to have been returned to long-term occupation by the end of 2020 (La Vanguardia 2020).

8. For the Register of Change of Use authorisations for STRs (open data), see Paris Data (n.d.).

9. In Barcelona the STR register is available online, which means that anyone is potentially able to check whether the address of a property appears on it. See Ajuntament de Barcelona (n.d.).

10. The City of Paris has administrative policing powers (*Code of Construction and Housing*). Any change of use made without prior authorisation is punishable by prosecution and civil fines. The BPLH is responsible for enforcement, with a staff of 33 agents, including 15 agents working specifically on STR issues and 11 change-of-use inspectors, all sworn in by the Tribunal de Grande Instance. They can carry out inspection visits in private dwellings in the presence of an occupant (owner, tenant, visitor). If an infringement is established, the BPLH requests that proceedings be initiated with the Public Prosecutor's Office of the Paris Tribunal de Grande Instance to enforce sanctions, including a civil fine of up to €50,000.

11. In Paris, one BPLH inspector was hit by a guest during an inspection in 2016.

12. In France, the law requires that rental leases for primary residences be for a minimum of three years in the case of an empty dwelling, barring professional or family exceptions, and of one year in the case of furnished accommodation (except in the case of student rentals, for which the lease may be for nine months). Another exception is the 'mobility lease' (*bail mobilité*), often used for seasonal workers or students, which can be from one to ten months. The civil lease (*bail civil*) enables two parties to sign a short-term furnished rental contract, in accordance with the conditions chosen by the parties.

13. See Hajdenberg (2015), which presents the results of a study by geographers Saskia Cousin, Sebastien Jacquot and Gaël Chareyron, who were among the first web scrapers of Airbnb data in France.

14. 2015: 503 on-site investigations into suspected offences, followed by 15 orders on 24 homes, leading to €162,500 in fines; 2016: 13 orders on 17 homes with €89,500 in fines; 2017: 70 units with €223, 000 in fines; 2021–2022: 420 orders with €14 million fines (interview, officers from BPLH, July 2022).

15. Court cases were interrupted due to the referral of the Parisian regulation to the Court of Justice of the European Union,then resumed in 2021 (see Chapters 6 and 7).

16. Article L631-7, *Code de la Construction et de l'Habitat*.

17. In Paris, see for example the Cabinet Demeuzoy, presenting itself as the 'must-have specialist for Airbnb regulation and real estate' (https://www.demeuzoy-avocat.com).

18. See Ajuntament de Barcelona (n.d.).

19. The city government of New York was one of the pioneers in the legal fight to request access to the data held by Airbnb, in 2013 (Hoffman and Schmitter Heisler 2020). After several years of contention, an agreement for the sharing of individualised data (with the consent of the host) was reached in June 2020 (Airbnb 2020a; City of New York 2020).

20. See Chapter 6. The data that Airbnb agrees to release upon request in an aggregate form is set out in its Policy Tool Chest (2016a). The company has also regularly released aggregated data as part of communication strategies.

21. Though a ruling by the Berlin administrative court in June 2021 confirmed that district administrations can require platforms to release personalised data if there is 'justified initial suspicion' against a STR landlord.

22. In the case of Airbnb, such occurrences remain relatively infrequent: in 2018 only 3,071 law enforcement inquiries for user information were lodged globally; for 1,739 of those, some form of legal process was served, and for 811 of those at least some account information was disclosed by the company (Airbnb 2019a). The company describes the way in which it deals with data requests from law enforcement agencies at Airbnb (n.d.-b).

23. A total of over 13,000 listings were deactivated across those platforms, of which about 12,000 were on Airbnb, according to information shared by the Department of Inspection in the summer of 2023.

24. In San Francisco, in 2017 Airbnb and HomeAway settled their lawsuit with the city and agreed to collect data from hosts that is then passed on to the city's Office of Short-Term Rentals, a system referred to as 'pass-through registration' (Bay Area Council Economic Institute 2018). This system prevents unregistered STRs from being listed online. Platforms also agreed to cancel reservations and deactivate listings if the city notifies them of an invalid registration. Airbnb noted that the pass-through registration system 'is an exception to our usual approach in which individual hosts are responsible for registering and securing any necessary licenses so their personal information is communicated directly to the jurisdiction, rather than via Airbnb. Pass-through registration can be difficult to implement, requiring significant technical cooperation between a city and a home-sharing platform to share data regarding individual hosts' (Airbnb 2016a:9).

25. See for instance the page for France, at Airbnb (n.d.-d).

26. The data gathered is the publicly available content of STR listings advertised on a platform's website; it does not contain any precise address, and hosts' names may be pseudonyms. The data is saved into a spreadsheet for ulterior analysis or use. Such processes of web scraping require some programming skills but are not overly complicated. See Wang et al. (2024) and Burrow (2021).

27. The Inside Airbnb website (https://insideairbnb.com) provides aggregate and mapped data on the number and approximate location of listings, the STR type, the estimated number of nights booked and income for each

listing for the last 12 months and the proportion of multi-listings. The aggregate data produced through such scraping methods is not perfect, as it is based on assumptions (e.g., the maximum number of days per year for a housing unit rented short-term to be no longer considered as someone's 'primary residence') and approximations (in particular because the data scraped from the Airbnb website does not allow users to distinguish true bookings from days on which a property is otherwise unavailable; occupancy is estimated through the assumption that 50% of bookings lead to a review). See explanations at Inside Airbnb (n.d.); Grisdale (2019), for a comparison of the data generated by Inside Airbnb and AirDNA; and Wang et al. (2024).

## CHAPTER 6. PLATFORM POWER, GRASSROOTS MOBILISATIONS AND POLITICAL CLIENTELES

1. Own calculation based on AirDNA data (average, 2024).

2. Semi and Tonetta (2021) first developed the idea of STR operators as a 'new rentiers class' that inspired our notion of 'short-term-rentiers'. Müller et al. (2021) also use the expression STR 'rentier coalition' in their work on Palma de Mallorca, and Wijburg et al. (2023) include the various actors we mention here in their concept of 'tourism-led rentier capitalism'. It is worth noting that some of the authors mentioned in Chapter 1 (section 'Who Owns and Runs STR?') nuance the labelling of all STR hosts as 'rentier capitalists' (Maier and Gilchrist 2022), by pointing out that some hosts engage in STR practices out of dire financial need.

3. Fairbnb was initially developed in 2016 in Venice, Amsterdam and Bologna. It is now present in Italy, Portugal, France, Slovenia, Croatia, Belgium, and Spain, though with a very small market share compared to that of commercial platforms. According to its website, Fairbnb aims to give 'travellers and locals the opportunity to participate in a more responsible and sustainable tourism model by supporting social and ecological projects', which are funded by redirecting 50% of the platform's booking fees. It promotes hosts who share their home and 'excludes large real estate investors who exclusively rent to tourists'. It works with local authorities to verify the lawfulness of the STRs on offer and 'promote[s] a fair regulation of the market'. (For a discussion of the

opportunities and limits of the project see Foramitti *et al.* 2020; Petruzzi *et al.* 2021; Cano *et al.* 2024).

4. Public lecture 'Airbnb and cities, shaping the future of travel' given by Chris Lehane in Sciences Po Paris, France, on 2 March 2017. Attended by the authors.

5. Calculated by the authors from the Budget orientation report of the city of Paris (2023).

6. A small agglomeration (Ile d'Oléron) took Airbnb to court in 2023 for 'incomplete and erroneous declarations' in the payment of the tourist tax in 2020 and 2021, demanding repayment of a €30 million fine.

7. One page on the Airbnb website ('News') is dedicated to this point; see Airbnb (2023).

8. According to Italian law, there are two types of medium-term contracts: transition contracts (1 to 18 months) and student contracts (6 to 36 months).

9. Airbnb (n.d.-c).

10. Airbnb has also opened a new "Patrimoine" section (https://www.airbnb .fr/d/patrimoine) to promote this strategy.

11. The campaign was presented on the website Airbnbcitizen in May 2017 under the title 'I am a host and I stand for home-sharing'. The website does not exist anymore. Slogans were in Italian, translated by the authors.

12. Officially, they are dedicated to help 'hosts come together to advocate for fair home sharing laws in their communities', 'share best practices around hosting and hospitality' and 'elevate the host voice locally.'

13. The Airbnb Citizen website has been shut and the information reorganised between the main website and the corporate social responsibility website (www.airbnb.org).

14. See their advocacy page (https://www.vrbo.com/discoveryhub/tips-and -resources/guest-management/regulations-resources#advocacy-101) and their Twitter page (https://twitter.com/vrbopolicy?lang=en).

15. Haute Autorité pour la Transparence de la Vie Publique (n.d.) (the French authority for the transparency of public life).

16. Entr'hôtes Collective (2017).

17. Data from Inside Airbnb (n.d.-b).

18. Data from Inside Airbnb (n.d.-b).

19. Data from Inside Airbnb (n.d.-b).

20. Tranquille Émile (n.d.).

21. Global ReformBnB is an international association of professional organisations representing the hotel industry 'with the aim of promoting fair rules in the field of tourism accommodation and digital distribution' (Global Reformbnb 2023). The conference was held in Paris 23 and 24 May 2022. We were invited to present our research and attended the conference, but we did not accept any funding by the organisers to do so.

22. The citizens' conference was organised by the City of Paris: 26 citizens were randomly selected to take part in 'training' and 'hearing' sessions over several days from January to February 2021. The sessions involved agents from the City of Paris and other French and European cities, activists, non-governmental organisations specialising in housing issues, researchers (we were invited to present our work on regulations in Europe on 6 February 2021), platforms, hotel associations, representatives of neighbourhood associations and the Airbnb Paris Host Club. At the end of the process, a citizens' opinion document was drafted. It recommended mobilising the national state and the EU to give city government more tools and made proposals to improve the enforcement of existing regulations. However, it rejected the proposal by Mayor Anne Hidalgo to lower the time cap from 120 to 30 days per year for the occasional STR of a primary residence (Errard 2021).

## CHAPTER 7. THE JUDICIALISATION AND TRANSNATIONALISATION OF LOCAL CONFLICTS

1. The cities covered in this book are all located in the EU, except London, following the UK's exit from the EU on 31 January 2020.

2. Any discussion of the EU's influence on national, regional and local regulatory debates should avoid the reification of the EU as a single entity with a single political agenda. Different EU institutions (the Council of Ministers that represents national governments, the European Parliament that represents EU citizens, the European Commission that acts as the public administration of the EU and the Court of Justice of the EU that has ultimate authority over the interpretation of EU law) have different agendas and positions on an issue. Such differences also exist *within* each institution. This is particularly the case

within the European Commission, where different Directorates-General are shaped by different policy communities and serve different aspects of the EU political project. This may lead to tensions and contradictions, in particular between the objective of economic integration and growth through a single market and the objectives of social/territorial cohesion and environmental sustainability, which are also key in the EU treaties (Dühr et al. 2010). This explains why digital platforms and STR activities have been perceived differently by different EU institutions (and within those institutions).

3. The *digital single market* is defined as one in which 'individuals and businesses can seamlessly access and exercise online activities under conditions of fair competition, and a high level of consumer and personal data protection, irrespective of their nationality or place of residence' (European Commission 2015:3).

4. Such stakeholders have also invoked privacy concerns and the General Data Protection Regulation (GDPR) that came into force in 2018. The GDPR stipulates that personal data may only be shared with third parties if a legal basis for this is determined. Such legal basis may exist if, first, the data subject has given consent to the data processing for a specific purpose. This means that platforms would have to request permission from hosts to share their personal data with public authorities at the stage when a user registers on the platform. The city government of Barcelona has negotiated with Airbnb for this to be the case from 2018 onwards. Second, a legal basis also exists if there is an obligation prescribed in EU or national legislation for specific operators to share specific personal data with public authorities. However, member states are only allowed to adopt such requirements if these are *necessary and proportionate* to safeguard legitimate public interest objectives (e.g., public security or taxation). In short, public authorities are not prevented by the GDPR from asking platforms for private customer data if it is in the public interest.

5. See European Commission (n.d.-b) for an overview. The *E-Commerce Directive* is the EU equivalent of Article 230 of the USA *Communications Decency Act*.

6. The ruling applies to this platform only.

7. The European Commission, however, has encouraged platforms to take voluntary action to fight illegal content, although this has mostly applied to social media platforms in relation to issues such as hate speech or child pornography.

8. See European Commission (n.d.-e) for an overview.

9. In that respect, it is worth mentioning that the European Commission encourages EU member states, in their regulations of STRs, to apply distinct rules for the occasional practice of homeowners or tenants renting out their primary home and for the professional activity of an operator managing several STRs as a business. This has been done, for example, by establishing time thresholds based on the level of activity (European Commission 2016a:7), as mentioned in Chapter 3. But EU legislation does not establish explicitly at what point a non-professional operator (sometimes referred to as 'peer') becomes a 'professional services provider'.

10. Arrêt n°195 du 18 février 2021 (17-26.156)—Cour de cassation—Troisième chambre civile-ECLI:FR:CCAS:2021:C300195, https://www.legifrance.gouv.fr/juri/id/JURITEXT000043200274.

11. In March 2020 the European Commission reached an agreement with large platforms Airbnb, Booking, Expedia and TripAdvisor, whereby the latter share aggregate data on the bookings made through them on a regular basis, at the level of municipalities, to help the European Statistical Office (Eurostat) produce STR accommodation statistics. Such aggregate data are, however, useless for local regulatory enforcement, as stated by a network of 22 European cities (Eurocities 2020a).

12. See European Commission (n.d.-g) and LobbyFacts.eu (n.d.-b).

13. In the case of Airbnb, as of July 2023 the Register listed 25 meetings held since November 2014 with commissioners, their cabinet members or directors-general at the European Commission. Other lobby meetings with lower-level staff may have taken place, but the European Commission does not publish information about such meetings. See LobbyFacts.eu (n.d.-a).

14. The power and discretion of the European Commission in monitoring compliance with Single Market rules and EU competition law to ensure a level playing field between economic actors is significant: it can carry out formal investigations in the member states, require a government to abolish or alter domestic rules deemed unlawful, prosecute a state in front of the CJEU for infringement of rules and impose fines.

15. This type of formal complaint launches a period of mediation between the European Commission and the relevant member state (in this instance

Germany, Spain, Belgium and France), starting with the issuing of a letter by the Commission to national governments, who have two months to respond to justify the regulations or propose modifications. If the Commission is not satisfied, a second notification letter is sent. If this does not solve the issue, the Commission can launch an 'infringement procedure' and ask the CJEU to make a ruling on the case (thus clarifying its interpretation of European law) and, if judged necessary, to impose a fine on the member state. National, rather than local, public authorities are usually targeted by such complaints, and it is national governments that have to respond to the Commission's letters. This may generate tensions between tiers of government in case of divergent approaches.

16. European Commission (n.d.-c.)

17. For an overview, see European Commission (n.d.-c.). It should be noted that the *Digital Services Act* will not repeal the *E-Commerce Directive*, but amend it.

18. See LobbyFacts.eu (n.d.-a).

19. European Commission (n.d.-c.).

20. European Commission (n.d.-f.).

21. The DG GROW document (2021) stated that the most likely legal basis for an EU legislative initiative would be Article 114 of the *Treaty on the Functioning of the European Union*, which enables EU initiatives to improve the conditions for the functioning of the internal market.

22. The meaning of the principle of subsidiarity in the EU context is discussed in European Commission (n.d.-d). It rules out EU intervention 'when an issue can be dealt with effectively by Member States themselves at central, regional or local level', and is fully spelled out in Article 5(3) of the Treaty on the EU.

23. It should also be noted that in its preliminary assessment of the expected impacts of a potential 'initiative', the Commission's document generally reproduced platforms' arguments about the positive impacts of STRs on job creation, extra income for citizens and less-visited areas. However, in the short section on the possible impacts on fundamental rights, while property rights and the right to conduct a business were emphasised, the impacts on the right to housing and on the right to peace and privacy of local residents were not mentioned.

24. Article 3(2) of the draft regulation (see European Commission 2022) defined a *host* as 'a natural or legal person that provides, or intends to provide, on a professional or non-professional basis, permanently or temporarily on a regular or on a temporary basis, directly or through an intermediary, a short-term accommodation rental service against remuneration through an online short-term rental platform'.

# References

Aalbers, M. B. (2016) *The Financialization of Housing: A Political Economy Approach*, Abingdon: Routledge.

Aalbers, M. B. (2017) 'The variegated financialization of housing', *International Journal of Urban and Regional Research*, 41(4), 542–554.

Aalbers, M. B. (2019) 'Introduction to the forum: From third to fifth-wave gentrification', *Tijdschrift voor Economische en Sociale Geografie*, 110(1), 1–11.

Aalbers, M. B. (2022) 'Towards a relational and comparative rather than a contrastive global housing studies', *Housing Studies*, 37(6), 1054–1072.

ACABA (2022) 'Who we are', https://www.associacioacaba.org/en.html.

Adamiak, C. (2022) 'Current state and development of Airbnb accommodation offer in 167 countries', *Current Issues in Tourism*, 25(19), 3131–3149.

Adkins, L., Cooper, M., and Konings, M. (2021) 'Class in the 21st century: Asset inflation and the new logic of inequality', *Environment and Planning A: Economy and Space*, 53(3), 548–572.

Aguilera, T. (2016) 'Governing (and resisting) the Tourist City. The conflicts over the regulation of Airbnb in Paris and London', Paper presented at the WHIG Project workshop, April, University of São Paolo.

Aguilera, T. (2017) *Gouverner les Illégalismes Urbains: Les Politiques Publiques face aux Squats et aux Bidonvilles dans les Régions de Paris et de Madrid*, Paris: Dalloz.

Aguilera, T., Artioli, F., and Colomb, C. (2021) 'Explaining the diversity of policy responses to platform-mediated short-term rentals in European cities: A comparison of Barcelona, Paris and Milan', *Environment and Planning A: Economy and Space*, 53(7), 1689–1712.

Airbnb (2014) 'Airbnb growth in Europe', *The Airbnb Blog—Belong Anywhere*, https://blog.atairbnb.com/airbnb-growth-europe.

Airbnb (2015) *Airbnb Community Compact*, https://www.airhttps://www.airbnb citizen.com/wp-content/uploads/2015/11/Airbnb-Community-Compact.pdf.

Airbnb (2016a) *Airbnb Policy Tool Chest*, https://www.airbnbcitizen.com/wp-content/uploads/2016/12/National_PublicPolicyTool-ChestReport-v3.pdf.

Airbnb (2016b) 'Airbnb, Comune di Milano e Casa delle Donne Maltrattate insieme per accogliere i famigliari dei pazienti in cura', *Airbnb Newsroom*, 31 August, https://news.airbnb.com/it/airbnb-comune-di-milano-e-casa-delle-donne-maltrattate-insieme-per-accogliere-i-familiari-dei-pazienti-in-cura/.

Airbnb (2017a) 'Il piano "Borghi Italiani"', *Airbnb Newsroom*, 6 October, https://news.airbnb.com/it/borghi-italiani/.

Airbnb (2017b) 'Italian Villages, il progetto di Airbnb con ANCI e MiBACT per promuovere i borghi italiani', *Airbnb Newsroom*, 9 October, https://news.airbnb.com/it/italian-villages-il-progetto-di-airbnb-con-anci-e-mibact-per-promuovere-i-borghi-italiani/.

Airbnb (2018a) 'Airbnb economic impact', *The Airbnb Blog—Belong Anywhere*, https://blog.atairbnb.com/economic-impact-airbnb/.

Airbnb (2018b) *Airbnb Submission: Draft London Plan*, https://www.london.gov.uk/sites/default/files/Airbnb%20%282301%29.pdf.

Airbnb (2018c) 'Firmato l'accordo tra Comune di Milano e Airbnb sull'imposta di soggiorno', *Airbnb Newsroom*, 16 March, https://news.airbnb.com/it/firmato-laccordo-tra-comune-di-milano-e-airbnb-sullimposta-di-soggiorno/.

Airbnb (2019a) *2018 Supplemental Airbnb Law Enforcement Transparency Report*, https://www.airbnbcitizen.com/transparency/2018-supplemental.

Airbnb (2019b) 'Locations meublées touristiques à Paris: Une tendance positive', *Airbnb Newsroom*, 20 December, https://news.airbnb.com/fr/locations -meublees-touristiques-a-paris-une-tendance-positive/.

Airbnb (2020a) 'A message to our New York City hosts', *Airbnb Newsroom*, https:// news.airbnb.com/a-message-to-our-new-york-city-hosts/.

Airbnb (2020b) 'Su Airbnb porte aperte a medici e infermieri impegnati nell'emergenza', *Airbnb Newsroom*, https://news.airbnb.com/it/airbnb-e-la -comunita-di-host-a-fianco-di-medici-e-infermieri-nellemergenza/.

Airbnb (2020c) *Digital Services Act Package: Open Public Consultation; Response Submitted by Airbnb*. Contribution ID: 7bfbf18a-a35e-4ba4-8c80-aa9b7cde042f D', https://www.politico.eu/wp-content/uploads/2020/09/Airbnb-DSA -consultation-response-8-Sept-2020-SUBMITTED.pdf.

Airbnb (2021a) 'Airbnb annonce une série d'engagements pour un tourisme responsable', *Airbnb Newsroom*, 7 February, https://news.airbnb.com/fr/airbnb -annonce-une-serie-dengagements-pour-un-tourisme-responsable/.

Airbnb (2021b) *The EU Host Action Plan*, https://news.airbnb.com/wp-content /uploads/sites/4/2021/12/The-EU-Host-Action-Plan_Dec-2021.pdf.

Airbnb (2022a) 'How destinations can benefit from the rise in remote workers', *Airbnb Newsroom*, 15 September, https://news.airbnb.com/how-destinations -can-benefit-from-the-rise-in-remote-workers/.

Airbnb (2022b) 'Ruralité connectée: Airbnb et l'AMRF encouragent le télétravail au vert', *Airbnb Newsroom*, 11 October, https://news.airbnb.com/fr /ruralite-connectee-airbnb-et-lamrf-encouragent-le-teletravail-au-vert/.

Airbnb (2022c) *Data Collection and Sharing Relating to Short-Term Accommodation Rental Services—Airbnb Position*, https://news.airbnb.com/wp-content /uploads/sites/4/2022/12/Airbnb-EU-Position-Paper-December-2022.pdf.

Airbnb (2023) '148 million euros of tourist tax paid to French municipalities in 2022', 12 January, https://news.airbnb.com/fr/148m-deuros-de-taxe-de -sejour-reverses-aux-communes-francaises-en-2022/#:~:text=La%20taxe %20de%20séjour%20reversée,le%20centre%20de%20l%27agglomération.

Airbnb (2024) *Airbnb Q4-2023 and Full-Year Financial Results*, https://news.airbnb .com/airbnb-q4-2023-and-full-year-financial-results/.

Airbnb (n.d.-a) 'Airbnb open', https://community.withairbnb.com/t5/Airbnb -Open/bd-p/airbnb-open.

Airbnb (n.d.-b) 'How does Airbnb respond to data requests from law enforcement?', https://www.airbnb.co.uk/help/article/960/how-does-airbnb-respond-to-data-requests-from-law-enforcement.

Airbnb (n.d.-c) 'Le patrimoine au service du développement touristique rural', https://www.fondation-patrimoine.org/fondation-du-patrimoine/partenaires-et-mecenes/airbnb.

Airbnb (n.d.-d) 'Responsible hosting in France', https://www.airbnb.com/help/article/1383/?locale=en&_set_bev_on_new_domain=1706098527_OGJkNjJlZmM1YzEw.

AirDNA (2020) 'COVID-19 short-term rental data: Analyzing the impact of COVID-19 on vacation rentals', https://www.airdna.co/covid-19-data-center.

AirDNA (2024) 'Short-term rental data', https://www.airdna.co.

Ajuntament de Barcelona (2016) *Barcelona desplega un pla de xoc per combatre amb contundència els habitatges d'ús turístic il·legals*, https://ajuntament.barcelona.cat/premsa/wp-content/uploads/2016/06/HUT.pdf.

Ajuntament de Barcelona (2017a) *Enquesta de Serveis Municipals 2017 Abril—Juny 2017 Evolució 1989–2017 (Taules)*, Ajuntament de Barcelona, https://ajuntament.barcelona.cat/premsa/wp-content/uploads/2017/11/r17008_ESM_Evoluci%C3%B3_Taules.pdf.

Ajuntament de Barcelona (2017b) 'About the PEUAT', https://ajuntament.barcelona.cat/pla-allotjaments-turistics/en/home.

Ajuntament de Barcelona (2018) 'Municipal inspections to get access to all data from Airbnb adverts', *InfoBarcelona*, https://www.barcelona.cat/infobarcelona/en/municipal-inspections-to-get-access-to-all-data-from-airbnb-adverts_668222.html.

Ajuntament de Barcelona (2019) 'Illegal tourist flats reduced to a minimum', *InfoBarcelona*, https://www.barcelona.cat/infobarcelona/en/illegal-tourist-flatsreduced-to-a-minimum_779808.html.

Ajuntament de Barcelona (2020) *Informe de La Unidad Antiacoso de Disciplina de Vivienda*, https://www.habitatge.barcelona/sites/default/files/informe_disciplina_2019_es_0.pdf.

Ajuntament de Barcelona, Direcció de Turisme (2017) *Barcelona tourism for 2020: A collective strategy for sustainable tourism*, https://ajuntament.barcelona.cat/turisme/en/strategic-plan.

Ajuntament de Barcelona (n.d.) 'Flat detector of tourist accommodation', https://meet.barcelona.cat/habitatgesturistics/en.

Alexandri, G. and Janoschka, M. (2020) '"Post-pandemic" transnational gentrifications: A critical outlook', *Urban Studies*, 57(15), 3202–3214.

Allen, J., Barlow, J., Leal, J., Maloutas, T., and Padovani, L. (2004) *Housing and Welfare in Southern Europe*, Oxford: Blackwell.

Almeida, H. (2016) 'Airbnb finds love in Lisbon after Berlin shies away', *Bloomberg.com*, 5 June, https://www.bloomberg.com/news/articles/2016-06-05/airbnb-finds-love-in-lisbon-after-berlin-barcelona-shy-away.

Alterman, R. and Calor, I. (2020) 'Between informal and illegal in the Global North: Planning law, enforcement and justifiable noncompliance', in Grashoff, U., ed., *Comparative Approaches to Informal Housing Around the Globe*, London: UCL Press, 150–185.

Ameri, M., Rogers, S. E., Schur, L., and Kruse, D. (2020) 'No room at the inn? Disability access in the new sharing economy', *Academy of Management Discoveries*, 6(2), 176–205.

Amnesty International (2019) 'Destination: Occupation: Digital tourism and Israel's illegal settlements in the Occupied Palestinian Territories', https://www.amnesty.org/en/latest/campaigns/2019/01/destination-occupation-digital-tourism-israel-illegal-settlements/.

Amore, A., Bernardi, C. de, and Arvanitis, P. (2020) 'The impacts of Airbnb in Athens, Lisbon and Milan: A rent gap theory perspective', *Current Issues in Tourism*, 25(22), 3329–3342.

Amsterdam Gastvrij (2023) 'Amsterdam Gastvrij', https://www.amsterdamgastvrij.com.

Andreotti, A., ed. (2019) *Governare Milano nel nuovo millennio*, Bologna: Il Mulino.

Andreu, M. (2015) *Barris, Veïns i Democràcia: El Moviment Ciutadà i La Reconstrucció de Barcelona (1968–1986)*, Barcelona: L'Avenç.

Ansell, B. (2014) 'The political economy of ownership: Housing markets and the welfare state', *American Political Science Review*, 108(2), 383–402.

Ansell, B. and Cansunar, A. (2021) 'The political consequences of housing (un)affordability', *Journal of European Social Policy*, 31(5), 597–613.

Ansell, B. W. (2019) 'The politics of housing', *Annual Review of Political Science*, 22(1), 165–185.

Anselmi, G., Chiappini, L., and Prestileo, F. (2021) 'The greedy unicorn: Airbnb and capital concentration in 12 European cities', *City, Culture and Society*, 27, 100412.

Anselmi, G. and Conte, V. (2021) 'Airbnb a Milano: Geografie, concentrazione ed attori', in Perrone, C., Masiani, B., and Tosi, F., eds., *Una geografia delle politiche urbane tra possesso e governo: Sfide e opportunità nella transizione*, Bologna: Dipartimento di Architettura dell'Università di Bologna, 274–281.

Anselmi, G. and Vicari, S. (2020) 'Milan makes it to the big leagues: A financialized growth machine at work', *European Urban and Regional Studies*, 27(2), 106–124.

APUR (Atelier Parisien d'Urbanisme) (2011) *Les Locations Meublées de Courte Durée à Paris: Etat des lieux et propositions*, Paris: APUR.

APUR (2020) 'Locations meublées touristiques à Paris—Situation 2020 et comparaison avec sept autres grandes villes', note 177, https://www.apur
.org/fr/nos-travaux/locations-meublees-touristiques-paris-situation-2020
-comparaison-sept-autres-grandes-villes.

APUR (2021) 'Quel impact de la crise de la Covid-19 sur les locations meublées touristiques à Paris?', note 205, https://www.apur.org/fr/nos-travaux/impact
-crise-covid-19-locations-meublees-touristiques-paris.

Aquaro, D. and dell'Oste, C. (2022) 'Imposta di soggiorno in ripresa nel 2022 anche per gli affitti brevi', *Il Sole 24 ORE*, https://www.ilsole24ore.com/art
/imposta-soggiorno-ripresa-2022-anche-gli-affitti-brevi-AEFsZykB.

Arbaci, S. (2019) *Paradoxes of Segregation: Housing Systems, Welfare Regimes and Ethnic Residential Change in Southern European Cities*, Hoboken, NJ: Wiley.

Arcidiacono, D., Gandini, A., and Pais, I. (2018) 'Sharing what? The "sharing economy" in the sociological debate', *The Sociological Review*, 66(2), 275–288.

Arias Sans, A. and Quaglieri Domínguez, A. (2016) 'Unravelling Airbnb: Urban perspectives from Barcelona', in Russo, A. P. and Richards, G., eds., *Reinventing the Local in Tourism: Producing, Consuming and Negotiating Place*, Bristol: Channel View Publications, 209–228.

Arias Sans, A., Quaglieri Domínguez, A., and Russo, A.P. (2022) 'Home-sharing as transnational moorings', *City*, 26(1), 160–178.

Armondi, S. and Bruzzese, A. (2017) 'Contemporary production and urban change: The case of Milan', *Journal of Urban Technology*, 24(3), 27–45.

Armondi, S., Coppola, A., Fedeli, V., Pacchi, C. and Pasqui, G. (2022) 'Milano tra poliarchia e nuove disuguaglianze', in Urbanait, *Settimo Rapporto sulle città. Chi possiede la città? Proprietà, poteri, politiche.* Bologna: Il Mulino, 51–68.

Artioli, F. (2016) 'Retrenchment of the center and conflict at the peripheries', *Revue Française de Science Politique*, 66(2), 229–250.

Artioli, F. (2018) *Digital Platforms and Cities: A Literature Review for Urban Research*, Working Papers du Programme Villes & Territoires de Sciences Po, https:// sciencespo.hal.science/hal-02385137.

Artioli, F. (2020) *La gouvernance urbaine à l'épreuve d'Airbnb: Locations de courte durée et groupes d'intérêt à Milan*, Paris: Plan Urbanisme Construction Architecture, https://www.urbanisme-puca.gouv.fr/IMG/pdf/la_gouvernance _urbaine_a_lepreuve_dairbnb.pdf.

Ash, J., Kitchin, R., and Leszczynski, A. (2018a) *Digital Geographies*, Thousand Oaks, CA: Sage.

Ash, J., Kitchin, R., and Leszczynski, A. (2018b) 'Digital turn, digital geographies?', *Progress in Human Geography*, 42(1), 25–43.

Ashworth, G. and Page, S. J. (2011) 'Urban tourism research: Recent progress and current paradoxes', *Tourism Management*, 32(1), 1–15.

Assemblea de Barris pel Decreixement Turístic (ABDT) (2016) 'Inside Airbnb, com i per què vam reservar i denunciar un pis turístic il·legal', September, https://assembleabarris.wordpress.com/2016/09/.

Assolombarda (2023) *Osservatorio Turismo 2023, Il Turismo a Milano Nel Post Pandemia: Caratteristiche Strutturali e Tendenze Recenti*, Assolombarda, Milano, https://www.assolombarda.it/centro-studi/osservatorio-turismo-2023-1#: ~:text=Tra%20il%202019%20e%20il%202020%20gli%20arrivi%20turistici %20a,milioni%20di%20visitatori%20nel%202020.&text=Il%202021%20e %20il%202022,5%2C8%20milioni%20nel%202022.

Avdimiotis, S. and Poulaki, I. (2019) 'Airbnb impact and regulation issues through destination life cycle concept', *International Journal of Culture, Tourism and Hospitality Research*, 13(4), 458–472.

Balampanidis, D., Maloutas, T., Papatzani, E., and Pettas, D. (2021) 'Informal urban regeneration as a way out of the crisis? Airbnb in Athens and its effects on space and society', *Urban Research & Practice*, 14(3), 223–242.

Balchin, P. (1996) *Housing Policy in Europe*, Abingdon: Routledge.

Barbrook, R. and Cameron, A. (1996) 'The Californian ideology', *Science as Culture*, 6(1), 44–72.

Barns, S. (2020) *Platform Urbanism: Negotiating Platform Ecosystems in Connected Cities*, Singapore: Palgrave Macmillan/Springer Nature Singapore.

Barry Born, T. (2021) 'Proactive state geographies: Geocoded intelligence in London's "suburban shanty towns"', *Environment and Planning D: Society and Space*, 39(4), 609–626.

Bauriedl, S. and Strüver, A. (2022) 'Platformized cities and urban life: An introduction', in Bauriedl, S. and Strüver, A., eds., *Platformization of Urban Life: Towards a Technocapitalist Transformation of European Cities*, Bielefeld: Transcript Verlag, 11–37.

Bay Area Council Economic Institute (2018) *Homesharing in San Francisco: A Review of Policy Changes and Their Impacts*, Bay Area Council Economic Institute, San Francisco, http://www.bayareaeconomy.org/files/pdf/BACEI_Homesharing_1112018.pdf.

Beck, L. (2018) 'Berlin had some of the world's most restrictive rules for Airbnb rentals. Now it's loosening up', *Washington Post*, 30 March, https://www.washingtonpost.com/world/europe/berlin-had-some-of-the-worlds-most-restrictive-rules-for-airbnb-rentals-now-its-loosening-up/2018/03/27/e3acda90-2603-11e8-a227-fd2b009466bc_story.html.

Beckert, J. (2009) 'The social order of markets', *Theory and Society*, 38(3), 245–269, https://www.jstor.org/stable/40587527.

Bei, G. and Celata, F. (2023) 'Challenges and effects of short-term rentals regulation: A counterfactual assessment of European cities', *Annals of Tourism Research*, 101, 103605.

Bekkerman, R., Cohen, M.vC., Kung, E., Maiden, J., and Proserpio, D. (2022) 'The effect of short-term rentals on residential investment', *Marketing Science*, 42(4), 637–837.

Belk, R. (2007) 'Why not share rather than own?', *The Annals of the American Academy of Political and Social Science*, 611(1), 126–140.

Benli-Trichet, M. C. and Kübler, D. (2022) 'The political origins of platform economy regulations: Understanding variations in governing Airbnb and Uber across cities in Switzerland', *Policy & Internet*, 14(4), 736–754.

Benoît, C. (2021) 'Politicians, regulators, and regulatory governance: The neglected sides of the story', *Regulation & Governance*, 15(S1), S8–S22.

Benson, M. and O'Reilly, K. (2009) 'Migration and the search for a better way of life: A critical exploration of lifestyle migration', *The Sociological Review*, 57(4), 608–625.

Berg, J. and Furrer, M. (2018) *Digital Labour Platforms and the Future of Work: Towards Decent Work in the Online World*, Report, International Labour Organization, http://www.ilo.org/global/publications/books/WCMS_645337/lang--en/index.htm.

Bergeron, H., Castel, P., and Saguy, A. (2014) *When Frames (Don't) Matter: Querying the Relationship Between Ideas and Policy*, LIEPP Working Paper, no. 8, 1–42, https://sciencespo.hal.science/hal-01503847.

Bernt, M. (2022) *The Commodification Gap: Gentrification and Public Policy in London, Berlin and St. Petersburg*, Hoboken, NJ: Wiley.

Bertolino, F. (2023) 'Airbnb paga 576 milioni: Chiuso il contenzioso fiscale con l'Agenzia delle Entrate- Corriere.it', *Il Corriere della Sera*, 13 December, https://www.corriere.it/economia/tasse/23_dicembre_13/airbnb-paga-576-milioni-chiuso-contenzioso-fiscale-l-agenzia-entrate-5of1f9be-99ad-11ee-97fb-911ff9649ac6.shtml.

Bertuzzi, L. (2023) 'Leading MEP wants to empower authorities to delist short-term rentals—EURACTIV.com', *Euractiv.com*, 9 May, https://www.euractiv.com/section/platforms/news/leading-mep-wants-to-empower-authorities-to-delist-short-term-rentals/.

BHA (2016) *Supplementary Evidence to the Business Innovation and Skills Committee Oral Evidence Session: The Digital Economy*, British Hospitality Association, London, https://www.parliament.uk/business/committees/committees-a-z/commons-select/business-innovation-and-skills/inquiries/parliament-2015/digital-economy/publications/.

Bibler, A., Teltser, K., and Tremblay, M.J. (2023) 'Short-Term Rental Platforms and Homeowner Displacement: Evidence from Airbnb Registration Enforcement', SSRN, https://doi.org/10.2139/ssrn.4390232.

Birch, K. and Muniesa, F. (2020) *Assetization: Turning Things into Assets in Technoscientific Capitalism*, Cambridge, MA: The MIT Press.

Blackwell, T. and Kohl, S. (2019) 'Historicizing housing typologies: Beyond welfare state regimes and varieties of residential capitalism', *Housing Studies*, 34(2), 298–318.

Blázquez-Salom, M., Blanco-Romero, A., Vera-Rebollo, F., and Ivars-Baidal, J. (2019) 'Territorial tourism planning in Spain: From boosterism to tourism degrowth?', *Journal of Sustainable Tourism*, 27(12), 1764–1785.

Bock, K. (2015) 'The changing nature of city tourism and its possible implications for the future of cities', *European Journal of Futures Research*, 3(1), 1–8.

Boeing, G., Besbris, M., Wachsmuth, D., and Wegmann, J. (2021) 'Tilted platforms: Rental housing technology and the rise of urban big data oligopolies', *Urban Transformations*, 3(1), 1–10.

Böhme, K. (2021) *Regional Impacts of the COVID-19 Crisis on the Tourist Sector*, European Commission—DG REGIO, https://ec.europa.eu/regional_policy /en/information/publications/studies/2021/regional-impacts-of-the-covid -19-crisis-on-the-tourist-sector.

Boon, W. P. C., Spruit, K., and Frenken, K. (2019) 'Collective institutional work: The case of Airbnb in Amsterdam, London and New York', *Industry and Innovation*, 26(8), 898–919.

Borja, J. (1977) 'Popular movements and urban alternatives in post-Franco Spain', *International Journal of Urban and Regional Research*, 1(1–3), 151–160.

Borraz, O. and Le Galès, P. (2010) 'Urban governance in Europe: The government of what?', *Métropoles*, (7), https://journals.openedition.org/metropoles /4297.

Bosma, J. R. (2022) 'Platformed professionalization: Labor, assets, and earning a livelihood through Airbnb', *Environment and Planning A: Economy and Space*, 54(4), 595–610.

Bosma, J. R. and van Doorn, N. (2022) 'The gentrification of Airbnb: Closing rent gaps through the professionalization of hosting', *Space and Culture*, 27(1), 31–47.

Botsman, R. and Rogers, R. (2011) *What's Mine Is Yours: The Rise of Collaborative Consumption*, London: HarperCollins Business.

Boyer, R. (2003) 'Les institutions dans la théorie de la régulation', *Cahiers d'économie Politique*, 44(1), 79–101.

Boztas, S. (2018) 'Amsterdam, other EU cities, urge Brussels to take action on Airbnb data', *DutchNews.nl*, 26 January, https://www.dutchnews.nl/2018/01 /amsterdam-other-eu-cities-urge-brussels-to-take-action-on-airbnb-data/.

Bricocoli, M. and Peverini, M. (2024) *Milano per chi? Se la città attrattiva è sempre meno abbordabile*. Milano: LetteraVentidue.

Brill, F., Raco, M., and Ward, C. (2023) 'Anticipating demand shocks: Patient capital and the supply of housing', *European Urban and Regional Studies*, 30(1), 50–65.

Brollo, B. and Celata, F. (2023) 'Temporary populations and sociospatial polarisation in the short-term city', *Urban Studies*, 60(10), 1815–1832.

Brossat, I. (2018) *Airbnb, La Ville Ubérisée*, Paris: La Ville Brûle.

Bürgisser, R. and Di Carlo, D. (2023) 'Blessing or curse? The rise of tourism-led growth in Europe's southern periphery', *JCMS: Journal of Common Market Studies*, 61(1), 236–258.

Burrow, S. (2021) *The Law of Data Scraping: A Review of UK Law on Text and Data Mining*, CREATe Working Paper Series, Glasgow, https://doi.org/10.5281/zenodo.4635759.

Busemeyer, M. R. and Thelen, K. (2020) 'Institutional sources of business power', *World Politics*, 72(3), 448–480.

Calavita, N. and Ferrer, A. (2000) 'Behind Barcelona's success story: Citizen movements and planners' power', *Journal of Urban History*, 26(6), 793–807.

Caldini, C. (2013) 'Les hôtels face à une concurrence accrue . . . et pas toujours loyale', *Franceinfo*, 7 May, https://www.francetvinfo.fr/france/les-hotels-face-a-une-concurrence-accrue-et-pas-toujours-loyale_319081.html.

Camera di Commercio Milano Monza Brianza Lodi (n.d.) 'Affiti brevi', https://www.milomb.camcom.it/affitti-brevi.

Câmara Municipal de Lisboa (2023) 'Alojamento Local', https://www.lisboa.pt/temas/economia/setores-estrategicos/alojamento-local.

Cañada, E. and Izcara Conde, C. (2021) 'Precariedad laboral y viviendas de uso turístico', https://www.albasud.org/noticia/es/1323/precariedad-laboral-y-viviendas-de-uso-turistico.

Cano, M. R., Espelt, R., and Morell, M.F. (2024) 'How to build alternatives to platform capitalism?', in Mezzadra, S., Cuppini, N., Frapporti, M., and Pirone, M., eds., *Capitalism in the Platform Age: Emerging Assemblages of Labour and Welfare in Urban Spaces*, Cham: Springer International, 249–271.

Carrigan, C. and Coglianese, C. (2011) 'The politics of regulation: From new institutionalism to new governance', *Annual Review of Political Science*, 14(1), 107–129.

Carvalho, L., Chamusca, P., Fernandes, J., and Pinto, J. (2019) 'Gentrification in Porto: Floating city users and internationally-driven urban change', *Urban Geography*, 40(4), 565–572.

Cassell, M. K. and Deutsch, A. M. (2023) 'Urban challenges and the gig economy: How German cities cope with the rise of Airbnb', *German Politics*, 32(2), 319–340.

Cassese, S. (2011) *L'Italia: Una Società Senza Stato?*, Bologna: Il Mulino.

Castells, M. (1983) *The City and the Grassroots: A Cross-Cultural Theory of Urban Social Movements*, Berkeley: University of California Press.

Celata, F. and Romano, A. (2020) 'Overtourism and online short-term rental platforms in Italian cities', *Journal of Sustainable Tourism*, 30(5), 1020–1039.

Celata, F., Sanna, V. S., and De Luca, S. (2017) *La 'Airbnbificazione' Delle Città: Gli Effetti a Roma Tra Centro e Periferia*, Università di Roma La Sapienza, Dipartimento MEMOTEF, https://memotef.web.uniroma1.it/sites/default/files/Celata_Airbnbificazione_Roma_2017_0.pdf.

Chareyron, G., Cousin, S., and Jacquot, S. (2015) 'Comment Airbnb squatte la France (résultats de recherche présentés par Michaël Hajdenberg)', *Mediapart*, 31 July, https://www-mediapart-fr-s.acces-distant.sciences-po.fr/journal/france/310715/comment-airbnb-squatte-la-france.

Charpantier, D. (2023) 'Airbnb a reversé 148 millions d'euros de taxe de séjour en 2022 en France', *leparisien.fr*, 13 January, https://www.leparisien.fr/economie/airbnb-a-reverse-148-millions-deuros-de-taxe-de-sejour-en-2022-en-france-13-01-2023-SZZFH23LR5H5JL2AJC575FRZNA.php.

Chee, F.Y. (2018) 'Airbnb says not property agent, French hoteliers say nonsense', *Reuters*, 28 September, https://www.reuters.com/article/us-airbnb-ahtop-court-idUSKCN1M82OR.

Chen, Y., Huang, Y., and Tan, C.H. (2021) 'Short-term rental and its regulations on the home-sharing platform', *Information & Management*, 58(3), 103322.

Cheng, M. and Foley, C. (2019) 'Algorithmic management: The case of Airbnb', *International Journal of Hospitality Management*, 83, 33–36.

Christophers, B. (2022) *Rentier Capitalism: Who Owns the Economy, and Who Pays for It?* London: Verso.

Cicognani, A. (2023) 'Il turismo in Italia è sempre più degli affitti brevi: Valgono il 42% del mercato', *La Repubblica.it*, 14 June, repubblica.it/economia/2023/06/12/news/affitti_brevi_airbnb_controlli-403692120/.

City of New York (2020) 'City of New York and Airbnb reach settlement agreement', 12 June, http://www.nyc.gov/office-of-the-mayor/news/432-20/city-new-york-airbnb-reach-settlement-agreement.

CJEU (2019) *Case C-390/18: Judgement of the Court (Grand Chamber) of 19 December, Request for a preliminary ruling under Article 267 TFEU from the investigating judge of the Tribunal de Grande Instance de Paris, made by decision of 7 June 2018, received at the Court on 13 June 2018, in the criminal proceedings against X, interveners: YA, Airbnb Ireland UC, Hôtelière Turenne SAS, Association pour un hébergement et un tourisme professionnels (AHTOP), Valhotel*, https://curia.europa.eu/juris/document/document.jsf?text=&docid=223715&pageIndex=0&doclang=en&mode=req&dir=&occ=first&part=1&cid=10381085.

CJEU (2020a) *Joined Cases C-724/18 and C-727/18 HX: Judgement of the Court (Grand Chamber) of 22 September in Cali Apartments v Procureur Général Près La Cour d'appel de Paris et Ville de Paris and HX v Procureur Général Près La Cour d'appel de Paris et Ville de Paris; Request for a Preliminary Ruling from the Court of Cassation*, http://curia.europa.eu/juris/documents.jsf?num=C-724/18.

CJEU (2020b) *Opinion of Advocate General Bobek Delivered on 2 April 2020: Cali Apartments SCI and HX v Procureur Général Près La Cour d'appel de Paris and Ville de Paris; Requests for a Preliminary Ruling from the Cour de Cassation (France); Requirements Relating to the Conditions for Granting Authorisations; Joined Cases C-724/18 and C-727/18*, https://eur-lex.europa.eu/legal-content/EN/TXT/?uri=CELEX%3A62018CC0724.

Cobb, R. W. and Coughlin, J.F. (1998) 'Are elderly drivers a road hazard? Problem definition and political impact', *Journal of Aging Studies*, 12(4), 411–427.

Cobb, R. W. and Ross, M. H. (1997) *Cultural Strategies of Agenda Denial: Avoidance, Attack, and Redefinition*, Lawrence, Kansas: University Press of Kansas.

Cockayne, D. G. (2016) 'Sharing and neoliberal discourse: The economic function of sharing in the digital on-demand economy', *Geoforum*, 77, 73–82.

Cocola-Gant, A. (2016a) 'Apartamentos turísticos, hoteles y desplazamiento de población', www.agustincocolagant.net.

Cocola-Gant, A. (2016b) 'Holiday rentals: The new gentrification battlefront', *Sociological Research Online*, 21(3), 1–10.

Cocola-Gant, A. (2018) *Struggling with the Leisure Class: Tourism, Gentrification and Displacement*, PhD dissertation, https://agustincocolagant.net/wp-content/uploads/2018/02/A-Cocola-Gant-PhD-Thesis.pdf.

Cocola-Gant, A. (2023) 'Place-based displacement: Touristification and neighborhood change', *Geoforum*, 138, 103665.

Cocola-Gant, A. and Gago, A. (2021) 'Airbnb, buy-to-let investment and tourism-driven displacement: A case study in Lisbon', *Environment and Planning A: Economy and Space*, 53(7), 1671–1688.

Cocola-Gant, A., Gago, A., and Jover, J. (2020) 'Tourism, gentrification and neighbourhood change: An analytical framework—Reflections from southern European cities', in Oskam, J. A., ed., *The Overtourism Debate: NIMBY, Nuisance, Commodification*, Leeds: Emerald Publishing Limited, 121–135.

Cocola-Gant, A., Hof, A., Smigiel, C., and Yrigoy, I. (2021) 'Short-term rentals as a new urban frontier—evidence from European cities', *Environment and Planning A: Economy and Space*, 53(7), 1601–1608.

Cocola-Gant, A., Jover, J., Carvalho, L., and Chamusca, P. (2021) 'Corporate hosts: The rise of professional management in the short-term rental industry', *Tourism Management Perspectives*, 40, 100879.

Cocola-Gant, A. and Pardo, D. (2017) 'Resisting tourism gentrification: The experience of grassroots movements in Barcelona', *Urbanistica Tre, Giornale Online di Urbanistica*, 5, 39–47.

Codagnone, C. and Martens, B. (2016) *Scoping the Sharing Economy: Origins, Definitions, Impact and Regulatory Issues*, Institute for Prospective Technological Studies Digital Economy Working Paper, 1, https://papers.ssrn.com/sol3/papers.cfm?abstract_id=2783662.

Colau, A. (2014) 'Mass tourism can kill a city—just ask Barcelona's residents', *The Guardian*, 2 September, https://www.theguardian.com/commentisfree/2014/sep/02/mass-tourism-kill-city-barcelona.

Cole, A., Harguindéguy, J.-B., Stafford, I., Pasquier, R., and de Visscher, C. (2015) 'States of convergence in territorial governance', *Publius: The Journal of Federalism*, 45(2), 297–321.

Collective (2020) 'La regolamentazione degli affitti brevi non è più rinviabile!', *Il Manifesto*, https://ilmanifesto.it/lettere/la-regolamentazione-degli-affitti-brevi-non-e-piu-rinviabile?fbclid=IwAR312OviMBxgloX9pmN1aXIqfSD4gtnQAJDpob6850xXNboVejoYRp-yUsg.

Collier, R. B., Dubal, V. B., and Carter, C. L. (2018) 'Disrupting regulation, regulating disruption: The politics of Uber in the United States', *Perspectives on Politics*, 16(4), 919–937.

Colomb, C. (2012) *Staging the New Berlin: Place Marketing and the Politics of Urban Reinvention Post-1989*, Planning, history, and environment series, London: Abingdon.

Colomb, C. (2023) 'Urban politics', in Grasso, M. T. and Giugni, M., eds., *Elgar Encyclopedia of Political Sociology*, Cheltenham, UK; Northampton, MA: Edward Elgar, 613–617.

Colomb, C. and Gallent, N. (2022) 'Post-COVID-19 mobilities and the housing crisis in European urban and rural destinations: Policy challenges and research agenda', *Planning Practice & Research*, 37(5), 624–641.

Colomb, C. and Kazepov, Y. (2023) 'Comparative urban studies in Europe', in Le Galès, P. and Robinson, J., eds., *The Routledge Handbook of Comparative Global Urban Studies*, Abingdon: Routledge, 87–103.

Colomb, C. and Moreira de Souza, T. (2021) *'Regulating short-term rentals: Platform-based property rentals in European cities; The policy debates'*, Property Research Trust, https://www.propertyresearchtrust.org/regulating_short_term_rentals.html.

Colomb, C. and Moreira de Souza, T. (2024) 'Illegal short-term rentals, regulatory enforcement and informal practices in the age of digital platforms', *European Urban and Regional Studies*, 31(4), 328–345.

Colomb, C. and Novy, J. (2021) 'Making sense of (new) social mobilisations, conflicts and contention in the tourist city: A typology', in Fregolent, L. and Nel·lo, O., eds., *Social Movements and Public Policies in Southern European Cities*, Cham: Springer International, 53–74.

Colombo, F. (2018) 'Airbnb contro il Pirellone: Siete l'ufficio complicazione affari semplici', 18 January, *Radio Lombardia*, https://www.radiolombardia.it/2018/01/17/42979/.

Comune di Milano (2014) *Approvazione Del Documento "Milano Sharing City". Approvazione Delle Linee Di Indirizzo per Promuovere e Governare Lo Sviluppo Di Iniziative Di Economia Della Condivisione e Collaborazione*, Delibera della Giunta Comunale n. 2676, Comune di Milano, Milano.

Comune di Milano (2016) 'Comune e Airbnb, parte percorso condiviso', *Comune di Milano*, http://www.comune.milano.it/wps/portal/ist/it/news/primopiano/archivio_dal_2012/lavoro_sviluppo_ricerca/comune_airbnb_percorso_condiviso.

Comune di Milano (2021) 'Politiche abitative: Comune e Airbnb, accordo per promuovere il canone concordato; Comunicato stampa 11 Maggio 2021', https://www.comune.milano.it/-/politiche-abitative.-comune-e-airbnb-accordo-per-promuovere-il-canone-concordato-1.

Comune di Milano (2023a) *Una Nuova Strategia per La Casa*, Comune di Milano, Milano, https://www.forumabitaremilano.it/nuova-strategia-per-la-casa.

Comune di Milano (2023b) *Forum dell'Abitare: Presentata la nuova strategia per la casa*, Comune di Milano, https://www.comune.milano.it/-/forum-abitare.-presentata-la-nuova-strategia-per-la-casa.

Consell Econòmic i Social (2016) *Informe Sobre l'ocupació i El Sector Turístic a Barcelona*, Consell Econòmic i Social, Barcelona, https://www.barcelona.cat/cesb/pdf/informes/i2016/Informe_Turisme.pdf.

Conte, V. and Anselmi, G. (2022) 'When large-scale regeneration becomes an engine of urban growth: How new power coalitions are shaping Milan's governance', *Environment and Planning A: Economy and Space*, 54, 1184–1199.

Cook, D. (2020) 'Remote-work visas will shape the future of work, travel and citizenship', *The Conversation*, 3 September, http://theconversation.com/remote-work-visas-will-shape-the-future-of-work-travel-and-citizenship-145078.

Corporate Europe Observatory (2018) 'Commission protects AirBnB lobby paper as "commercial secret"', https://corporateeurope.org/en/power-lobbies/2018/06/commission-protects-airbnb-lobby-paper-commercial-secret.

Coslovsky, S., Pires, R., and Silbey, S.S. (2011) 'The pragmatic politics of regulatory enforcement', in Levi-Faur, D., ed., *Handbook on the Politics of Regulation*, Cheltenham: Edward Elgar, 322–334.

Costa, N. and Martinotti, G. (2003) 'Sociological theories of tourism and regulation theory', in Hoffman, L. M., Fainstein, S. S. and Judd, D. R., eds., *Cities and Visitors*, Oxford: Blackwell, 53–71.

Cox, M. and Haar, K. (2020) *Platform Failures: How Short-Term Rental Platforms like Airbnb Fail to Cooperate with Cities and the Need for Strong Regulations to Protect Housing*, The Left—GUE/NGL group in the European Parliament, Brussels, https://left.eu/issues/publications/platform-failures-how-short-term-rental-platforms-like-airbnb-fail-to-cooperate-with-cities-and-the-need-for-strong-regulations-to-protect-housing/.

Coyle, D. and Yu-Cheong Yeung, T. (2016) *Understanding AirBnB in Fourteen European Cities*, Jean-Jacques Laffont Digital Chair Working Papers, https://www.tse-fr.eu/sites/default/files/TSE/documents/ChaireJJL/PolicyPapers/2016_30_12_pp_understanding_airbnb_in_14_european_cities_coyle_yeung_v.3.1.pdf.

Cress, D. M. and Snow, D. A. (2000) 'The outcomes of homeless mobilization: The influence of organization, disruption, political mediation, and framing', *American Journal of Sociology*, 105(4), 1063–1104.

Cristino, S. (2024) 'Ilegalidades fazem disparar fecho de alojamentos locais', *Jornal de Notícias*, 5 March, https://www.jn.pt/7514215041/ilegalidades-fazem -disparar-fecho-de-alojamentos-locais/.

Croft, A. (2015) 'Barcelona mayor's tourism crackdown puts Airbnb in firing line', *Reuters*, 26 August, https://www.reuters.com/article/us-spain-tourism -airbnb-idUSKCN0QV1LR20150826.

Crommelin, L., Troy, L., Martin, C., and Pettit, C. (2018) 'Is Airbnb a sharing economy superstar? Evidence from five global cities', *Urban Policy and Research*, 36(4), 429–444.

Cucca, R. and Ranci, C., eds. (2019) *Unequal Cities: The Challenge of Post-Industrial Transition in Times of Austerity*, Abingdon: Routledge.

Culpepper, P. D. and Thelen, K. (2020) 'Are we all Amazon primed? Consumers and the politics of platform ower', *Comparative Political Studies*, 53(2), 288–318.

de Frémont, L. (2020) *Les Transformations de Bureaux, Commerce, Artisanat et Entrepôt En Meublés de Tourisme*, Rapport de stage sous la direction de Francesca Artioli, Paris: Université Paris Est-Créteil, Lab'Urba.

De Vito, L. (2017) 'Airbnb apre le case ai rifugiati, a Milano primo esperimento in Italia: Già 100 host hanno detto sì', *la Repubblica*, 5 July, https://milano .repubblica.it/cronaca/2017/07/05/news/airbnb_rifugiati_milano_ospitalita _-170023682/.

Degen, M. and García, M. (2012) 'The transformation of the "Barcelona Model": An analysis of culture, urban regeneration and governance', *International Journal of Urban and Regional Research*, 36(5), 1022–1038.

Degoli, O. (2017) 'A scuola di sharing economy: Per portare l'economia della collaborazione dove serve', *Collaboriamo!*, 23 February, https://collaboriamo.org /a-scuola-di-sharing-economy-per-portare-leconomia-della-collaborazione -dove-serve/.

Della Porta, D. (2008) 'Comparative analysis: Case-oriented versus variable-oriented research', in Della Porta, D. and Keating, M., eds., *Approaches and Methodologies in the Social Sciences: A Pluralist Perspective*, Cambridge: Cambridge University Press, 198–222.

Deloitte Property Index (2020) *Overview of European Residential Markets*, 9th ed., https://www2.deloitte.com/content/dam/Deloitte/cz/Documents/real -estate/Property_Index_2020.pdf.

Demir, E. and Emekli, G. (2021) 'Is Airbnb no longer a sharing economy platform? Evidence from Europe's top 10 Airbnb destinations', *Anatolia*, 32(3), 470–488.

Department for Business, Innovation and Skills (2015) *Sharing Economy: Government Responses to the Independent Review*, https://www.gov.uk/government /publications/sharing-economy-government-response-to-the-independent -review.

Department of Communities and Local Government (2015) *Promoting the Sharing Economy in London: Policy on Short-Term Use of Residential Property in London*, https://assets.publishing.service.gov.uk/government/uploads/system /uploads/attachment_data/file/402411/Promoting_the_sharing_economy _in_London.pdf.

DeVerteuil, G. and Manley, D. (2017) 'Overseas investment into London: Imprint, impact and pied-à-terre urbanism', *Environment and Planning A: Economy and Space*, 49(6), 1308–1323.

Dinamopress (2018) 'Nasce SET: Una rete di città contro l'attuale modello turistico', *DINAMOpress*, 25 April, https://www.dinamopress.it/news/nasce-set -rete-citta-lattuale-modello-turistico/.

Direction Générale des Entreprises (2022) 'Expérimentation lancée entre communes et intermédiaires de meublés volontaires', https://www.entreprises .gouv.fr/fr/presse/tourisme/conseils-strategie/experimentation-lancee -entre-communes-et-intermediaires-de-meubles-volontaires.

Doling, J. and Ronald, R. (2010) 'Home ownership and asset-based welfare', *Journal of Housing and the Built Environment*, 25(2), 165–173.

D'Ovidio, M. and Pacetti, V. (2020) 'Milano, hub creativo per il sistema moda', *Sociologia urbana e rurale*, 42(121), 32–51.

Dredge, D. and Gyimóthy, S. (2015) 'The collaborative economy and tourism: Critical perspectives, questionable claims and silenced voices', *Tourism Recreation Research*, 40(3), 286–302.

Ducarroz, A.-S. and Jankel, S. (2011) 'Les locations meublées de courte durée à Paris —état des lieux et propositions', APUR, https://www.apur.org/fr/nos -travaux/locations-meublees-courte-duree-paris-lieux-propositions.

Duhatis, J., Cruz, H., and Buhigas, M. (2016) *Impacte Del Lloguer Vacacional en el Mercat de Lloguer Residencial de Barcelona*, Ajuntament de Barcelona, https://ajuntament.barcelona.cat/turisme/sites/default/files/160921_informe_impacte_lloguer_vacacional.pdf.

Dühr, S., Colomb, C., and Nadin, V. (2010) *European Spatial Planning and Territorial Cooperation*, Abingdon: Routledge.

Durst, N .J. and Wegmann, J. (2017) 'Informal housing in the United States', *International Journal of Urban and Regional Research*, 41(2), 282–297.

Edelman, B. and Luca, M. (2014) *Digital Discrimination: The Case of Airbnb.Com*, SSRN, https://papers.ssrn.com/sol3/papers.cfm?abstract_id=2377353.

Edelman, B., Luca, M., and Svirsky, D. (2017) 'Racial discrimination in the sharing economy: Evidence from a field experiment', *American Economic Journal: Applied Economics*, 9(2), 1–22.

Edelman, B .G. and Geradin, D. (2016) 'Efficiencies and regulatory shortcuts: How should we regulate companies like Airbnb and Uber?', *Stanford Technology Law Review*, 19, https://papers.ssrn.com/abstract=2658603.

Edelman, M. J. (1971) *Politics as Symbolic Action: Mass Arousal and Quiescence*, New York: Academic Press.

EHHA (2016) 'Industry submits official complaint to European Commission about excessive and contradictory local rules stifling short-term rental sector', European Holiday Homes Association press release, 22 September, https://ehha.eu/2016/09/22/industry-submits-official-complaint-to-european-commission-about-excessive-and-contradictory-local-rules-stifling-short-term-rental-sector/.

EHHA (2021) *EHHA Position Paper: Short-Term Rental Initiative [Response to the Consultation of the European Commission DG GROW]*, Ref. Ares(2021)7831630, https://ec.europa.eu/info/law/better-regulation/have-your-say/initiatives/13108-Tourist-services-short-term-rental-initiative/F2688598_en.

EHHA and ETTSA (2018) *Roadmap for the Short-Term Rental Sector*, https://ehha.eu/2018/10/11/roadmap-for-the-short-term-rental-sector/.

Eizaguirre, S., Pradel-Miquel, M., and García, M. (2017) 'Citizenship practices and democratic governance: "Barcelona en Comú" as an urban citizenship confluence promoting a new policy agenda', *Citizenship Studies*, 21(4), 425–439.

Entr'hôtes Collective (2017), 'Furnished tourist accommodation: Open letter to Anne Hidalgo', *Les Echos*, 17 May, https://www.lesechos.fr/2017/05/meubles-touristiques-lettre-ouverte-a-anne-hidalgo-168260.

Errard, G. ( 2021) 'Airbnb: La mesure phare d'Hidalgo rejetée par une confé-
rence citoyenne', 21 April, *Le Figaro*, https://immobilier.lefigaro.fr/article
/airbnb-la-mesure-phare-d-hidalgo-rejetee-par-une-conference-citoyenne
_439ca358-a1ef-11eb-8442-d220dfaddfb3/.

Errard, G. and Visseyrias, M. (2018) 'Airbnb assigné en justice par les hôteliers pour
"concurrence déloyale"', *Le Figaro*, 6 November, https://immobilier.lefigaro
.fr/article/airbnb-assigne-en-justice-par-les-hoteliers-pour-concurrence
-deloyale-_1a6ab06c-e0d9-11e8-83d1-fc7ebc69ae48/.

Esposito, A. (2023a) *Le Case Degli Altri*, Firenze: Editpress.

Esposito, A. (2023b) 'Tourism-driven displacement in Naples, Italy', *Land Use
Policy*, 134, 106919.

Estevens, A., Cocola-Gant, A., López-Gay, A., and Pavel, F. (2023) 'The role of
the state in the touristification of Lisbon', *Cities*, 137, 104275.

Eurocities (2020a) 'European cities call for action on short-term holiday rentals:
Position paper on better EU-legislation of platforms offering short-term holiday rentals', https://eurocities.eu/wp-content/uploads/2020/08/european
_cities_alliance_on_short_term_rentals_final.pdf.

Eurocities (2020b) 'Making digital opportunities work for people and the public good', https://eurocities.eu/latest/making-digital-opportunities-work
-for-people-and-the-public-good/.

Eurocities (2020c) '22 cities call for stronger European regulation of holiday
rental platforms—Eurocities', https://eurocities.eu/latest/22-cities-call-for
-stronger-european-regulation-of-holiday-rental-platforms/.

Eurocities (2020d) 'Opportunities and challenges in a digital era—Cities meeting with Margrethe Vestager', https://eurocities.eu/latest/opportunities
-and-challenges-in-a-digital-era-cities-meeting-with-margrethe-vestager/.

Eurocities (2022) 'Short term rentals: Cities ask Europe's help—Eurocities',
https://eurocities.eu/latest/short-term-rentals-cities-ask-europes-help/.

European Cities Marketing (2019) 'Benchmarking Report 2018–2019', https://
citydestinationsalliance.eu/european-cities-marketing-benchmarking
-report-2019-shows-continuous-growth-of-european-city-tourism/.

European Commission (2015) *Communication from the Commission: A Digital
Single Market Strategy for Europe*, https://eur-lex.europa.eu/legal-content/EN
/TXT/?uri=celex%3A52015DC0192.

European Commission (2016a) *Communication from the Commission: A European Agenda for the Collaborative Economy*, https://eur lex.europa eu/legal-content /EN/TXT/?uri=COM%3A2016%3A356%3AFIN.

European Commission (2016b) *Communication from the Commission: Online Platforms and the Digital Single Market Opportunities and Challenges for Europe*, https:// eur-lex.europa.eu/legal-content/EN/TXT/?uri=CELEX%3A52016DC0288.

European Commission (2018) *Collaborative Short-Term Accommodation Services: Policy Principles & Good Practices*. Conference on Collaborative Economy: Opportunities, Challenges, Policies, Brussels, 11 October, https://ec.europa .eu/docsroom/documents/32062.

European Commission (2019) 'Commission takes action to ensure professionals and service providers can fully benefit from the EU Single Market for services', https://ec.europa.eu/commission/presscorner/detail/en/IP_19_467.

European Commission (2022) *Proposal for a Regulation of The European Parliament and of The Council on Data Collection and Sharing Relating to Short-Term Accommodation Rental Services and Amending Regulation (EU) 2018/1724*, https:// eur-lex.europa.eu/legal-content/EN/TXT/PDF/?uri=CELEX:52022PC0571.

European Commission (n.d.-a) 'Collaborative economy', https://single-market -economy.ec.europa.eu/single-market/services/collaborative-economy_en.

European Commission (n.d.-b) 'E-Commerce directive', https://digital-strategy .ec.europa.eu/en/policies/e-commerce-directive.

European Commission (n.d.-c) 'The Digital Services Act package', https:// digital-strategy.ec.europa.eu/en/policies/digital-services-act-package.

European Commission (n.d.-d) 'The principle of subsidiarity', https://www .europarl.europa.eu/factsheets/en/sheet/7/the-principle-of-subsidiarity.

European Commission (n.d.-e) 'The services directive', https://single-market -economy.ec.europa.eu/single-market/services/directive_en.

European Commission (n.d.-f) 'Tourist services—short-term rental initiative', https://ec.europa.eu/info/law/better-regulation/have-your-say/initiatives /13108-Tourist-services-short-term-rental-initiative_en.

European Commission (n.d.-g) 'Transparency register', https://transparency -register.europa.eu/index_en.

European Commission, DG GROW (2021) *Short-Term Rental Initiative: Inception Impact Assessment*, Ares(2021)5673365, https://ec.europa.eu/info/law/better

-regulation/have-your-say/initiatives/13108-Tourist-services-short-term
-rental-initiative_en.

European Committee of the Regions (2020) *Opinion of the European Committee
of the Regions—A European Framework for Regulatory Responses to the Collaborative Economy*, https://eur-lex.europa.eu/legal-content/EN/TXT/?uri=
CELEX%3A52019IR1951.

European Parliamentary Research Service (2024) *Briefing, EU Legislation in
Progress: Data Collection and Sharing Relating to Short-Term Accommodation
Rental Services*, https://www.europarl.europa.eu/RegData/etudes/BRIE/2023
/739334/EPRS_BRI(2023)739334_EN.pdf.

Eurostat (2023) 'In 2022, more than 1.5 million tourists per night slept in a bed
booked via the platforms', https://ec.europa.eu/eurostat/statistics-explained
/index.php?title=Short-stay_accommodation_offered_via_online
_collaborative_economy_platforms.

Eurostat (n.d.-a) 'Regions and cities', database, https://ec.europa.eu/eurostat
/web/regions/database

Eurostat (n.d.-b) 'Short-stay accommodation offered via online collaborative
economy platforms—monthly data', https://ec.europa.eu/eurostat/statistics
-explained/index.php?title=Short-stay_accommodation_offered_via_online
_collaborative_economy_platforms_-_monthly_data&stable=1

European Union Joint Research Centre (2019) 'Cultural and creative cities monitor', https://composite-indicators.jrc.ec.europa.eu/cultural-creative-cities
-monitor.

Facchini, M. (2021) 'Dove finisce l'imposta di soggiorno: Inchiesta sui bilanci
dei Comuni', *Altreconomia*, 1 May, https://altreconomia.it/dove-finisce
-limposta-di-soggiorno-inchiesta-sui-bilanci-dei-comuni/.

FAVB (2011) 'La creu del turisme a Barcelona', *Carrer*, 121, https://carrer.cat
/portada/la-creu-del-turisme-barcelona/.

Federalberghi and Incipit Consulting (2016) *Sommerso Turistico e Affitti Brevi: Le
Bugie Della Sharing Economy a Confronto Con Dati Reali*, Roma: Istituto Internazionale di Studi e Documentazione Turistico Alberghiera.

Fernández Medrano, H. and Pardo Rivacoba, D. (2017) 'La lucha por el decre-
cimiento turístico: El caso de Barcelona', Ecología Política, https://www
.ecologiapolitica.info/la-lucha-por-el-decrecimiento-turistico-el-caso-de
-barcelona/.

Ferreri, M. and Sanyal, R. (2018) 'Platform economies and urban planning: Airbnb and regulated deregulation in London', *Urban Studies*, 55(15), 3353–3368.

Ferreri, M. and Sanyal, R. (2019) 'Corporatised enforcement: Challenges of regulating AirBnB and other platform economies', *Planning Theory & Practice*, 20(2), 279–282.

Fields, D. and Raymond, E. L. (2021) 'Racialized geographies of housing financialization', *Progress in Human Geography*, 45(6), 1625–1645.

Fields, D. and Rogers, D. (2021) 'Towards a critical housing studies research agenda on platform real estate', *Housing, Theory and Society*, 38(1), 72–94.

Filandri, M., Olagnero, M., and Semi, G. (2020) *Casa dolce casa? Italia, un paese di proprietari*, Bologna: il Mulino.

Finck, M. (2018) 'Digital co-regulation: Designing a supranational legal framework for the platform economy', *European Law Review*, 43(1), 47–68, https://doi.org/10.2139/ssrn.2990043.

Fligstein, N. (1996) 'Markets as politics: A political-cultural approach to market institutions', *American Sociological Review*, 61(4), 656–673.

Foramitti, J., Varvarousis, A., and Kallis, G. (2020) 'Transition within a transition: how cooperative platforms want to change the sharing economy', *Sustainability Science*, 15(4), 1185–1197.

Fossati, S. (2020) 'Affitti brevi, la stretta in un emendamento (già arenato) al Dl "Milleproproghe"', *Il Sole 24 ORE*, 28 January, https://www.ilsole24ore.com /art/affitti-brevi-stretta-un-emendamento-gia-arenato-dl-milleproproghe -ACCYv6EB.

France Info and AFP (2023) 'Le gouvernement dévoile un plan contre le surtourisme', 19 June, https://www.francetvinfo.fr/economie/tourisme/le -gouvernement-devoile-un-plan-contre-le-surtourisme_5897596.html.

Fregolent, L. and Torri, R. (2018) *L'Italia senza casa: Bisogni emergenti e politiche per l'abitare*, Milano: Franco Angeli.

Frenken, K. and Schor, J. (2017) 'Putting the sharing economy into perspective', *Environmental Innovation and Societal Transitions*, , 23, 3–10.

Friedman, U. (2014) 'Airbnb CEO: Cities are becoming villages', *The Atlantic*, 29 June, https://www.theatlantic.com/international/archive/2014/06/airbnb -ceo-cities-are-becoming-villages/373676/.

Furukawa, N. and Onuki, M. (2022) 'The design and effects of short-term rental regulation', *Current Issues in Tourism*, 25(20), 3245–3260.

Gabor, D. and Kohl, S. (2022) *My Home Is an Asset Class: Study about the Financialization of Housing in Europe*, The GREENS/EFA in the European Parliament, Brussels, https://www.greens-efa.eu/en/article/document/my-home-is-an-asset-class.

Gadeix, D. (2011) *Locations meublées de courte durée: Le point sur la pratique*, Agence Départementale pour l'information sur le logement de Paris, https://www.anil.org/documentation-experte/etudes-eclairages/etudes-et-eclairages-2011/locations-meublees-de-courte-duree-le-point-sur-la-pratique/.

Gainsforth, S. (2019) *Airbnb città merce: Storie di resistenza alla gentrificazione digitale*, Roma: DeriveApprodi.

Gallagher, L. (2018) *The Airbnb Story: How to Disrupt an Industry, Make Billions of Dollars . . . and Plenty of Enemies*, London: Virgin Books.

Garcia-López, M.-À., Jofre-Monseny, J., Martínez-Mazza, R., and Segú, M. (2020) 'Do short-term rental platforms affect housing markets? Evidence from Airbnb in Barcelona', *Journal of Urban Economics*, 119, 103278.

Garriga, A., Rigall, R., and Saló, A. (2015) *L'impacte Econòmic de l'activitat Turística a La Ciutat de Barcelona*, L'impacte econòmic de l'activitat turística a la ciutat de Barcelona, https://ajuntament.barcelona.cat/turisme/sites/default/files/documents/151115_informe_impacte_economic_bcn_2013-actualitzacio.pdf.

Gascó, M., Trivellato, B., and Cavenago, D. (2016) 'How do southern European cities foster innovation? Lessons from the experience of the smart city approaches of Barcelona and Milan', in Ramon Gil-Garcia, J., Pardo, T. A., and Nam, T., eds., *Smarter as the New Urban Agenda*, Cham: Springer International, 191–206.

Gerritsma, R. (2019) 'Overcrowded Amsterdam: Striving for a balance between trade, tolerance and tourism', in Milano, C., Cheers, J., and Novelli, M., eds., *Overtourism: Excesses, Discontents and Measures in Travel and Tourism*, Wallingford: CABI, 125–147.

Gil, J. (2024) 'Not gentrification, not touristification: Short-term rentals as a housing assetization strategy', *Journal of Urban Affairs*, 46(6): 1125–1145.

Gil, J., Martínez, P., and Sequera, J. (2023) 'The neoliberal tenant dystopia: Digital polyplatform rentierism, the hybridization of platform-based rental markets and financialization of housing', *Cities*, 137, 104245.

Gil, J. and Sequera, J. (2022) 'The professionalization of Airbnb in Madrid: Far from a collaborative economy', *Current Issues in Tourism*, 25(20), 3343–3362.

Gil, J., Vidal, L., and Martínez, M. A. (2023) *¿Cómo afectará el control del precio de los alquileres a los caseros?*, Barcelona: IDRA, https://idrabcn.com/es/publicacion/como-afectara-el-control-del-precio-de-los-alquileres-a-los-caseros/.

Gilheany, J., Wang, D., and Xi, S. (2015) 'The model minority? Not on Airbnb .com: A hedonic pricing model to quantify racial bias against Asian Americans', *Technology Science*, 31 August, https://techscience.org/a/2015090104/.

Gimat, M., Guironnet, A., and Halbert, L. (2022) *La financiarisation à petits pas du logement social et intermédiaire en France. Signaux faibles, controverses et perspectives*, Working Paper de la Chaire Villes, Logement et Immobilier, Sciences Po, Paris, https://shs.hal.science/halshs-03745166.

Global Reformbnb (2023) 'Global Reformbnb home', https://globalreformbnb .com/.

Gold, A. E. (2020) 'Redliking: When redlining goes online', *William & Mary Law Review*, 62, 1841, https://heinonline.org/HOL/Page?handle=hein.journals /wmlr62&id=1874&div=&collection=.

Goldsmith, M. J. and Page, E. C. (2010) *Changing Government Relations in Europe: From Localism to Intergovernmentalism*, Abingdon: Routledge.

Gössling, S., Scott, D., and Hall, C. M. (2021) 'Pandemics, tourism and global change: A rapid assessment of COVID-19', *Journal of Sustainable Tourism*, 29(1), 1–20.

Gotham, K. F. (2005) 'Tourism gentrification: The case of New Orleans' Vieux Carre (French Quarter)', *Urban Studies*, 42(7), 1099–1121.

Gottlieb, C. (2013) 'Residential short-term rentals: Should local governments regulate the "industry"?', *Planning & Environmental Law*, 65(2), 4–9.

Goyette, K. (2021) '"Making ends meet" by renting homes to strangers', *City*, 25(3–4), 332–354.

Grabher, G. and König, J. (2020) 'Disruption, embedded: A Polanyian framing of the platform economy', *Sociologica*, 14(1), 95–118.

Gravari-Barbas, M. and Fagnoni, É., eds. (2013) *Métropolisation et Tourisme: Comment le Tourisme Redessine Paris*, Paris: Belin.

Gravari-Barbas, M. and Guinand, S., eds. (2018) *Tourism & Gentrification in Contemporary Metropolises: International Perspectives*, Abingdon: Routledge.

Gravari-Barbas, M. and Jacquot, S. (2016) 'No conflict? Discourses and management of tourism-related tensions in Paris', in Colomb, C. and Novy, J., eds., *Protest and Resistance in the Tourist City*, Abingdon: Routledge, 31–51.

Grisdale, S. (2021) 'Displacement by disruption: Short-term rentals and the political economy of "belonging anywhere" in Toronto', *Urban Geography*, 42(5), 654–680.

Guardian, The (2016) 'Berlin's government legislates against Airbnb', *The Guardian*, 1 May, https://www.theguardian.com/technology/2016/may/01/berlin-authorities-taking-stand-against-airbnb-rental-boom.

Guardian, The (2022) 'The Uber files', https://www.theguardian.com/news/series/uber-files.

Guironnet, A., Attuyer, K., and Halbert, L. (2016) 'Building cities on financial assets: The financialisation of property markets and its implications for city governments in the Paris city-region', *Urban Studies*, 53(7), 1442–1464.

Gurran, N. (2018) 'Global home-sharing, local communities and the Airbnb debate: A planning research agenda', *Planning Theory & Practice*, 19(2), 298–304.

Gurran, N., Maalsen, S., and Shrestha, P. (2022) 'Is "informal" housing an affordability solution for expensive cities? Evidence from Sydney, Australia', *International Journal of Housing Policy*, 22(1), 10–33.

Gurran, N. and Phibbs, P. (2017) 'When tourists move in: How should urban planners respond to Airbnb?', *Journal of the American Planning Association*, 83(1), 80–92.

Gurran, N. and Sadowski, J. (2019) 'Regulatory combat? How the "sharing economy" is disrupting planning practice', *Planning Theory & Practice*, 20(2), 261–287.

Gusfield, J. R. (1984) *The Culture of Public Problems: Drinking-Driving and the Symbolic Order*, Chicago: University of Chicago Press.

Gutiérrez, J., García-Palomares, J. C., Romanillos, G., and Salas-Olmedo, M. H. (2017) 'The eruption of Airbnb in tourist cities: Comparing spatial patterns of hotels and peer-to-peer accommodation in Barcelona', *Tourism Management*, 62, 278–291.

Guttentag, D. (2015) 'Airbnb: Disruptive innovation and the rise of an informal tourism accommodation sector', *Current Issues in Tourism*, 18(12), 1192–1217.

Gyódi, K. (2024) 'The spatial patterns of Airbnb offers, hotels and attractions: Are professional hosts taking over cities?', *Current Issues in Tourism*, 27(17), 2757–2782.

Hajdenberg, M. (2015) 'Comment Airbnb squatte la France', *Mediapart*, 31 July, https://www.mediapart.fr/journal/france/310715/comment-airbnb-squatte -la-france.

Hall, P. A. (1986) *Governing the Economy: The Politics of State Intervention in Britain and France*, Oxford: Oxford University Press.

Hall, P. A. and Soskice, D. (2001) *Varieties of Capitalism: The Institutional Foundations of Comparative Advantage*, Oxford: Oxford University Press.

Halpern, C. and Galès, P.L. (2011) 'No autonomous public policy without ad hoc instruments', *Revue française de science politique*, 61(1), 51–78.

Harris, R. (2018) 'Modes of informal urban development: A global phenomenon', *Journal of Planning Literature*, 33(3), 267–286.

Harvey, D. (1989) 'From managerialism to entrepreneurialism: The transformation in urban governance in late capitalism', *Geografiska Annaler: Series B, Human Geography*, 71(1), 3–17.

Haute Autorité pour la Transparence de la Vie Publique (n.d.) 'Consulter le répertoire des représentants d'intérêts', https://www.hatvp.fr/le-repertoire/.

Hay, C. (2004) 'Common trajectories, variable paces, divergent outcomes? Models of European capitalism under conditions of complex economic interdependence', *Review of International Political Economy*, 11(2), 231–262.

Hay, C. and Rosamond, B. (2002) 'Globalization, European integration and the discursive construction of economic imperatives', *Journal of European public policy*, 9(2), 147–167.

Hayes, M. and Zaban, H. (2020) 'Transnational gentrification: The crossroads of transnational mobility and urban research', *Urban Studies*, 57(15), 3009–3024.

Hearns, A. (2010) 'Structuring feeling: Web 2.0, online ranking and rating, and the digital "reputation" economy', *Ephemeral Journal*, 10(3/4), 421–438.

Heinelt, H. (2017) *The Role of Cities in the Institutional Framework of the European Union*, European Parliament, https://www.europarl.europa.eu/RegData /etudes/STUD/2017/596813/IPOL_STU(2017)596813_EN.pdf.

Henley, J. (2019) 'Ten cities ask EU for help to fight Airbnb expansion', *The Guardian*, 20 June, https://www.theguardian.com/cities/2019/jun/20/ten -cities-ask-eu-for-help-to-fight-airbnb-expansion.

Hery, J.-J. (2015) 'AirBnb : Paris en guerre contre les meublés touristiques', *Europe 1*, 22 May, https://www.europe1.fr/economie/airbnb-paris-en-guerre -contre-les-meubles-touristiques-969890.

Hijrah Hati, S. R., Balqiah, T. E., Hananto, A., and Yuliati, E. (2021) 'A decade of systematic literature review on Airbnb: The sharing economy from a multiple stakeholder perspective', *Heliyon*, 7(10), e08222.

Hilgartner, S. and Bosk, C. L. (1988) 'The rise and fall of social problems: A public arenas model', *American Journal of Sociology*, 94(1), 53–78.

Hodson, M., Kasmire, J., McMeekin, A., Stehlin, J. G., and Ward, K. (2020) *Urban Platforms and the Future City: Transformations in Infrastructure, Governance, Knowledge and Everyday Life*, Abingdon: Routledge.

Hofäcker, J. and Gebauer, M. (2021) 'Airbnb in townships of South Africa: A new experience of township tourism?', in Rogerson, C. M. and Rogerson, J. M., eds., *Urban Tourism in the Global South: South African Perspectives*, Cham: Springer International, 129–147.

Hoffman, L. M., Fainstein, S. S., and Judd, D. R. (2003) *Cities and Visitors: Regulating People, Markets, and City Space*, Oxford: Blackwell.

Hoffman, L. M. and Schmitter Heisler, B. (2020) *Airbnb, Short-Term Rentals and the Future of Housing*, Abingdon: Routledge.

Holleran, M. (2017) 'Falling off the tourism ladder: Spanish tourism from Franco to the housing bubble of 2008', *Radical History Review*, 2017(129), 144–163.

Holman, N., Mossa, A., and Pani, E. (2018) 'Planning, value(s) and the market: An analytic for "what comes next?"', *Environment and Planning A: Economy and Space*, 50(30), 608–626.

Hong, S. and Lee, S. (2018) 'Adaptive governance, status quo bias, and political competition: Why the sharing economy is welcome in some cities but not in others', *Government Information Quarterly*, 35(2), 283–290.

Hood, C. (1983) *The Tools of Government*, New York: Macmillan.

Hooghe, L., Marks, G., and Schakel, A. H. (2023) 'Multilevel governance', in Caramani, D., ed., *Comparative Politics*, Oxford: Oxford University Press, 214–232.

Horn, K. and Merante, M. (2017) 'Is home sharing driving up rents? Evidence from Airbnb in Boston', *Journal of Housing Economics*, 38, 14–24.

HOTREC (2015) 'Levelling the Playing Field: HOTREC Policy Paper on the "Sharing" Economy', https://www.hotrec.eu/policy/levelling-the-playing -field-hotrec-policy-paper-on-the-sharing-economy/.

HOTREC (2017) *5 Policy Priorities for a Responsible and Fair 'Collaborative' Economy*, https://www.hotrec.eu/wp-content/customer-area/storage/c6ab98527c30a95

foa51ca21205f469d/Policy-Priorities-for-a-responsible-and-fair-collaborative-economy.pdf.

Hübscher, M. and Kallert, T. (2023) 'Taming Airbnb locally: Analysing regulations in Amsterdam, Berlin and London', *Tijdschrift voor Economische en Sociale Geografie*, 114(1), 6–27.

Iacovone, C. (2023) 'Debate on regulation and professionalisation in the short-term rental housing market', *Geoforum*, 146, 103870.

Iborra, Y.S. (2017) 'Airbnb pide a sus usuarios que presionen al Ayuntamiento de Barcelona y a la Generalitat contra su regulación', *elDiario.es*, 10 March, https://www.eldiario.es/catalunya/airbnb-presionen-ayuntamiento-barcelona -generalitat_1_3539402.html.

ICIJ (2022) 'The Uber files', International Consortium of Investigative Journalists, https://www.icij.org/investigations/uber-files/.

Inside Airbnb (n.d.-a) 'About Inside Airbnb', http://insideairbnb.com/about .html.

Inside Airbnb(n.d.-b) 'Top Hosts', http://insideairbnb.com/barcelona, http:// insideairbnb.com/milan, http://insideairbnb.com/paris.

Inside Airbnb (n.d.-c) 'Adding Data to the Debate', https://insideairbnb.com/.

International Union of Tenants (IUT) (2023) 'Feedback from the International Union of Tenants on the Proposal for a Regulation of the European Parliament and of the Council on Data Collection and Sharing Relating to Short-Term Accommodation Rental Services', https://ec.europa.eu/info/law/better -regulation/have-your-say/initiatives/13108-Tourist-services-short-term -rental-initiative/F3374244_en.

Jacquot, S. and Halpern, C. (2015) 'Aux frontières de l'action publique', in Boussaguet, L., Jacquot, S., and Ravinet, P., eds., *Une French touch dans l'analyse des politiques publiques ?*, Paris: Presses de Sciences Po, 57–84.

Jaeger, B. and Sleegers, W. W. A. (2023) 'Racial disparities in the sharing economy: evidence from more than 100,000 Airbnb hosts across 14 countries', *Journal of the Association for Consumer Research*, 8(1), 33–46.

Janoschka, M. and Haas, H. (2014) *Contested Spatialities, Lifestyle Migration and Residential Tourism*, Abingdon: Routledge.

Jefferson-Jones, J. (2015) 'Airbnb and the housing segment of the modern "sharing economy": Are short-term rental restrictions an unconstitutional taking?', *Hastings Constitutional Law Quarterly*, (42), 557–576.

Jolivet, V. (2024) 'Havana's transnational gentrification: Highest and best use from elsewhere', *Tijdschrift voor Economische en Sociale Geografie*, 115(1), 142–154.

Jover, J. and Cocola-Gant, A. (2023) 'The political economy of housing investment in the short-term rental market: Insights from urban Portugal', *Antipode*, 55(1), 134–155.

Jover, J. and Díaz-Parra, I. (2022) 'Who is the city for? Overtourism, lifestyle migration and social sustainability', *Tourism Geographies*, 24(1), 9–32.

Judd, D. R. and Fainstein, S.S. (1999) *The Tourist City*, New Haven, CT: Yale University Press.

Kadi, J., Plank, L., and Seidl, R. (2022) 'Airbnb as a tool for inclusive tourism?', *Tourism Geographies*, 24(4–5), 669–691.

Kafkadesk (2020) '#OccupyAirbnb: Fighting back against short-term rentals in Prague—Kafkadesk', *Kafkadesk*, 20 February, https://kafkadesk.org/2020/02/20/occupyairbnb-fighting-back-against-short-term-rentals-in-prague/.

Kassam, A. (2014) 'Naked Italians spark protests against antics of drunken tourists in Barcelona', *The Guardian*, 21 August, http://www.theguardian.com/world/2014/aug/21/naked-italians-protests-drunken-tourists-barcelona.

Katsinas, P. (2021) 'Professionalisation of short-term rentals and emergent tourism gentrification in post-crisis Thessaloniki', *Environment and Planning A: Economy and Space*, 53(7), 1652–1670.

Kelling, E. (2021) *Urban Informality: Space, Power and Legitimacy in Addressing London's Housing Need*, PhD dissertation, https://depositonce.tu-berlin.de/handle/11303/13149.

Kemeny, J. (1995) *From Public Housing to the Social Market: Rental Policy Strategies in Comparative Perspective*, Abingdon: Routledge.

Kenney, M. and Zysman, J. (2016) 'The rise of the platform economy', *Issues in Science and Technology*, 32(3), 61–69.

Kenney, M. and Zysman, J. (2020) 'The platform economy: Restructuring the space of capitalist accumulation', *Cambridge Journal of Regions, Economy and Society*, 13(1), 55–76.

King, D. and Le Galès, P. (2017) *Reconfiguring European States in Crisis*, Oxford: Oxford University Press.

Kingdon, J.W. (1984) *Agendas, Alternatives and Public Policies*, Harlow: Pearson.

Kitchin, R. (2018) 'Thinking critically about and researching algorithms', in Beer, D., ed., *The Social Power of Algorithms*, Abingdon: Routledge.

Kluzik, V. (2022) 'Governing invisibility in the platform economy: excavating the logics of platform care', *Internet Policy Review*, 11(1), online.

Knill, C. and Tosun, J. (2020) *Public Policy: A New Introduction*, London: Bloomsbury.

Koens, K., Postma, A., and Papp, B. (2018) 'Is overtourism overused? Understanding the impact of tourism in a city context', *Sustainability*, 10(12), 4384.

Koop, C. and Lodge, M. (2017) 'What is regulation? An interdisciplinary concept analysis', *Regulation & Governance*, 11(1), 95–108.

Koster, H. R., Van Ommeren, J., and Volkhausen, N. (2021) 'Short-term rentals and the housing market: Quasi-experimental evidence from Airbnb in Los Angeles', *Journal of Urban Economics*, 124, 103356.

Kovács, B., Morris, J., Polese, A., and Imami, D. (2017) 'Looking at the "sharing" economies concept through the prism of informality', *Cambridge Journal of Regions, Economy and Society*, 10(2), 365–378.

Kriz, M. (2023) *Platform Work in Municipal Contexts: A Multi-Level Governance Analysis of Madrid, Milan, and San Francisco*, PhD dissertation, https://theses .gla.ac.uk/83687/.

La Repubblica (2018) 'Turismo Milano, Airbnb firma l'accordo con il Comune sulla tassa di soggiorno', *la Repubblica*, 13 March, https://milano.repubblica .it/cronaca/2018/03/13/news/tassa_soggiorno_airbnb_accordo_comune _milano-191189892/.

La Repubblica (2020) '"Milano può ancora permettersi Airbnb?": La provocazione dell'assessore sulla questione degli affitti brevi', *la Repubblica*, 19 February, https://milano.repubblica.it/cronaca/2020/02/19/news/milano_airbnb _affitti_brevi_maran_polemiche-249005665/.

La Vanguardia (2020) 'Barcelona pide a Airbnb la retirada de un millar de "pisos turísticos ilegales"', *La Vanguardia*, 8 December, https://www.lavanguardia .com/local/barcelona/20201208/6103791/barcelona-pisos-turisticos-ilegales -airbnb.html.

Lange, P. and Regini, M. (1989) *State, Market and Social Regulation: New Perspectives on Italy*, Cambridge: Cambridge University Press.

Langley, P. and Leyshon, A. (2017) 'Platform capitalism: The intermediation and capitalization of digital economic circulation', *Finance and Society*, 3(1), 11–31.

Lascoumes, P. and Le Galès, P. (2007) 'Introduction: Understanding public policy through its instruments—From the nature of instruments to the sociology of public policy instrumentation', *Governance*, 20(1), 1–21.

Lasswell, H.D. (1936) *Politics: Who Gets What, When, How*, New York: Whittlesey House.

Le Galès, P. (1998) 'Regulations and governance in European cities', *International Journal of Urban and Regional Research*, 22(3), 482–506

Le Galès, P. (2002) *European Cities*, Oxford: Oxford University Press.

Le Galès, P. (2016) 'Neoliberalism and urban change: Stretching a good idea too far?', *Territory, Politics, Governance*, 4(2), 154–172.

Le Galès, P. (2022) 'Policy instrumentation with or without policy design', in Peters, G. and Fontaine, G., eds., *Research Handbook of Policy Design*, Cheltenham: Edward Elgar, 88–103.

Le Galès, P. and Robinson, J. (2023) *The Routledge Handbook of Comparative Global Urban Studies*, Abingdon: Routledge.

Le Galès, P. and Vitale, T. (2013) *Governing the Large Metropolis: A Research Agenda*, Working Papers du Programme Cities Are Back in Town, Sciences Po Paris, https://sciencespo.hal.science/hal-01070523/document.

Le Monde (2023) 'Le Sénat vote à l'unanimité un projet de loi pour "sécuriser et réguler l'espace numérique"', *Le Monde.fr*, 6 Jul, https://www.lemonde.fr/pixels/article/2023/07/06/le-senat-vote-a-l-unanimite-un-projet-de-loi-pour-securiser-et-reguler-l-espace-numerique_6180758_4408996.html.

Lee, D. (2016) 'How Airbnb Short-Term Rentals Exacerbate Los Angeles', *Harvard Law and Policy Review*, (10), 230–253.

Leloup, D. (2022) '"Uber Files": Révélations sur le deal secret entre Uber et Emmanuel Macron à Bercy', *Le Monde.fr*, 10 July, https://www.lemonde.fr/pixels/article/2022/07/10/uber-files-revelations-sur-le-deal-secret-entre-uber-et-macron-a-bercy_6134202_4408996.html.

Lerena Rongvaux, N. and Rodriguez, L. (2024) 'Airbnb in Latin America: A literature review from an urban studies perspective', *Journal of Urban Affairs*, 46(6), 1146–1160.

Leshinsky, R. and Schatz, L. (2018) '"I don't think my landlord will find out:" Airbnb and the challenges of enforcement', *Urban Policy and Research*, 36(4), 417–428.

Li, Y. and Canelles, G. (2021) 'Governing Airbnb in Amsterdam and Singapore: A comparative study on governance strategies and styles', *Sage Open*, 11(4), 21582440211052257.

Lijphart, A. (1971) 'Comparative politics and the comparative method', *The American Political Science Review*, 65(3), 682–693.

Lindblom, C. E. (1977) *Politics and Markets: The World's Political-Economic Systems*, New York: Basic Books.

Lipsky, M. (2010) *Street-level bureaucracy: Dilemmas of the individual in public services*, 30th anniv. ed., New York: Russell Sage Foundation.

LobbyFacts.eu (n.d.-a) 'Airbnb Ireland UC', https://www.lobbyfacts.eu/datacard /airbnb-ireland?rid=823871417098-42&sid=178702.

LobbyFacts.eu (n.d.-b) 'Welcome to LobbyFacts', https://lobbyfacts.eu/.

Local AT, The (2021) 'Airbnb removes all Viennese municipal apartments from its site', *The Local Austria*, 15 October, https://www.thelocal.at/20211015/vienna -municipal-apartments-social-housing-rental-airbnb.

Logan, J. R. and Molotch, H. L. (1987) *Urban Fortunes: The Political Economy of Place*, Berkeley: University of California Press.

Lomas, N. (2021) 'Court overturns Amsterdam's three-district ban on Airbnb rentals', *TechCrunch*, 15 March, https://techcrunch.com/2021/03/15/court -overturns-amsterdams-three-district-ban-on-airbnb-rentals/?guccounter=1.

López-Gay, A., Cocola-Gant, A., and Russo, A.P. (2021) 'Urban tourism and population change: Gentrification in the age of mobilities', *Population, Space and Place*, 27(1), e2380.

Lorrain, D. (2005) 'Urban capitalisms: European models in competition', *International Journal of Urban and Regional Research*, 29(2), 231–267.

Losada, A. (2024) El lloguer de temporada es descontrola a Barcelona a l'espera d'una llei estatal, *Tot Barcelona*, 25 January, https://www.totbarcelona.cat /societat/lloguer-temporada-descontrola-barcelona-espera-llei-estatal-468680/.

Luca, M., Pronkina, E., and Rossi, M. (2024) 'The evolution of discrimination in online markets: How the rise in anti-Asian bias affected Airbnb during the pandemic', *Marketing Science*, 20 February, https://doi.org/10.1287/mksc .2023.0112.

Mahoney, J. and Thelen, K. (2010) *Explaining Institutional Change: Ambiguity, Agency, and Power*, Cambridge: Cambridge University Press.

Maier, G. and Gilchrist, K. R. (2022) 'Women who host: An intersectional critique of rentier capitalism on AirBnB', *Gender, Work & Organization*, 29(3), 817–829.

Maitland, R. and Newman, P. (2009) *World Tourism Cities: Developing Tourism Off the Beaten Track*, Abingdon: Routledge.

Mansilla, J. A. (2023a) *Los Años de La Discordia: Del Modelo a La Marca Barcelona*, Barcelona: Apostroph.

Mansilla, J. A. (2023b) 'Social movements and class struggle: Against unequal urban transformations from the neighborhood', *Journal of Urban Affairs*, 45(1), 2–16.

Mansilla, J. A. and Milano, C. (2022) 'Becoming centre: Tourism placemaking and space production in two neighborhoods in Barcelona', *Tourism Geographies*, 24(4–5), 599–620.

Marchenko, A. (2019) 'The impact of host race and gender on prices on Airbnb', *Journal of Housing Economics*, 46, 101635.

Marcuse, P. and Madden, D. (2016) *In Defense of Housing: The Politics of Crisis*, London: Verso Books.

Marcuse, P. and Van Kempen, R. (2000) *Globalizing Cities: A New Spatial Order?* Oxford: Blackwell.

Marques, E. (2021) 'Introduction', in Marques, E., ed., *The Politics of Incremental Progressivism: Governments, Governances and Urban Policy Changes in Sao Paulo*, Hoboken, NJ: Wiley, 1–43.

Marques, E. (2024) 'Continuities and transformations in the studies of urban politics and governments', *Nature Cities*, 1(1), 22–29.

Marques Pereira, S. (2022) 'Regulation of short-term rentals in Lisbon: Strike a balance between tourism dependence and urban life', *Urban Research & Practice*, 15(4), 477–504.

Martínez, M. A. and Gil, J. (2024) 'Grassroots struggles challenging housing financialization in Spain', *Housing Studies*, 39(6): 1516–1536.

Martínez, M. A. and Wissink, B. (2022) 'Urban movements and municipalist governments in Spain: alliances, tensions, and achievements', *Social Movement Studies*, 21(5), 659–676.

Martínez Mata, Y. (2017) 'Bolkestein revisited in the era of the sharing economy', *Revista Electrónica de Estudios Internacionales*, 33, https://doi.org/10.17103/reei.33.09.

Martínez Mata, Y. (2021) 'The Digital Services Act and tourist rentals: A challenge or an opportunity for cities?', *CIDOB Opinion 685*, https://www.cidob

.org/en/publications/publication_series/opinion/2021/the_digital_services
_act_and_tourist_rentals_a_challenge_or_an_opportunity_for cities.

Martinotti, G. (1993) *Metropoli: Nuova Morfolgoia Sociale Della Cita*, Bologna: Il
Mulino.

Marvel, M. (2017) 'Sharing economy and the hotel industry', HotelAnalyst,
https://hotelanalyst.co.uk/shop/sharing-economy-and-the-hotel-industry
-2017/.

MasterCard (2016) 'Global destination cities index 2016', https://www.weforum
.org/stories/2016/09/these-are-the-worlds-most-visited-cities-in-2016/.

Mazur, J. and Serafin, M. (2023) 'Stalling the state: How digital platforms contribute to and profit from delays in the enforcement and adoption of regulations', *Comparative Political Studies*, 56(1), 101–130.

McCabe, S. (2005) '"Who is a tourist?": A critical review', *Tourist Studies*, 5(1),
85–106.

McCloskey, J. (2018) 'Discriminatorybnb: A discussion of Airbnb's race problem,
its new anti-discrimination policies, and the need for external regulation',
*Washington University Journal of Law & Policy*, 57, 203, https://heinonline.org
/HOL/Page?handle=hein.journals/wajlp57&id=213&div=&collection=.

McCourt Institute (2023) *EU Digital Services Act and US Section 230: Decision-
Making Processes and Expected Consequences*, https://mccourtinstitute.org
/wp-content/uploads/2023/03/MCI_EU-Digital-Services-Act-and-US
-Section-230_-Decision-making-processes-and-expected-consequences.pdf.

McElroy, E. (2020) 'Property as technology', *City*, 24(1–2), 112–129.

McKay, S. (2003) 'Sheriffs and outlaws: In pursuit of effective enforcement', *The
Town Planning Review*, 74(4), 423–443.

McLaren, D. and Agyeman, J. (2015) *Sharing Cities: A Case for Truly Smart and
Sustainable Cities*, Cambridge, MA: MIT Press.

McLaughlin, B.R. (2018) '#AirbnbWhileBlack: Repealing the Fair Housing
Act's Mrs. Murphy exemption to combat racism on Airbnb', *Wisconsin Law
Review*, 2018, 149, https://heinonline.org/HOL/Page?handle=hein.journals
/wlr2018&id=153&div=&collection=.

McMillan Cottom, T. (2020) 'Where platform capitalism and racial capitalism
meet: The sociology of race and racism in the digital society', *Sociology of
Race and Ethnicity*, 6(4), 441–449.

McNeill, D. (2016) 'Governing a city of unicorns: Technology capital and the urban politics of San Francisco', *Urban Geography*, 37(4), 494–513.

Medina, F. (2020) Opinion: After Coronavirus, Lisbon is turning away from Airbnb and using holiday rentals as key worker homes, *The Independent*, 4 July, https://www.independent.co.uk/voices/coronavirus-lisbon-portugal -airbnb-homes-key-workers-a9601246.html.

Medvedeva, N. (2023) 'The romantic anti-capitalisms of short-term rental hosting', *Antipode*, 55(6), 1841–1859.

Mendes, L. (2018) 'Tourism gentrification in Lisbon: Neoliberal turn and financialisation of real state in a scenario of austerity urbanism', in David, I., ed., *Crisis, Austerity, and Transformation: How Disciplinary Neoliberalism Is Changing Portugal*, London: Lexington Books, 25–48.

Menegus, G. (2019) 'Locazioni per finalità turistiche: il codice identificativo lombardo supera lo scrutinio di costituzionalità', *Le Regioni*, 47(3), 825–836.

Menegus, G. (2020) 'Recenti interventi delle Regioni ordinarie in materia di locazioni per finalità turistiche', *Osservatorio sulle fonti*, 1, 1–13.

Mermet, A.-C. (2021) 'Who is benefiting from Airbnb? Assessing the redistributive power of peer-to-peer short-term rentals', *The Professional Geographer*, 73(3), 553–566.

Milano, C. (2017) *Overtourism y Turismofobia: Tendencias Globales y Contextos Locale*, Barcelona: Ostelea School of Tourism & Hospitality, http://www.aept.org/archivos/documentos/ostelea_informe_overtourism_y _turismofobia.pdf.

Milano, C., Cheer, J. M., and Novelli, M., eds. (2019) *Overtourism: Excesses, Discontents and Measures in Travel and Tourism*, Wallingford: CABI.

Milano, C., Novelli, M., and Cheer, J. M. (2019) 'Overtourism and degrowth: A social movements perspective', *Journal of Sustainable Tourism*, 27(12), 1857–1875.

Milone, F. L., Paolucci, E., and Raguseo, E. (2022) 'Airbnb e gli affitti brevi in Italia: Le prospettive di un mercato in forte ascesa', *Agenda Digitale*, 21 December, https://www.agendadigitale.eu/mercati-digitali/airbnb-e-gli-affitti-brevi-in -italia-le-prospettive-di-un-mercato-in-forte-ascesa/.

Ministère Chargé du Logement (2022) *Guide Pratique De La Réglementation Des Meublés De Tourisme À Destination Des Communes*, https://www.ecologie.gouv .fr/sites/default/files/09.02.2022_GuideReglementationMeubleTourisme Communes_def_light_vdef.pdf.

Monaci, S. (2023) 'Airbnb, maxi sequestro da 779 milioni di euro per evasione fiscale', *Il Sole 24 Ore*, 6 November, https://www.ilsole24ore.com /art/sequestrati-oltre-779-milioni-ad-airbnb-il-mancato-pagamento-cedolare -secca-AFMQXHXB.

Montalban, M., Frigant, V., and Jullien, B. (2019) 'Platform economy as a new form of capitalism: A Régulationist research programme', *Cambridge Journal of Economics*, 43(4), 805–824.

Montezuma, J. and McGarrigle, J. (2019) 'What motivates international home-buyers? Investor to lifestyle "migrants" in a tourist city', *Tourism Geographies*, 21(2), 214–234.

Morar em Lisboa (2017) 'Open letter living in Lisbon', Morar em Lisboa, http:// moraremlisboa.org/open-letter-living-in-lisbon/.

Mosaad, M., Benoit, S., and Jayawardhena, C. (2023) 'The dark side of the sharing economy: A systematic literature review of externalities and their regulation', *Journal of Business Research*, 168, 114186.

Mossberger, K., Clarke, S.E., and John, P. (2012) 'Studying politics in an urban world: Research traditions and new directions', in John, P., Mossberger, K., and Clarke, S. E., eds., *The Oxford Handbook of Urban Politics*, Oxford: Oxford University Press, 3–8.

Müller, N., Murray, I., and Blázquez-Salom, M. (2021) 'Short-term rentals and the rentier growth coalition in Pollença (Majorca)', *Environment and Planning A: Economy and Space*, 53(7), 1609–1629.

Musterd, S. and Ostendorf, W., eds. (1998) *Urban Segregation and the Welfare State: Inequality and Exclusion in Western Cities*, Abingdon: Routledge.

Navarrete Escobedo, D. (2020) 'Foreigners as gentrifiers and tourists in a Mexican historic district', *Urban Studies*, 57(15), 3151–3168.

Navarro, N. (2014) 'La concejala que dijo "no" a la corrupción', *El Periódico*, 19 February, https://www.elperiodico.com/es/dominical/20140219/itziar -gonzalez-3117332.

Nel·lo, O. (2015) *La Ciudad En Movimiento: Crisis Social y Respuesta Ciudadana*, Madrid: Díaz & Pons.

Neveu, E. and Surdez, M., eds. (2020) *Globalizing Issues: How Claims, Frames, and Problems Cross Borders*, Cham: Palgrave Macmillan.

NHL Stenden University of Applied Sciences (2018) *'Overtourism'?— Understanding and Managing Urban Tourism Growth Beyond Perceptions*,

World Tourism Organization (UNWTO), https://doi.org/10.18111/978928
4419999.

Nieuwland, S. and van Melik, R. (2020) 'Regulating Airbnb: How cities deal
with perceived negative externalities of short-term rentals', *Current Issues in
Tourism*, 23(7), 811–825.

Nofre, J., Giordano, E., Eldridge, A., Martins, J. C., and Sequera, J. (2018) 'Tourism, nightlife and planning: Challenges and opportunities for community
liveability in La Barceloneta', *Tourism Geographies*, 20(3), 377–396.

Novy, J. (2016) 'The selling (out) of Berlin and the de- and re-politicization of
urban tourism in Europe's "Capital of Cool"', in Colomb, C. and Novy, J.,
eds., *Protest and Resistance in the Tourist City*, Abingdon: Routledge, 52–72.

Novy, J. (2018) 'Urban tourism as a bone of contention: Four explanatory
hypotheses and a caveat', *International Journal of Tourism Cities*, 5(1), 63–74.

Novy, J. (2021) 'Amsterdam is laying down a model for what tourism should
look like after COVID', *The Conversation*, 16 June, http://theconversation
.com/amsterdam-is-laying-down-a-model-for-what-tourism-should-look
-like-after-covid-162271.

Novy, J. and Colomb, C. (2016) 'Urban tourism and its discontent: An introduction', in Colomb, C. and Novy, J., eds., *Protest and Resistance in the Tourist
City*, Abingdon: Routledge, 1–30.

Novy, J. and Colomb, C. (2019) 'Urban tourism as a source of contention and
social mobilisations: A critical review', *Tourism Planning & Development*, 16,
358–375.

Novy, J. and Huning, S. (2009) 'New tourism (areas) in the "New Berlin"', in
Maitland, R. and Newman, P., eds., *World Tourism Cities*, Abingdon: Routledge, 87–108.

Numbeo (2021) 'Cost of living database', https://www.numbeo.com/cost-of
-living/.

Observatori del Turisme a Barcelona (2024) *Barcelona 2023: Tourism Activity
Report*, Observatori del Turisme a Barcelona, https://ajuntament.barcelona
.cat/turisme/en/data-and-studies.

O'Regan, M. and Choe, J. (2017) 'Airbnb and cultural capitalism: Enclosure and
control within the sharing economy', *Anatolia*, 28(2), 163–172.

Oskam, J. (2019) 'The future of Airbnb and the "sharing economy": The
collaborative consumption of our cities', in *The Future of Airbnb and the*

'Sharing Economy', Channel View Publications, https://doi.org/10.21832/978
1845416744.

Oskam, J. (2020a) 'Eiffel Tower and Big Ben, or "off the beaten track"? Centrip-
etal demand in Airbnb', *Hospitality & Society*, 10(2), 127–155.

Oskam, J. (2020b) 'Introduction', in A. Oskam, J., ed., *The Overtourism Debate*,
Leeds: Emerald Publishing Limited, 1–8.

Oskam, J. and Boswijk, A. (2016) 'Airbnb: The future of networked hospitality
businesses', *Journal of Tourism Futures*, 2(1), 22–42.

Oskam, J., van der Rest, J.-P., and Telkamp, B. (2018) 'What's mine is yours—
but at what price? Dynamic pricing behavior as an indicator of Airbnb host
professionalization', *Journal of Revenue and Pricing Management*, 17(5), 311–328.

Oskam, J. and Wiegerink, K. (2020) 'The unhospitable city: Residents' reactions to tourism growth in Amsterdam', in A. Oskam, J., ed., *The Overtourism Debate*, Leeds: Emerald Publishing Limited, 95–118.

Pace, G. (2020) 'Le proposte delle grandi destinazioni turistiche su turismo
sostenibile e affitti brevi', *TgTourism*, 25 February, https://www.tgtourism
.tv/2020/02/le-proposte-delle-grandi-destinazioni-turistiche-su-turismo
-sostenibile-e-affitti-brevi-91794.

Pack, S. (2006) *Tourism and Dictatorship: Europe's Peaceful Invasion of Franco's
Spain*, Basingtoke: Palgrave Macmillan.

Pais, I., Polizzi, E., and Vitale, T. (2019) 'Governare l'economia collaborativa
per produrre inclusione: Attori, strumenti, stili di relazione e problemi di
implementazione', in Andreotti, A., ed., *Governare Milano Nel Nuovo Millennio*, Bologna: Il Mulino.

Palier, B. (2004) 'Les instruments, traceurs du changement: La politique des
retraites en France', in Lascoumes, P. and Le Galès, P., eds., *Gouverner par les
instruments*, Académique, Paris: Presses de Sciences Po, 273–300.

Palou i Rubio, S. (2012) *Barcelona, Destinació Turística: Un Segle d'imatges i Promo-
ció Pública*, Barcelona: Vitel·la.

Paris, C. (2009) 'Re-positioning second homes within housing studies: Household investment, gentrification, multiple residence, mobility and hyper-con-
sumption', *Housing, Theory and Society*, 26(4), 292–310.

Paris Data (n.d.) 'Register of authorizations for change of use for furnished
tourist accommodation', https://opendata.paris.fr/explore/dataset/registre
-des-autorisations-de-changement-dusage-pour-les-meubles.

Paulauskaite, D., Powell, R., Coca-Stefaniak, J. A., and Morrison, A.M. (2017) 'Living like a local: Authentic tourism experiences and the sharing economy', *International Journal of Tourism Research*, 19(6), 619–628.

Peck, J. and Phillips, R. (2020) 'The platform conjuncture', *Sociologica*, 14(3), 73–99.

Peck, J. and Theodore, N. (2007) 'Variegated capitalism', *Progress in Human Geography*, 31(6), 731–772.

Peeters, P., Gössling, S., Klijs, J., Milano, C., Novelli, M., Dijkmans, C., Eijgelaar, E., Hartman, S., Heslinga, J., Isaac, R., Mitas, O., Moretti, S., Nawijn, J., Papp, B., and Postma, A. (2018) *Research for TRAN Committee—Overtourism: Impact and Possible Policy Responses*, European Parliament, https://www.europarl.europa.eu/RegData/etudes/STUD/2018/629184/IPOL_STU(2018)629184_EN.pdf.

Pérez Mendoza, S. and Casado, D. (2021) 'Los propietarios de pisos turísticos de Madrid se resisten a pasarse al alquiler tradicional', *El Diario*, 2 January, https://www.eldiario.es/madrid/propietarios-pisos-turisticos-madrid-resisten-pasarse-alquiler-tradicional_1_6513788.html.

Petruzzi, M. A., Marques, C., and Sheppard, V. (2021) 'To share or to exchange: An analysis of the sharing economy characteristics of Airbnb and Fairbnb.coop', *International Journal of Hospitality Management*, 92, 102724.

Picascia, S., Romano, A., and Teobaldi, M. (2017) 'The airification of cities: Making sense of the impact of peer to peer short term letting on urban functions and economy', SocArXiv, https://osf.io/preprints/socarxiv/vs8w3.

Pierson, P. (1994) *Dismantling the Welfare State? Reagan, Thatcher and the Politics of Retrenchment*, Cambridge: Cambridge University Press.

Piganiol, V. (2021) 'Le système Airbnb bordelais face à la crise du Covid-19: Gestion, adaptation et réinvention', *Mondes du Tourisme*, (20), https://doi.org/10.4000/tourisme.4040.

Pinson, G. (2023) 'Odious comparisons in urban studies: A plea for comparative monographs', in Le Galès, P. and Robinson, J., eds., *The Routledge Handbook of Comparative Global Urban Studies*, Abingdon: Routledge, 232–245.

Pinson, G. and Journel, C. M. (2017) *Debating the Neoliberal City*, Abingdon: Routledge.

Pinson, G. and Morel Journel, C. (2016) 'The neoliberal city—Theory, evidence, debates', *Territory, Politics, Governance*, 4(2), 137–153.

Pixová, M. (2020) *Contested Czech Cities: From Urban Grassroots to Pro-Democratic Populism*, Singapore: Palgrave Macmillan/Springer Nature Singapore.

Pixová, M. and Sládek, J. (2016) 'Touristification and awakening civil society in post-socialist Prague', in Colomb, C. and Novy, J., eds., *Protest and Resistance in the Tourist City*, Abingdon: Routledge, 87–103.

Pollman, E. and Barry, J. M. (2017) 'Regulatory entrepreneurship', *Southern California Law Review*, 90(3), 383–448.

Post, A. E. (2023) 'The role of comparison in urban political science', in Le Galès, P. and Robinson, J., eds., *The Routledge Handbook of Comparative Global Urban Studies*, Abingdon: Routledge, 132–141.

Prassl, J. (2018) *Humans as a Service: The Promise and Perils of Work in the Gig Economy*, Oxford: Oxford University Press.

Prayag, G. and Ozanne, L. K. (2018) 'A systematic review of peer-to-peer (P2P) accommodation sharing research from 2010 to 2016: Progress and prospects from the multi-level perspective', *Journal of Hospitality Marketing & Management*, 27(6), 649–678.

Pressman, J. L. and Wildavsky, A. (1973) *Implementation: How Great Expectations in Washington Are Dashed in Oakland*, Berkeley: University of California Press.

Quattrone, G., Proserpio, D., Quercia, D., Capra, L., and Musolesi, M. (2016) 'Who benefits from the sharing economy of Airbnb?', *Proceedings of the 25th International Conference on World Wide Web*, http://dl.acm.org/citation.cfm?id=2872427.2874815.

Querol Mayor, J. and Santos Gordillo, A. (2015) *El Problema de La Massificació Turística a Barcelona i El Seu Conflicte Polític: Universos Simbòlics i Propostes*, Barcelona: FAVB.

Rabari, C. and Storper, M. (2015) 'The digital skin of cities: Urban theory and research in the age of the sensored and metered city, ubiquitous computing and big data', *Cambridge Journal of Regions, Economy and Society*, 8(1), 27–42.

Rahman, K. S. and Thelen, K. (2019) 'The rise of the platform business model and the transformation of twenty-first-century capitalism', *Politics & Society*, 47(2), 177–204.

Randle, M. and Dolnicar, S. (2019) 'Enabling people with impairments to use Airbnb', *Annals of Tourism Research*, 76, 278–289.

Rauch, D. and Schleicher, D. (2015) *Like Uber, But for Local Government Policy: The Future of Local Regulation of the 'Shared Economy'*, Working Paper 21, Marron

Institute of Urban Management, https://marroninstitute.nyu.edu/uploads /content/The_Future_of_Local_Regulation_of_the_Shared_Economy .pdf.

Ravenelle, A. (2016) 'Belong Anywhere? How Airbnb Is Dismantling Generations of Civil Rights in the Name of Progress', SSRN, https://papers.ssrn .com/sol3/papers.cfm?abstract_id=2838219.

Regione Lombardia (n.d.) 'Strutture Ricettive Alberghiere e extra-alberghiere', https://www.dati.lombardia.it/Turismo/Strutture-Ricettive-Alberghiere-e -extra-alberghier/745d-3uyg/data.

Reichenberger, I. (2018) 'Digital nomads—a quest for holistic freedom in work and leisure', *Annals of Leisure Research*, 21(3), 364–380.

Reuters (2018) 'Airbnb homes in on African growth story', *Reuters*, 22 November, https://www.reuters.com/article/idUSKCN1NR24Y/.

Richon, J. (2022) 'Les stratégies de contournement des loueurs et les limites des textes existants', paper presented at the conference '"La plateformisation" du logement—Observer et maîtriser les locations de meublés saisonniers', 18 November, Paris, CEREMA.

Richon, J. (2024) 'Les loueurs Airbnb parisiens face à la loi: Stratégies d'adaptation et contournements', *Espace et Société*, 191, 11–29.

Rihoux, B. and Ragin, C. G. (2009) *Configurational Comparative Methods: Qualitative Comparative Analysis (QCA) and Related Techniques*, Thousand Oaks, CA: Sage.

Ríos, P. (2010) 'Tres mujeres contra la mafia de Ciutat Vella', *El País*, 9 October, https://elpais.com/diario/2010/10/09/catalunya/1286586440_850215.html.

Rittel, H. W. J. and Webber, M. M. (1973) 'Dilemmas in a general theory of planning', *Policy Sciences*, 4(2), 155–169.

Rius Ulldemolins, J. (2014) 'Culture and authenticity in urban regeneration processes: Place branding in central Barcelona', *Urban Studies*, 51(14), 3026–3045.

Robertson, C., Dejean, S., and Suire, R. (2024) '"Airbnb in the City": Assessing short-term rental regulation in Bordeaux', *The Annals of Regional Science*, 72, 647–682.

Robinson, J. (2006) *Ordinary Cities: Between Modernity and Development*, Abingdon: Routledge.

Rodríguez, P. (2018) 'Barcelona pide a Airbnb que verifique las licencias turísticas mientras pacta acceder a sus datos para comprobarlo', *El Diario*, 29 May,

https://www.eldiario.es/catalunya/Barcelona-Airbnb-verifique-turisticas
-comprobarlo_0_776572531.html.

Rodríguez-Pose, A. and Storper, M. (2020) 'Housing, urban growth and
inequalities: The limits to deregulation and upzoning in reducing economic
and spatial inequality', *Urban Studies*, 57(2), 223–248.

Rolnik, R., Guerreiro, I. de A., Marín-Toro, A., Rolnik, R., Guerreiro, I. de A.,
and Marín-Toro, A. (2021) 'Rental housing—formal and informa—as a new
frontier of housing financialization in Latin America', *Revista INVI*, 36(103),
19–53.

Rossini, L., Martínez, M. A., and García Bernardos, A. (2023) 'The configuration of a multi-pronged housing movement in Barcelona', *Partecipazione E
Conflitto*, 16(1), 63–86.

Rushe, D. (2020) 'Airbnb soars to near $100bn valuation as shares more than
double in IPO', *The Guardian*, 10 December, https://www.theguardian.com
/technology/2020/dec/10/airbnb-ipo-wall-street-share-sale.

Russo, A. P. and Arias Sans, A. (2016) 'The right to Gaudí: What can we learn
from the commoning of Park Güell, Barcelona?', in Colomb, C. and Novy, J.,
eds., *Protest and Resistance in the Tourist City*, Abingdon: Routledge, 261–277.

Russo, A. P. and Scarnato, A. (2018) '"Barcelona in common": A new urban regime
for the 21st-century tourist city?', *Journal of Urban Affairs*, 40(4), 455–474.

Ryan-Collins, J. and Murray, C. (2023) 'When homes earn more than jobs: The
rentierization of the Australian housing market', *Housing Studies*, 38(10),
1888–1917.

Sadowski, J. (2020) 'Cyberspace and cityscapes: On the emergence of platform
urbanism', *Urban Geography*, 41(3), 448–452.

Salerno, G.-M. and Russo, A. P. (2022) 'Venice as a "short-term city": Between
global trends and local lock-ins', *Journal of Sustainable Tourism*, 30(5), 1040–1059.

Samaan, R. (2015) *AirBnB, Rising Rent, and the Housing Crisis in Los Angeles*,
LAANE, https://laane.org/research/airbnb-rising-rent-and-the-housing-crisis
-in-los-angeles/.

Scarnato, A. and Quaglieri Domínguez, A. (2017) 'The Barrio Chino as last
frontier: The penetration of everyday tourism in the dodgy heart of the
Raval', in Gravari-Barbas, M. and Guinand, S., eds., *Tourism & Gentrification
in Contemporary Metropolises: International Perspectives*, Abingdon: Routledge,
107–133.

Schattschneider, E. E. (1960) *The Semisovereign People: A Realist's View of Democracy in America*, New York: Holt, Rinehart and Winston.

Schmidt, V. A. (2016) 'Varieties of capitalism: A distinctly French model?', in Elgie, R., Grossman, E. and Mazur, A. G., eds., *The Oxford Handbook of French Politics*, Oxford Handbooks Online, Oxford: Oxford University Press.

Scholz, T. and Schneider, N. (2016) *Ours to Hack and to Own: The Rise of Platform Cooperativism, A New Vision for the Future of Work and a Fairer Internet*, New York: OR Books.

Schor, J. (2021) *After the Gig: How the Sharing Economy Got Hijacked and How to Win It Back*. Oakland: University of California Press.

Schor, J. B. (2017) 'Does the sharing economy increase inequality within the eighty percent? Findings from a qualitative study of platform providers', *Cambridge Journal of Regions, Economy and Society*, 10(2), 263–279.

Schor, J. B. and Attwood-Charles, W. (2017) 'The "sharing" economy: Labor, inequality, and social connection on for-profit platforms', *Sociology Compass*, 11(8), e12493.

Schor, J. B. and Vallas, S. P. (2021) 'The sharing economy: Rhetoric and reality', *Annual Review of Sociology*, 47(1), 369–389.

Schwartz, H. and Seabrooke, L. (2009) *The Politics of Housing Booms and Busts*, Basingstoke, New York: Palgrave Macmillan.

Schwyter, A. (2018) 'Face à la mairie de Paris et aux hôteliers, Airbnb en pleine guérilla judiciaire', *Challenges*, 12 April, https://www.challenges.fr/entreprise/tourisme/face-a-la-mairie-de-paris-et-aux-hoteliers-airbnb-en-pleine-guerilla-judiciaire_580378.

Scott, J. C. (1999) *Seeing Like a State: How Certain Schemes to Improve the Human Condition Have Failed*, New Haven, CT: Yale University Press.

Selby, M. (2004) *Understanding Urban Tourism: Image, Culture and Experience*, London: Bloomsbury Academic.

Semi, G. and Tonetta, M. (2021) 'Marginal hosts: Short-term rental suppliers in Turin, Italy', *Environment and Planning A: Economy and Space*, 53(7), 1630–1651.

Sénat (2018) *Airbnb, Booking . . .: Pour une régulation équilibrée et efficace*, Rapport d'information no. 587, https://www.senat.fr/rap/r17-587/r17-587.html.

Sente, A. (2019) 'Face à l'Europe, Bruxelles ne compte pas adapter sa réglementation "Airbnb"', *Le Soir*, 19 March, https://www.lesoir.be/213229/article/2019

-03-19/face-leurope-bruxelles-ne-compte-pas-adapter-sa-reglementation
-airbnb.

Sequera, J. and Nofre, J. (2018) 'Shaken, not stirred: New debates on touristification and the limits of gentrification', *City*, 22(5–6), 843–855.

Sequera, J. and Nofre, J. (2020) 'Touristification, transnational gentrification and urban change in Lisbon: The neighbourhood of Alfama', *Urban Studies*, 57(15), 3169–3189.

Sequera, J., Nofre, J., Díaz-Parra, I., Gil, J., Yrigoy, I., Mansilla, J., and Sánchez, S. (2022) 'The impact of COVID-19 on the short-term rental market in Spain: Towards flexibilization?', *Cities*, 130, 103912.

Serafini, T. (2015) 'Airbnb, les effets pervers d'un monde appart'', *Libération*, 25 February, https://www.liberation.fr/societe/2015/02/25/airbnb-les-effets-pervers-d-un-monde-appart-_1209947/.

SET (2021) 'Nasce SET—Sud Europa di fronte alla Turistificazione', Facebook, 14 March, https://www.facebook.com/notes/400760154255009/.

Shade, L.R. (2018) 'Hop to it in the gig economy: The sharing economy and neo-liberal feminism', *International Journal of Media & Cultural Politics*, 14(1), 35–54.

Sharexpo (2014) 'Documento d'Indirizzo Sharexpo: Milano città condivisa per Expo 2015', https://issuu.com/sharexpo/docs/documento_d_indirizzo_sharexpo/7.

Sharp, D. (2018) 'Sharing cities for urban transformation: Narrative, policy and practice', *Urban Policy and Research*, 36(4), 513–526.

Shaw, J. (2020) 'Platform real estate: Theory and practice of new urban real estate markets', *Urban Geography*, 41(8), 1037–1064.

Sheppard, S. and Udell, A. (2016) *Do Airbnb Properties Affect House Prices?*, Department of Economics Working Paper 2016-03, Department of Economics, Williams College, http://econpapers.repec.org/paper/wilwileco/2016-03.htm.

Short, J.L. (2021) 'The politics of regulatory enforcement and compliance: Theorizing and operationalizing political influences', *Regulation & Governance*, 15(3), 653–685.

Shrestha, P., Gurran, N., and Maalsen, S. (2021) 'Informal housing practices', *International Journal of Housing Policy*, 21(2), 157–168.

Sigala, M. (2018) 'Market formation in the sharing economy: Findings and implications from the sub-economies of Airbnb', in Barile, S., Pellicano, M. and Polese, F., eds., *Social Dynamics in a Systems Perspective*, Cham: Springer International, 159–174.

Sigler, T. and Wachsmuth, D. (2020) 'New directions in transnational gentrification: Tourism-led, state-led and lifestyle-led urban transformations', *Urban Studies*, 57(15), 3190–3201.

Sindicat de Llogateres de Barcelona (2024) 'Acció de denúncia contra els lloguers de temporada', https://sindicatdellogateres.org/accio-de-denuncia -contra-els-lloguers-de-temporada/.

Smart, A. and Zerilli, F. M. (2014) 'Extralegality', in Nonini, D. M., eds., *A Companion to Urban Anthropology*, Chichester: Wiley, 222–238.

Smith, N. (1979) 'Toward a theory of gentrification: A back to the city movement by capital, not people', *Journal of the American Planning Association*, 45(4), 538–548.

Smith, T. and Gillet, K. (2020) 'Europe's startups battle Airbnb for digital nomad market', *Sifted*, 22 October, https://sifted.eu/articles/mid-term -rental-digital-nomads/.

Söderström, O. and Mermet, A.-C. (2020) 'When Airbnb sits in the control room: Platform urbanism as actually existing smart urbanism in Reykjavík', *Frontiers in Sustainable Cities*, 2, https://doi.org/10.3389/frsc.2020 .00015.

Spangler, I. (2020) 'Hidden value in the platform's platform: Airbnb, displacement, and the un-homing spatialities of emotional labour', *Transactions of the Institute of British Geographers*, 45(3), 575–588.

Spector, M. and Kitsuse, J. I. (1977) *Constructing Social Problems*, Menlo Park, CA: Benjamin-Cummings.

Spirou, C. (2011) *Urban Tourism and Urban Change: Cities in a Global Economy*, Abingdon: Routledge.

Srnicek, N. (2016) *Platform Capitalism*, Cambridge, UK; Malden, MA: Polity.

Stabrowski, F. (2017) '"People as businesses": Airbnb and urban micro-entrepreneurialism in New York City', *Cambridge Journal of Regions, Economy and Society*, 10(2), 327–347.

Stark, D. and Pais, I. (2020) 'Algorithmic management in the platform economy', *Sociologica*, 14(3), 47–72.

Stephens, M. (2020) 'How housing systems are changing and why: A critique of Kemeny's theory of housing regimes', *Housing, Theory and Society*, 37(5), 521–547.

Stephens, M., Lux, M., and Sunega, P. (2015) 'Post-socialist housing systems in Europe: Housing welfare regimes by default?', *Housing Studies*, 30(8), 1210–1234.

Stone, B. (2018) *The Upstarts: Uber, Airbnb, and the Battle for the New Silicon Valley*, New York: Back Bay Books/Little, Brown.

Storto, G. (2018) *La Casa Abbandonata: Il Racconto Delle Politiche Abitative Dal Piano Decennale Ai Programmi per Le Periferie*, Roma: Officina edizioni.

Streeck, W. and Thelen, K. (2005) *Beyond Continuity: Institutional Change in Advanced Political Economies*, Oxford: Oxford University Press.

Sundararajan, A. (2017) *The Sharing Economy. The End of Employment and the Rise of Crowd-Based Capitalism*, Cambridge, MA: MIT Press.

Surak, K. (2022) 'Who wants to buy a visa? Comparing the uptake of residence by investment programs in the European Union', *Journal of Contemporary European Studies*, 30(1), 151–169.

Taşan-Kok, T., Özogul, S., and Legarza, A. (2021) 'After the crisis is before the crisis: Reading property market shifts through Amsterdam's changing landscape of property investors', *European Urban and Regional Studies*, 28(4), 375–394.

Tedds, L. M., Cameron, A., Khanal, M., and Crisan, D. (2021) 'Why Existing Regulatory Frameworks Fail in the Short-Term Rental Market: Exploring the Role of Regulatory Fractures', https://papers.ssrn.com/abstract= 4048253.

Terrasse, P. (2016) *Rapport au Premier Ministre sur l'Economie Collaborative*, Paris: Hôtel de Matignon.

Thelen, K. (2018) 'Regulating Uber: The politics of the platform economy in Europe and the United States', *Perspectives on Politics*, 16(4), 938–953.

Therborn, G. (2023) 'Cities in their states', in Le Galès, P. and Robinson, J., eds., *The Routledge Handbook of Comparative Global Urban Studies*, Abingdon: Routledge, 333–343.

Tonetta, M., Esposito, A., and Conte, V. (2022) 'Questa casa (non) è un albergo: La gestione speculativa del patrimonio residenziale in Italia', *cheFare*, 21 December, https://www.che-fare.com/almanacco/politiche/questa-casa

-non-e-un-albergo-la-gestione-speculativa-del-patrimonio-residenziale-in
-italia/.

Törnberg, P. (2021) 'Short-term rental platforms: home-sharing or sharewashed neoliberalism?', in Sigler, T. and Corcoran, J., eds., *A Modern Guide to the Urban Sharing Economy*, Cheltenham: Edward Elgar, 72–86.

Törnberg, P. and Chiappini, L. (2020) 'Selling black places on Airbnb: Colonial discourse and the marketing of black communities in New York City', *Environment and Planning A: Economy and Space*, 52(3), 553–572.

Törnberg, P. and Uitermark, J. (2022) 'Urban mediatization and planetary gentrification: The rise and fall of a favela across media platforms', *City & Community*, 21(4), 340–361.

Tourmis (n.d.) 'Marketing-Information-System for tourism managers', https://www.tourmis.info/index_e.html.

Tozzi, L. (2023) *L'invenzione di Milano: Culto della comunicazione e politiche urbane*, Napoli: Cronopio.

TPN/Lusa (2022) 'L'ASAE se concentre sur les inspections du secteur du tourisme en 2023', *The Portugal News*, 12 October, https://www.theportugalnews.com/fr/nouvelles/2022-10-12/asae-focusing-on-tourism-sector-inspections-in-2023/71072.

Tranquille Émile (n.d.) 'Investir dans un Local Commercial!', https://www.tranquilleemile.com/local-commercial-airbnb.

Tulumello, S. and Allegretti, G. (2021) 'Articulating urban change in Southern Europe: Gentrification, touristification and financialisation in Mouraria, Lisbon', *European Urban and Regional Studies*, 28(2), 111–132.

Turner, A. (2020) 'The rise of the "half-tourist" who combines work with a change of scene', *The Guardian*, 25 September, https://www.theguardian.com/travel/2020/sep/25/the-rise-of-the-half-tourist-who-combines-work-with-a-change-of-scene.

Tussyadiah, I. P. and Pesonen, J. (2018) 'Drivers and barriers of peer-to-peer accommodation stay—an exploratory study with American and Finnish travellers', *Current Issues in Tourism*, 21(6), 703–720.

UK Ministry of Housing, Communities & Local Government (2015) 'Boost for Londoners as red tape slashed on short term lets', Press release, 26 May, https://www.gov.uk/government/news/boost-for-londoners-as-red-tape-slashed-on-short-term-lets.

United Nations (2008) *International Recommendations for Tourism Statistics*, https://unstats.un.org/unsd/publication/Seriesm/SeriesM_83revie.pdf#page=21.

UNWTO (2015) 'UNWTO tourism highlights', http://mkt.unwto.org/publication/unwto-tourism-highlights-2015-edition.

UNWTO (2021) '2020: A year in review; COVID-19 and tourism', https://www.unwto.org/covid-19-and-tourism-2020.

Urry, J. (1990) *The Tourist Gaze: Leisure and Travel in Contemporary Societies*, London: Sage.

Valdez, J. (2023) 'The politics of Uber: Infrastructural power in the United States and Europe', *Regulation & Governance*, 17(1), 177–194.

Valente, R., Bornioli, A., Vermeulen, S., and Russo, A. P. (2023) 'Short-term rentals and long-term residence in Amsterdam and Barcelona: A comparative outlook', *Cities*, 136, 104252.

Valente, R., Zaragozí, B., and Russo, A. P. (2023) 'Labour precarity in the visitor economy and decisions to move out', *Tourism Geographies*, 25(8), 1912–1928.

Vallas, S. P. (2018) 'Platform capitalism: What's at stake for workers?', *New Labor Forum*, 28(1), 48–59.

Van de Walle, S. and Raaphorst, N., eds. (2019) *Inspectors and Enforcement at the Front Line of Government*, London: Palgrave Macmillan.

van der Borg, J., Costa, P., and Gotti, G. (1996) 'Tourism in European heritage cities', *Annals of Tourism Research*, 23(2), 306–321.

Van Doorn, N. (2017) 'Platform labor: On the gendered and racialized exploitation of low-income service work in the "on-demand" economy', *Information, Communication & Society*, 20(6), 898–914.

Van Doorn, N. (2020) 'A new institution on the block: On platform urbanism and Airbnb citizenship', *New Media & Society*, 22(10), 1808–1826.

Van Doorn, N. (2022) 'Platform capitalism's social contract', *Internet Policy Review*, 11(1), 1–18.

van Holm, E. J. (2020) 'Evaluating the impact of short-term rental regulations on Airbnb in New Orleans', *Cities*, 104, 102803.

Vaughan, R., Daverio, R., and PWC UK (2016) *Assessing the Size and Presence of the Collaborative Economy in Europe*, Brussels: European Commission, https://op.europa.eu/en/publication-detail/-/publication/2acb7619-b544-11e7-837e-01aa75ed71a1.

Verhaeghe, P.-P., Martiniello, B., Endrich, M., and Landschoot, L.V. (2023) 'Ethnic discrimination on the shared short-term rental market of Airbnb: Evidence from a correspondence study in Belgium', *International Journal of Hospitality Management*, 109, 103423.

Vianello, M. (2016) 'The No Grandi Navi campaign: Protests against cruise tourism in Venice', in Colomb, C. and Novy, J., eds., *Protest and Resistance in the Tourist City*, Abingdon: Routledge, 171–190.

Vidal, L. (2019) 'Cities versus short-term rental platforms: The European Union battle', *CIDOB Notes Internacionals*, 222, https://www.cidob.org/en /publications/publication_series/notes_internacionals/n1_222/cities_versus _short_term_rental_platforms_the_european_union_battle.

Vignon, E. (2023) 'Pour Thierry Marx (Umih), Airbnb "dépasse les bornes"', *L'Echo Touristique*, 2 February, https://www.lechotouristique.com/article /pour-thierry-marx-umih-airbnb-depasse-les-bornes.

Ville de Paris (2021) 'Le tribunal judiciaire de Paris condamne Booking à verser une amende de 1,234 million d'euros à la Ville de Paris', *Presse.Paris*, 18 October, https://presse.paris.fr/pages/19929.

Vith, S., Oberg, A., Höllerer, M. A., and Meyer, R .E. (2019) 'Envisioning the "sharing city": Governance strategies for the sharing economy', *Journal of Business Ethics*, 159(4), 1023–1046.

Von Briel, D. and Dolnicar, S. (2020) 'The evolution of Airbnb regulation—An international longitudinal investigation 2008–2020', *Annals of Tourism Research*, 87, 102983.

Voytenko Palgan, Y., Mont, O., and Sulkakoski, S. (2021) 'Governing the sharing economy: Towards a comprehensive analytical framework of municipal governance', *Cities*, 108, 102994.

Vyas, N. (2021) '"Gender inequality—now available on digital platform": An interplay between gender equality and the gig economy in the European Union', *European Labour Law Journal*, 12(1), 37–51.

Wachsmuth, D. (2017) 'How do we measure Airbnb's impact on housing and gentrification?', https://davidwachsmuth.com/2017/03/17/how-do-we -measure-airbnbs-impact-on-housing-and-gentrification/.

Wachsmuth, D., Chaney, D., Kerrigan, D., Shillolo, A., and Basalaev-Binder, R. (2018) *The High Cost of Short-Term Rentals in New York City*. A report from the Urban Politics and Governance research group, School of Urban Planning,

McGill University, https://www.mcgill.ca/newsroom/channels/news/high -cost-short-term-rentals-new-york-city-284310.

Wachsmuth, D. and Weisler, A. (2018) 'Airbnb and the rent gap: Gentrification through the sharing economy', *Environment and Planning A: Economy and Space*, 50(6), 1147–1170.

Wallut, P. (2015) 'De la destination à l'usage: Pratique de l'article L. 631-7 du CCH', *Droit et Ville*, 80(2), 67–76.

Wang, Y., Livingston, M., McArthur, D .P., and Bailey, N. (2024) 'The challenges of measuring the short-term rental market: An analysis of open data on Airbnb activity', *Housing Studies*, 39(9), 2260–2279.

Wegmann, J. and Jiao, J. (2017) 'Taming Airbnb: Toward guiding principles for local regulation of urban vacation rentals based on empirical results from five US cities', *Land Use Policy*, 69, 494–501.

Wetzstein, S. (2017) 'The global urban housing affordability crisis', *Urban Studies*, 54(14), 3159–3177.

Whitehead, C. (2016) 'Housing as asset based welfare: A comment', *Critical Housing Analysis*, 3(1), 10–18.

Wijburg, G. and Aalbers, M. B. (2017) 'The alternative financialization of the German housing market', *Housing Studies*, 32(7), 968–989.

Wijburg, G., Aalbers, M. B., Conte, V., and Stoffelen, A. (2023) 'Tourism-led rentier capitalism: Extracting rent and value from tourism property investment', *Antipode*, 56(2), 715–737.

Wilson, J., Garay-Tamajon, L., and Morales-Perez, S. (2021) 'Politicising platform-mediated tourism rentals in the digital sphere: Airbnb in Madrid and Barcelona', *Journal of Sustainable Tourism*, 30(5), 1080–1101.

Wolifson, P., Maalsen, S., and Rogers, D. (2023) 'Intersectionalizing housing discrimination under rentier capitalism in an asset-based society', *Housing, Theory and Society*, 40(3), 335–355.

Woll, C. (2016) 'Politics in the interest of capital: A not-so-organized combat', *Politics & Society*, 44(3), 373–391.

Woodcock, J. and Graham, M. (2019) *The Gig Economy: A Critical Introduction*, Cambridge, UK: Polity.

Yates, L. (2021) *The Airbnb 'Movement' for Deregulation: How Platform-Sponsored Lobbying Is Changing Politics.* Manchester: The University of Manchester and Ethical Consumer, https://pure.manchester.ac.uk/ws/portalfiles/portal

/192396608/Yates_2021_The_Airbnb_Movement_Corporate_Sponsored _Grassroots_Lobbying_in_the_Platform_Economy.pdf.

Yates, L. (2023) 'How platform businesses mobilize their users and allies: Corporate grassroots lobbying and the Airbnb "movement" for deregulation', *Socio-Economic Review*, 21(4), 1917–1943.

Yates, L. (2025) *Platform Politics: Corporate Power, Grassroots Movements and the Sharing Economy*, Bristol: Bristol University Press.

Yeon, J., Kim, S. 'James', Song, K., and Kim, J. (2022) 'Examining the impact of short-term rental regulation on peer-to-peer accommodation performance: A difference-in-differences approach', *Current Issues in Tourism*, 25(19), 3212–3224.

Yeung, K. (2018) 'Algorithmic regulation: A critical interrogation', *Regulation & Governance*, 12(4), 505–523.

Yrigoy, I. (2019) 'Rent gap reloaded: Airbnb and the shift from residential to touristic rental housing in the Palma Old Quarter in Mallorca, Spain', *Urban Studies*, 56(13), 2709–2726.

Yrigoy, I., Morell, M., and Müller, N. (2022) 'Why do middle-class positions matter? The alignment of short-term rental suppliers to the interests of capital', *Antipode*, 54(3), 959–978.

Zekan, B. and Wöber, K. (2022) 'Urban tourism: Major trends', in van der Borg, J., ed., *A Research Agenda for Urban Tourism*, Cheltenham: Edward Elgar, 19–30.

Zervas, G., Proserpio, D., and Byers, J. (2016) 'The Rise of the Sharing Economy: Estimating the Impact of Airbnb on the Hotel Industry', SSRN, https://papers.ssrn.com/sol3/papers.cfm?abstract_id=2366898.

Zuboff, S. (2019) *The Age of Surveillance Capitalism: The Fight for a Human Future at the New Frontier of Power*, London: Profile Books.

# Index

overtourism in, 47–49; robust housing institutions in, 134–36; STR regulatory instruments in, 107–8; temporary city users, 39–44; three worlds of STR regulation in, 99–139; transnational gentrification in, 60

citizens: collective, 150, 169, 171, 186, 284; conference on short-term rental for, 283–84; mobilisation, 17; movement, 85–86, 277–78, 282–83, 340–44, 350

clienteles: economic, 249, 267, 286, 323–24; political, 69, 166, 249–50, 256, 267–68, 286, 321–24, 335

collaborative economy, 31, 42, 105, 290, 302–4. *See also* sharing economy

comparison, 13–14, 66, 69, 78, 82, 87, 351, 362; agenda-setting in comparative perspective, 86–88; case-oriented, 20–21; and case selection, 92–93; comparative political economy, 19–20; cross-case comparison of Paris, Barcelona and Milan, 189–96; debates on, 335; ideal-typical comparison, 94–95; instrumentation and measuring intensity, 106–16; multi-dimensional approach allowing, 100; multi-level governance, 14–21, 79–80, 194–96; potential for, 334; variable-oriented, 20–21; within-country comparison, 77. *See also* mixed methods

conciergeries, 221, 250, 275–75, 367n6

corporate platforms, 7, 22, 106, 162, 244; agility of, 246; as multi-level policy entrepreneurs, 247–64; political relevance of, 240–42; property managers and, 273; rise of, 29–64;

shifting away from sharing economy ideal, 184; STR regulation targeting, 102–3; types of, 364n3

Court of Justice of the European Union (CJEU), 170, 371n40; Airbnb ruling, 292–94; and data wars, 229–30; defining STRs, 102; and Italian fiscal law, 179, 188; ruling on Parisian regulation, 167, 172; and *Services Directive*, 295–99, 303; in situation of uncertainty, 291

court(s): administrative court, 179, 257, 293, 375n21; cases, 164, 167, 222, 225, 229, 246–47, 257, 259; Constitutional Court, 178, 181, 183, 188, 193, 229; national court, 254, 288, 291, 298; stalling, 256–60, 374n15

data: activists, 236; contentious release of, 229–32; datactivism, 235–37; data wars, 229–37; methods, 337–62; sources of, 337–62; towards EU-wide framework for sharing, 311–15; turning platform into enforcement tool, 232–35. *See also* web scrapping

digital platform: ambiguous nature of, 292–94; compliance, 229–37; as new kind of firm, 33–35; regulation of furnished rentals before, 161–62; STR practices mediated by, 102. *See also* Airbnb; corporate platforms; Uber

effects: measuring, 73–75; perceived, 75, 242; of regulations, 13, 23, 67, 73–75; of STRs, 5, 165, 186, 197, 199, 282, 325–26; testing, 116–29; of tourism, 116–29. *See also* instruments

enforcement, 205–6; court trials/
sanctions, 222–29; institutionalising,
215–29; limited staffing and, 208–12;
with little political support, 208–12; of
new STR regulations, 207–8; and
symbolic power of implementation,
212–15; turning platform into tool of,
232–35; understanding, 73–75. *See also*
instruments; judicialisation
ethnographic observation, 338–39, 351. *See
also* interviews
Europe, 73–74; case selection for cities,
92–93; changing visitor economy in,
39–49; democratic governance in,
332–35; explaining diversity of
regulation in, 5–10; number of guest
nights spent at short-stay accommodation in, 42; public debates over
overtourism in, 47–49; Southern
Europe, 150, 180, 276, 283, 366n3; three
worlds of STR regulation in, 99–139
European Commission, 315–17; DG
GROW document, 290, 307–11, 381n21;
drafting legislative initiatives, 304–6;
harmonisation *versus* diversity of local
STR regulations, 306–11; publishing
STR Data Regulation, 311–15
European Parliament, 378n2; DSA
preparation, 304–6; towards EU-wide
framework for data sharing, 314–16
European Union (EU), 315–17; addressing
Airbnb, 34; ambiguous nature of
digital platforms, 292–94; application
of *Services Directive*, 295–99, 308;
EU-wide framework for data sharing,
311–15; harmonisation *versus* diversity
of local STR regulations, 306–11;

judicialisation of local regulatory
conflicts, 290–91; legal context
regarding role of platforms, 235; new
EU *Digital Services Act*, 303–6; policy
agenda of, 106; pushing for/resisting
application of EU law, 300–302;
reforming regulatory framework of,
299–315; as regulatory battleground,
288–90, 288–317; *Services Directive* of,
275, 292, 296, 298, 367n4; towards
EU-wide framework for sharing data,
311–15; towards new EU *Digital
Services Act*, 303–6
Europeanisation, 80, 91

financialisation, 7, 14, 18, 24, 33, 49, 54, 60,
82, 84. *See also* assetisation
fines, 167–68, 220–22, 224, 227, 233, 294
firms, 8, 29, 43, 63; collaboration between
governments and, 71–73; digital
platforms as new type of, 31, 33–35;
market power to political power, 35–37;
and platformisation of the urban,
37–39; political-economic dimension,
81–82; and regulation of urban
capitalism, 14–21; STR market presence
of, 54; transnationalisation of, 93
framing: connecting STRs to broader
sectoral agendas, 189–91; STRs
becoming public problem, 85–86

governance: modes of, 71–73; multi-level,
14–21, 194–96; profiling cities, 67–69;
urban, 20, 23–24, 79–80, 91, 240, 285,
320–21, 323
government: city governments against
STRs, 136–38; contentious relations

with, 256–60; datactivism for, 235–37; levels of, 103–6; local, 86–88, 198–99, 235–37; majorities in, 125–29; national, 103–6, 133, 170–71, 181–82, 194–96, 268, 274, 294, 316, 378n2; new municipalist government in Barcelona, 152–56; regional, 103–4, 133, 157, 176, 180, 183, 190–96, 243; responsiveness of, 199–201

grassroots movements: mobilisation in Barcelona, 147–48; mobilisation in Italy, 187–89; mobilisation in Paris, 168–69; rescaling, 282–84. *See also* citizens

guests, 22, 67, 254, 309, 373n2; identity of, 173, 179; in sharing economy, 31–32; STR promotion and, 45–46; and street-level inspectors, 220–22

home sharing clubs, 270–72, 346; and local spaces of contention, 244. *See also* host clubs; hosts, association of

homeowner(s): homeowners' cities, 123–34; privileged position of STR property interests in cities of, 265–68; share of homeownership, 120–22

host clubs, 271, 300, 339, 378n22

hosts, association of, 269–73

hotel (industry): mobilisation, 176–78; unlikely alliance of hoteliers and social movements, 278–84

housing: activating protection instruments, 198–99; assetisation, 29–64, 331, 335; cities with robust housing institutions, 134–36; financialisation, 54–55, 60; home-sharing, 50–56; housing market rentierisation, 54–55;

impact of STRs on market, 56–59; importance of conditions of, 121–25; inputs for, 353–61; shifts in market of, 30, 331; slow emergence of STRs as housing problem, 185–89; understanding enforcement, 73–75; welfare/housing regimes, 82–84

illegality, 12, 206–7, 217–18, 222, 235, 275, 372n1

implementation: challenges of, 205–39; investigating, 84–90; scrutinising, 88–90; symbolic power of, 212–15. *See also* enforcement; instruments

informality, 173, 184, 191, 335

Inside Airbnb, 3, 53, 119, 143, 234, 269, 357, 359

inspection, 237, 341, 373n10; announcing, 155; court trials and sanctions, 222–29; evasion of, 20–22; street-level strategies of, 215–20

inspectors, 89, 149, 155, 208, 373n10; court trials and sanctions, 222–29; ethnographic observation of, 339, 347–48; evading, 220–22; regulation enforcement, 213–14; street level, 215–20

institutionalisation, 76, 88, 90; of different STR rules, 140–42; policy mechanisms leading to different STR regulations, 189–201; of political mode of action, 222–29; and three worlds of STR regulation, 320–26

institutions: administrative enforcement work, 215–29; bringing back into STR regulation field, 12–14; infrastructural power and, 247–50; institutionalising administrative enforcement work,

digital age, 205–39; regulatory instruments in European cities, 107–8; rise of, 29–64; shaping of new accommodation offer, 44–47; sociology of regulations of, 84–90; theorising/researching regulation of, 65–95; three worlds of STR regulation in European cities, 99–139; types of practices, 102; understanding enforcement of regulation on, 73–75; urban public problem in Europe, 2–5; and urban rent extraction, 320–26; welfare/housing regimes, 82–84

short-term rentiers: groups in European cities, 265–68; local spaces of contention (Figure 21), 243–45; weight/organisation of, 268–75. See also hosts; lobbying; power

social mobilisations, 14–15, 36, 48–49, 201, 338; governing majorities and, 125–29

social movements: allying with responsive city governments, 199–201; in Barcelona, 142–59; and city governments against STRs, 136–38; unlikely alliance of hoteliers and, 278–84

sociology: of multi-level urban governance, 79–80; policy instrumentation, 88–90; political sociology of public policies, 19; of social movements, 127–29, 136–38, 142–89; of STR regulations, 84–90

statistics, 120, 122, 301, 353, 365n5, 380n11

STR accommodation, 365n8; describing, 31; expansion of, 4; legal/illegal, 372n1; operating, 196; producing statistics, 380n11; providers, 301–2; quantity of, 17; types of, 68–69

STR operators: finding and sanctioning, 215–29; grasping new illegalities, 207–15; making street-level inspection harder, 220–22; procedures, 144, 160, 173; professionals, 243–44, 251, 273, 291, 328. See also conciergeries; host clubs; hosts, association of; short-term rentiers

tax: collection, 161, 166, 183, 210–11, 249, 250–55, 285, 310; evasion, 47, 165, 178, 191, 211, 296, 372n1; flat tax, 178–79, 181, 189, 193, 230, 257; minimisation, 47; tourist tax collection, 107–8, 140, 160, 161, 166, 173, 183, 210–11, 251–52, 255, 310

taxation, property-friendly, 178–82

tourism: digital nomads, 39–44; growing discontent around impact of, 145–48; growth model, 178–82; inputs for, 353–61; 'politicisation from below' of, 148–52; saturation of, 117–21; temporary city users, 39–44; testing/nuancing effects of, 116–29; tourist tax collection agreements, 252

tourist accommodation. See short-term rentals (STRs); STR accommodation

touristification. See overtourism: public debates over; tourism

typology: ideal-typical comparison, 94–95, 139, 321, 352; regulatory approaches, 69–71; three worlds of STR regulation, 129–38. See also research design

United Nations World Tourism Organization (UNWTO), 39–40. See also cities: temporary city users

Founded in 1893,
UNIVERSITY OF CALIFORNIA PRESS
publishes bold, progressive books and journals
on topics in the arts, humanities, social sciences,
and natural sciences—with a focus on social
justice issues—that inspire thought and action
among readers worldwide.

The UC PRESS FOUNDATION
raises funds to uphold the press's vital role
as an independent, nonprofit publisher, and
receives philanthropic support from a wide
range of individuals and institutions—and from
committed readers like you. To learn more, visit
ucpress.edu/supportus.